Stonewall Inn Editions
Michael Denneny, General Editor

W9-BZF-036

Also by the Reverend Troy D. Perry
The Lord Is My Shepherd and He Knows I'm Gay

Also by Thomas L. P. Swicegood
Our God Too!

Don't Be Afraid Anymore

THE STORY OF
REVEREND TROY PERRY AND
THE METROPOLITAN COMMUNITY CHURCHES

REVEREND TROY D. PERRY
WITH
THOMAS L. P. SWICEGOOD

ST. MARTIN'S PRESS NEW YORK

Library of Congress Cataloging-in-Publication Data

Perry, Troy D.
   Don't be afraid anymore : the story of Reverend Troy Perry and the Metropolitan Community Churches / Troy D. Perry with Thomas L. P. Swicegood.
      p.   cm.
   Includes index.
   ISBN 0-312-06954-5 (pbk.)
   1. Perry, Troy D.   2. Metropolitan Community Church   3. Church work with gays.
I. Swicegood, Thomas L. P.   II. Title.
BX9896.Z8P47   1990
289.9—dc20
[B]   90-36143
                                                                  CIP

First Paperback Edition: March 1992
10 9 8 7 6 5 4 3 2 1

Contents

Don't Be Afraid Anymore

1

The Double Helix:
1940–1958

For the body is not one member but many.
Now has God set the members every one of
them in the body as it has pleased God.
  —1 Corinthians 12: 14, 18

A DOUBLE helix consists of two twisting chains of chromosomes without which life as we know it would not exist. So also, all of my adult life has consisted of a pair of indivisible threads, religion and sexuality, forever intertwined. This inherent, unsought union of religion and sexuality has brought me the greatest joy although, initially, it was accompanied by genuine despair.

Before I was born, President Franklin D. Roosevelt said, "We have nothing to fear but fear itself." His words have endured, although many years of my life would pass before I truly understood their truth. Until that time of enlightenment, I lived with anxiety and terror. My journey toward maturity was beset with ignorance and doubt before I could understand that, truly, fear is the greatest enemy.

During the decade beginning in 1940, our world seemed a simpler place than we know today, and in that brief period, the bold American spirit became free. World War II was fought and won in three and a half years. Nobody ever dreamed that we might lose the peace. My mother lived happily with my father, her second husband, and they had five healthy sons, including myself, the oldest, born on July 27, 1940. My father was Troy Perry and I was named after him. My brothers are Eugene, Jimmy, Jack, and Jerry.

We lived comfortably in our home in Tallahassee, Florida, where Mother devoted herself to our family. With my dad's income, there was never any want. We owned a gasoline station, and in Jasper, about eighty miles away, also held title to a 168-acre farm that was sharecropped by one of my uncles. My father was a loving man, never vulgar in front of my four brothers or me, religious in moderation, and a good provider—he knew how to make money and babies, and was always very concerned that his children not know what he did for a living.

When I was eight, Dad introduced me to a wonderful part of the Old South about which books are still being written. He took me to see *Silas Green from New Orleans,* a black road show that came into town with a big canvas tent, featuring terrific gospel and blues singers like Bessie Smith. It was before integration, but my father took me anyway and he bought seats for the two of us up front, the best seats in the house!

Our grandest times were in the summer when all of us went swimming, or at the end of the year when everything my brothers and I had ever mentioned wanting would be found, wrapped and tied with pretty ribbons, under a brightly decorated Christmas tree. The quantity of gifts was nearly endless. And life was often filled with relatives from near and far. My mother and father had an equal share of brothers and sisters; the result was a world filled with loving Baptist and Pentecostal aunts and uncles.

I cannot remember a time when religion did not attract me. Church was like an extended family, with social warmth, emotion, and a strong spiritual magnetism. At age ten, I was attending prayer services on every occasion without prompting. The fascination was not derived from any example set by either of my parents, who went to church on special days like funerals and weddings, Christmas and Easter, and when they visited family, but were not otherwise often inclined to attend. My father believed in *sending* children to church.

Concurrently with religion, my sexuality developed. I was nine when another young boy and I went into Tallahassee's Bird's Woods to cut our own Christmas trees, and I had my first sexual encounter. The two of us sat in a forest clearing and played with tumescent flesh that I had never previously shared with anyone. The stimulation we enjoyed was magical, a gift at the earliest onset of puberty. There was no fear or shame—there was only delight, the wonderful pleasure and happiness of a harmless and minor transgression. For me, those were the greatest years, the innocent time of religious and sexual discovery.

I knew nothing about my father's work, but I did know that, although unable to read or write, he could do mathematics in his head. I was content to believe the source of his considerable income was the large farm we owned in Jasper, Florida, about eighty miles from Tallahassee.

Not until after Dad's death did my brothers and I learn the truth about what he did for a living.

Our tragedy was linked to my energetic, eighteen-year-old cousin Clayton, who had come to live with us when I was nearly twelve. Clayton rode a motorcycle and liked to be the local center of attention. That was unfortunate because, when Clayton became associated with my father, Clayton brought the scrutiny of the law upon their business, which I later learned was bootlegging—an illegal vocation better left unnoticed. Tallahassee, the capital city of Florida and seat of Leon County, was "dry" by vote of its electorate who cast ballots against alcoholic beverages but made no secret about crossing the county line. In Gadsden County they bought whiskey at package stores or drank in Quincy's American Legion Hall. Even though federal prohibition had ended years before, because of the hypocrites in Leon County, my father became the most successful bootlegger in North Florida, selling bonded whiskey to the governor's mansion and moonshine to everybody else.

When local authorities made the connection between high-profile Cousin Clayton and my more conservative father (who preferred that everybody not be aware of his business), trouble became inevitable. To make matters worse, there came a day when Troy D. Perry, Sr., who was capable of revealing his own wild streak on rare occasions, suddenly decided to make a speed run in his big, new Lincoln—with the law chasing in hot pursuit! Dad and Clayton were not transporting moonshine at the time, only large demijohns of regular Texaco from the family's gasoline station. The gasoline was legal fuel intended for machinery on our farm in Jasper. But the police did not know.

On that fatal morning, according to the *Tallahassee Democrat,* my father passed a police car heading in the opposite direction, and the patrolmen turned their vehicle around and gave chase while firing a barrage of bullets. The fast and deadly race that ensued lasted about four miles over country roads through the outskirts of Tallahassee. What happened at the conclusion is only surmise. Perhaps some of the law's ammunition hit a tire. At any rate, the Lincoln flipped over on a curve and its cargo burst into flames. My father and Clayton were trapped inside.

That same morning, not many hours later, a friend of the family came to our house and told us my father and cousin were dead. Mother became totally distraught. For what seemed like a very long time, she was inconsolable. My mother and my father had been fortunate to have a special, loving relationship, but because Mother was not accustomed to being alone, she was ill equipped to handle five boys, all under the age of twelve, without assistance.

As months passed, extreme grief turned to anger, then paled into sorrow and eventually dissipated. Six months after becoming a widow, my mother—who as an adult had always been married—felt compelled to marry again. Her new suitor, aware of the ample estate left for Mother to manage, hastily offered his help.

Bob Martin was very aggressive. As soon as he met my mother, he pushed himself on her and passed himself off as part owner of a bakery, which was untrue. Accepting Bob Martin's proposal was, unquestionably, Mother's greatest mistake. My brothers and I knew immediately that we were going to have problems. It quickly became apparent, but only to us, that our stepfather was a terrible man.

I had been attending the First Pentecostal Holiness Church in Tallahassee, and after my father's demise, I felt drawn toward religious meetings considerably more than ever before. I urgently needed to fill the paternal void, and never having had a relationship with my mother that encouraged discussion, I substituted my talking to God for talks I had previously enjoyed with my father.

There is no denying that I, unlike even my brothers, was one of those people who found excitement in a prayer meeting. I often won prizes for memorizing Scripture. There was something wonderful about worship, friendly Southern people, and congregational dinners—plus all the other social activities in which church people are joyfully involved. Everybody knew everybody and called each other "brother" and "sister." It is a beautiful part of the South that has remained unchanged for hundreds of years. But then Bob Martin came along and made me quit. He said church was a place for sissies!

In some ways, Bob Martin attempted to become friendly with me, but I refused to accept him. I resented many things about his manners, including the crude jokes he told about women and the disrespect he showed toward Mother. Before long it was obvious that our stepfather became hateful on the days when he overindulged himself with alcohol. Sometimes on those occasions, when I was aware of nothing I had done to antagonize him, he would become angry, pick up a hose, and beat me. It was an agonizing world into which I was suddenly plunged: church was wrong, innocence was punishable, and I was beginning to learn the meaning of fear.

In accordance with archaic state laws, Bob Martin, as husband, legally assumed full control of what had been my father and mother's property, and in three months saw to it that everything we had owned in and around Tallahassee was sold. Thereafter, Martin moved us to Daytona

Beach, Florida, away from my church, our family, and all our friends. He had convinced my mother that the purchase of a fishing camp consisting of motel, restaurant, and charter boats was a good investment. In theory he was correct, although the results were anything but happy. The problem was my stepfather's inability to regulate his consumption of liquor. He began alienating tourists who had been customers of the previous owner, causing continual damage to our business, which dwindled day after miserable day.

I was certain there was something wrong with the man, and as the situation worsened, it was obvious he and I were headed for a showdown. Shortly before sunset on a humid evening at the end of summer, when my stepfather had been intoxicated for hours, all of us were seated around a large table in our restaurant. For dinner we were having both liver and chicken, which mother had fixed to go with ample side dishes, including vegetables. In my family it has always been customary to serve a good country meal, and we help ourselves to whatever we please.

Nevertheless, that night in Daytona, Bob Martin decided for some reason that my baby brother, Jerry, was going to eat liver. But Jerry hated liver and wouldn't swallow. A contest of wills developed. Jerry was forbidden to leave the table. As the little boy repeatedly gagged and expelled the food he detested, our stepfather became infuriated. Eugene and I had just gone behind the counter to wash the dinner dishes, as was our custom, when Bob Martin jumped up from his seat, grabbed a large piece of liver from the serving platter, and viciously began using his fingers to force chunks of the meat down Jerry's throat. As our little brother, unable to breathe, struggled frantically to get free, Mother tried without success to pull Martin away, all the while screaming for his madness to cease.

That fracas was to be an important turning point in my life, but those of us involved thought merely of saving Jerry's life. My mother hit Martin over the head with a Coca-Cola bottle. The heavy green glass broke, causing no damage to my stepfather's head, but it distracted him long enough for the child to escape. Angrily, Martin turned, made a fist, and knocked my mother to the floor.

It was horrible.

I ran to the telephone, intending to call the sheriff. Martin saw me. He prevented me from dialing out by picking up an extension. Then I knew I was in danger as he moved in my direction to vent his meanness.

Propelled by fear, I fled the building. I ran along the main highway until I reached our neighbor, a woman who knew my stepfather's temper well enough to be certain he could be violent. She immediately called the sheriff. She also produced a loaded pistol for our protection in case Bob Martin should decide to brave the mosquitoes and come up the highway looking for me.

When the sheriff arrived, he drove the neighbor and me back to the fishing camp. Mother was sitting on the front porch with her head down. She was crying. In those days, lawmen strenuously avoided involvement in domestic squabbles, but the sheriff that evening decided there was sufficient reason to incarcerate Bob Martin. Therefore, disheveled and wet with perspiration, my stepfather was handcuffed. The last I saw of him that terrible evening was immediately after he was forced into the backseat of the sheriff's car. He looked up at me, his sullen face not far from mine. I have rarely seen such hatred and, as though everything that had just happened was my fault, I read clearly what my mother's husband was thinking. "Just you wait," said his intimidating eyes, and in that unnerving instant I understood—as far as Bob Martin was concerned— the days of my life were numbered.

I was certain that if he returned home, he would try to kill me. I was in harm's way, and I knew it!

Three days later, my stepfather was released from jail. He was capable of saying anything to get back in the good graces of my mother, and indeed, spoke his words cleverly. "I'm going to treat you all better," he promised, and as a result, mother allowed him to return "one more time." At first I avoided the man, but when that was impossible, I glanced into his eyes and saw something in them that warned me of continuing danger. Convinced that the man still wanted to murder me, I became increasingly nervous, and with good reason.

Martin had been returned from jail less than a week when, at his invitation, a frightening fellow with a mustache and grotesque tattoos arrived. My stepfather passed the man off as his brother, although the two bore no family resemblance. The fellow could just as likely have been an inmate Martin had encountered during his recent sojourn in jail. Martin also claimed that the "brother" had worked on swamp boats and therefore would be a help around the fishing camp.

On the day of his arrival, the "brother" and my stepfather spent a considerable amount of time together, whispering and laughing, and on several occasions I was aware that both were looking at me. At bedtime I felt relieved to have gotten through another day, unaware in my youthful naiveté that my private bed would no longer mean refuge or safety.

"Brother needs a place to sleep," announced my stepfather. "We'll bunk him in with the boys tonight." Whether or not Martin's decision was planned with malice, I never did know.

Two of my brothers and I shared a small bedroom. They slept in a double-decker bunk bed, and I had a single because I was the oldest. I had just turned thirteen. Soft light filtered in through our bedroom window that was open because, although there was the prospect of a cool autumn, the weather was still warm. From the wooded area near the Halifax River, which ran through our property, came the incessant sound of crickets.

Both of my brothers were asleep when Martin's "brother" came to my bed. He sat on my mattress without a word, noisily dropped both shoes on the floor, and tossed his clothing aside. When he rolled against me, he pushed as though he had a right to all of the space. I moved as best I could and kept very still with my back to him, hoping the rude, unwelcome intruder would soon be asleep—but it was quickly apparent that the grown man had no such intentions.

He clutched me roughly. When I resisted, he tightened his grip and whispered threats against my ear. Then suddenly, with strength greater than mine, he forced pain into my body. I am certain it mattered not to him whether I was male or female. I wanted to scream, but false shame outweighed the terror. The last thing I desired was for my own brothers to look over and see what was happening. Nor could I imagine tortures worse than what I was suffering—yet I was afraid that if this was a punishment conceived by my stepfather, any immediate response on my part might result in no end of the two men's awful misdeeds.

I lay awake until shortly before dawn when the Lord took pity on me. I was finally able to fall asleep. In the morning, my physical hurt remained, but it was nothing compared with the lingering mental agony that I suffered. During the next week I made desperate plans, while careful never to be alone with the men. Day or night, I awkwardly contrived to find sleeping places where and when I could sleep unmolested.

The school bus driver, a big, kind matron, suspected what I was going to do. She did not see the toothbrush in my pocket, but she could read me like a book. I had told her a little of my troubles, and on the day I intended to run away, she could tell, somehow. "Don't do it," the woman counseled. "Your momma loves you."

But I was not about to remain where I was.

At Seabreeze High School, the bus driver watched me all the way to the front entrance, and before driving away, she waited until I had gone inside. But I kept going, exiting from the back of the building, walking as fast as I dared toward the Greyhound Bus Station. I had saved my allowance, plus money earned from tips for baiting the fishhooks of tourists, so I could afford a bus ticket. Being tall belied my youthful age, and nobody questioned my purchase. Nevertheless, not until we crossed Florida's state line would I get off the bus or even leave my seat. There was always the nervous fear that someone would realize I was running away, and would send me back home.

When the bus finally arrived at Moultrie, a small county seat in southern Georgia, I hitchhiked out of town along dark country roads. In general, I knew where I was, having often visited my father's brother, Uncle Arthur, and his wife, Aunt Sarah, on their farm during summer vacations. Although they were aware from my letters that I was having problems with Bob Martin, they were shocked to find me on their doorstep. However, once they had listened in horror to my stories, both agreed it was best that I stay with them.

In the morning, Aunt Sarah awakened me with my cousins, J.B., James, and Hortense, and loaded us on the rural school bus for Norman Park Junior High. That afternoon, when the Georgia sheriff came to the farm and told my aunt and uncle, who had no telephone, that my mother had called, concerned about my disappearance, my aunt informed him, "I sent Troy to school this morning. We're not sending him back."

The sheriff, who had known Aunt Sarah since they were children, and whose families had known each other since the Civil War, replied, "Fine, we'll let it go. I'll send them a telegram. I'm satisfied the boy is here and that he's safe."

Fifteen miles away on another farm lived my Uncle Wes and Aunt Siney. Also in the area lived Aunt Lizzy Smithy and her husband who were "shirttail" relatives, a country term of affection for people one loves even if a precise blood relationship cannot be traced. All of these aunts and uncles my brothers and I refer to as the South Georgia Perrys.

It was the right place at the right time for me. The Perrys were deeply religious (although each in slightly divergent, offbeat ways). Uncle Arthur and Aunt Sarah were Pentecostals, as were Uncle Wes and Aunt Siney, but the latter belonged to the "established" Pentecostal group, the Church of God, headquartered in Cleveland, Tennessee. Uncle Arthur was involved with other Pentecostals in what was called the Free Holiness movement. The name meant that they didn't believe in organized religion, but in spite of what they said, they were organized in their disbelief.

Free Holiness meetings were rotated from one farm to another and held in members' homes. Their houses would fill with friendly people. Away from my disapproving stepfather, I was thrilled to be back with Jesus, and I submerged myself in rural Pentecostal worship where miracles of Scripture exist, where people believe God heals, where kids continually run in and out of services but never seem to bother anybody.

When a meeting began, you could expect to be there all day. And the wonderful thing was that everybody was encouraged to stand up and sing, testify, or preach as he or she wanted. Now add to all of that Aunt Lizzy Smithy, who lived in nearby Lenox, a town of eight hundred persons. Aunt Lizzy was the snake handler in the family. Her religion was patterned after Uncle Arthur's Free Holiness movement in that they were both very independent. But Uncle Arthur never handled serpents. There are degrees of fanaticism!

Snakes were brought to Aunt Lizzy's meetings in fruit jars and boxes. Sometimes they were bought from strangers. And I can honestly tell you, those snakes were *real*—and they were not defanged! Snake handling did not happen in every meeting; yet it could occur at any time, usually after the sermon when there was an altar call. By then the music would have reached a fever of hand clapping, with people (popularly known as Holy Rollers, a term we considered slanderous) exuberantly jumping up and down, shouting and speaking in tongues as they felt empowered by heaven. It was then that Aunt Lizzy, or somebody, would reach down into a box or jar and grab a venomous snake, or three or four venomous snakes, and hold them wriggling aloft while shouting claims that he or she had been moved upon by the Holy Spirit.

It was a test of faith, claimed to prove that true believers were undaunted by Satan who (as in the Garden of Eden) could take the form of a serpent. Steadfast in their devotion, members of the congregation would not back away when poisonous reptiles were brandished about the room, but curiosity seekers, who infrequently were in attendance, usually sprang from their seats and rapidly headed for the nearest exit!

I was at a farmhouse with Uncle Arthur and Aunt Sarah when Aunt Lizzy Smithy was bitten during a service at New River Holiness Church. By the time we were notified and arrived, she had recovered on her own, but two men, who were subsequently bitten by the same snake, fared less well. One was the church pastor whose arm swelled to the elbow, and the other was a farmer who refused a doctor because he did not believe in medicine. The farmer went into convulsions and died two hours later. At his funeral, the farmer's widow and children handled the viper before an enormous crowd, then vigorously proclaimed the Devil conquered, and buried the living snake with the dead man in his coffin.

Ordinances against handling snakes at worship services have been in existence for years in Tennessee, Alabama, and Georgia, but peace officers generally refuse to enforce those laws. A local sheriff said, "I wouldn't mess with any of them people's way of doing prayers. Be damned if I want somebody getting into a holy fit and slinging rattlers and copperheads up to my face!" Those were sentiments I understood. Aunt Lizzy, nevertheless, tried hooking me into giving her brand of religion a try.

"Troy, I want to tell you," she would say with focused intensity, "the final verses in the Book of Mark tell us that if you're a true believer, there are things you've got to do. The Scriptures describe Jesus talking to his disciples in the final seconds before being taken up into heaven, when he declared, 'Signs shall follow them that believe—they shall speak with new tongues—they shall take up serpents!' And Jesus didn't say *may* take up serpents, he said *shall* take up serpents! That's why you have to—if you're going to heaven!"

Though I was only thirteen, I knew my own mind. "I'm frightened by four kinds of snakes," I said. "Big snakes, little snakes, live snakes, and dead snakes. If I have to pick one up to get into heaven, then more than likely I'm going to go the other way—for I will never, never handle a snake!"

Three and a half decades have passed since those days when I was a little boy with the South Georgia Perrys, yet, as long as I live, I will forever cherish the genuine love and affection I received from all of them. Aunt Lizzy Smithy is unforgettable not only because she was the most radical (oh yes, she handled fire, too!), but because she had the insight to aim me toward a path in life that our Lord has approved.

It was in Aunt Lizzy Smithy's home during a prayer meeting when she came to me while I was kneeling and, in the midst of all our friends and relatives, placed her strong hands behind my head and held the side of my face tightly against hers. My heart raced as I listened to her deliver a prophecy. In a clear voice, Aunt Lizzy announced that she had been given most certain knowledge that I was called to reveal and preach the Will of God. "Henceforth," she said, "you, Troy Perry, shall also be of such an understanding."

Among people accustomed to Divine Inspiration, it seemed surprising to me how great was the feeling of awe which developed in that room. Hours later, when the service eventually ended, I was congratulated by everyone, including my own proud aunts and uncles. But the most awed person was unquestionably myself. Aunt Lizzy arranged for me to preach my first sermon a week later, and I resolved not to be a disappointment. After that, in the days and weeks that followed, I was generally encouraged to preach in every home and at every prayer meeting. I even declaimed on street corners in nearby Adel, which was a small community of four thousand people. My early sermons probably left much to be desired, but I gained priceless experience. And I was constantly surrounded by considerate, salt-of-the-earth friends who were consciously guiding me toward a religious vocation.

In Daytona Beach, on the night of my disappearance (I later learned from my brothers), my mother, who feared I had been drowned or otherwise murdered, finally stood up to my stepfather. She warned him, "If you've touched one hair on Troy's head, I'll kill you!" For a time Bob Martin was truly uneasy. He was fully aware of a great heritage in the South of determined women; like Margaret Mitchell's vivid Scarlett O'Hara, they are quite capable of meaning what they say, and doing what they mean!

However, upon news of my safe arrival in Georgia, my stepfather's anxiety level dropped rapidly. When he felt there was no more danger to his person, his drinking increased. He told my brothers stories about his "brother" going into town with him and both of them "getting a little." Worst of all, he resumed a dangerous bullying attitude. Week after week, my mother and brothers found themselves being unmercifully intimidated, and even I, reading letters from 250 miles away, felt threatened.

Mother bided her time until a day came when Martin took a party charter-fishing in one of our boats. That morning, as soon as the tourists and my stepfather were out of sight on the river sailing toward the Atlantic Ocean, Mother hastily began giving orders to all my brothers, whom she had kept close at her side. "Start grabbing your things," she told them. "Get your clothes and everything else you ever want to see again. We're leaving!" In a short time, excited but composed, they were all in Mother's car, happily heading toward the home of her sister, Aunt Eutha Bell, and Aunt Eutha Bell's husband, Uncle Roy Wynn. The Wynns lived in Winter Haven, a city in the heart of central Florida's orange groves.

Immediately following the family's success in relocating, Mother began insisting I return to her and my brothers, but I was uncertain that she could continue to resist Bob Martin's wiles and would not go back with him in Daytona. I also had a fear that if my stepfather could not get at Mother, he would come for me. Consequently, I endeavored to move not closer to, but considerably farther away from his area of influence.

I had been writing Aunt Bessie, another of so many favorite relations, who lived in Texas. After learning of my situation, Aunt Bessie sent me a letter accompanied by a bus ticket to El Paso. Whereupon Uncle Arthur, who preferred that I remain in Georgia but was nevertheless understanding, gave me some of his old clothing, including my first three-piece suit. He said it would be good for attending church in the big city! I was not quite fourteen, but my uncle's coat and trousers were nearly a perfect fit.

Inevitably, the hour for departure arrived, and it was celebrated with gentle tears and kind wishes from assembled relatives. We had lived in pleasant proximity for months and I regretted leaving Uncle Arthur, Aunt Sarah, Uncle Wes and Aunt Siney, cousins, friends, and, of course, my special shirttail relative, Aunt Lizzy Smithy. Yet my heart was filled with anticipation as I boarded a Greyhound bus headed for the westernmost tip of Texas.

In El Paso, my Aunt Bessie wasted no time putting me back into school—as had Aunt Sarah before her. And Aunt Bessie introduced me to members of the formal Pentecostal church where they worshiped. Schooling did not have the attraction religion held for me. I did not mind missing school, but I was at the church on every occasion when its doors were open. Upon learning that I had a call to the ministry and had already been preaching, the Assemblies of God pastor welcomed me to speak. I readily accepted, and afterward, a love offering was collected from the congregation, enabling me to purchase some new clothes.

My religious education increased rapidly, particularly with moves from one city to another and between different Baptist and Pentecostal denominations. Perhaps for that reason, it never occurred to me (and never has) that one form of Christianity should be correct and another false or less correct. My feeling was that all the genuine modifications of religion to which I had been exposed were valid, although from one to another, devotion was unquestionably affirmed with varying degrees of intensity. For several years, particularly in Georgia and Texas, I enjoyed Pentecostal exuberance. The emotionalism fit me like a glove! But after a month in El Paso, the time arrived for me to join a considerably more sedate religious branch of my family.

The fishing camp in Daytona was declared bankrupt and Mother filed for divorce. On the subject of my returning to Florida, she could become nearly hysterical. Mother wanted me back with her—immediately—and was threatening a lawsuit against calm and collected Aunt Bessie if I was not returned without delay. On my part, I was homesick, and only fear caused me to keep my distance. Then, when I learned my Uncle Roy Perry (I had two Uncle Roys in Winter Haven) and my Aunt Eula Mae had been to Daytona Beach to get some things out of our house, and that he had really been able to put the fear of God into the wicked and cowardly man who would soon be an ex-stepfather, my courage returned. Uncle Roy Perry, a powerful Baptist minister who had suffered spinal meningitis in his youth, was only four feet ten inches from the floor to the top of his head!

Nobody in Winter Haven was forewarned of my coming when I arrived at Aunt Eutha Bell and Uncle Roy Wynn's home, and I waited in the dark until they and my cousins came home. For a moment they were shocked to discover a "person" lurking on their front porch, but everybody hugged me as soon as I was identified. Five minutes later, my mother arrived in her car. It was a wonderful reunion. Surprised and happy, Mother made it clear to me that no matter what my fears were about Bob Martin's hold on her, she was never going back to him.

The next Sunday I started going to the West Winter Haven Baptist Church. My brothers and mother were nominal Baptists. When visiting our maternal grandmother, we had always known we *would* attend Corinthian Baptist Church in North Florida. In Winter Haven, likewise, my relatives were all staunch Baptists. To me, although I had become so closely associated with the South Georgia and Texas Pentecostals, it did not matter what the Florida Wynn and Perry affiliations were—so long as we were worshiping.

Several weeks after my return, Uncle Roy Perry said to his Baptist churchgoers, "Now all of you know my nephew Troy has a call to ministry, and we want him to preach. Tonight, let's have a business meeting on the matter."

That evening the church was full of people, and using experience I had gained in preaching during the past year, I spoke with the assurance of youth. I had little nervousness, and did sufficiently well that when I was finished, a devout and respected member of the group stood and made a motion that their church license me. Such local approval is the means by which a Baptist's call is recognized. It does not mean the person is ready for ordination. In Baptist tradition, an individual—when old enough, which I was not—must first seek a congregation and then successfully pastor the group for approximately a year prior to being ordained. Nevertheless, at fifteen, I was licensed to preach.

When Mother, who had never before in her life been required to work for wages, realized that seasonal jobs picking and packing fruit would not support us, we considered our options and decided to take the advice of her sister. My Aunt Mattie, who lived in Alabama, said there was more opportunity to earn a living in Mobile than in Winter Haven, and it was obviously true, so we moved there. My brothers and I were able to find odd jobs, and Mother and Aunt Mattie went into business together.

They liked each other and worked well as a team, operating a Tastee Freeze at one end of a building and a juke joint at the other. The combination was bizarre, but all of us survived and Mother soon managed to have our own home for us with our name on the mortgage.

By that time I had become the most fanatical human being with which any scholastic institution has ever had to contend. I was enrolled at Murphy High School where I annoyed teachers as well as students by forever preaching Salvation on the entrance steps. Not surprisingly, after the eleventh grade I became a dropout. Algebra, chemistry, and most other required subjects seemed pointless to me. I only wanted to evangelize because I had been taught that Jesus was coming any day—and in my mind, "any day" meant this afternoon or early tomorrow!

Concurrently, my sexual development was maturing in the same non-exclusive direction as my religion. When it came to worship, the spirited Pentecostals and the inhibited Baptists were both part of my being, although I knew I felt happier with the Pentecostals. It was not that I was ever anti-Baptist. They were just different. By the same token, I felt an ever increasing desire to be physically close with boys, yet part of me sought the social approval of being with girls. There was, however, a difference. My acceptance of two religions troubled me not at all, but an attraction toward two sexes was, and for a number of years would continue to be, troublesome and very disturbing.

In junior high school I met a girl whom I wanted to date. I had been going to the Tolmanville Baptist Church since my arrival in Alabama, but that changed when I learned the girl's father was a Pentecostal pastor in Mobile. Realizing that the only way I could be with the daughter was to be watched by the father, I was pleased to switch my affiliation back to the Church of God and sit in the front pew of her daddy's church. So, in 1956, for better and for worse, I was again with the Pentecostals. I was sixteen, and it was a wonderful time! I felt as though I had returned home to again be a part of their joyful exuberance—revelations of the Holy Spirit (which Baptists view with suspicion), speaking in tongues, and the belief in miracles, all of which had been vividly instilled in me when I lived in Georgia.

I became a paid evangelist, traveling throughout Alabama, preaching. Young women liked me, as did their boyfriends and their brothers, and occasionally the male attraction led to pleasant sexual interludes that never went beyond the stage of tender exploration in which most healthy boys engage. As for my relationship with girls, I dated frequently, but compromising acts of love were easily avoided, particularly because of the strong Pentecostal belief that sexual intercourse outside of marriage is a terrible sin. Perhaps that was another reason why I was attracted to a fundamentalist church. I was trying to keep the lid on a pressure cooker as far as my inescapable sexuality was concerned.

Two years after rejoining the Pentecostals to be with one young woman, I prepared to marry another. Her name was Pearl. She was slender, had reddish blond hair, and was typically Southern in many ways. Pearl's father, perhaps not by coincidence, was another Church of God pastor in Alabama. Before I was really even aware of Pearl's existence, I had attempted to discuss with her father my increasingly troublesome homosexual tendencies, inclinations that confused and bothered me. But in the true Pentecostal tradition of the late 1950s, when sex was not considered a proper subject for conversation, Pearl's father abruptly insisted that I stop trying to express my feelings. He said flatly, "All you need is to marry a good woman, and that will take care of everything!" Therefore, as a result of Reverend Pinion's not too subtle suggestions, I began dating his daughter.

Pearl played the piano, and I needed a pianist. Every pastor's dream is a wife who can play the piano. And she was bright. I did not love Pearl when we were wed, but to become ordained in Pentecostal churches you need to be married. The Church of God pushes you into a union. One month after Pearl was graduated from high school, we smiled our way through a sparkling wedding ceremony. At that time, I believe neither of us knew what lovers-in-love are supposed to feel.

My lack of understanding concerning love also applied to a handsome lad who was well entrenched in the congregation of my prospective father-in-law. While dating Pearl, I was, nevertheless, occasionally closer to the always available young man. Our secret relationship seemed like a playful, uncomplicated affair of "little boy sex"—presumably noncommittal— but what began as an intimate friendship would become a nightmare in the not too distant future.

Meanwhile, I fell in love with my wife.

2

God Knows I'm Gay:
1958–1968

*In the house of my Lord are many mansions;
if it were not so, I would have told you; for
I go to prepare a place for you. And if I go
and prepare a place for you, I come again,
and will receive you unto myself; that where
I am, there ye may be also.*
                                   —John 14: 2, 3

IN Pentecostal factions, education was fought for many years. It was believed that for individuals with a calling, God would grant knowledge without any work. Some of our ministers would quote Scripture which said that you would stand before kings, and God would fill your mouth with words you were supposed to say.

When our Bible colleges were first started, people would sneer, "Aha—so you're going to the seminary. They ought to call it the cemetery—because when young men and young women come back from getting all that learning, they've lost all their natural zeal and fire! Education kills spirit—dead as a doornail!"

Nevertheless, the old ways were slowly beginning to improve, and Pearl encouraged my enrollment in a college for Bible studies. The curriculum required a high school diploma, or an educational equivalent. Fortunately, there is such a thing as the General Educational Development test which I took in Chicago and passed. After some preliminary work at Moody Bible Institute, I attended a nonaccredited Bible college for the better part of two years. My high school marks had only been average, but the study of biblical courses made a difference to me, and in extensive religious studies my grades kept me near or at the head of the class.

Being a conscientious student did not deter my working for a living while also pastoring a little Church of God congregation in Joliet, Illinois. We had only eight people in attendance on the first Sunday I preached, but the group grew rapidly, and near the end of my second year in Bible college, we had sufficient church members to schedule a gala rally and fundraiser to purchase our own building. In the lull after everything was planned, Pearl and I drove to Florida for a quick vacation. Mother was again living in the Sunshine State. When we returned to Illinois, just prior to what we expected to be our gala Sunday, Pearl's world would be shaken—mine was nearly destroyed. I was nineteen years old.

The first suggestion of trouble came on Saturday morning when I telephoned Wayne Proctor, our district coordinator for a large number of Church of God churches around Chicago. I wanted to remind Wayne that he had promised to be at our rally the following day, but Wayne was evasive, and I could tell from the tone of his voice that something was wrong.

"The state overseer is here," he told me, "and we must talk with you. Would you meet us at the church at noon?"

Naturally, I agreed, but with unspoken dread. At a quarter past eleven I was at the church, waiting. Busy around me were several women. Typical of fundamentalist churches, they did most of the work but were never allowed to vote. Men had all of the power.

I tried to do little things to appear occupied, although I felt no enthusiasm for the work. In my heart I knew what had happened. I knew my homosexuality had suddenly become much more than a "worrisome little secret" and, without having all of the details, I thought I knew why. I wanted to be sick, but the thing that saved me from losing control was a very small glimmer of hope—a desperate, slim chance that my fears might be unfounded.

The state overseer also arrived early, by about twenty minutes, and he and the district coordinator bristled with authority as they allowed me to go through the motions of showing them the church premises. After a polite and brief interval, the overseer looked directly into my eyes and without any trace of friendliness said, "Let's go out to the car where we can have a private talk."

I knew the truth then and I was frightened.

As we walked to the overseer's polished Chrysler, I felt hot all over and knew my body was damp from shock. The shiny automobile looked like an expensive metal casket, and I had no choice but to open the door and step inside. I sat alone in the back. Reverend Proctor and the overseer sat in front and they solemnly turned around and observed me.

"I guess you know why I'm here," said the overseer, wasting no time.

I didn't reply. My head was warm and I knew my face was probably flushed and red. The hair on the back of my neck was already wet. It was horrible the way those church leaders could so quickly change their mood from appearing to care for me, to regarding my existence as though I was the worst form of life crawling on earth.

"He told us everything," said Proctor, and his words said more than I needed to know. Proctor was talking about the young man from my father-in-law's congregation, the sweet young lad of nearly my same age with whom, nearly three years earlier, I had become accustomed to sharing "little boy sex." He was talking about the young man I will never forget, a young man who believed he loved me, who lost a long and terrible battle against his own jealousy. What occurred in the years to follow might never have happened had I not been denounced by a youth who loved me, the young man who rationalized that destroying me was "the Christian thing to do." He may have thought it was the Will of God, but on that humid June morning in Joliet, Illinois, as the hands of my watch moved toward noon, it seemed like work of the Devil.

"I'm excommunicating you," said the state overseer of the Church of God, "and I would advise you to get out of town. I don't want you around Illinois anymore." He looked at me as though I was a pervert, and in his eyes I was.

I began sobbing. My fall from grace had been so sudden. The horrible thing was that when I most needed the church, it was not there to help me. When my entire being cried out for compassion, the hierarchy was sanctimonious instead. I had no way of knowing, at the time, that the manner in which I was treated was not uncommon.

"Do you want me to tell your wife?" the district coordinator asked.

I looked at him through tears of despair and disbelief, trying to gather my wits, finally managing to shake my head and say no. Having Proctor tell Pearl about me was the last thing I needed.

The overseer glanced at the coordinator, then shrugged. "You better get back to Florida where you belong," he said.

"I don't have any money," I replied.

"I'll give you a twenty," said the overseer. "Take it, and don't show up here again."

I accepted the money, aware that it would barely pay for the gas for my Studebaker. The district coordinator stepped out of the car, opened the door where I was sitting, and waited for me to leave. He said not a word.

I returned to my wife.

18

"What's the matter?" asked Pearl, looking into my eyes.

"We have to return to Florida," I said.

"Why, Troy?"

"I'll tell you later."

Pearl stared at me until I could only look away. Then she sighed and agreed to leave. Our bags were still packed from the vacation. "I have to say goodbye to my folks before we get started," she said. I agreed, and dropped her off at their house without going inside. Present was Pearl's entire family, including her brother and sisters who were currently living in Joliet. I knew it was the last place on earth I would be welcome. They had been informed about everything, even before I was. I learned later that the nervous young man who had denounced me was inside with them, trimming and reshaping the facts of our involvement to protect himself.

"I'll return for you in an hour and a half," I said to Pearl as I tried to resign myself to the inevitability of what was happening. "Come out if you still want to go back to Florida with me," I added wearily. Pearl nodded, got out, and very quietly closed the door of our car. I watched as she entered the house where her sister was peering at us from behind a curtain.

I drove a distance away.

Ninety minutes seemed like forever to wait. I kept thinking about what had so inflamed my unhappy young boyfriend. Not my marriage, certainly. He was Pentecostal and automatically understood our church's traditional demand. He knew that essentially all Pentecostal men and women are required to be joined in the bonds of Holy Matrimony. That was an ingrained part of his heritage. It was a man I had met in Mobile, shortly before my marriage, who unintentionally precipitated the jealous exposé.

The man was several years older than I. He was unapologetically gay. To me, he made no pretense of being anything else. He happily embraced his homosexuality, and that made a profound impression upon my way of thinking. I had never before experienced anyone with a similar attitude. His lack of inhibitions when it came to being sexually honest aroused my admiration, while at the same time I found such candor disturbing.

I was attracted to the stranger on many levels. He stretched my horizons. He filled me with desire, and also with fear. The full extent of the physical contact I had with him in Mobile was the touch of our hands, but when we parted, it was with his promise that one day we would be more intimate. The accomplishment of that fantasy seemed unlikely because I never expected to see him again. My marriage was only a month away. Already there were plans for Pearl and me to move to Illinois.

Two months later, however, the man located me in Chicgo. When he arrived in an impressive new car and came to my door, I knew why he was there. Part of my being fought to send him away, but the rest of me, the dominant part, knew that he would have to stay, at least for one night. Like magnets, we were attracted, and my sister-in-law unwittingly contrived to bring us together. She moved Pearl into her room overnight, and hospitably arranged for our visitor to sleep in the family bed with me.

Before we undressed, I was experiencing feelings of guilt. I knew there was going to be sex, and not "little boy sex," but the fulfillment of yearnings of an adult nature. With my eyes completely open, and for the first time ever in my life, I knew in advance what I wanted and would have. But at the same time, nagging anxieties persisted. I kept thinking, God, I'm a married man—with a wife in the next room! What will happen if I disregard a lifetime of inhibition?

Eventually, I came to realize that what we were doing seemed right for me. No force was employed during that long night. Everything was different from anything I had known. It stopped short of being love, but was a marvelous education. When morning arrived, my visitor dressed and departed. I never saw or heard from him again. Apparently he had absconded with some money from a relative and the authorities were on his trail. Nevertheless, despite the larcenous side of his nature, the man had revealed something to me about my inherent sexuality. I realized that if I had had such an eye-opening experience with him before I was married, the marriage would never have happened.

We were having dinner, sometime after that one-night visit, when Pearl casually mentioned to my young Pentecostal admirer that police had come looking for the man with whom I had shared our bed. Instantly, my secretly enamored boyfriend became suspicious and subsequently started seeking "the truth." He began probing with persistent and none too subtle questions. His curiosity was not satisfied with my noncommittal answers; failing to obtain information, he would wait several days and resume his interrogation.

"That guy who was up here from Mobile," he would ask. "Who was he really? Did anything ever happen between you? You can tell me— what did you do?"

That went on for a long time, until finally I told my young friend what he really did not desire to know. Afterward, following an extended period of months in which his moods alternated between terrible threats and jealous attention, his simmering anger came to a boil. He waited until Pearl and I were out of town on vacation, and then went to our leaders in the Church of God. With a calculated denunciation, my dear religious friend repaid me for not sharing his infatuation.

Those were some of the thoughts running through my head as I waited for the full hour and a half to elapse before returning to pick up my wife. I also had feelings of being very much alone, and plenty of time to wonder if Pearl would rejoin me. I tried to stop my tears, but it seemed they would never be gone. When I drove back to the in-laws' home and parked my car at the curb, Pearl's family intentionally remained out of sight. I honked the car horn, wondering if my wife would join me in exile. I could understand why she might not, but after several minutes Pearl walked with measured determination across their lawn, opened the car door, and took her seat beside me.

I waited for Pearl to speak. Her words eventually began. "My mom and dad, my brother in particular, and everybody, tried to get me to stay, but I figured I didn't have the right," she said, pausing thoughtfully. Then Pearl surprised me. "I don't say I completely forgive you," she continued, "but Troy, I do love you. We could try one more time? And I'll try and do better for you."

What relief Pearl's words brought to me! There was considerable truth in what she said, delicately referring to our private relationship. My ardor had been hot when we were married; hers was less than I desired.

"Improvement may solve our problem," I replied. With the Studebaker still at the curb, I put my arm around Pearl. We kissed. Both of us began to feel more comfortable.

The storm was far from over, but as we drove to Florida, we discovered that even our cloud had its silver lining. Thus, very soon after I was excommunicated for homosexuality, my first son was conceived! When he was born, we named him Troy after his father and his grandfather.

Less than a year had passed when Pearl, little Troy, and I returned to Illinois. We felt a need to pick up the pieces and start again. Pursuing that objective I managed an audience with the same overseer who had pronounced my sentence of excommunication. He had an education superior to that of many of his peers, and was very intelligent (as are numerous people in his denomination today).

Unlike my remembrance of our previous meeting, the overseer tried to be compassionate, but had little choice in what the denomination permitted him to say. "Troy, you can never again be a minister for the Church of God," he explained. "Don't you realize that the Church of

God says once you've been thrown out for homosexuality, you can never be in it again?"

I replied, "You forgive adultery—and that is breaking one of the Ten Commandments!"

"But," he said, "I'm sure that's something God understands."

"Well, God called me to preach. I can't not do what God called me to do."

The overseer looked sadly in my direction, and answered resolutely, "Troy, you can never be licensed in the Church of God again. There's no room to argue. You can never pastor. They will watch you the rest of your life. It is over."

That same evening, I nevertheless attended a Church of God function, and as fate would have it, met a young couple who belonged to a very similar, but completely separate, rival denomination. They were members of the Church of God of Prophecy. The two organizations had split from a single source in 1923, and although continuing to have very similar doctrine, they almost entirely avoided speaking to each other on religious subjects.

It seemed like Divine Intervention that night when the couple asked me to come to their church. Since my denomination almost never communicated with theirs, it was highly unlikely that the Church of God of Prophecy would ever learn from the Church of God that I had been accused of being homosexual.

In an instant, I realized my ministry would continue.

Pearl and I stayed in Illinois for a time. I worked for a company that manufactured plastics, and I preached. Pearl took care of our boy baby, a pretty sight that I never failed to enjoy, but Pearl wanted no more children. It seemed as though she felt her sexual obligation to me as her husband had been fulfilled. For my part, still shaken by the merciless punishment recently received from the Church of God, I had no wish to do anything but stay close to home—which, at the zestful age of twenty-two, undeniably resulted in amorous frustration. On a rare occasion, the very last time when I insisted upon our having a physical relationship, it resulted (as heaven would decree) in Pearl's second pregnancy. She went to term without hiding her displeasure, and gave birth to James Michael, our second son. Thereafter, in regard to the marriage bed, I might as well have been single.

When the plastics firm I worked for opened a new plant in Torrance, California (adjacent to Los Angeles), I was offered an opportunity to relocate. The decision to move was easy. As a result, my little family packed and we journeyed west. Making our trip even more attractive, a church in Santa Ana (thirty-six miles southeast of Torrance) needed a new pastor for their small congregation. I applied and was selected.

The small church was a wood and stucco building shaped like a rectangle. It seated about a hundred people. Living quarters were petitioned off from the auditorium and made up the smaller end of the plain structure. Our boys, Troy, then three, and Michael, close to his first birthday, slept in the bedroom with us.

More than half of the people who attended our fundamentalist church were Southerners who had migrated to California, bringing their religion with them. They disapproved of cosmetics and jewelry. Women were not permitted to cut their hair. Nobody went to dances, motion pictures, or the theater. A good person was also expected to avoid a large number of disapproved books and publications.

I watched my congregation grow week after week, and that was encouraging, even flattering. But simultaneously, my marital frustrations combined with my increased awareness of many petty things the Church of God of Prophecy (like other fundamentalist churches) refused to permit. After the elimination of marital bliss and other secular amusements from my daily routine, there seemed very little joy remaining in life. As a result, I began to have a constant conflict with Pentecostal teachings. I became convinced that too often their advice was "Don't! Don't! Don't!" when life should be more positive—"Do! Do! Do!"

Eventually, I came to realize that our church majored in minor and questionable transgressions. The realization caused me to become depressed. With increasing frequency I became moody, and there would be two or three days at a time when Pearl and I would not speak even though there had been no argument. The time was fast approaching when we would need to make some decisions.

I began reading books, and in one particular respect the Pentecostals were proven correct: I gained knowledge. It was information that had previously eluded me, awareness (however vague) that rapidly altered the course of my life. When I discovered and digested a book entitled *The Homosexual in America* by Donald Webster Cory, I almost instantly knew that it was I who was being discussed. And I also concluded that not only would my life as a pseudoheterosexual *never* work, but that such deception would probably lead to disaster for all of us.

Pearl was in the East with our children, visiting her parents, when I grasped the opportunity to take a large step in the altering of our lives. I went to visit our district overseer, a large man in his late forties who had been a farmer in Tennessee. He was an excellent minister (without having a lot of education) and a hard worker. He had raised a large family. I knew that speaking candidly with the overseer would force the issue of who was the real Troy Perry. Ultimately, the matter of my sexuality would be communicated from him to higher religious authorities and, whether consciously or subconsciously, that obviously was what I wanted—even though it would surely mean again being forced out of a church.

"What do you want to tell me?" he asked.

Gathering my courage, I said, "Well, I'm a homosexual."

The overseer blanched, becoming very upset. "You're nothing of the sort!" he declared, and wanting very much to help me, asked, "What makes you think you're homosexual?" When I informed him that a book I had read stated that I was gay, he answered, "It's just a trick of the Devil!" He said, "Get down on your knees. We're going to pray, and we know the Lord can help you."

Our prayer was intense, lasting ten or fifteen minutes, although it seemed longer. When we had said the last Amen, the overseer told me to return to Santa Ana, tear up the educational sex book, read no more, and forget all the homosexual nonsense. I replied, "All right, but do this for me—when you talk with the bishop, tell him what I told you!" The overseer agreed, and I knew that was not the end of the matter. I knew how Pentecostal churches work.

My wife and the babies were home the following week. Late one afternoon, I returned after being away most of the day. Pearl met me at the door where, obviously distraught, she quickly informed me that something was wrong—our bishop had come to the house on church business and had left a message that he wanted to see me and would return in the evening.

Pearl went into our bedroom and she said, "Oh, I took one look at the bishop and the two ministers who were with him, and I knew the day of reckoning was here." We shed a few tears. After the sobs subsided, Pearl asked, "What are we going to do?"

I had no suggestions. She had always known, possibly even before we were married, that there was something "different" about me, but even in Joliet when I was excommunicated, we had not discussed our mutual difficulties with any frankness. At that time her solution had been for us to be closer, but after five years of marriage, Pearl was considering another solution, one in which she was not required to participate sexually.

"You know, I found your book, *The Homosexual in America*," she told me, "and I read in it that there are homosexual men who are married

24

and their wives let the husbands have a night out with the 'boys' sometimes. Maybe we could work something out like that?"

"No, we couldn't!" I said. "The time has come for me to stand up and find me. I've got to know who I am."

"Then I want to go home," Pearl said.

A little later, the bishop arrived and asked me to go before my congregation, which, unbeknownst to me, he had called to an emergency meeting that evening. "I want you to get up and tell them you feel like you've failed the Lord, and leave," he told me without any trace of compassion.

I agreed.

"And of course you will move out of the parsonage first thing tomorrow?" the bishop said, his question sounding very much like an order.

"No, I can't," I replied, "It will take a week."

The bishop backed down immediately. I had little fear of him. I was experienced. I had been run out of town before.

My mother and I had many traits in common. One seemed to be that we were often moving from one city to another. When my wife and I separated, Mother was living in Los Angeles with her fourth husband, and they insisted that I, then twenty-three, stay with them. I did so, briefly, until I found a new job and a place of my own to live.

I began to meet gay people and to think of gay people as part of my extended family. Willie Smith was the first homosexual man with whom I became acquainted in Hollywood, and we became trusting companions. He and I were always the best of friends, not lovers, and several years later, Willie would become very important in my life. Another friend, during that same period, caused me to do something I had never considered before. I entered a bar. It was a gay establishment called The Islander, located in Huntington Park. When I drank my first beer, all of my Pentecostal fears came forward, and I was afraid God might strike me dead on the spot!

Two years later, in 1965, I was drafted into the U.S. Army. Being a soldier was not my idea of what I wanted to do with my life. I was still a very timid person who had just begun enjoying a newfound freedom, but the military changed all that. Refusing to believe my outspoken assertions of being homosexual, the army put me through boot camp, sent me to teletype school, and then transferred me to Kaiserslautern, Germany. There, for a year and a half, along with other men with high security clearances, I was charged with coding and decoding top secret messages. So sensitive was our position that we were forbidden to enter East Germany and even had to sign papers stating that we would not travel within five miles of the Czechoslovakian border.

Kaiserslautern boasted the largest Pentecostal church for GIs in Germany, supported primarily by churchgoers in the United States. The chapel seated only about sixty persons, but once a year a gigantic prayer meeting was held and four or five hundred GIs from all over Europe would come by plane or train or bus for a get-together of religious shouting, the laying on of hands, everything! The Church of God minister, who had once been my wife's pastor, was aware of our separation. Nevertheless, he tried to involve me with his church, and when he returned to North America for a month's leave, insisted I preach in his absence. I did as he asked, but found the experience disturbing. I could not convince myself that I still believed what Pentecostals said they believed. I felt I was being hypocritical, and I also felt they were being hypocritical, too.

I met a young black man on the post. Ted Cobb was an Episcopalian and he became my best buddy during our tour of duty in Germany. I instantly knew Ted was gay even though he had a high security clearance and wore a pistol. When Ted threw a parka over his shoulders, he gave the impression that it was the only mink coat on the post. Sissy-prissy Ted got away with being one of the campiest individuals in the U.S. Army because of his genial personality and genuine charm.

One day, a very proper soldier boy came to me and warned, "Perry, you'd better stay away from that black guy. They're investigating and they're gonna catch him. He'll get you into trouble." As it turned out, the discreet boy was somehow caught in bed with a German gentleman. The boy was quickly out of the service, whereas Ted spent his full two years in the army with never any problems. Just being near Ted Cobb was an education in public relations.

He and I took thirty days' leave and traveled around the continent with a guidebook called *Europe on $5 a Day*. The book worked for us because we stayed at recommended hotels and caught space-available hops on military aircraft. In Spain we went to Madrid's art museums. In Greece we walked through Athens' cypress-lined streets and touched the Parthenon's ancient marble. The Italian countryside was beautiful, and Rome, despite filthy streets, was wonderful from a religious point of view. We went to all the churches. St. Peter's and the Vatican museums were at the head of our list. Our vacation ended in Amsterdam, which is the gayest city in the world!

Being drafted at the age of twenty-five resulted in my being older than everyone who lived in the barracks, with the exception of officers and sergeants. The unwanted result was that I became a confessor to young soldiers. They brought me all their teenage problems at a time when the last thing I wanted was to find myself in the role of minister without a church. Some of the men had questions about being gay. If they asked me, "Should I talk to a chaplain?" I quickly told them, "Yes, but by all means pick a Roman Catholic chaplain who is under a vow of silence—and remind him of his vow. I had once seen a Protestant chaplain who could not wait to run to his company commander and repeat what he had just been told!"

On the other hand, Ted and I were so open about being gay, making known the fact on frequent occasions, that nobody took us seriously.

I was lying on my bunk when one of several roommates, a truly nice Southern kid named Tim, who had always looked up to me, asked if I would be best man at his wedding. His fiancée was due to arrive at Kaiserslautern from North Carolina in several weeks. I didn't immediately answer, and the hesitation bothered my roommate, particularly when I said, "Tim, there's something you gotta know and I'm gonna tell you right now."

"What?" he said.

I said, "Don't you know I'm homosexual?"

Tim looked at me, not certain whether he should be amused or perturbed, and after a moment said, "Oh, no you're not. What do you mean by saying that?"

"I mean just that. I *am* homosexual!" I insisted. "I'm telling you because it might embarrass you. Someday Army Intelligence might come in here, and if they know I was best man at your wedding, it might embarrass you. They might think something's funny."

The soldier never faltered. "It won't embarrass me," he said. "I don't give a damn!"

When the bride-to-be arrived, I met the sweetest young woman in the world. Tim told her everything he knew about me, and it didn't upset her. So I was the best man at their wedding, and they became two of my favorite people in Europe.

All the while I was growing up, thanks to the army, developing a potential for leadership. Everywhere there was exposure to the real world. Occasionally, I would listen to our minister from the Church of God and return with him to worship. Sometimes Ted Cobb would accompany me, but he would shake his head and say, "It's your business if you want to keep going to that church, but you're gay and they really don't want you. Going there doesn't make any sense. What are you going to do when you get home?"

"I don't know."

"Then, Troy, why don't you think about starting your own church?" asked Ted, after which he declared, "*That* would make sense!"

In 1967, at the age of twenty-seven, I was a civilian again. Willie Smith met me at the bus station in Los Angeles, and we rented part of an old two-bedroom house which our penny-pinching landlord, in a gross display of insensitivity, had painted *watermelon pink!* (He was saving money by mixing leftover exterior paint, mostly white and a little red.)

Divided down the middle from front to back, the house was occupied by Willie and me on one side, and by Madeline Nelson and her three teenage sons on the other. Madeline was a free spirit, a wonderful human being, and pretty good at telling fortunes in which she employed her highly developed intuition. Willie Smith and I were like godfathers for Madeline's bright, well-behaved boys.

Willie was a motion picture projectionist and worked mostly at night. Often we only passed each other coming and going. I returned to my daytime job at Sears Roebuck where I had been employed before being drafted for two years in the army. My work was in Sears's display department where we printed all the many signs that were used throughout the store. My boss was Steve Sands, a kind and considerate gay man who, although he had a lover, was not yet out of the closet.

In the year that followed, I became reacquainted with the gay scene in Hollywood. I met more homosexual men and women than I had ever before dreamed existed in the entire world. I heard our people called "faggot" and "queer" by the Los Angeles police, and I knew that persecution by law was a reality of life. Also, I had fallen in love!

Larry Drane was my height, over six feet tall, with fair skin, blond hair, and blue eyes. My heart went to him at first sight. It was a unilateral attraction, however, because although I convinced the radiant young man to come live in the pink house with me, what followed were six of the best and worst months of my life. Delightful times as well as terrible arguments existed from the very beginning.

On one occasion, it came into my head that our presence in church might miraculously solve my problems with him, so I urged my disapproving friend into a Pentecostal service. That did not sit well with Larry. He didn't care for the style of worship, and spared no adverse adjectives in telling me. I began to feel terrible. I wondered, What's going to happen?

What am I going to do? Almost immediately, I found myself turning away from God. I was deluded into believing my friend was everything. I put Larry on a pedestal of love—and was blinded by his physical beauty! But I would soon be punished.

Within several months, the end of our torturous affair arrived unexpectedly after what had been a particularly erotic and enjoyable night. In the morning, Larry said, "I'm moving out." I was startled. He said, "Last night didn't mean anything."

A sickness invaded my stomach. I didn't want to believe what I had heard, but by afternoon, the reality of his leaving was confirmed. I went home after work, locked myself in the bathroom, and decided it wouldn't be such a bad thing to die. In the tub I slashed both my wrists with a clean razor blade.

When I regained consciousness, Willie had broken open a lock on the bathroom door facing his bedroom, and Larry and Madeline came in through a rarely used rear entrance. They quickly wrapped cloth around my wrists to staunch the flow of blood, and Madeline, with her sons, loaded me into her car and rushed me to the hospital. Sometime later, with tourniquets on both arms, I sat in an antiseptic room crying uncontrollably while waiting for a doctor. A nurse came toward me instead, and she unexpectedly shoved a magazine in front of my face. Her intention was to capture my attention.

"I don't know why you did this," the woman said as my eyes turned toward hers, "but what you did tonight was crazy—why don't you look up?"

With my Pentecostal background, I knew the nurse's words meant, "Why don't you get your act together and get in touch with God?"

And she added, "You're too young for this sort of thing!" Then the woman showed me scars on her wrists. "I did it, too, one time. But I went on and I made something out of myself. You should do the same. Get hold of yourself. Nothing can be that bad!"

There was no opportunity to answer. The nurse walked away without waiting to hear if I had anything to say. I don't know if she even suspected that she had reached the raw pain inside of me, but I began to pray with heart and soul.

"Lord, forgive me for my sins," I said silently to God. "For all these long months, I've committed the sins of Romans One: twenty-six–twenty-eight. I've served and worshiped the creature more than the Creator. Larry became my God. Please, Lord, if you can see your way, forgive me for that." Immediately thereafter, I felt soothed by an inspirational influence which had been absent for years. It was a wonderful feeling.

Not many minutes later, my wrists received medical attention. When they were neatly bandaged, my doctor leaned toward me, looking down into my eyes. He told me to wiggle my fingers. When my fingers wiggled, he said, "It's a pretty deep cut but I think you'll be all right."

I said, "Do you think I should see a psychiatrist?"

He said, "No, what I think you need is a good swift kick in the ass!" So much for sympathy.

I was home the next morning. Larry had moved out. Willie wanted to go to work but was careful to make certain that I would be all right by myself. "Yes, I will," I assured him. "Go!"

When I was alone, I tried talking to our Creator again. I said, "You know, God, I'm awfully sorry. If you'll just put up with me, I want to talk to you. You know I learned to love and worship somebody more than I worshiped you. Now, I ask you to forgive me because I've really been off the track."

Instantly, the peace and joy that I had felt after praying and renewing my acquaintance with God the night before, returned. The effect was so sudden that I was close to becoming frightened. "Wait a minute, God!" I exclaimed. "I don't know what you expect from me—I'm still a homosexual—a practicing homosexual!"

Then God spoke to my heart, and God said to me, "Troy, do not tell me what I can and cannot do. I love you. You are my son. I do not have stepdaughters or stepsons!"

Many divergent ideas about love, sex, religion, and marriage came into my head. In the days that followed, friends offered conflicting philosophies. When, in my desperation, I said to Willie Smith (for the thousandth time), "I've got to get straight with God. He's punishing me. I have to try one more time to be heterosexual!" Willie would become angry, and impatiently impress me with a blitzkrieg of his best advice.

Willie had been excommunicated by the Seventh Day Adventists because he would not deny being homosexual, but it was Willie's strong feeling that he was not in need of blessings from fallible men in imperfect churches. "God loves me!" was Willie's steadfast belief. Therefore, with contagious conviction, he was able to say, "Listen, Troy, you *are* a homosexual. You will *always* be a homosexual until the day you die. God knows that you are a homosexual. God made you the way you are, and God loves! Nothing you or I can do will change it!"

Madeline Nelson would tell me that God had put me here on earth for some special purpose, but God had yet to reveal the plan. As I discovered, Madeline was more often right than wrong. She had also told me, before I went into the army, that she felt no person had the right to come between any other person and God. Her sons, to the best of our knowledge, were not homosexual, but Madeline said to me, "If I had a daughter who was a lesbian, how dare anybody say she couldn't go to church! If one of my sons was a homosexual, he'd have a right to worship God just like anybody else—because my God is his God, and his God is our God, too!"

There never was any need for me to argue with Madeline. She made me think, however, and I never forgot her suggestion that God had a plan for me as yet unrevealed. Then, my thoughts would flash back to the army base in Germany where Ted Cobb often asked me how I could bear attending a church where homosexuals not only were not welcome, but were condemned. Ted's idea had been that I should start a church of my own, and time and again I wondered, Should it really be done, and when?

I went dancing on a summer evening in 1968. With me was a slender, very attractive man named Tony Valdez who was about twenty-two and married. Tony and I had known each other for several months. Our shared interest was that both of us liked going to The Patch, a very large gay dance bar in Wilmington, across the river from Long Beach and south of Los Angeles. I knew little about music, but Tony introduced me to La Bamba and taught me to enjoy fast dances. Popular were the Madison, the Monkey, and the Jerk, which were primarily massed male chorus lines with loud music and dance routines that rivaled sweaty calisthenics. Large, dramatically lit rooms were filled with cigarette smoke. People drank plenty of beer and behaved themselves better than many men and women in similar heterosexual establishments.

The difference, however, was twofold. One, we were gay, and two, the people with power in Los Angeles, for many homophobic reasons, endorsed vicious policies generally used against us. The police, without fear of retribution, sometimes murdered homosexuals, but more often laughed at us as they attempted to ruin our lives. Gay dance bars and overtly gay enterprises, no matter how well they were managed, rarely were able to stay in business as long as a year during the 1960s.

The Patch, widely known as a "groovy" bar, was running out of time. The manager was Lee Glaze, a tall, fast-speaking blond who said loud and often, "I may be a queen, honey, but I'm going to stand up for my rights." When Lee said, "There's something around here I'm allergic to, and it's giving me an itch," his words were an obvious signal that plain-clothesmen had infiltrated the premises. A bar owner could be arrested for breaking police cover, but Lee never refrained. His reply to angry officers was, "You're not here to do anything but harass us!"

The night Tony and I were dancing at The Patch was a dangerous evening. It seemed the music often stopped, either because uniformed police seemed to keep coming in and asking for people's identification, or because Lee needed to use the band's microphone to inform frightened customers that they had some constitutional rights and should not give in to gestapo tactics. Around midnight, many cautious customers had departed, but there were newcomers. Band music was loud. Scores of men were dancing as Tony went to the bar and purchased two beers, one for himself and one for me. When he returned to where I was standing, after about ninety seconds, a plainclothesman walked up to us and flashed a police badge into my face. "Follow me outside," he demanded.

"Are you talking to me?" I asked.

"Not you, him," snarled the officer, pointing to Tony.

Minutes later, Tony was charged with lewd and lascivious conduct, a standard but meaningless accusation used against homosexuals. It could mean anything, or nothing. In Tony's case, he had been in my field of vision the entire time when he went to the bar, and if he had done anything illegal, he would have needed to be a magician. Or I needed to have my eyes examined.

Nevertheless, in spite of all protests, Tony was handcuffed and pushed into one of many squad cars that, for some irrational reason, were parked in front of the bar with their red lights flashing. Tony was hauled off to jail accompanied by a forty-year-old man named Bill who was also in handcuffs. Bill was accused of being lewd with Tony although the older man had merely slapped the latter on the rump in a casual fashion (exactly the way football players do). Therefore, a few infuriating minutes after the patently discriminatory arrests, Lee Glaze again took a microphone away from the band. He made a rousing speech that galvanized everyone, including myself, to action.

"Two people who are totally innocent have just been arrested," Lee declared. "The cops are trying to put us out of business by keeping us frightened. I think all of us are familiar with the routine. We all know about harassment and entrapment. So let me tell you what we're going to do. We're going to fight! We have rights just like everybody else. Together we can beat the police-state tactics these lousy cops are using. We'll all go get Tony and Bill out on bail, and we'll carry bouquets of flowers to the jail, and we'll stand in the light so everybody will know we're no longer afraid! What do you say?"

Lee's words thrilled me. There were still police around, listening and scowling, but he did not care. It was all a great revelation. In those moments I found courage within myself that I had never known existed. I suddenly realized that we, as gay people, could stand up and fight for our rights which had too long been denied.

I was already at the Harbor Jail when Lee arrived with a colorful procession of assertive, flower-bedecked homosexuals whom he led into the building. Imperiously, he announced to a shocked desk sergeant, "We are here to get our sisters out of jail!"

The moment was delicious, exciting, and certainly memorable. But it faded. We stunned the police, standard-bearers of our oppression, but time was on their side. As the hours of night marched toward dawn, our expensive array of flowers wilted. Yet we waited. When most of us had tired we began singing "We Shall Overcome"—over and over, louder with every refrain. The irritated police were not pleased, but Bill and Tony were released.

There was no celebration for Tony. He managed to make his way into my automobile before I saw the full extent of his mental agony. To say he was upset would be a colossal understatement. He was REALLY upset! His clenched fists showed white knuckles. Moans of agony came from deep inside him. He refused to be touched by so much as a fingertip, and he resisted any word of consolation.

"Have you got anything to drink at your place?" Tony said while I was driving. I nodded, and twenty minutes later, as he sat at my breakfast table with early rays of the sun on his face, I let Tony pour his own glass of bourbon. When he had drunk a little of it, he was no less upset, but appeared calmer.

"Man, you know I never been arrested in my life for anything before," he said, wiping his mouth with the back of his hand. "What am I going to do?" Before I could think of a reply, Tony began reflecting on something that had particularly galled him in jail. "You know," he said, "there was a Chicano cop in there, talking to me through the bars, in Spanish. He called me a *puto*, a male whore, and he said he was going to call where I work and tell my boss there's a *puto* working for him!"

"Tony, you just have to ignore—"

"I tried to ignore! But do you know how it feels?"

"Yes."

"No, Troy, you only think you know. You never been arrested! You don't know how it is when the cell door bangs shut and you're in their cage. I felt like a freak in a sideshow. *Puto Latino!*"

"Take it easy."

"Do you know what everybody says about queers?"

"Come on, listen, it'll work out all right."

"No, it won't," growled Tony, standing. "I'm going to get a bus and go home. Nothing's going to be all right. I don't want to hear that crap. You live in an ivory tower. We're just a bunch of dirty queers and nobody cares about dirty queers!"

"Somebody cares."

"Who?"

"God cares."

Tony had walked to the front door. He paused and uttered a terrible, painful laugh. "No, Troy," he said, "God doesn't care. What do you mean, 'God cares.' Be serious! I went to my priest for guidance when I was fifteen and he wouldn't even let me come back to Sunday school. I guess he thought I might contaminate somebody! He said I couldn't be a homosexual and a Christian, so that was the end of church. And for me, in my religion, that meant the end of God!"

"You don't need the church to speak to God."

"I do."

"Just get down on your knees and pray."

"I can't."

"God will hear you."

A look of increased sadness seemed to envelop Tony's face. In his culture, religious exaltation was all-consuming, as it was in mine, but in a different way. He could not go to God without the intercession of a priest—but I could—because I knew it was possible to meet God anywhere.

"I'll catch the bus," my friend said.

Tony shut the door. As he walked out of my line of vision, I was still Pentecostal enough that I knelt down and urgently lifted my clenched hands in prayer. Somehow I knew I was approaching the culmination of my life, and I felt a building excitement. I went out of the house. The rest of the world still seemed to be sleeping as the bright sun arose.

A short time later, I lay on the bed in my room upstairs, tired from a night without rest, but nevertheless unable to sleep. I said, "Lord! You know I've prayed and I know you love me. You've told me that. I feel your Holy Spirit. What should I be doing? I can't help thinking of Tony, alone, bitter, cut off from talking to you. I wish I could find a church somewhere that would help him. I wish there was a church somewhere for all of us who are outcast."

Suddenly, as if there was an electric spark in my head, I began asking myself, "What's wrong with Troy Perry? Why are you waiting for somebody else?"

Then I prayed a little later that same morning, harder than ever before, and in the sort of talking I do, I said, "Lord, you called me to preach. Now I think I've seen my niche in the ministry. We need a church, not a homosexual church, but a special church that will reach out to the lesbian and gay community. A church for people in trouble, and for people who just want to be near you. So, if you want such a church started, and you seem to keep telling me that you do, well then, just let me know when?"

Whereupon, I received my answer to an impossible dream. A still, small voice in my mind's ear spoke, and the voice said, "Now."

3

What Did Jesus Say?
1968–1970

*For there are some eunuchs which were so
born from their mother's womb: and there
are some eunuchs which were made eunuchs:
and there are eunuchs which have made
themselves eunuchs for the kingdom of heav-
en's sake. They that are able to receive this,
let them receive it.*
                              —Matthew 19:12

ON October 6, 1968, twelve people attended the first service of Metropolitan Community Church. It was held in the right half of the little
pink house in Los Angeles that Willie Smith and I called home. Instead
of a suit and tie, I departed from Pentecostal fashion and wore black
robes for the first time in my life. The change was initiated because an
older friend, Reverend Revel Quigley, a gay Congregational minister,
knew that my outreach would attract people from a wide spectrum of
very different religious backgrounds. Revel impressed upon me that many
worshipers, including Lutherans, Catholics, and Episcopalians would feel
comfortable if they saw liturgical robes, even though they might find my
style of Pentecostal preaching unusual. Reverend Quigley's advice was
some of the best I ever received. Revel lifted my parochial Pentecostal
view of religion to a more sophisticated level where individuals worshiped
God with a devotion similar to mine, but without the great public display
of emotion I had previously assumed was the only way to be a good
Christian.

   All of my plans for our prayer meeting were completed when Mother
arrived, passing through Los Angeles on her way from Florida to Las
Vegas to visit my brother, Eugene. I knew I had to tell her something.

Mother was already aware by that time that I was gay, but she needed to know I was starting a church. After I told her, Mother responded philosophically. "Well, Troy, you've always been trying to be a preacher, even with all the problems," she said. "If this will make you happy, have a try at it."

(I think Mother was pleased that the congregation would not be Pentecostal. She wore makeup and smoked cigarettes, things Pentecostals condemned. Mother would have liked me to be a Baptist, but that was not to be.)

Willie Smith could not imagine gay people being interested in my church, but Madeline Nelson said, "Do what God has called you to do! I think it's a wonderful idea." Madeline watched the service from our kitchen door. Her most important contribution was encouragement. However, since those were still the 1960s, when minorities in America were too often beaten and jailed for seeking their civil rights, Madeline was not speaking entirely in jest when she added, "We'll probably all be arrested during the service—but go ahead anyway!"

Between the night Tony was arrested and the sixth of October, about two and a half months had passed. During that time I had been planning, figuring, and talking to people. I knew what I wanted to accomplish and I never wavered. I was a person obsessed. Not that I was brave. Very much to the contrary, I was merely ignorant of the generally accepted wisdom of the day. I was not aware that when you took out an advertisement in a gay newspaper (*The Advocate*), you were not supposed to use your real home address! The only way I knew to begin a church was the way I had been taught in the South, and I still do not know any other—that is, to tell people openly who you are and where they can find you.

Before the service, in the morning when I was cleaning house, Tony Valdez came for a very brief visit. He had read the newspaper. "Just came by to say I hope everything goes okay for you."

"I'm sure it will," I replied. "Don't you want to stay?" I asked my Hispanic friend.

"No," he said. Then, abruptly, Tony waved and walked out of the house. Across the street he started his old car and drove away. That was the last I saw of Tony.

Steve Sands, my boss at Sears, was in the minority of people who believed I would actually hold the service, and Steve's worry was that Sears would learn what I was doing and terminate my employment. But he and his lover, despite their anxiety, came to the house (departing before the service began) and brought me a silver Jefferson cup from which to serve communion wine. Wafers were placed in a candy dish that Madeline donated.

As I prepared to receive people for worship early on that Sunday afternoon, I had two fears. Worst was my fear that nobody would come. My other fear was that people would attend for a week or two, and then everything would collapse. My best friend, Willie, who worked late running movies at the Encore Theater, was not optimistic and slept until after twelve o'clock on that important Sunday. Just prior to the beginning of the service, Willie walked through our living room wearing a bathrobe, and he inquired, in a hateful but friendly manner, why people were present at such an indecent hour (1:30 P.M.). I couldn't help laughing, but it was a relief when Willie returned a second time, dressed and ready to lead the singing of hymns.

Beginning the service, I told our gathering what Metropolitan Community Church was going to be, and I told them I would preach what God had told me to preach, a three-pronged Gospel:

> SALVATION—God so loved the world that God sent Jesus to tell us that whoever believes shall not perish but have everlasting life; and "whoever" included me as a gay male, unconditionally, because salvation is free—no church can take it away.

> COMMUNITY—for those who have no families who care about them, or who find themselves alone or friendless, the church will be a family.

> CHRISTIAN SOCIAL ACTION—We would stand up for all our rights, secular and religious, and we would start fighting the many forms of tyranny that oppressed us.

I called my first sermon "Be True to You."

I said to everybody, "If you believe in yourself, then God will help you. God cares about you. He created you. He wants you to survive. I found out the hard way, but now I know—and I want you to know! And I don't want you to ever forget: God really cares!"

A fundamentalist friend, Jim Bilbrey, came to me at our home reception following communion. Of importance to him were the questions "What does the Bible say about homosexuality?" and "What did Jesus say?"

They were questions that had to be answered with absolute correctness, but I needed to return to my Bible before I could give Bilbrey an adequate answer. Therefore, in that instant I said to myself, Troy, you know God loves you without a shadow of a doubt. You know you're God's child. You know God called you to the ministry and you know God told you to start this work. Now be able to defend what has been given you to do.

For the next two weeks I lived with my Bible, even during work at Sears. I started by reading and rereading the chapters and verses themselves, beginning with scriptures from the Old Testament. And as I read, I prayed, saying, "God, you've given me the message, but you've got to teach me more if I'm to teach others." For two weeks I studied my Bible until God revealed answers to me, and then to Jim Bilbrey and others I related what I had learned.

I said, "God's Great Commandment was not 'You shall not commit adultery,' or even 'You shall not kill.' The Great Commandment is given to us in the twenty-second chapter of Matthew.

"Jesus said, 'You shall love the Lord your God with all your heart, and with all your soul, and with all your mind. . . . and the second commandment is like unto it, You shall love your neighbor as yourself. On these two commandments hang all the law and the prophets.'"

In my entire Bible I counted 362 admonitions concerning sexual behavior between men and women, and many of those passages were never mentioned by holier-than-thou preachers. On the subject of homosexuality, however, I could find only a total of six references in the entire Bible. With the exception of two graphic verses in the Old Testament (which every bigoted, antigay preacher this side of the eternal fires has committed to memory), there is nothing to rival the biblical condemnations of adultery, lust, or other prohibited acts committed by heterosexual sex fiends in or out of the ministry of the "moral" majority! By sheer weight of numbers, 6 versus 362, you can see who God was worried about!

To condemn homosexuals, many denominations have intentionally misread and misinterpreted their Bibles to please their own personal preferences, remembering only verses that suit themselves, forgetting or ignoring many other scriptures. As I started reading, I began comparing things I had heard preached in the churches with what I actually found in the Bible.

On several occasions my initial reading brought acute discomfort. I read in Leviticus that mankind who lies with mankind should be stoned to death! That it is an abomination and their blood shall be upon their own head! It says exactly that. But then I reread the rest of the dos and don'ts and I discovered something else: the verses also said the same thing in reference to witches and wizards (whoever they are). Did that mean fortune-tellers should be stoned to death?

My study progressed. I went forward to the New Testament and back to the Old Testament, reading Deuteronomy and Numbers and Leviticus again and again. As I read and reread every verse, the puzzling pieces of God's picture miraculously fell into place. I said to myself, "Just look here a minute! If we as Christians are going to blindly accept some parts of the Bible, then we have to take them all! You must consider that there are scriptures which say clearly that it is an abomination to mix fabrics— in other words, one is forbidden to wear cotton and linen at the same time. There are scriptures which state clearly that you may not eat shrimp, lobster, oysters, or have your steak cooked too rare.

"If you follow every verse of Scripture in the Old Testament, then multimillion-dollar sewers in our cities need to be abandoned because there are Bible verses in which every descendant of the children of Israel is told to walk around with his or her little paddle for digging holes. That may once have been the ancient method of getting rid of human waste, but today, our police would certainly arrest us for slavishly adhering to scripture!"

Repeatedly rereading verses, it became clear to me that literally following every word of the Bible was to deny the capacity for reasoning God gave to the human race. And as I searched through the Old Testament, I found more and more things we were told to do that nobody in his or her right mind would even consider anymore.

As for the question "What did Jesus say about homosexuality?" the answer is simple. Jesus said nothing.

Not one thing.

Nothing!

Jesus was more interested in *love*. What Jesus condemned was lust, no matter in what form lust occurred. That is what Jesus talked about.

The apostle Paul added more things. In Romans, Paul disapproved of women engaging in vile affections contrary to nature, and men burning in their lust one toward another. Those things Paul called "unseemly" and he labeled them as "error." But Paul was also concerned with *lust* (including homosexual lust) as opposed to love.

Nevertheless, Paul does seem to have disapproved of gay men and lesbians. He also disapproved of women becoming teachers or preachers. He did not like men with long hair or women with short hair. And let us not forget, Paul was completely in favor of slavery. As a result of

Paul's written opinions, eighteen centuries later (in 1848—slightly more than a decade before America's Civil War), slave-owning Baptists split away from their parent organization; the Southern Baptists quoted the apostle Paul as their authority for their "God-given right" to own people as slaves. In this day and age, nobody in her or his right mind would say such a thing. But Paul not only said it, he wrote it in the Bible.

Scholars, theologians, and tyrants have picked through biblical verses for hundreds of years, choosing only what pleased them. My coming to that realization provided me with scriptural ammunition to fight back, because I knew that people who would want to use Scripture against me would only understand our defense if Scripture was used. I decided to memorize obscure passages as never before. It was essential to stand on my own two feet and be able to say, "All right, certainly the Bible says thus and so—but the Bible also says this! What do you have to say about that?"

I knew I would have few if any problems with the so-called liberal churches. Liberal churches do not usually deeply involve themselves with Scripture. But I knew the fundamentalists would want to hurl selected chapters and verse at me, picking and choosing the approved quotations as they delight in doing. However, from my background, I was aware that Bible-quoting fundamentalists have few unrehearsed answers. Thus, I wanted to be able, always, particularly with impressionable young people, to be able to say, "Wait a minute! Sure, the Bible says what you said. Yes, that's absolutely right—but your verses have been taken out of context.

"Let us see what else the Bible says!"

The Holy Spirit had been with us in Los Angeles, then as now, but not everyone was optimistic about our future. If you had asked Willie Smith in 1968 what he anticipated would be Metropolitan Community Church's ultimate size and number of churches, he would candidly have said, "Our parlor in Los Angeles, and maybe another living room in San Francisco!"

Growth was rapid, nevertheless, even if not always easy. In our community were many gay people who were, despite our "gay" label, anything but happy. Tremendous need existed for a bold ministry. Literally tens of thousands of homosexual sons and daughters, sisters and brothers, plus our friends and the friendless in every age group from puberty on, who had been robbed of their self-esteem, were waiting to find and heed our basic message, "God loves you!" They came to us with tears and newfound hope. We were the first Christian bulwark against a determinedly ignorant society whose homophobic cruelty masked a callous indifference to humanity.

Once we knew we would succeed, we moved with utmost speed, and although caution was advised, it was frequently disregarded, often for reasons beyond our control. During the first two years, our fast-growing congregation continuously outgrew the dimensions of available meeting places, but also, on several occasions, our moves occurred when the landlords of various civic and fraternal organizations discovered they were renting to "queers who meet on the premises every Sunday."

The membership of Metropolitan Community Church was primarily homosexual, but we did have a membership of 5 to 15 percent who were heterosexual. For various good reasons, the latter were genuinely unconcerned about the sexuality of the majority of worshipers. Together, all of us worked to expand our outreach toward a tide of scorned unfortunates who we knew were being swept into oblivion every day by unpublicized acts of self-destruction.

My practice was to preach wherever I was welcome and, sometimes, to preach where I was not welcome. The first time Metropolitan Community Church was invited to hold a service outside of the greater Los Angeles area, the location was a gay bar in Orange County, not far from Disneyland. When I arrived, the bar's owner, who had invited me, was not present. To make the situation more difficult, the bartender-in-charge, unsympathetic and suspicious of my motives, was unaware of the owner's invitation.

Yet I was not to be denied!

Adjoining the bar, through a broad doorway, I could see a dining room that was empty at the moment. "How would it be if I preached in there?" I asked.

The bartender's relief became apparent. "Oh yes," he said quickly. "If you must, off in there would be okay—anywhere would be better than here. Just don't start preaching at the counter where I sell drinks."

"Oh, no!" I agreed.

Before long, about fifteen residents of the area who had heard of the meeting arrived for prayer, and several bar patrons with drinks joined us in the dining room. We then began what was probably the most disconcerting worship service I have ever held.

There was no door to close the opening between the bar and the dining room. The bartender would not turn off the jukebox or even consider lowering its volume. On several occasions, bar patrons, fortified with ample amounts of alcohol, decided we were from the Salvation Army and wanted to know if we were collecting money—and where were our tambourines?

Every person present was a male homosexual. Toward the end of the hectic service, just as I lifted a silver chalice to consecrate communion, from the monstrous jukebox in the barroom Tammy Wynette's voice blared forth at full volume, singing "Stand By Your Man"!

That was our initial outreach from the Los Angeles Mother Church. With it, as with other instances in the gay tradition of camp, we have learned and never forgotten that God has a sense of humor.

Another ultimately humorous occasion began with what at first seemed like a disaster. It occurred on a wintry day in December 1970 when a feature article was carried as front page news in the *Washington Post.* The story reported that I, besides proclaiming that God loves gay people, would be in the nation's capital to perform a holy union, often referred to as a "gay marriage" in the press.

Reverend Paul Breton, founder of a small religious gay group (destined to become the first of many strong Metropolitan Churches in the District of Columbia, met me when I arrived. He thrust his copy of the *Washington Post* into my hands and I read it with delight. In those days, any reference to a gay event, whether positive or negative, was sufficiently unusual that we considered it a triumph of public relations. There were even celebrations if the reportage was not entirely prejudicial or derogatory, even though general public knowledge of our whereabouts or our doings very often brought repercussions.

I was scheduled to give my sermon at an Episcopal church Reverend Breton had rented, and the holy union was to follow at the same location. As it happened, our greeting at the church was not quite what we anticipated. The temperature was 23 degrees Fahrenheit when we arrived, and snow on the ground was five inches deep. I was wearing a suit that would be comfortable year-round in Los Angeles, but in Washington, D.C., although at first I made an attempt to ignore the cold, I soon admitted to being a Southern boy and began to contemplate the undesirable aspects of freezing fingers and feet.

Unfortunately, a problem much worse than temperature existed. The bishop responsible for Episcopal churches in the District of Columbia was a reader of the *Washington Post,* and he did not like what he read about us. Furthermore, the bishop was adamantly opposed to any marriage joining persons of the same gender. On his forceful orders, we were, without any notice or prior warning, locked out in the snow, unable to enter the church Paul had rented for the afternoon.

Later, we were told that the Episcopal vestry who manage the temporal affairs of that church attempted to resist their bishop. They said to him, "The people of Metropolitan Community Church are Christians, and in the spirit of good faith, the least we can do is to honor our commitment!"

Those words of reason were not well received. "I don't care what you want," ranted the irate prelate. "I don't want homosexuals using an Episcopal building. Can I make myself any clearer? No? Then, since accepting my wishes seems to cause you some difficulty, I'll go further. I invoke canon law. I will be obeyed. All authority is hereby out of your hands!"

Given any choice, our shivering little band of seventeen persons, after holding nothing more than a simple service of worship, would gladly have settled for moving to a different location to witness vows of holy union. None of us had been aware of any problem until faced with the church's locked door. Others, however, did have advance information. In the snow and the cold, we were outnumbered and surrounded by reporters, press photographers, and television crews lugging their cumbersome equipment.

"What are we going to do now?" asked one member of Paul Breton's congregation, rubbing his frigid hands together for a moment of warmth.

"We'll hold our service out here," I said. "Right here and right now." Under my breath I added, "And fast!" Then I said, in a grandstand play for the media, "All of us realize how icy cold it is here today, where we have been locked out in the snow, but as Christians, we're not moving away from where God has given us a right to be! Hallelujah! Amen?"

"Amen!" echoed several voices.

The group gathered near me on the side lawn of the church and I preached—until my jaw felt like a block of ice. The entire prayer meeting moved along in double-time. It only lasted about eight minutes from start to finish, including my sermon. I usually try to preach not much over twenty minutes, but that service in the snow was, and remains, the shortest sermon I ever delivered!

Metropolitan Community Churches celebrate communion every Sunday. That icy service was no exception. Our people knelt in the snow to partake of the body and blood of Christ. It must have been a picturesque sight although, for those of us who participated, it was very painful. One young woman was shivering almost uncontrollably in the bitter cold, but everyone, including a fragile old man, endured long enough to complete the abbreviated program.

Afterward, we were brushing wet snow from our knees when a television commentator in an Arctic-proof overcoat unexpectedly thrust a microphone in front of my face. "What do you intend to do now?" he demanded.

My plan, until that precise second, was to seek a warm coffee shop and drink hot chocolate. But a new idea flashed into my head. Without hesitation, I told the newsman, "We are going to pray for the soul of the Episcopal bishop who denied shelter to this small band of Christians you see here, locked out in the freezing cold. The bishop is in need of salvation, and in order to pray for him, we are now on our way to the National Cathedral!"

Reverend Breton's head swiveled in my direction. "We are?" he said.

"Yes," I replied with bravado to accompany my sudden inspiration. "Get the cars, Paul. Load up your church members and let's go!" To the press I said, "The National Cathedral is a building that also belongs to the Episcopalians. Let's find out if their bishop has enough power to also keep us out of there!"

Our congregation had dwindled to eight when we arrived at the cathedral, but the press corps and television crews with their cameras had somehow increased. The National Cathedral is a tourist attraction, and hundreds of people in overcoats and mufflers were milling around on the inside. We worked our way through the crowds into the sanctuary. When we had progressed beyond most of the tour groups, we discovered that an iron fence separated us from a breathtakingly beautiful altar. Meanwhile, because the media stayed close to us and followed our every move with their cameras, we became a secondary tourist attraction, although few observers had any idea of who we were.

We moved forward, realizing that anything we could do would probably be anticlimactic. Then, as I entered a wide aisle which led directly to the iron fence, a youthful clergyman appeared from off to the side and suddenly blocked my progress. He was obviously perturbed, and willing to fight Lucifer to protect the cathedral.

Television cameras moved closer. It was showdown time, and I suspected that the balloon of interest we had created was about to pop. But Jesus was with us, and a small but wonderful miracle occurred.

Before I could say anything to the young man, his eyes widened appreciably, and I could see a glint of friendly recognition. Unexpectedly, a warm smile appeared on his face and, in a loud whisper, he asked, "You're Reverend Troy Perry, aren't you?"

I quickly returned his smile. I know a friend when I see one. "Yes," I acknowledged, grasping the outstretched hand of the clergyman and proceeding to shake it.

"Reverend Perry," he blurted out, "I am so happy to meet you! I'm an Episcopal seminary student and I've read all about you in *The Advocate*. Can you tell me, why are you here?"

It was definitely a time to be candid. "Your bishop had us locked out of one of your churches we rented. Because of him, our members have nearly caught their death kneeling in the snow. So I've come here to pray for your bishop!"

"That's terrible," frowned the perturbed seminary student who obviously wanted to help us. When a sly, conspiratorial glint brightened his features, I knew there was a solution. "Look," he said, producing a key from his pocket and holding it for my perusal, "this will open that iron gate. Would you like to pass inside and use our main altar?"

"Would I!" was my instant response.

The seminary student turned his key in the lock, the gate opened, and I advanced to the splendid altar where I immediately fell on my knees and thanked God for watching over us. Directly behind me, the media charged toward the alter, popping flash guns and hauling battery packs for their television cameras.

I began to pray.

Quiet spread through the inner recesses of the National Cathedral. Tourists who had been moving aimlessly, took seats in the pews, and some knelt. Many Catholics who were still present in the Episcopal cathedral after attending the funeral of a founder of Alcoholics Anonymous were fingering their rosaries as my prayers continued.

We savored the moment. Eventually I stood and, with both arms raised, turned to face the assembled crowd. My booming voice echoed in the chamber as I prayed: "God, I want you to cure the Episcopal bishop of his homophobia! Let the bishop know that homosexuals are everywhere, and that we have been here in this wonderful building with you today! Let the bishop realize right now that you love us, because gay men and lesbians are your people just as much as anybody else. Throughout the world we suffer under the yoke of civil and religious oppression! So, Lord, we ask now that you release us. Set homosexuals free! Amen!"

Amid gasps of shock, tourists clutched parcels, grabbed their children, and hastened for the nearest exits. Episcopalians were merely stunned, but some of the Catholics released the grip on their rosaries and actually dropped beads all over the floor.

The Episcopal seminary student who opened the gate to the altar for us was Jack Isbell. Jack is now a minister ordained in the Universal Fellowship of Metropolitan Community Churches. Neither he nor I ever again emptied people from a building so fast in all of our lives!

4

Gifts of the Spirit:
September 1972

*Now there are varieties of gifts, but the same
Spirit; and there are varieties of service, but
the same Lord; and there are varieties of
working, but it is the same God who inspires
them all in every one. To each is given the
manifestation of the Spirit for the common
good.*
　　　　　　　—1 Corinthians 12: 4–7

RECOLLECTIONS of some services of worship come gloriously to
mind, while others bring tears and varying measures of sadness. In the
short time our denomination has existed—not much longer than a score
of years since October 6, 1968—we have founded hundreds of churches
and offered devotion within the boundaries of many nations, always
praising the Almighty, believing our Creator helps those who help themselves, carrying our inspirational message "God loves you," and quoting
Matthew (22: 37–40), wherein Jesus never spoke more clearly.

Each of us who became a part of Metropolitan Community Church
has been ever anxious to proclaim the Good News that is ours to give,
but in the early years, before we had hundreds of churches and tens of
thousands of members, we traveled on faith—with little more than enthusiasm to sustain us.

In the second year of our existence, when the Universal Fellowship of
Metropolitan Community Churches came into being and I became its
moderator, my mother had come to live with me, and we survived on
the small salary I received. Sometimes we were hungry. Once all my
credit cards were revoked for nonpayment, and for a while we existed
on a limited diet of spaghetti and canned asparagus which charitable

members had donated to what was called the Deacon's Closet. Our congregations were, for the most part, blissfully unaware that their pastor and his family were forced to feed themselves with provisions for the needy.

All of us worked with unceasing fervor, and before long the success of the church brought various rewards. For me it meant, among other blessings, a steady income and hot meals on the dining room table. For the membership it meant a beautiful building of our own in which to pray. But in some nonfinancial ways, Metropolitan Community Church had struggled into desperate times.

The church, which had grown with vitality from its infancy, suddenly was threatened with becoming nonevangelical. Conservative members struggled for a retreat toward social invisibility. They were unsure about continuing our involvement with Christian liberation theology. They shrank from our participation in vocal or visible gay community action. Their idea was that we had done all we should to promote public enlightenment. To the contrary, my idea was that we should never abandon our mission, and that like the Early Christian Church, social action was required of us by God.

It may seem peculiar to say that during the first two years of Metropolitan Community Church—when we met to pray, when we were derided, when we were frequently evicted and forced to move from one place to another—we were, unknowingly, experiencing the easiest years of our existence. Then, our philosophy and our motivations were uncomplicated: we loved God, we came to realize that God loved us in return, and all we needed seemed to be a building of our own where we could worship without apprehension. Every accomplishment, even the smallest, was an exciting milestone on a divine course that nobody had ever previously traveled. Unfortunately, after we bought, renovated, and (on March 7, 1971) consecrated our first church, the large, imposing edifice which stood at the corner of Twenty-second and Union in Los Angeles, many of us thought we had accomplished our final objective, thought we had arrived in the daylight at the end of a long, dark tunnel. But thereafter, problems began, and our destiny became less clear.

Somewhere along the way many of us, myself included, had developed the habit of saying that Metropolitan Community Church's only reason for being was to encourage long-established denominations to reexamine their homophobic interpretations of theology. A substantial number of members in our congregation agreed that once we revealed the extent of hyprocisy in other churches, their unchristian attitudes would surely be corrected and—continuing with that overly optimistic theory—each of us then would happily be welcomed back into the *reformed* denomination of his or her previous persuasion.

Baptists, Catholics, Methodists, Episcopalians, Mormons, Presbyterians, and a long roll call of members from a long list of other denominations could prepare to be joyfully welcomed back into the churches where they had been baptized or were once associated—if only the day of acceptance might ever be achieved! Many of us who should have known better more than once commented, "We are working to work ourselves out of business."

Some thought otherwise.

We were beset with soul-searching questions: Was it a proper course for Metropolitan Community Church to cease to exist when—if—other denominations eventually accepted gay Christians as God's children? Or was it God's intention that the Universal Fellowship of Metropolitan Community Churches should remain viable and continue to grow?

There was no consensus.

After nearly four years of existence, when our Third General Conference was held in Los Angeles during the Labor Day weekend, we were at a crossroads. The year was 1972, and it happened that an analytical business-management consultant, an ex-Mormon on the threshold of becoming one of our ordained ministers, quietly challenged the overall perception of what Metropolitan Community Church should become. The results he precipitated were too miraculous to be foretold. James E. Sandmire did not know he was about to preach the most important sermon of his life.

Jim was born a Mormon, the healthy son of robust pioneer parents with genealogical ties to the powerful leaders of their denomination. His grandfather was president of their own congregation. In high school, Jim learned easily and was an honor student, but not exactly a saint in the Mormon tradition. However, following his graduation from Harvard Business School, Jim bid farewell to a "wild and riotous life" and undertook a two-year period of missionary work, which was expected of him and his peers. Soon afterward, Jim and an attractive young woman were unceremoniously informed by authorities in the church that it was "God's will that they should wed." The marriage lasted nine years. Mrs. Sandmire's pregnancies were periods of joy which never lasted, for none of their infants survived childbirth. Others were adopted to fill the void.

During this same period when Jim Sandmire was becoming a leader in the Mormon church, he simultaneously, as so often occurs, arrived at the stage in life when maturing sexual urges refused to be denied. Jim foreswore living the life of a closeted homosexual. The result was divorce,

49

a major reorganization of his life, and the particularly painful rejection of a homophobic theology he could not, with any integrity, continue to accept.

Jim moved to California, settled down with a lover (with whom he has lived for over twenty-seven years), and started a very successful business. According to Jim, the business world would have made him wealthy had he not crossed the path of Troy Perry, after reading about me in a popular gay newspaper called *The Advocate*.

Sandmire was glancing at the paper one evening in his living room when he discovered a prominent article. "Will you just look at this!" declared Jim, shoving the newspaper into his lover's hands, "A gay church! Can you imagine? What will they think of next? It has to be a travesty—or some terrible joke!"

But curiosity is a great propellant. Jim came to hear our message, then had to begin rearranging his life all over again. One week after hearing my sermon, he joined the congregation of Metropolitan Community Church. Two Sundays after that he became a deacon. Within another fortnight, at the urging of Reverend Howard Wells, pastor of our first church in the San Francisco Bay Area, Jim organized a midweek prayer group, which rapidly evolved into the Metropolitan Community Church of Oakland, California. After a little time, while still a deacon, he became our pastor in San Francisco.

On September 3, 1972, the final day of our Third General Conference held in Los Angeles, Jim Sandmire, having become highly regarded as a licensed minister in our Fellowship, was scheduled to preach the main sermon. Then later, prior to the completion of the same morning service, he was to be ordained. The church at Twenty-second and Union was filled to capacity by eleven o'clock that Sunday morning. Thirty-five Metropolitan Community Church congregations from cities as far away as Chicago, Boston, and Miami were represented.

The Mother Church had two renovated auditoriums consisting of a pleasant, spacious sanctuary with stage and altar, and a smaller adjoining chamber. Above the rear of the main room was a wide strip of balcony. All locations, including standing areas, were full. Outside, late arrivals stood, prayed, and listened to the ensuing service from loudspeakers. All in all, fifteen hundred persons were present.

As usual, the sanctuary had a clean, fresh appearance with its bright green carpet, upholstered theater seats secured in neat rows, and antique-white walls. Suspended from the center of the high ceiling was one large, highly polished brass chandelier. An impressive, multicolored stained glass window in the east wall depicted gentle Jesus beckoning to us from a bright meadow where he appeared to be slightly suspended without earthy support.

On the stage, Reverend Ploen, Reverend Hose, and a number of others, including myself, were seated as Jim Sandmire, wearing his black ministerial robe, approached the pulpit. Jim's hair, prematurely silver and white, was neatly combed back from the top and sides of his head, accentuating the penetrating eyes and dark eyebrows.

He was not an emotional speaker. His manner has always been intellectual. If you wanted to know what Jim wished to convey to you, it was necessary to be attentive. When the congregation hushed, following a rousing hymn led by white-robed Willie Smith, Jim began a spiritually provocative exhortation.

"One of the most attractive doctrines of our early Fellowship," said Jim with characteristic sincerity, "was that we were building a refuge— a refuge for people of all Christian faiths who had been unable to worship comfortably in other established churches. In so doing, we said that Metropolitan Community Church would endure only so long as it was needed, and not any longer.

"Now, I know a lot of us believe that means M.C.C. is simply in business until such time as the churches of our childhood decide to open their doors to those of us who are gay—which assumes that the more they become willing to accept us as whole and healthy Christians, the less M.C.C. will need to remain in existence. In my opinion, that is incorrect.

"Dissolution of M.C.C. under any circumstances would be a terrible tragedy, particularly if God has truly called us to be an authentic voice of our time!"

A few persons in the auditorium said "Amen," more out of habit than conviction. They were not certain where Sandmire's sermon would lead.

"I believe we are the new establishment church," Jim said with an increased note of optimism, temporarily allaying any apprehension. "I believe we are a new expression of the Gospel. I believe God has called us to be a guide for other churches which need to be shown the way toward a rediscovery of Jesus' love."

"Amen!" from a few more members of the gathered congregations.

Jim raised his hand. "But," he said firmly, a measure of admonition entering his voice, "I fear we have allowed ourselves to become complacent, satisfied with our own situation now that we have a grand building here in L.A., and so many other fine churches in the Fellowship. Have we become too satisfied? Are we becoming less than dedicated to the outreach God has called upon us to accomplish?

"My concern is that although most of us are gay, we are in danger of becoming a pale reprint of all the self-righteous, do-nothing churches we came from. The irony is that as we seem to become less active in pursuit of gay and lesbian rights, several of the denominations we fled years ago seem finally to be responding to renewal, partly because of us, and they are attempting to change their direction in order to view the humanity of homosexuals with a more positive attitude.

"Therefore, if the Fellowship is to continue as a meaningful religious experience, we need to make these essential assumptions: our theology needs to remain basic, centered on the love of God, with genuine expressions of goodness and responsibility to others. An earlier example of what I mean was set nearly two thousand years ago by Jesus—who consorted with outcasts, championed the weak, and raised the humble.

"Jesus believed religion should serve to bring all people close to God, and to one another in spiritual love. If Metropolitan Community Church is here to stay, I urge an end to middle-class introversion and the beginning of a greater commitment to opening the Fellowship to more young people, to more heterosexuals, more minority groups, and a lot more on the distaff side!"

Among the listeners that day were a few women who clapped hands enthusiastically at the suggestion of their greater representation. The women's applause was joined by our male majority, and Jim Sandmire was pleased. He smiled in his own thoughtful, unhurried manner, and then continued. "We should not be too concerned," he said, "that different churches in our Fellowship may adopt varying spiritual trappings. Devotion need not be a wholly rigid ritual.

"The love of God, need for a Savior, the sacrifice of Christ, salvation through the grace of God, the value of Christian life, renewal of our spirit in baptism, Holy Communion, and honest prayer, these are the minimum all must believe. No more should be required.

"Our religious services should remain open, participative, and particularly attentive to the needs of individual congregations. An exciting thing is that we are not bound by anything other than devotion to God, divine scriptures, and the Holy Spirit. The result, constantly restated in vital and living ways, can be an ecumenical faith grounded in what we have been taught by Jesus Christ."

"Amen, amen," murmured a sprinkling of voices throughout the sanctuary.

Jim's voice became more intense, but only slightly louder. He said, "I believe God would desire that we stop talking about going out of business and start actually being the new prophetic voice to the world!"

Applause began spontaneously, but Sandmire motioned for his audience to withhold approval. "A church like Metropolitan Community Church has never before existed anywhere on earth," he said, hesitating until he had everyone's attention. Then he resumed with simple eloquence.

"If it is God's will," said Jim, standing motionless with his arms at his sides, speaking as if to each individual in the auditoriums and the balcony, "we shall be available to spiritual manifestations. If it is God's will that Metropolitan Community Church shall continue to grow and go forward, then all gifts of the Holy Spirit that identify the church will be ours."

The approbation that followed was accepted by Jim who quietly remained beside the podium for a few moments. "Amen," he said before modestly resuming his seat.

Afterward, there was an air of uncertainty, the muted excitement of expectancy as though a high level of energy had entered the building. The overall feeling was electric. Something was happening.

Our Fellowship choir sang an anthem as silver plates were passed to take the offering. I pushed back into my chair, mentally anticipating the next part of the service when my function would be to ordain new ministers into the Universal Fellowship. There was time to reflect on Jim's sermon which suggested that if we should continue to exist, expressions of the Holy Spirit would identify the church. Did he mean that in the absence of spiritual manifestations, we should cease to exist? The acolyte had challenged heaven!

Opening my Bible to First Corinthians, I read silently, "Now concerning spiritual gifts, brethren, I would not have you ignorant—to one is given wisdom, to another knowledge, to another faith, to another gifts of healing, to another the working of miracles, to another prophecy, to another discerning of spirits, to another divers kinds of tongues, to another the interpretation of tongues."

What I read seemed, at first, not difficult to understand, but I knew from experience that identical words have different meanings for different people. Reverend Sandmire's expectation for manifestations of the Holy Spirit undoubtedly were unlike my expectations because we came from very dissimilar religious backgrounds. Mormons, to the best of my knowledge, do not view speaking in tongues as an authentic tradition. I do. Mormons are not expected to rely upon faith healers, but Pentecostal preachers are occasionally known to yank people from their sickbeds and proclaim them healed upon the spot!

It is because the membership of Metropolitan Community Churches derives from nearly every Christian denomination or sect imaginable that our understanding of scripture is so vast and richly varied, like a beautiful country quilt. For that reason alone, it was essential we continue as Jim had said, bound by our devotion to God and the Holy Spirit.

When the offering was over, our ordination service began. The candidates kneeled in one row, and as I moved before them, I quietly prayed with my head close to each person, then lifted my voice for the benefit of the assembled congregations and related something personal about each particular individual:

Bob Cunningham had owned a gay bar. He first came to church because he thought it would appeal to his customers and be good for business. As it happened, Bob became a minister and left the bar.

Joseph Gilbert had spent a cruel period of time in jail for describing sexually explicit fantasies in his private love letters to a consenting adult. Postal inspectors, in what was once considered their duty, had unsealed and read Joe Gilbert's mail. His sentence for posting "unacceptable" letters was five years in a federal prison.

Howard Williams had been a Presbyterian minister. His persistence persuaded Reverend "Papa" John Hose and myself to preach in San Diego where, in the very early days of our religious existence, the first Metropolitan Community Church that would join the Fellowship was established. (The Mother Church in Los Angeles was second, joining the Universal Fellowship of Metropolitan Community Churches after San Diego.)

There were also others to be ordained, including Jim Sandmire, with whom I prayed. After Jim was ordained, I paused for a moment with my eyes shut. That was the moment when, without warning, somebody started speaking aloud in a strange language.

My immediate reaction was annoyance. I had grown up with fanaticism all around me, and felt a residue of shame. Glossolalia is not an uncommon event in my Pentecostal background, but until that moment, a speaking in tongues had never been heard in the Mother Church. I did not feel comfortable discussing it with others and never mentioned glossolalia from the pulpit. God forgive me, because what happened in the crowded sanctuary that Sunday morning was so public, so powerful, so real, that there was no denying it.

We heard a voice that was male, rich in quality, and powerful. Some said the language sounded like Spanish but others suggested Latin. It was neither.

When I heard the unexpected, I looked up immediately. The person speaking was not where I could see him but that did not seem important.

My visual attention was diverted to something I had never dreamed of before—a grayish, slightly blue haze that filled the entire sanctuary. It was as though a cloud had settled around the church on that day of sunshine, and a soft, edgeless fog found its way inside.

The voice in tongues continued briefly with a deliberate, mesmerizing effect. I closed my eyes again, as if on command, and listened a short time longer. Then it was over, but my heart was pounding. I felt soothed, then excited, with emotions alternating as though governed by a pendulum.

One moment later, in the blink of an eye, translation of the message began from a separate source. The second voice was also male, purposeful and unwavering. "I have called you, my children," said the interpreter, "I have established you to be my church. If you will listen to me and follow my precepts, you will continue to grow."

Witnesses by the hundreds, the majority being intelligent and successful businessmen attracted from an entire spectrum of religious backgrounds, listened in awe. Each later seemed to have observed the moment as if viewing slightly different facets of a single splendid gem. They were not people to be overwhelmed by hallucinations or engulfed in mass hysteria.

Paul Peachy has been a Baptist for many years, and in accordance with the holdings of the Baptists, Paul had always disbelieved in the gift of tongues. By chance, however, when the speaking in tongues occurred as it did during our service, Paul was seated beside a person conditioned from childhood to believe what Paul did not believe. While the public interpretation of the spoken cryptic message was happening, Paul became aware that the quiet but intense individual beside him was, in a soft unmodulated voice, also interpreting the message—simultaneously—and nearly word for word. Paul's negative and well-entrenched ideas about gifts of the Spirit were instantly converted to a newly enhanced perception.

"There will be persecutions," said the prophetic interpretation. "There will be heartaches and difficulties, but if in faith you seek your needs, whatever they be, they will be met. Signs will follow believers in My Name. You will cast out devils and witness great achievements. This will happen so long as you continue to repeat the message that I have given— God loves you."

It is reported that our interpreter for the deaf, signing on the stage behind me, was immediately busy with his hands converting the unintelligible syllables into a silent language, and that he was promulgating the tidings in tongues with a meaning identical to, but slightly *ahead* of, the translation being spoken. Other extraordinary spiritual manifestations, akin to those reported at the original Pentecost, continued for several breathtaking minutes. During that span, every gift of the Holy Spirit was expressed, and the cumulative effect was so overwhelming that beholders were in absolute awe of what was happening.

After a time, when we were able to begin communion, rays of golden sunlight began to stream into the sanctuary through our stained glass windows. The rays shone on those in a line to partake of the sacrament. Among them was a man of about sixty who was a member of the Metropolitan Community Church in Denver. He wore a bulky, old-fashioned hearing aid which, even at full volume, was practically useless to him because his hearing had been essentially nonexistent for a considerable number of years. He also wore earplugs to alert strangers that he was deaf.

As the man moved forward to the altar, his hearing device suddenly emitted a loud, ear-piercing squeal of which he, and those of us anywhere in the vicinity, became very much aware. Believing that the hearing contraption had shorted itself, the embarrassed man ripped the tiny speaker from his ear, hastily stuffed the device into his pocket, and kneeled to take communion. It was during that devout moment when it slowly dawned upon him what had happened.

No longer was he imagining sound. He was actually hearing sound. And for the better part of a minute I saw him repeatedly touching his fingertips first to one ear and then the other. On his face there was an extremely pleased, yet dazed, expression.

"Are you okay?" I asked, not knowing what had transpired.

The man's eyes drifted toward mine. With almost no inflection in his voice, he said, "I can hear." He repeated it several times. Finally he stood, and nearly delirious with joy, hurriedly returned to his seat where he immediately began volubly telling his acquaintances what had happened.

Freda Smith was another who shared the benevolence of God's Spirit on that wonderful day. She had come to General Conference from Sacramento with the hope of becoming a licensed minister; nursing that objective she had spent all of Saturday night and the small hours of Sunday morning in the bleak, semidark confines of a carpeted foyer in the Mother Church.

In her midthirties, Freda was slender, blond, attractive—and determined. After midnight she had still been awaiting her turn to be interviewed by the ministerial credentials committee. Her application was last on their agenda, and although she received periodic encouragement from her mother who was accompanying her, Freda knew she had a genuine reason for being nervous: the licensed ministers in the Universal Fellowship of Metropolitan Community Churches were all men, and no woman had ever received the credentials committee's formal approval to pastor. Furthermore, female members of the churches were then only a small minority in the mostly male congregations.

Freda continued waiting for hours. The large church building seemed almost deserted except for herself, her mother, two preceding male applicants, and the committee itself, which was generally invisible behind closed doors. During the course of time, Freda read all available magazines in the foyer. Conversations with her mother dropped to short whispers in the stillness of the dark hours of Sunday morning. Hands on a loud, ticking clock dragged inexorably in the direction of sunrise. And Freda continued waiting, tired, wondering if the delay could be intentional, praying that it was not.

An hour and fifteen minutes after midnight, she was finally called to address the committee, fully aware that the men who preceded her had advantages she could never claim. One of them had previously been a minister in another denomination. The other had completed two thirds of the required curriculum at an established seminary. Nevertheless, Freda's credentials were unique, consisting of practical tutoring by Reverend Joseph Gilbert, her pastor at Metropolitan Community Church in Sacramento, plus many years of service as a dedicated evangelist in the Salvation Army.

Standing bravely before the ministerial credentials committee, Freda steeled herself to face men who were no less tired than she. A trained speaker, Freda was willing, if called upon, to face the Devil himself— or herself. "It touches my heart," she said with sincerity, "that some gay brothers have been disenfranchised from other churches because of their sexuality, have been terminated as pastors, or have not been allowed to complete seminary training. But will you consider the plight of women? We have had less advantages than any of your men.

"Metropolitan Community Churches won't have many female applicants who were thrown out of the well-known seminaries—because we were, on account of being women, rarely ever accepted by those institutions in the first place. Nor do I know of any women who have been thrown out of pastoring positions—for the same reason. But women do have the best of qualifications. You must surely realize that some of us are also called by God!"

Freda's listeners asked her a few questions and then she returned to the dreary hall again, to wait for their decision. A tedious half hour passed. "I'm going down to the kitchen in the basement for some coffee," she told her mother. "Do you want some?"

"No, but I'll go with you."

Freda shook her head. "Never mind. I'll only be a minute."

The time was nearly two-thirty in the morning. Freda was physically drained and in a hurry. Concrete stairs down to the basement were steep. As she ran, Freda's foot slippped on a slick tread. Her ankle twisted. Freda fell, trying to catch a metal rail, striking the sharp edges of steps until her body slammed down on the cold, uncarpeted floor below.

She tried desperately to cushion the fall as, at the same time, she became acutely aware of agony exploding within her ankle. Freda screamed once, but afterward, lying in shock on the hard basement floor, she uttered only moans of misery, clutching herself into a fetal position when the horrible pain was made worse by sickening waves of nausea.

Fortunately, Freda's mother heard the commotion and located her daughter with minimal delay, but there was little anyone could do until the consuming pain subsided, a matter of several minutes. During that same time, Freda's ankle was rapidly swelling. Soon the injury was grossly out of proportion to her foot and leg.

"I don't have time for having anything broken!" groaned Freda, annoyed by her own carelessness. Fortunately, her sympathetic mother could do more than listen to complaints. For some fortuitous reason, she had an Ace elastic bandage in her purse. Thus, Freda's ankle was tenderly bound and she was able to very carefully ascend the stairs and hobble back to the room where the credentials committee was finally ready to reveal their decision.

After the verdict was rendered, with tears streaming down her face, Freda emerged from the committee's private room and returned to her mother. "I'm licensed," she said, brushing aside the moisture on her cheeks. "Wonder of wonders, they approved me!"

All of Freda's pain was momentarily overriden.

At eleven in the morning, when Reverend Freda Smith arrived at that fateful Third General Conference, she sat for the first time in seats reserved for clergy. Her ankle, which was turning dark, ugly shades of blue, had been carefully rebound just prior to the service.

Freda listened intently as Jim Sandmire preached, and she was impressed by his every word. When she heard Jim say, "Stop talking about going out of business, and start being the new prophetic voice to the world," those words were the beginning of her own personal revelation. As a member of the Salvation Army which asked everything of its soldiers—asked time and life if necessary—Freda had never questioned orders, but the revolutionary idea of dedication to a predominantly homosexual religious organization, where men originally outnumbered women by a large margin, was more than Freda had thoroughly considered. So it was that exciting thoughts began echoing in Freda's mind. Could exemplary gay men and lesbians actually create a shining example of Christian love and evangelize the two-thousand-year-old words of Jesus Christ? Could Metropolitan Community Church address not only the lesbians and gay men in the community, but also reach out to other spiritually repressed people (and denominations) around the world?

Moments later the gifts of the Spirit would begin. Meanwhile, I was completing the ritual of ordaining our new ministers. (Ordination grants lifetime recognition in our ministry, whereas a license requires renewal.) The procedure was that as I completed praying individually with each newly ordained minister, that person would turn and reach out a hand to whoever was behind, and that person would turn and reach out a hand, and so forth, until everyone in the building was joined hand to body and heart to soul in a tactile human network. The result was a flood of joined spiritual emotion, and there seemed not to be a dry eye in the entire church.

At the moment when Freda, newly licensed, reached out her hand to James Sandmire, newly ordained, and their fingers touched, the message in tongues began.

Immediately after the message came the interpretation. "I have called you, my children," said our earthly translator, but Freda recalls knowing what each word was going to be *before* it was spoken. While she was in the Salvation Army, Freda had been taught that speaking in tongues is nearly as "wrong" as being homosexual, but she nevertheless describes what came to her ear that Sunday morning as the most beautiful sound she has ever heard.

While the translation continued, Reverend Smith raised both her arms until they were stretched upward. A lump formed in her throat. When tears entered her eyes, she thought, "No, I don't want to cry. I want to be sane. I must be sensible. All of this is contrary to what I was taught as a child!"

Freda began shaking. Her tears continued flowing. Then, abruptly, she changed her mind and decided, "If this is happening, I want all there is! I want to experience everything God is giving—this is for me!"

Other people were similarly stunned.

From his viewpoint, Jim Sandmire watched a confirmation of what he had felt strongly urged to preach, although for Jim, the voices were inaudible. "It was as though I was a spectator and not a participant," he said, "yet I could see what was happening. All around me I could feel the spiritual emotion!"

After the service was concluded, people did not want to leave the interior of the building. They seemed to be clinging to each other, wanting to prolong the moment, wanting to stop time in a blessed period of comfort, communion, and warmth. Time was moving, however, although remarkable events continued.

Freda, beautiful and flushed with excitement, started to walk away from her chair and placed all of her weight on her injured ankle without thinking about the consequences. But there was no pain! With delight, she realized that she could walk without the ankle hurting.

Freda unzipped the borrowed, overlarge boot wherein her foot had been encased. The elastic bandage was hanging loose. "I guess I didn't break anything," she casually told her lover. "Maybe I just knocked the ankle out of joint, and moving around has slipped it back into place?"

Freda's friend looked closer.

The bruise was gone.

"That's impossible!" said the friend, staring at Freda's leg. "Bruises don't instantly disappear. They change from black and blue to a greenish color, and then to an ugly yellow before they heal. The process of healing for a bad bruise like yours takes weeks!"

True, but nevertheless, there was no evidence remaining of the injury that had been so forbidding less than two hours before.

Outside, the large crowd stayed close to the church. They were in no great hurry to leave. Many were conversing on the sidewalk, and an equal number, or more, stood in the side street where there was never much traffic. The overwhelmed, no longer deaf man from Colorado was sitting on the curb with both of his feet in the street. He kept putting plugs into his ears and taking them out, over and over again, pausing now and again to explain to the curious that in a moment of wonder, his hearing had returned.

Freda walked toward me and there was the look of angels on her face. "I will know from this day forward that God has called to us with a power beyond imagination," she said. "I will never again question myself, or have any doubt concerning what this Fellowship is, and what the Fellowship is to be."

I looked at Freda, and I looked beyond.

"Amen!" said the man who would never be deaf again.

I am no stranger to miracles. The existence of Metropolitan Community Church has seemed like a wonder to many, particularly foundering gay men and women who at one time had lost their faith in the Almighty. Additionally, sincere people have occasionally testified to receiving very special attention from the Lord, to being healed of major physical afflictions while in our sanctuaries. There is genuine substance to many of the claims, but I hesitate to represent as factual individual gifts of which I have no personal knowledge.

There was, however, one healing (considerably less than miraculous in nature) with which I was directly involved. The main participant was a fifty-year-old, thin, nervous man who, with his attentive lover, frequently attended services. At first sight, it was obvious even to nonmedical observers, that he craved attention. Toward that end, he often wore a neck brace or used crutches although there seemed to be nothing substantially wrong with him.

Eventually, the man appeared at a service in a wheelchair, causing considerable consternation with a pronouncement that doctors had decided it was necessary to amputate his legs. My reaction was to have one of our staff ministers contact his physician to obtain precise information.

"The problem is entirely psychosomatic," the physician told me without any reticence. "There's nothing wrong with his legs. There's nothing at all wrong with him except he's a constant pain in the buttocks. If I was going to amputate any part of his body, it would be his head!"

Three weeks later, the petulant hypochondriac was in church again. Our Gospel choir was in the middle of a hymn when the brother let out a bloodcurdling scream from the rear of the building. Everybody, including myself and Reverend Carlton who was directing the choir, looked around. Ninety seconds later, another louder, more horrible scream shattered the tranquility of our sanctuary. By that time, I had determined the source of disruption, and my main reaction was a growing irritation.

During the next several minutes, the loud boor propelled his wheelchair into the back part of the church aisle where he let out a third heart-chilling scream, after which he made the mistake of falling out of the chair, face forward on the floor. Four or five ushers rushed to him and began trying to help. All were being very sympathetic, an emotion I had difficulty sharing.

"Leave him on the floor and move away!" I told the ushers as I arrived on the scene moments later. When a space opened, I kneeled beside the man and, as I leaned toward him, he unleashed a fourth bloodcurdling yell not many inches away from my ear.

"Stop it!" I demanded.

"I just want to praise the Lord," he moaned.

"Well, praise the Lord, but quit screaming!"

Defiantly, he looked directly into my eyes, and bellowed again! Around us, most of our audience watched, appalled.

I said, "You shut up now! You're not praising the Lord—you're screaming." Remembering that his doctor had told me there was nothing wrong with the man, I asked, "Do you want to spend the rest of your life in a wheelchair?"

"No," he replied tearfully, "of course not."

"Then we are going to claim a healing for you right now!" I said. Reaching down, I picked him up, literally by the hair of his head, and pulled him unceremoniously to his feet. Once he was up, I immediately walked to the front of the building, turned to the congregation before anything more could happen, and announced, "God has healed our brother—of whatever was wrong with him!"

The crowd went wild.

Those who were emotional rejoiced and thanked the Lord. Others, correctly hearing the tone of my voice, knew what had really happened. But it was, in either case, a definite healing. The brother could no longer play his games because I knew the truth and had taken away the fun. Nevertheless, he was out of his wheelchair, and when our "healed" brother eventually returned to church, there was no more foolishness. He is living proof that the Lord works for us in many and mysterious ways.

5

Providence:
January 1973

*Let two or three prophets speak, and let the
others weigh what is said. If a revelation is
made to another sitting by, let the first be silent. For you can all prophesy one by one, so
that all may learn and all be encouraged;
and the spirits of prophets are subject to
prophets. For God is not a God of confusion
but of peace.*
—*1 Corinthians 14: 29–33*

THE overabundant profusion of religious sects around the world exists
not because of important differences in religious perceptions, but because
in all human endeavors there have inevitably been individuals with the
obsessive need to grasp control. I would prefer to be able to say such
conflict has never been the case in the Universal Fellowship of Metropolitan Community Churches, but like all existing denominations, we
have more than once been shaken by divisive takeover attempts.

The first venture was in the summer of 1970. While I was fasting on
the steps of the Federal Building in Los Angeles to protest laws that
discriminated against homosexuals, some members of our board of directors (those who were opposed to Christian social action) called a special
congregational meeting. Their objective was to remove our denomination
from any future public involvement in secular gay activism and, in the
process, to elevate their own positions. Fortunately, our membership
understood the mission of Metropolitan Community Church better than
most of the church's directors, and voted by a lopsided count, 110 to 11,
to reject the usurpers and to maintain our original three priorities—

salvation, community, and Christian social action—which I had explained in detail at our very first service on October 6, 1968.

Much more unsettling was a second hostile effort, beginning in 1972, to overthrow the stability of our Fellowship. Unlike the first challenge, it would never include any elements of reconciliation. When it was over, I felt betrayed by a man I had believed in, a man I had felt could, with some experience, have become one of the important leaders of our Universal Fellowship.

Ron Carnes, originally from Altoona, Pennsylvania, had been an Evangelical Methodist. His features were cleanly chiseled but severely pockmarked. Plaguing Ron as an adult was his apparent inability to integrate a puritanical Methodist heritage with what he considered a debilitating burden, his burgeoning homosexual passion.

In one of Carnes' attempts to repress what he described to me as distressing sexual desires, Ron sought to endure a celibate life-style. Failing that, he unfortunately fell into the hands of a misguided minister who gave him bad advice. "What you are doing is sinful," Ron's odiously pious counselor had told him, compounding the error of prejudice by adding, "You can be cured by God!"

But homosexuality was not Ron Carnes' problem. God already knew Ron was homosexual. God had made him homosexual. (The choice never was his because there is no "cure." Those who testify and make claims to the contrary are charlatans, or are inadequately informed persons who for any of many possible reasons try to delude themselves or their associates.)

When Ron came to me, he poured out fears and misgivings, indicating that Metropolitan Community Church was his last great hope to attain salvation. He made known to us that we were a beacon in his time of wretched despair. All of us who were in contact with Ron felt tremendous compassion for the young man, particularly when copious tears streamed down his face.

"God loves you," I told Ron, and after considerable elaboration on the subjects of God, the Bible, and homosexuality, I thought Ron's uneasy months of self-punishing introspection might have ended. He seemed to brighten suddenly, exerting a charming influence on everyone with whom he came into contact.

"I've seen what M.C.C. is doing in the gay community," Ron said, "and I want to be a part of this living church!"

The words were well spoken. Less happily, all of us, including myself, misunderstood Ron's intentions. We were too ready to congratulate ourselves for exorcising homophobia in a homosexual man when (we would later learn to our dismay) within him were other equally destructive psychological forces of which we had never dreamed.

It is difficult not to blame Ron Carnes for what occurred. He was both intelligent and clever. At age twenty-one, he claimed one degree in theology, and later, another in education. Using his ability to make new friends easily, Ron deserved the credit he received when his assigned congregation of Metropolitan Community Church flourished in Denver. And so successful was he as a preacher there, and so quickly did his reputation spread throughout our Fellowship, that in only six months after becoming a viable minister in Denver, he was flattered by a couple of offers to relocate and take over as a pastor in either of two very large American cities.

In his meteoric rise as a personality in our denomination, Ron was appointed interim district coordinator for all of our churches in a wide area designated as "the mid-American district." Also, it was likely that at Metropolitan Community Church's Fourth General Conference in 1973, which was initially scheduled to be held in Denver, Ron's newly adopted city, Ron would have been the odds-on favorite to be elected to our Universal Fellowship's prestigious Board of Elders!

But none of the foregoing was sufficiently speedy or exalted for Ron. His anxiety to personally control all the theology and all the activities of our denomination, which he secretly wanted to transform into a "closeted" institution with regressive ideas, was something I had not suspected. Although Ron was not the first with that objective, nor the last, our Denver pastor's partial success was decidedly the most disruptive.

A portent of trouble appeared in 1972 at the Third General Conference in Los Angeles. Ron's egocentric discontent boiled to the surface for the first time when he learned that a highly respected black politician, State Assemblyman Willie Brown (who would eventually become Speaker of the Assembly in California's legislature), was invited to our conference to speak concerning a bill Brown and many others, myself included, wanted voted into law. The bill would allow sexual privacy for consenting adults, something all gay leaders and many others advocated—but which few dared hope could become a law within any living person's lifetime.

Ron became furious when he learned Assemblyman Brown had been invited to speak. "We absolutely must not ask this partisan politician into the church!" Ron vociferously declared. "I will not have it! Brown must not speak at our General Conference!"

At first, Carnes was difficult to take seriously, but when his rancor failed to be dissipated by any reasonable arguments from several persons, it was necessary to end the futile disagreement. "It's too late to do anything now," I said, trying to maintain a semblance of calm. "Assemblyman Brown has been invited—and Assemblyman Brown has accepted!"

"I don't care. Cancel it anyway!" snapped Carnes.

"That's not possible," I replied.

The importance Ron gave to his objection seemed oddly inappropriate. "Mr. Brown is not coming here to talk partisan politics," I tried to explain. "Give us a little credit! He's coming here to talk about gay rights, and about what we can do to make certain our rights are obtained. Whether Willie Brown is a Republican or a Democrat makes no difference in my head."

Nevertheless, when nothing I or anyone else could say seemed to soothe Ron's fury, he made his opening move. Waiting outside the Mother Church were fifty members of the Denver congregation Ron had brought with him in a chartered Greyhound bus. After I refused to reconsider the withdrawal of Willie Brown's invitation, Ron revealed that he was prepared to show his own authority. Angrily, he loaded the majority of his congregation into their bus and took them away from the General Conference for an afternoon and an evening at Disneyland. While they were at the amusement park, our other delegates applauded the assemblyman's speech.

Then (as if Ron Carnes had not already caused sufficient disruption), he initiated another commotion at the same 1972 General Conference. His rage erupted immediately following the completion of the memorable service in which the speaking in tongues occurred. Ron was extremely upset. As I was walking toward an exit via a crowded aisle, Ron, with visible wrath, blocked my path, repeatedly attempting to anger me with his accusations that there was something terribly wrong with that worship service because glossolalia was permitted.

"Babel is not a message from God!" snarled Ron.

"You're welcome to your opinion," I said.

"It's a Pentecostal trick," he snapped.

"I don't believe it was."

"Bull crap!"

"God speaks through us," I insisted.

Ron stared at me. Suddenly, his hostility exploded. His eyes, often watery, seemed brighter than usual. His voice came at me through lips drawn into a snarl. "I don't believe in this damn glossolalia!" he screamed. "If that translation had been real, I would have received it, too. I can't believe you dared any of this!"

Members of my congregation, concerned that the confrontation was about to deteriorate into a physical brawl, wordlessly moved between us.

"I'm sorry you don't believe," I said to Ron, "but I do believe. I believe in the gifts of the Spirit. I believe in the Holy Ghost. I believe in things I don't understand. I haven't any explanations. All I know, and the best I can tell you, is I'm certain this was real."

Ron took a breath and exhaled. Then, abruptly, he took one step back, turned, and marched out of the church. From that moment on, he seemed irrevocably involved in a concerted attempt to break the church in Denver away from the Universal Fellowship, and with it began his efforts to take with him all the churches in our denomination's mid-American district.

Thus, battle lines were already in existence on a fateful, final weekend in January 1973, when I met with Ron Carnes' board of directors in Denver. A real blizzard was blowing through Colorado. Howling winds were heavy with snow outside, as I, within the only slightly more hospitable meeting place, made an impassioned but losing effort to determine why members of the Metropolitan Community Church in Denver, alone of all our many congregations, were increasingly having a problem with the theology of our Universal Fellowship.

No matter what I asked, members of Ron's Denver board of directors responded to me with answers that were so obtuse that not only were they impossible to answer, they were also impossible to understand. It was additionally obvious that Ron's secular directors had been coached into making intolerant pronouncements about the personal religious beliefs of others. I deduced that Ron had prodded his group into feeling that all who had observed gifts of the Spirit, myself included, were heretics. That assessment only increased the weird feeling I had of having been thrust unprepared into a meeting in the Twilight Zone.

The encounter lasted two and a half hours. Throughout that period, I struggled to fathom the meaning of their endless, illogical verbiage. When the session was over, I had, to the best of my ability, answered every question they had seemed to be asking, but they never asked genuine questions about what was actually perturbing them. Whatever it may have been, prompting on my part elicited no enlightening responses. Therefore, toward the end of that strange and terrible meeting, I knew in my heart that there was only a single problem—Denver's pastor, my ambitious host!

I was scheduled to spend the night in the guest bedroom at Carnes' home in the city. There was no denying the convenience of those quarters because our District Conference was scheduled to begin the next day.

Our representatives from Texas, Louisiana, and Colorado would join us at the Unitarians' big Gothic church nearby, where I was expected to be the principal speaker.

My primary reason for staying in Ron's home was that I anticipated Ron and I might have the opportunity on Friday night, after the meeting with his board of directors, to have a private conversation which might somehow prevent the church in Denver from breaking away from the Fellowship. Events proved me wrong, but while the wind hammered against Ron's comfortable house and snowdrifts became deeper without, I imagined nonexistent reasons for hope.

As the stormy evening wore on, Ron drank and talked. Alcohol made him loquacious, and I let him ramble from one subject to another; sometimes he was laughing, sometimes he broke into tears. Eventually, he repeated his complaints about the speaking in tongues in Los Angeles.

"If the gifts of the Spirit had any validity, I would have received them!" Ron insisted.

Nothing I could say on the subject was helpful. Midnight passed. I realized Ron was doing most of the talking and all of the drinking. Liquor was one of his problems, impatience another.

Carnes' protracted monologue revealed clues to his motivation. Simultaneously, there were veiled hints that all of our inland churches in Texas, Oklahoma, Utah, and Colorado—in the heartland of the United States—were ready to rally beneath his secessionist banner. He would be their leader, and they, he said, would tumble to him, one after another, like dominoes.

I am a fighter, but there was no winning where my host was concerned, neither for me nor for him. Sometime, well after midnight, I had heard more than enough.

"I'm going to bed now," I said. "Hook up your telephone. There may be some messages at your service." The telephone jack had been unplugged for hours.

I was already in my room when Ron shouted, "Troy, there was a call for you!" Half a minute later as I came to the telephone, Ron, who had just heard another message, exclaimed, "Oh, Jesus, Troy!"

"Well, what is it?" I demanded, suddenly frightened. "For Pete's sake, what is it? What's happened?"

"Sit down."

"No, please, just tell me. What's wrong? Tell me what's happened!"

There was no malice in my enemy at that moment. True concern showed in his face. "There's a message that the L.A. church is on fire! It's burning!"

Shock hit me like a locomotive.

"Burning? You mean—burning now?" I managed to ask.

"Yes! Somebody just tried to call. Didn't leave a number."

"It's a joke. Somebody's trying to be funny, but I don't think fire's funny!"

Ron handed me the telephone. "You call L.A.," he said.

I could tell from Ron's expression that as far as he was concerned, the message was valid. I dialed the number for the Mother Church where our crisis intervention center operated an anti-suicide hotline all night, every night, but there was no answer. I hung up and dialed a second time, without success.

One after another, I attempted to contact every member of the Los Angeles board of directors, but nobody answered. Then, when I was nearly frantic with apprehension, Reverend Lee Carlton answered the second time I dialed his home.

Hearing my assistant pastor's voice was a relief. "Thank the Lord, Lee! Why didn't you answer before?" I asked.

"I just got home, Troy. Just walked in the door."

"Is there a fire?" I blurted.

"Where?" he asked.

"At the church!" I roared in exasperation.

A brief silence followed. After a few seconds that seemed forever, Lee said patiently, "We were over near the church. Went by on the freeway coming from the Shrine Auditorium. Didn't see anything."

I began to relax.

The earlier telephone message started to seem bogus, but my anxiety persisted. "Lee," I said, "Do me a favor—please. Find out for sure! If you can't get the church by telephone, go back by there, okay? And then call me?"

Reverend Carlton readily agreed and immediately departed. In the meantime, the idea dawned upon me that I could call the Los Angeles Fire Department. They would have information. Within several minutes, I was on the line with the department and my call was being transferred to a public relations officer who was part of the city's fire program. His duty was to disseminate knowledge to the press, television, and sometimes, even the general public.

"I'm Reverend Troy Perry," I told him. "I've received a telephone message that my church is on fire—at Twenty-second and Union. Can you tell me if someone's pulling a hoax?"

"I'll check it for you," replied a much too cheery voice on the other end of the line.

My fingers trembled as I waited. I hoped for the best but tried to be prepared for anything. When the public relations officer returned, as he began to speak, I tightly gripped the edge of the table.

"Reverend Perry?"

"Yes?" I answered nervously.

"Twenty-second and Union is involved in a major-alarm fire. Seventeen units have responded."

The words were like a knife plunged into my stomach, but robotlike, the public relations officer's voice continued. It was just another fire for him and he was professionally undisturbed. I wondered if that was his general manner and training, or if he was unsympathetic because a gay church might be burning to the ground. In Denver, nevertheless, the crisis temporarily shoved aside any animosity that existed between my host and me.

There would be no sleep. I felt impelled to be in Los Angeles in the morning. At least an hour was consumed arranging emergency air transportation at an hour when ticket agents prefer to be asleep (particularly when weather conditions indicate the futility of departure attempts). Our pastor from Salt Lake City, who was visiting Denver for the District Conference on the morrow, had driven to Colorado in his four-wheel-drive Jeep. It was one of the few vehicles which could navigate Denver's nearly unmanageable drifts of snow that night. The pastor came to Ron's home.

"Can you get me to the airport?" I asked, telling him, "They hope to get a plane off the ground at dawn if there's a lull in the storm."

Around four o'clock in the morning I loaded my bags into the Jeep and we started off without regard for ice or snow. In the windy, forbidding darkness, we slipped and skidded along almost totally abandoned roads all the way to Denver's partially deserted airport. There was no encouragement that any planes could take off during the coming day, but fortunately, a brief after-dawn lull in the blizzard occurred. As a reduced but still icy wind blew across airport runways, a score of shivering passengers hurried from the heated terminal to a waiting airliner. Because of efficiently operated snowplows, which had been working much of the night, the flight managed what seemed like a miraculous departure.

Colorado's skies were a blanket of ominous gray. As the airplane hurtled aloft into dark, swirling forms, we had only a moment to look down upon the white-mantled city of Denver before we were encased in foreboding clouds. Lightning discharges were accompanied by horrendous crashes of thunder. I said a prayer. Several exhilarating minutes later, having rapidly gained altitude, our plane lifted into clear sky. Passengers applauded to express relief. Behind us, a beautiful dawn was in the east and rays of sunlight were like flashes of gold.

I stared at the skyscape with aching eyes, aware of the fantastic beauty of storm clouds while looking down upon them from on high. In my imagination I could picture a rainbow that arched up out of the troubled clouds, with Denver at one end and Los Angeles at the other. And so it was, flying between two cities; I was temporarily above turmoil at both ends of my journey.

Long descent patterns, consuming a distance of forty miles or more, bring passenger airplanes into Los Angeles, sometimes affording spectacular views of the city. When the aircraft I was in lowered its wing flaps as it rapidly flew just south of the Civic Center, I tried to get a glimpse of our church. The weather was clear with visibility good for over a hundred miles, but all I had time to do was find the general locations where many freeways come together in Los Angeles. Several heartbeats later, the plane taxied toward its terminal at LAX.

Lee Carlton was waiting when we deplaned. He saw me hurrying off the ramp and shouted my name. I thought he wanted to say more after that, but for the moment his speech failed. Instead, he threw his arms around me and began to sob. Words became unnecessary. I felt my strength ebb as I stood there, unshaven, in my rumpled ministerial suit, as Lee and I braced each other against our grief.

Our church at the corner of Twenty-second and Union had been an important building. It was the first property ever owned by any gay organization in America—but it was much more than a building! We had performed services of Holy Union there. We had buried our dead from there. We had made it a wellspring for rejoicing and communion.

It had been our center—and it was destroyed.

I found myself remembering how we had struggled to raise enough money for a down payment on what was already an old building in a sorry state of repair. I remembered how much physical labor industrious people had put into the church. And when it became our property, I remembered how inspired individuals, mostly gay, had donated seemingly limitless talent to restore it.

Our congregation completed reconstruction projects that some people had never thought were possible. Members taught each other how to lay tile, how to glaze windows, how to patch large holes in plaster walls, how to repair plumbing and electrical wiring, how to build, panel, paint and perform hundreds of other tasks required to restore a virtually abandoned building and make it a useful church again.

But that was history.

Several hundred people were standing in the vicinity when we arrived at the water-soaked ruins. It was shortly after eleven on that Saturday morning, January 27, 1973. Several fire trucks remained and firemen were removing hoses from the street. John Hose and Willie Smith were there. They came to me with sadness in their eyes. Richard Ploen touched my arm and expressed regret. The gesture was repeated by many who felt our loss.

Everywhere, the waiting crowd was solemn, offering sympathy, sharing the sorrow. Many were not members of the church. Not all were Christians. But the majority were friends. They came with more than despair. They came with a whisper of hope, to learn if Metropolitan Community Church, a community symbol of achievement and worthiness would, like the phoenix, rise from the ashes again.

Thinking about what might happen in the future was not my concern that morning. My worst anxiety was that someone might have been killed or injured—death by fire is a nightmarish fate. I thanked God when I knew nobody was hurt. We had escaped what could have been a far worse tragedy.

As for Los Angeles' Mother Church, many parts of the structure that still stood were obviously unsound. Ignoring barriers, I ducked under a rope the fire department had put up to keep people out of the ruins, and walked into a disarray of burned timbers. What had been the sanctuary was reduced to sodden ash-black debris. Some walls were horizontal. Fragments of our large stained glass window were among the rubbish. I picked up a charred memento, then discarded it, preferring to remember good times in the building.

No strangers had worked on this building. Gay women had painted the interior of the high sanctuary—because some gay men were afraid to get up on three-story ladders! Terry Luton and Robert Quinn, professional carpet layers, had brought in their best crew and worked overtime to carpet the floors the night before our first service. Actors, authors, and engineers were among enthusiastic workers who had paneled my pastoral offices.

It was my idea to remove badly worn pews from the main sanctuary, because they took up too much space and provided seating for too few. Theater seats would accommodate a larger congregation, and with that in mind, Willie Smith approached the owner of a chain of theaters and asked for a donation. "You've got hundreds and hundreds of repairable seats wasting your valuable storage space," said Willie, pleading our case, "and we could use them."

In a few days, the seats were delivered to us, and the task of renovation began. The work was supervised by a mother and father in the upholstery business whose son was a church member. The parents enlisted every gay person they could find with sewing talent and made them upholstery students, whereupon the group stitched for many evenings until every chair had a neat and professionally tailored look.

After months of work, the building was ready. Love was the cornerstone, and on March 7, 1971, we held the first service in our very own building after having worshiped for a year and a half in the Encore Theater where Willie worked as the projectionist. Crowds of people came to Twenty-second and Union. Representatives and friends of the entire gay community were present that Sunday. I saw agnostics and atheists who came and prayed for us, or at least offered us their good wishes in their own way.

Images of that service were among a hundred memories rushing through my bowed head as I stood in the ruins. Many kinds of success had been celebrated within those walls. The church had been a reasonable source of pride.

But it was all gone!

I kicked my foot in the ashes.

I thought, Dear God, when will people ever leave us alone? Did whoever threw the match that started the fire receive enough pleasure to compensate for our grief? Why should anyone feel compelled to commit such a desecration?

In my sorrow, I could not help blaming famous television evangelists whose self-serving, fund-raising tirades against homosexuals fan the life-threatening flames of unchristian bigotry. They could better accomplish Jesus' work by gloriously proclaiming from housetops the Good News: God loves the people God created—and that God does not differentiate among people because of national origin, or race, or sexuality.

How plain can a message be? Why cannot people, no matter what their belief, listen to the message of Jesus? Why do too many people find *love* so impossible to understand? It is the key to peace. It is our best if not our only means of salvation.

The antithesis of everything Jesus ever preached created the debris in which I stood. So it was difficult not to be depressed on that Saturday in Los Angeles, even when surrounded by caring people standing behind the barrier rope. I knew, however, that they were watching me to take their cue from my reactions. They could not be permitted to see that inside myself there was raw despair, a contagious emotion I wanted to hide.

My fear was not that Metropolitan Community Church would end. We had progressed too far for that. My problem was the very uncomfortable thought of having to return to the same people who had already contributed so much energy and money—and asking them to give all over again!

More immediately, I needed a fast answer to the question of where we would hold our next worship service. We had, in the church's infancy, moved many times. And ready or not, it was moving time again! But it would be Sunday in only a few hours, and where can you go at a moment's notice when your local congregation has increased to fifteen hundred people?

While those and similar bleak thoughts raced through my mind, I realized I was crying. With little success, I tried to dry my tears on a sleeve. Finally, someone put his comforting arm around my shoulder and touched soothing fingers to the tense cords in my neck. I looked up at Willie Smith. Willie's face was filled with compassion, but there was strength, too. In retrospect, it is difficult to know what would have happened without the stability my dear friend provided.

"My God, Troy!" Willie exclaimed, trying not to lose patience with me, "The Church didn't burn down! These ruins are just the closet. The Church is still intact. Look around. Look at all of us out here in the open—we are the Church!"

Willie's fingers pressed into my shoulder and he gave me a little shake. "They call us faggots," he continued, "They say, 'Throw another faggot on the fire!' But we will not run. No matter what some damn fools may do to us. We bend but we will not break. We are the Church, and the Church will survive!"

On the next day, we held our church service on Union Street beside the ruins. A thousand people were seated on folding chairs directly in front of our temporary altar, and unanticipated hundreds more were standing as far as a block and a half away. The crowd consisted almost entirely of gay men and lesbians, many who had never previously offered their support. They came in a time of adversity to worship under the clear blue sky. It was an astounding event! A CBS television crew was present to record the good news.

Exuberantly, almost defiantly, more than two thousand of us stood in the sunshine and smiled for the cameras. There was no wake. We sang hymns and showed our faces to the world. Willie Smith was right—the closet had burned down!

One month later, the Denver church voted to leave the Universal Fellowship. No other church followed Ron Carnes. A new Metropolitan Community Church now exists in the "Queen City of the Plains."

6

In Memoriam:
June 1973

These all died in faith, not having received the promises, but having seen them afar off, and were persuaded of them, and embraced them, and confessed that they were strangers and pilgrims on the earth. But now they desire a better country, that is, heavenly: wherefore God is not ashamed to be called their God: for the Lord has prepared for them a city.

—Hebrews 11: 13, 16

WE have become familiar with fire.

Not by choice!

Seventeen sites where we have worshiped have been intentionally burned, three in 1973 alone. Our Mother Church was the first, burned in January. Two months later, in March, our meeting place in Nashville, Tennessee was torched, destroying sacred items upon the altar. Authorities called it a fire "of suspicious origin." As in Los Angeles, no one was injured and no one was ever apprehended.

The third fire, in June 1973, was by far the worst, a nightmare in a city where unsuspected intolerance festered like an unclean wound. The tragedy did not become a part of my life until after it happened. The location, a New Orleans bar, had been but was no longer used on Sundays to conduct our religious services. Many of the victims were not members of Metropolitan Community Church. You may, therefore, wonder why the grim affair is vital to my story of the birth and growth of our denomination.

The reason is because some members of Metropolitan Community

Church were included among the victims, and because almost all of the victims were homosexual. The reason is because in our community there was, and continues to grow, a genuine sense that each of us must stand with our sisters and brothers, united against adversity. The reason is because members of my church, and millions of increasingly uncloseted homosexuals in our gay and lesbian community, felt that the flaming violence in New Orleans was a personal attack.

It was something that could have happened to any homosexual, and still could happen, at any time, in any city! The memory remains within us. Therefore, it is a part of our legacy which, like other holocausts in history, we dare not forget.

The disaster occurred on the last Sunday in June, which traditionally has come to be celebrated as Gay Pride Day in most large American cities. (Gay Pride Day began as a celebration of the 1969 Stonewall Rebellion, named for a bar, the Stonewall Club, in Greenwich Village. Patrons of the bar, after refusing to further endure antigay brutality that was being liberally dispensed by New York's police, poured out onto Christopher Street where they were joined by two thousand brothers and sisters. What happened then was something extraordinary. Homosexuals united and created a full-scale riot, outmaneuvering the tyrannical police who had long deserved to be embarrassed. The result was an enlightenment of many local politicians who thereafter rapidly retreated from their old policies of automatically endorsing the official abuse of homosexuals!)

Our Gay Pride Day celebration in 1973, in Los Angeles, consisted of a well-attended march called the Christopher Street West parade, followed by Metropolitan Community Church's huge, free wiener roast at Santa Monica Beach. A thousand members and friends sat around a camp fire, exuberant, watching bright glowing sparks swirling upward. It was one of those nights when everything seemed perfect. Had we known about the horror that was happening in New Orleans during those same moments, our songs of joy that evening would never have been sung. We would have been choked with sorrow and our faces drenched with tears.

My knowledge of the catastrophe began well after midnight, when I arrived home. A note was tacked to my front door. It read, "Where are you? They had a fire in New Orleans. People from all over the country are trying to get in touch. Long distance calls are ringing phones off the wall!" The note was signed by Bill Thorne, head of our local board of deacons.

My telephone began to ring as I entered my living room. With some apprehension, I lifted the receiver. The caller was Reverend John Gill who at the time was our southeastern district coordinator, the pastor in Atlanta, Georgia, and a marvelous preacher.

"Troy, at last!" John Gill exclaimed. "I'm about to catch a plane to Louisiana."

"Why? What's the big problem?"

"Then you haven't heard?"

"I just got a note saying New Orleans had a fire."

Reverend Gill hesitated before answering. His silence spoke more than I wanted to hear. Then his words changed dread into reality.

"There's been a terrible fire," John said. "They were having a beer bust late in the afternoon—you know, all you can eat and drink for a dollar, with lots of people in the bar, crowded, typical of New Orleans. It's a place called the UpStairs, same location where M.C.C. used to hold prayer meetings. Some of our members were there."

I could picture the bar. I had been in it less than three months before when I preached in New Orleans. The UpStairs was primarily, although not exclusively, homosexual. The premises were located on the second floor of a run-down building that looked like masonry on the exterior but was framed with wood inside. It was one of three separate drinking establishments occupying one unremarkable three-story structure.

The UpStairs was reached by walking up enclosed wooden steps from the sidewalk where a canvas canopy, with the name of the bar painted on it, extended from the building to the street. Inside the UpStairs, I recalled being surrounded by fireplaces, red-flocked wallpaper, and a cheerful pretense of elegance. It was a place to relax, to meet friends, and to enjoy the pleasure of a spirited conversation.

"Tell me nobody's hurt!" I exclaimed.

Reverend Gill sighed. As he responded I could imagine him shaking his head. "You realize I don't have many details here in Georgia," he told me. "I'll know more after I arrive in New Orleans, but from all first reports, it's serious."

"What does that mean?"

"It means people are dead."

"How many?"

"I don't know. More than twenty. Maybe fifty."

"You're saying injured?"

"No, Troy. Dead."

I heard myself cry, "Oh, God!" In my mind, featureless faces from our congregation in New Orleans began to materialize.

"Many are burned beyond recognition," Gill continued, "Sometimes two and three bodies are cooked together and hard to count."

I began to feel sick.

Images of charred flesh intruded upon my consciousness. I couldn't stop myself from imagining the awful horror of people in panic, twisting and screaming and dying. Then I visualized corpses, a scene from which the psyche immediately recoils.

I began searching my memory for the names of people I knew in Louisiana. There was Reverend William Larson, of course. Bill had been the dedicated pastor of our little church in New Orleans during the past five months. He was tall, nearly fifty, average in appearance, and a fatherly sort of person with a deep concern for others. He was also a hard worker with lots of common sense and a driving obsession to make Metropolitan Community Church a success in a city where every previous effort had failed.

"What about Reverend Larson?" I asked, "How is Larson?"

"I don't know," replied Gill from the other end of our long-distance connection, "I think someone said Larson was at the UpStairs before the fire. I don't know if he stayed, or left, or escaped. There is conflicting information. And considerable confusion."

Gill had told all he knew, but many questions remained unanswered. I had to know who had lived and who had died, and who and how many were hurt? How badly? And what could I do to help?

Two more names came to me, that of a playful, fun-loving Southerner everybody called Mitch, and his lover, Louis Broussard. Mitch's given name was George Mitchell. Mitch was a talkative person who dressed like an unmade bed, interrupted everybody's conversations, and was still impossible not to like. He was thirty-six and employed by a beauty company. Most vividly, I remembered that Mitch adored his handsome lover, Louis, who was about ten years younger. Louis worked as a barber.

They had a tumultuous relationship, particularly whenever a little jealousy was ignited, but their flare-ups were not frequent. For the most part, from what I observed, they enjoyed a cheerful and caring life. You did, however, need to understand the couple. Both attended Metropolitan Community Church. Mitch was a deacon, even though he had a wild and woolly manner and was far from sophisticated.

I also recalled that Mitch, who was divorced, was the father of two young children, a boy and a girl, one under ten and the other a little over. It was said by those who knew their playful nature (on any weekend when Mitch had the youngsters), that if it were not for the physical size of Mitch and Louis, bystanders would have difficulty telling who were the adults and who were the children. If, by unhappy chance, Mitchell had custody on Gay Pride Day, it would have been characteristic of him to have taken the children to the UpStairs for a Coke or a glass of milk.

Even though I realized more futile questions would try the patience of Reverend Gill, I nevertheless had to ask, "What about George Mitchell and Lou Broussard? Were they at the UpStairs? And did Mitch have custody of his children this weekend?"

"Troy, I told you," John patiently replied, "I don't know anymore. I have no news of Mitch or his kids. I'm sorry but there aren't any specifics. All I know is that our M.C.C. congregation in New Orleans has a regular habit of going to the UpStairs bar. Today they apparently had several reasons for being there. The Sunday beer bust—Gay Pride Day—and to celebrate the gift of an air-conditioning unit somebody gave the church. Yes, I imagine most of them went today—but I wouldn't expect they'd take children.

"What I know, Troy, boils down to just this: a lot of gay people are dead, and more than a dozen badly burned survivors have been taken in ambulances to the hospital. I know it seems like too little information, but in a way, it feels like too much!"

The horror, as yet incompletely defined, was overwhelming. I wanted to comfort Reverend Gill when he lost his composure and began crying into the telephone. Eventually, when he was able to speak again, he said, "I'm booked on a plane in little over an hour. Can you meet me in New Orleans?"

"On the first available flight," I replied, rubbing my head which had begun to ache.

Telephone calls continued throughout the night, to and from all corners of the United States. In only a matter of hours, concerned leaders of important gay organizations were on airplanes, converging upon the southernmost big city on the Mississippi River. Morris Kight, the well-spoken director of Los Angeles' Gay Community Services Center, who had been in Manhattan for their celebration of Gay Pride Day, and Morty Manford, President of the Gay Activists Alliance, were en route from New York City. Reverend Paul Breton, district coordinator and pastor of Metropolitan Community Church in Washington, D.C. (whom I telephoned at 4 A.M. his time) would travel on Tuesday. Reverend John Gill from Atlanta was already hastening to New Orleans. Gill would be the first to arrive.

Our mutual destination was the home of well over a hundred thousand gay brothers and lesbian sisters who were residents of a city insensitive to their existence, a city which, in spite of its raucous, world-famous Mardi Gras, was very embarrassed by the idea of gay liberation. Part of those one tenth of a million homosexuals lived incognito lives in the French Quarter, New Orleans' internationally infamous demighetto where the city's gay bars, a total of perhaps twenty-four, were sandwiched between other tourist attractions.

John Gill met me at the airport, and we drove to Reverend Larson's home on Magazine Street near Coliseum Square. As we drove, Gill informed me that in New Orleans there was a near vacuum of gay leadership which needed to be filled. The University of Tulane's Gay Students Union was the only homosexual group in the city, in addition to our small congregation, who were even minimally organized to plead for the rights of dead and dying gay people, but the gay students were disbanded for summer vacation, and our surviving church members were in a state of shock.

Reverend Larson's home, a long, narrow house, had become Metropolitan Community Church's place of worship for all of the sweltering month of June. Living quarters were in the back. The front of the building was where Larson, who had once been a lay minister in the Methodist church, held services. The nearly completed layout was the result of hard work by the Reverend himself, whose hands had become rough from carpentry. Often he worked late into the night, employing a hammer, a saw, and any persons who might be available and willing to help.

Sorrow pervaded Larson's house on the morning following the fire. Bill's lover opened the door and ushered us inside. Other friends, mostly grieving New Orleans members of our church, were present, including Lucien Baril, a former Orthodox priest who had accepted an appointment to be their worship coordinator. All were certain Bill was dead, although the coroner had yet to make an identification.

I moved to the fireplace and stood beside a religious print carefully centered over the mantel. We prayed that all of us in the difficult days to follow would have sufficient strength to assist injured survivors, to comfort the lovers and the parents and the friends of those whose lives were unexpectedly terminated.

Then we heard our first detailed account of the tragedy. It was André, a heavyset gay schoolteacher and a close friend of Reverend Larson, who insisted on relating to us the events of the previous evening. We listened because we knew that eventually we must.

We listened, also, because the schoolteacher had actually been in the midst of the terror. With one arm and a part of his shoulder bandaged for burns, André needed to retell his terrible story until retelling it somehow mitigated the pain of his and our remembrance. Staring at the floor, André momentarily seemed transported somewhere else. When his eyes lifted, he focused on none of us.

"At five o'clock the bar was jammed solid with a hundred and twenty-five people," André began, with a slight French accent, "but they started leaving at seven when the price of drinks went up. Seven o'clock was the official end of the beer bust. When it was over, there was a tradition in the bar for everyone to link their arms together and sing:

> *United we stand, divided we fall—*
> *And if our backs should ever be against the wall,*
> *We will be together—*
> *Together—you and I.*

After André had softly recited the prophetic little song, he continued. "Between seven and seven forty-five, half the customers, the lucky half, went home. About sixty, or more, remained. Everybody was mellow. David Gary, a nice young fellow, was playing ragtime melodies on the UpStairs' white baby grand. Inez Warren was there with her two sons, Eddie and Jim. And I remember talking to Dr. Waters. He's a dentist. Doc didn't charge much if you couldn't afford it. Two years ago he filled a cavity in my tooth for free.

"Trouble was the last thing we wanted—but incidents have a way of occurring. In midafternoon, a creep was caught taking other people's near-empty beer mugs for their return deposits, and he was told to leave. Later, a homophobic barhopper had too much to drink, and was given the boot for trying to provoke a fight. Either man could have returned looking for trouble. But mostly, people were in a good mood.

"Then, about a quarter to eight, the buzzer from below sounded. That meant there was a taxi waiting. But nobody had called a taxi and nobody wanted to go anywhere, so Buddy—Buddy Rasmussen—the bartender, asked Jimmy Warren to open the door and call downstairs to say none of us wanted a cab. When Jimmy pulled open the door, which acted as a fire barrier, a gigantic blast of flames shot up from the enclosed wooden stairwell. It looked like a red-hot furnace. The protective door was impossible to reshut because an inferno roared into the room with jet speed. One second was calm, the next—oh, God!

"Rasmussen shouted a warning, 'Fire! Fire' and added something about an exit, but few heard. Orange flames were already racing across the acoustical drop-ceiling, fed by oxygen from a space above. Cardboard and plastic decorations exploded into fire.

"Electric power failed within half a minute and all the lights went out. Black smoke filled the room. Chemical extinguishers were useless against the onslaught. In a matter of seconds, we were all breathing hot, suffocating fumes. A lot of people, many who'd been drinking most of the afternoon, panicked. I pissed my pants.

"Sweaty bodies began scrambling in all directions. Some struggled toward barred windows where the last rays of daylight appeared through the smoke. We were a mass of desperate humanity.

"Somebody clawed at me, screaming, and knocked off my useless spectacles. I stumbled and nearly tripped over a fleshy, motionless body that was being trampled. I reached down to help, but the chivalrous idea was madness. In that instant, carpet on the floor burst into a sheet of flame! I was certain all of us would die.

"Then, in the charnel house, my expectations changed again. I was suddenly wrenched from the Valley of Death when someone violently lurched against my back, causing me to be propelled toward a window. A very lean fellow there was frantically trying to push another man in front of him out through vertical iron bars. When the first man had miraculously squeezed through the opening, he jumped sixteen feet to the sidewalk below—where luck ran out. His head struck concrete. The slender fellow in front of me, undaunted, easily wriggled through the burglar bars, managed to get hold of a rain pipe and, with considerable agility, climbed down to safety. Almost automatically, I jumped for my turn on the sill, but when I also tried to slip through the iron rods, I discovered there was too much of me to fit. I became wedged.

"Tourists, who were looking down at us from the forty-one-story Marriott Hotel across the street, saw us only as performers in a tragedy, but our mounting toll of sudden death was never anything but real. I actually felt people who were collapsing against me. Their agony was ended by superheated air.

"Unconscious bodies were beginning to burn while I pushed desperately to get out through the bars. My cheeks and the side of my head, my chest, stomach, and rear end pushed hard against hot iron. I didn't care what or how much it hurt. Every muscle in me was working for release when the saints smiled in my direction. My skin pinched, then slipped—and I was free!

"The guy before me had climbed down a rain pipe, but I couldn't reach it. Closer, there was a Jimini Bar sign which extended perpendicularly from the building. Jimini is the bar below the UpStairs. By the grace of God, I jumped and managed to catch the top of the sign where I held on for several seconds until I fell. The back of my shirt was burning. People ran to my assistance from all directions. With bare hands, a man beat out the fire in my clothing.

"I know I'm very fortunate to be here!"

André paused and looked around at the group of us gathered in Bill Larson's small living room. We were disturbed by what André had described, but other horrible memories were stored in his brain.

"Immediately after I got out," André continued, "I looked back, and I saw Reverend Larson. Bill was screaming in an unbarred window where he had been struck by a falling object, perhaps an air-conditioning unit. Seeing the pastor reach out, crying for help as his body burned, was a scene of incredible horror.

"Some say it wasn't Reverend Larson silhouetted against the flames, but I'm certain it was. His half-cremated body remained in the window for hours for everybody on Chartres Street to see."

André's voice faltered. His entire upper torso began shaking and he was pitiful to behold. I was surprised when he attempted, with considerable effort, to continue. Nevertheless, it became necessary for André to surrender the completion of his narrative to Peter, a meticulous bank clerk and notary who also survived the ordeal. Along with eighteen others, including Courtney Craighead, a deacon in New Orleans' Metropolitan Community Church, Peter had been led from the holocaust to safety by the bartender, Buddy Rasmussen. Rasmussen had guided them out through an obscure fire-door that led to the roof of another building. Few of the UpStairs customers had apparently been aware of the back exit—or they died unable to reach it. One of the casualties was Rasmussen's truly devoted lover, Adam Fontenoit, an artistic, educated man with an unfortunate and fatal tendency to panic.

"You could hear the sirens from fire engines almost as soon as the fire started," said Peter. "The station is only two blocks away. A waitress employed at the bar close to the UpStairs called in the alarm. Firemen responded immediately and they were good. They were already attaching hoses to hydrants when I emerged on the street.

"Spectators were attracted like flies. A crowd formed, unaware, as were the firemen and myself, of the full extent of the catastrophe. I saw men pushing through burglar bars in the UpStairs windows. Two who jumped, struck the concrete wrong and died before they were moved.

"Everybody saw Reverend Larson in the window. His face was covered with grime and perspiration. His favorite green shirt, which some of us recognized, was covered with soot. We thought he could get out, but something interfered. It's difficult to know exactly what happened. Debris came down and must have struck Bill a blow on the head.

"Precious seconds were lost. In a very few moments it was all too late. Fire engulfed Reverend Larson. His face burst into a ball of flame. His hair flashed into a gray ash, and was gone. The skin burned. Some witnesses claimed he was already unconscious when fire enveloped him, but I regret that wasn't so. I saw him move. And I heard him scream!

"But there was nothing firemen could do to save Bill. They were helpless and so were we. No one could get to him in time. His lover was hysterical and had to be held. The rest of us were devastated."

Affected by his own words, Peter sank back into a plastic lawn chair that had been brought into the room. He closed his eyes and tried to relax for the better part of a minute while all of us watched and waited. Then, after several deep breaths, Peter continued:

"After Bill burned, no one else escaped. The fire was extinguished only sixteen minutes after combustion started. Does it seem possible that so much destruction could happen so fast?

"Not until the coroner began his work did we learn the death toll was greater than anyone at first imagined. Bodies that had fallen on each other were laminated together. As their lifeless forms were taken away, three good priests who had been in the neighborhood administered conditional absolution.

"Bill's body was not quickly removed. I don't know what the reason was, but like a fire-damaged manikin, the corpse remained upright in the window until after midnight, staring down at hundreds of curiosity seekers. It gave them a chill! The grim sight will haunt me forever."

Peter dropped his head, sighed, and then looked around. It was obvious he had said all he wanted. I was in tears and John Gill was using his handkerchief. Our worst fears were realized. But there was no information about George Mitchell.

It seemed encouraging that nobody had once mentioned the boisterous deacon who had temporarily been their assistant pastor. I like to believe that no news is good news, but the moment had arrived to inquire. "Does anybody know if Mitch is okay?" I asked, looking around.

"He should be!" said a member of the church, breaking into a smile. "His children had custody of him for the the weekend."

Somebody laughed.

There was relief, but only for a moment. Another person present, an older man who had previously been silent, said, "I saw Mitch at the

UpStairs. I was in the room toward the rear, behind the arch. Mitch was in the room behind that, where the stage is." Turning to me, he added for my benefit, "We put on little silly dramas, you know, with an admission charge to raise money for charities."

"Were his children in that other room with him? Playing around the stage or anything?" I asked.

"I don't know," replied the older man, "I didn't see them."

Worried, and frustrated, I looked around.

Peter said, "Troy, I definitely saw Mitch come out on the back roof. He was alone. But he was terribly upset. He seemed to be looking for somebody. I didn't see him again after that."

Nobody had any further information. The fact that Mitchell was not with us in the aftermath of tragedy was very unsettling. It was even worse to contemplate that no one had seen his children since the fire.

Reverend Gill and I were invited to room at the home of Reverend Larson during the remainder of our stay in New Orleans, but we decided any efforts on our part to assist the local gay community would better be undertaken where the atmosphere of grief was not so overwhelming. Therefore, in the middle of the afternoon, we registered at the new Marriott Hotel. A bellhop put my bags beside a bed in one of two rooms that Morris Kight, Morty Manford, Paul Breton, John Gill and myself would share.

We had been alone only a minute when Gill walked to the window and parted the draperies. We were on the tenth floor. Below us was a sparkling swimming pool and beyond that, a parking lot edging on Chartres Street. John called me to the window and pointed.

No imagination was necessary to know what I was to observe. Directly across the street, we had an unobstructed view of dilapidated structures, including the gutted, three-story building that contained whatever remained of the UpStairs. Black carbon streaked the outside of the building from its rectangular second-story windows up to the top of the flat roof.

While we were looking, Morris Kight and Morty Manford joined us. Morris had a newspaper, the *States-Item,* which he thrust into my hands, indicating an article he wanted me to read. It was a statement attributed to Major Henry Morris, chief of detectives of the New Orleans Police Department who, in a depreciatory reference to the UpStairs and its deceased customers, said, "Some thieves hung out there—and you know it was a queer bar!"

86

My blood pressure pushed upward. The quoted statement derived from the same type of official prejudice we had fought in California for years. Homosexuals in the Golden State had been equated with underworld personalities by puffy leaders of Los Angeles police who were often allowed to function with an inaccurate understanding of sex and sociology.

"This slander must not go unchallenged!" declared Morris Kight.

I agreed.

"We have a press conference set up for five o'clock," said Morty. "All of us should be present. There seems to be lots of paranoia in New Orleans. I understand many of the reporters in this city may be gay, but they're not doing anything to help the community."

Kight turned, frowning. "Indeed they are not!" he said. "The local press refers to the UpStairs as a 'hangout for homosexuals'—as prejudicial-sounding a turn of words as could possibly be imagined. And adding insult to injury—not one city or state official has uttered a single word of sympathy. So many dead and injured require our assistance, and it is a black day in our country when the state of Louisiana and the city of New Orleans have no apparent regrets!"

Morty quickly added his own comments. "If a fire like this had happened anywhere other than in a gay bar, the press, the police, the mayor's office and every public authority from here to Timbuktu would be tearing this city apart demanding investigations! But New Orleans is acting like a stupid bunch of jackasses. At the airport when we arrived, I mentioned to a man that we were here because of the tragedy. He laughed and said, 'What tragedy? I don't know of any tragedy. Only some faggots got burned!' "

Half an hour later, we carried yellow chrysanthemums to the UpStairs, which was around the corner from the front of the Marriott. We placed our remembrance with other flowers at the UpStairs' entrance where, surprisingly, the canvas canopy above the door was still intact.

In the aftermath of that terrible inferno, everything seemed unreal. Only hours before, the street had been filled with bodies, survivors, spectators, hook and ladder units, thirteen fire engines, and nearly a hundred firemen, but the frantic activity with its accompanying sounds was gone, replaced by normal daytime noises.

Nothing moved inside the dark and damaged windows. It was as though when the violence had ended, all life was emptied out for a very long time. Were it not for the lingering odor of fire, dirty glass, and dried blood on the sidewalks at the corner of Chartres and Iberville

Streets, strangers might have ignored the worst bar fire in New Orleans' incendiary history.

Our press conference was held on the high roof of the Marriott. The press arrived, eager to hear what a delegation of "fairy carpetbaggers" (as one of them called us) would have to say. Inasmuch as I was as Southern born and bred as any of them, and inasmuch as I had heard more insults directed at homosexuals than had all of the New Orleans press corps combined, I was not only irritated by their callous attitude, but also ready and able to address them. It mattered not to me that I had been a day and a night and most of another day without sleep.

"I want to tell you something!" I said angrily to the reporters. "I've seen yellow journalism before, and quotes from cops in your newspapers and on television about the UpStairs being a queer bar and a hangout for thieves won't do. The words are un—ack—cept—able!

"We are demanding an apology from your police department. Will you criticize the police for calling us queer and equating us with thieves—or do you condone it?

"The time in history for calling people niggers—and kikes—and queers is over in the United States of America. And it's high time that you people in New Orleans, Louisiana, got the message and joined the rest of the Union!

"Incidentally, I know some of you in front of me are gay. If you think you're fooling anyone by sniping at your own community, you're wrong. So listen to Reverend Perry's advice and get your act together—even if you aren't yet ready to come out of the closet. Too many people are now being hurt and suffering from your complacency!

"I would like to tell those who repeated the story about a redneck who said, 'I hope the fire burned their dresses off'—I don't think it's funny. And as for a woman quoted as saying, 'The Lord had something to do with this. He caught them and punished them,' I'd like to ask, Would you say anything so dreadful about thousands of other human beings who have been trapped and burned in thousands of other fires? I think not!

"What kind of city is this where the sick joke of the hour is the question, 'What will we bury the ashes of queers in? Answer—fruit jars.'

"I know such humor cannot really please any of us. One of our tasks here is to help raise the level of rhetoric. If that's accomplished, I think we can work together."

I had been harsh, but not unfair, and the media's response was generally favorable to my reprimand. When other members of our delegation completed their statements, we fielded questions. Asked repeatedly about the probability of arson being responsible for the inferno at the UpStairs, each of us in turn tried to explain to the media that we were only in New Orleans to assist the city's grieving gay community. We were not on the scene to act as private detectives solving a crime!

"We must depend upon the New Orleans Police Department to apprehend the culprits," said Morris, adding, "I'm terribly sorry their detective has made such a prejudicial statement at this time when everyone needs a little more understanding. It is our desire only that he does his job—and he lets us do ours—for we are all human beings in this complex society. Our efforts are concerned with trying to eliminate a prejudice for which there is absolutely no justification."

After our press conference, the city of New Orleans assigned a public relations officer to speak for their police department and, without admitting guilt, an apology was made for the derogatory comments attributed to their chief of detectives.

Shortly before sunset that same evening, at the exact hour when the fire had occurred, we held a memorial service in St. George's Episcopal Church. Nearly two hundred souls attended an emotional gathering conducted by Reverend William Richardson, the elderly rector of St. George's, who had been disposed to minister to gay people in his parish. Reverend Richardson spoke, deploring the untimely deaths of Reverend Larson and a third of his small congregation. Closing remarks and announcements were left to me.

"They were my sisters and brothers who were destroyed in the fire," I said. "They are at peace now. They are joined with Jesus. It is the individual or individuals who committed this crime—they are the ones we have to pray for. They have to live with themselves, and if I were them, that's something I wouldn't want to do. This crime before heaven will be upon their consciences for the rest of their lives!

"I have it from reliable sources that when the arson investigators went through the ruins, a large can of Ronson Lighter Fluid was found on the burned steps to the UpStairs bar! Doesn't that make you want to get sick?"

Many faces looking up at me nodded.

I shook my head. "It is not easy to think that anyone intended to murder so many people," I said. "My reason turns into outrage, refusing to think that whoever started the fire ever imagined such devastating results. Who hates homosexuals so much? Don't answer. In my heart, I find it difficult to believe human beings can sink so low.

"A National Memorial Fund will collect what we need to bury our unclaimed dead and to help surviving victims. We must assist those who are fortunate to be alive but are now unemployed, either because of burns that leave them presently unable to work, or because they were fired from their jobs this morning after being labeled 'gay' and having their photographs printed in newspapers.

"We have been flooded with telegrams throughout the day. Gay people from Florida to Washington, from New Hampshire to California, have expressed shock, horror, and anger. Therefore, we have decided it would be comforting and proper for us to join together on Sunday next, the first of July 1973, for a national day of mourning. Gay bars and gay nightclubs throughout the United States will be asked to close for sixty minutes in the evening. I further declare that all churches of the Universal Fellowship of Metropolitan Community Churches, in every city, will hold special memorial services during the same hour.

"We will gather across America and kneel to express our sorrow. Afterward, in the days which follow, we will stand with clear eyes to face misguided people who wish us harm. Tragedy is not defeat. Death is not the end. We will each of us survive to witness glory in this world as well as the next.

"And next Sunday, after we pray, I would like to hear a hundred church bells ringing. I would like to hear an anthem in the air to soothe the anguish of the living, to sanctify the memory of our dead. I would like this city that has seemed so harsh, indifferent, and uncaring, to join with us in all its separate churches, to pray for holy understanding. In memoriam, we ask that every bronze bell in every church steeple in New Orleans be tolled with fierce determination."

My brave words were to be tested in the days to follow. Since 1915, when a disastrous hurricane struck New Orleans, the often hot and ever humid metropolis has been pleased to refer to itself as "The City That Cares." It is a slogan which in our time of greatest need proved not entirely accurate.

During the days and nights following the fire, a rowdy band of hoodlums roamed through the French Quarter stealing money for themselves by claiming they were soliciting donations for victims of the UpStairs. The authorities were never notified, because those who were robbed expected their protests would be met with reprisals from the thugs and with inaction from the police.

A network affiliate irresponsibly broadcast to the public that it had received an anonymous telephone call from a so-called vigilante group threatening to firebomb the gay community in retaliation for homosexual attacks (which were nonexistent). Because harmful terrorist behavior is totally uncharacteristic of gay organizations, the Channel 8 news director should have checked his facts before airing a hoax designed solely to cause additional fear and paranoia in an already nervous community. After the fraudulent story was reported on television, anonymous threatening calls started being received at several gay bars. The result was official "protective activity" which resulted only in the further harassment of homosexual customers by uniformed police officers. Gay businesses suffered declines in patronage ranging from 30 to 50 percent.

Gay entrepreneurs suddenly wanted to have a meeting with those of us who had come into their city. They were of the opinion that we were the causes of their problems. "How dare you hold your damn news conferences!" one of them, a muscular disco owner with gold-rimmed glasses, wearing a smartly tailored linen suit, demanded.

Looking at him and his mercenary associates, who had never done anything to repay the gay community for wealth they derived from it, I felt a growing warmth about my collar. "I'll tell you something," I replied, intentionally accentuating my Southern accent. "You all think the way to take care of things in New Orleans is not to talk about them? That's a grand old Southern mistake! Well, Troy Perry's from Dixie, too, and I want to tell you, the reason I'm here in New Orleans is because when it comes to city officials and business leaders like you, I find you're a greedy lot that cares about nobody but yourselves! The fact is that somebody had to do something about the oppression in this city! It's terrible! And instead of you speaking out for what is right, instead of you caring for people that need assistance now, you call us on the carpet and ask how dare we address the press!

"In case you haven't heard, people have died here! Gay people are hurt and official New Orleans isn't lifting a finger to help. Are you going to keep letting this be just 'another queer happening'? Are you just going to sleep and forget? No, no! The time has come, my friends, for you to reexamine your priorities. What are you able and willing to do?"

Morris Kight put out his hand to touch my shoulder, reminding me that it was desirable to exercise restraint. I agreed, and gave Morris his opportunity to speak.

"Have you seen the front of the UpStairs bar lately?" Morris asked the businessmen, his mellow voice theatrical and controlled. "We had a wreath-laying ceremony, and the front of that burned building began to look like a shrine. Neighborhood people brought roses and lilies from their gardens. Bouquets arrived from everywhere, from around the world—but no sooner did we place our tributes at the door of that forever-sad old structure than people started stealing the flowers!

"This is a bittersweet world!

"Now, there's a wiry, aging sailor off a shrimp boat that has taken it upon himself to guard the bouquets. He's not exactly one of us. By that, I mean he's not homosexual. But from what I understand, the gay men who died were his friends. They had a habit of slapping him on the back when he was down and out, without a paycheck, and saying, 'You look thirsty, old fellow, how about having a drink with us?'

"That's what I call caring!"

As days passed, we continued talking to the press; and we often found ourselves being interviewed on television programs with hosts and host-esses who became increasingly familiar with, and less afraid of, words like gay, lesbian, and (gulp!)—homosexual.

At the same time, the people of New Orleans that were not politically involved began to show that in some respects they did care. Doctor Isidore Brickman, director of Charity Hospital, ordered their new burn unit opened ahead of schedule to accommodate three men who were burned the worst. A small army of medical students and registered nurses vol-unteered to attend the trio, employing the finest treatment modern tech-nology could supply.

From Louisiana State University, the Young Democrats bravely issued a bulletin supporting our national day of mourning. They were the only political group—executive, legislative, or judicial—in the entire state of Louisiana to utter a single word of sympathy concerning the tragedy of which anybody who read a newspaper or listened to radio or watched television must have been very much aware.

Most newspaper editorials in New Orleans carefully limited themselves to impeccable but gutless fire-code discussions. Letters to the editors, however, spoke of humanity, and those letters became kinder after we had frequently demonstrated to the media that we were neither alien devils nor child molesters. Here is a typical letter, written to the *Times-Picayune* by Mrs. C. W. Jacob:

I have heard and read numerous unpleasant comments about the people who burned to death. I would like to express my deepest sympathy for the victims, and to their families and friends. I would also like to apologize for the lack of compassion and understanding of my fellow citizens and for the obvious absence of official expressions of sympathy that usually abound following tragedies such as this. I feel all human beings should be treated with dignity and respect.

The task of accounting for the dead, comforting the injured, and consoling loved ones was led by Reverend Paul Breton who had previous experience in that difficult task. Paul became better acquainted with the three patients isolated at Charity Hospital's burn unit than anyone except medical personnel who were in around-the-clock attendance.

Forty-five-year-old Jim Hambrick, who had jumped from the burning building, was in critical condition. Every inch of his skin was charred. When gangrene developed, it was necessary that his hands be amputated. Jim died on Thursday, June 28.

Luther Boggs was forty-seven. On the second day after the tragedy, Luther, bravely clinging to life, was notified that he was fired from his job as a teacher. When I met him at the burn unit, he asked me to arrange interviews for him to seek new employment. Luther died on July 10.

Youngest of the three was Larry Stratton, age twenty-four. Completely encased in a sterile tent, he tried joking with nurses and others to allay his suffering. "Next time I go out drinking," Larry told an orderly, "I'm wearing an asbestos jock!" Larry died on July 14, 1973.

Larry was the thirty-second fatality.

Parents of the dead often had had no idea of their offsprings' sexual orientation. After the fire, in some instances, the unavoidable revelation of *where* a son had died, rather than the fact of his death, was unfortunately the primary cause of distress.

Reverend Larson's mother, having seen her deceased son referred to as homosexual in Louisiana's newspapers, wanted nothing to do with the minister's final disposition. She made it clear that she could not face her neighbors if his funeral or burial was held in her small hometown. Furthermore, we were told, should his remains be cremated, we were welcome to keep the ashes.

When Tuesday, June 26, dawned, the mysterious absence of George Mitchell and his children remained unexplained. His name was not on the coroner's list—but at that time many bodies were still unidentified.

At least one worry evaporated. We learned that Mitch's two children had been found and were safe. The youngsters had been left at a small movie theater to see a Disney film, and their father had instructed that he would pick them up when the motion picture was over. If Mitch and his lover were a little late returning, the children were instructed to wait inside the lobby. Mitch and Louis never returned. Eventually, the theater manager contacted authorities, and the children rejoined their mother.

Days later I learned of Mitchell's fate. It was true that he had been fortunate enough to be in the group at the UpStairs who were led to safety by the bartender, Buddy Rasmussen. But once outside, upon discovering that Louis was still inside the burning building, Mitch pulled free from men who tried to stop him, and rushed back into the bar. Retracing his steps, irrepressible Mitchell plunged back into hell in a desperate attempt to save the man he loved.

I have no way of knowing if George Mitchell was the bravest of those who died in that terrible inferno, but his courage and devotion I want never to forget.

We sent a telegram to the governor of Louisiana on Wednesday, June 27. Our message read, in part:

GOVERNOR EDWIN EDWARDS:
THE TRAGIC FIRE OF JUNE 24TH IN THE UPSTAIRS LOUNGE SHOCKED AND NOW SADDENS THE NATION. GAY, AS WELL AS NON-GAY, CHURCHES AND ORGANIZATIONS AROUND THE COUNTRY WILL BE OBSERVING A NATIONAL DAY OF MOURNING. THE HEARTFELT SYMPATHY OF AMERICA HAS FOCUSED HERE IN LOUISIANA AT THIS TIME OF NEED. WE RESPECTFULLY CALL UPON YOU TO JOIN IN THE SPIRIT OF COMPASSION AND LOVE BY DE-CLARING SUNDAY, JULY 1, 1973 A STATEWIDE DAY OF MOURNING FOR THE VICTIMS OF THE NEW ORLEANS CATASTROPHE.

Although the telegram was delivered by hand to the office of Louisiana's top executive, when Morty Manford attempted by telephone to pry a response from Governor Edwards, Morty was at first told by the governor's secretary that the telegram had not been received. When the telegram was located, Morty was told no answer was yet available. When Morty asked to speak to the governor, he was informed that Edwards would be away from his office for an extended period of time.

No reply was ever forthcoming.

Later, Mayor Landrieu of New Orleans, returning from a European holiday, was quoted as saying, "I'm not aware of any lack of concern in this community."

Politicians are easy targets. Elected officeholders in Louisiana, however, were not my primary disappointment. That dubious honor I unhappily reserve for a number of the largest and wealthiest churches in Christendom. Their leaders did routinely kneel and pray, but they rarely showed any true consideration for the teachings of Jesus Christ.

Money for the needy and consolation for the grieving poured into New Orleans from gay communities around the world in a manner that had never before occurred. Nevertheless, in "The City That Cares," a major problem existed. We needed a church large enough to hold many people who would attend our special services on the declared day of mourning. St. George's Episcopal Church, which had allowed us to use its premises on Monday night, was no longer available. Having read about that simple service in his morning newspaper, the bishop of the Episcopal diocese of New Orleans had sternly chastised the priest of St. George for even allowing us to enter. Furthermore, the bishop warned the priest and his colleagues that they would all be in serious trouble if any of them ever committed a similar indiscretion. I contacted the bishop's office, hoping I could speak to and reason with him, but my request was denied with undisguised hostility.

My telephone calls to New Orleans' Roman Catholic archbishop were intercepted by an officious priest, and his hostility varied from that of the Episcopal vestry only in that his responses took the form of long pauses before each of my various requests was denied. The Catholic priest was possibly the same rigid cleric who informed Bill Rushton (a very competent journalist for a weekly newspaper, the *Vieux Carré Courier*) that even with the positive knowledge that one of the persons who burned to death at the UpStairs was Roman Catholic, their human relations committee had not and would not consider issuing any statement of regret.

Working exhausting hours every day to assist physically and psychologically wounded survivors, our Reverend Paul Breton was incensed by the callous attitude of an archbishopric that sought to wash its hands of the affair. Paul had been born and bred a Catholic, but soon after the ordeal in New Orleans was concluded, he transcribed his thoughts:

> For many years I believed the ideals nuns taught us in grammar school, but in my adult life I have gotten to see more and more the lack of concern of the hierarchy of the church to live up to those ideals. Never have I felt so far removed from the Roman Catholic church as I do now, and it is because of the lack of plain, decent

95

humanity on the part of the hierarchy. It was reported to me that one of the deceased was denied a church burial by his priest who commented in a derogatory manner concerning his homosexuality. And the archbishop's office could not issue one single statement of sympathy!

A clergyman in New Orleans referred to the archbishop as a hypocrite. Perhaps the term is not strong enough. I thank heaven that God led me to Christ in spite of the Roman church, for I could well be as many ex-Catholics in the gay community now are—very bitter and opposed to religion.

Still seeking a place to hold our memorial service, I visted a Baptist church in the Vieux Carré and asked for assistance. They laughed in my face.

The board of a Lutheran church smugly informed us that they could not authorize use of their building for the purpose we intended. What a pity!

Then, two rays of God's golden sunlight shined upon us.

First, as our frustration reached its nadir, we were unexpectedly approached by Evelyn Barrett from a Unitarian church, offering us the use of their premises. It was a commendable gesture. We wanted to accept the Unitarians' gift, but being realistic, realized that their facility was too far removed from downtown New Orleans.

Second, while we were remembering how Mary and Joseph could only find shelter in a stable, and while we were obtaining permission from the Vieux Carré Commission to hold our memorial service in the open street, a man I had never seen before suggested a building which had somehow escaped our attention, St. Mark's Methodist Church.

St. Mark's is not a large church. It is a typical wooden building on Rampart Street in the historical section of the Vieux Carré. The congregation is white, but the minister, Reverend Kennedy, was black, an unusual situation in the Deep South.

Reverend Kennedy shook our hands and welcomed us into his church. Immediately upon hearing our request, he consented to host our memorial in St. Mark's, and in spite of our solemn mission, we could not contain our relief and joy.

"I wish it was always so easy to make people happy," said Reverend Kennedy, pleased yet surprised, unaware of the frustration that preceded our reaction.

With a sense of triumph, we had three thousand leaflets printed that same afternoon. To avoid more unnecessary problems, the word gay was intentionally not mentioned. The fliers read:

MEMORIAL WORSHIP
SERVICE

IN MEMORY OF THE

NEW ORLEANS

FIRE VICTIMS

SUNDAY, JULY 1

ST. MARK'S UNITED METHODIST CHURCH

2:00 P.M.

Reverend Paul Breton, Reverend John Gill, Morris Kight, Morty Manford, two or three other people and I started walking through the Vieux Carré, handing our leaflets to every person who would take one. People were frightened wherever we went, and we went everywhere! Rumors were going around that another bar was about to be firebombed. Our adrenaline was pumping. We had to show gays that we were beyond fear.

People knew who we were and what we were doing. Surprisingly, nobody threatened to beat us or called us names. We began to witness growing support. The response was very encouraging. Businesses started putting our leaflets in their windows. Many of those establishments were not gay, but with agreeable frequency we found friendly people in them. Buds of compassion were beginning to blossom. We felt as if we were walking out of the Dark Ages.

Newspaper people arrived. They started taking notes and asking the "right" questions. Individuals took time to read our leaflets. Some asked if it was possible to attend the memorial service without having their picture appear on television. I replied, "We will not allow television cameras in the church," and I added, "No cameras—period!"

That was my mistake.

When we arrived for the service at St. Mark's that Sunday afternoon, the first person I met was a woman about my mother's age who was all smiles and full of vitality. Mrs. Harold was one of five white females on St. Mark's board of directors. "I want to thank you for permitting us to use the church," I told her with sincerity.

The response, a hearty laugh, was not what I expected. "Oh, this is very controversial!" Mrs. Harold replied with some glee, "but we're not worried. Here in the South, when you have a church with a black pastor and five white women on the board—! Oh, my dear, we've been called everything!" Then, when her merriment subsided, Mrs. Harold inquired, "Reverend Perry, is your mother's name by any chance Edith? Are you from Tallahassee?"

I nodded, and soon learned that Mrs. Harold had once been a neighbor and a close friend of my mother when I was a little boy.

Ten minutes before services were to start, she came to me, pulled at the sleeve of my robe and whispered, "Troy, Reverend Finis Crutchfield, the Methodist bishop of Louisiana, is here!"

My heart sank.

The expression I could not hide must have appeared in my eyes, because Mrs. Harold saw my concern, and with a chuckle, quickly assured me that all was well.

"The bishop's a fine man," she said, "and you will both get along real well. Would you like to meet him?"

"Yes, ma'am, sure would," I replied with a relieved grin.

Preparations for the service were nearly completed when we left the back room. I followed Mrs. Harold to where Bishop Crutchfield was seated. He was not the least disturbed by the numerous gay people who surrounded him. About fifty-five, small and slender, the bishop was responsible for all Methodist congregations throughout the state of Louisiana.

He stood for me as I approached.

"You must be Reverend Perry," the bishop said, "I am pleased to meet you."

In a conservative area like New Orleans, even a bishop can encounter problems. I realized that his decision to be present at our memorial service would leave him vulnerable to criticism no matter how unjustified such criticism might be. In a spiritual sense, I immediately fell in love with him.

"I want to tell you how delighted I am you have chosen to be with us," I said. "You and Reverend Kennedy are the only representatives of any religious denomination other than our own."

The bishop's eyes twinkled. "Reverend Kennedy called me and I agreed with him that your service should be here in our church," said the bishop. "A lot of the people who died in that fire were my good friends, and by my presence I want every Methodist to know Reverend Kennedy is not a renegade pastor acting without permission. I would like to read in the

Times-Picayune tomorrow that not everybody in Louisiana can be called a redneck!"

Our service was to be traditional and ecumenical. The soft organ music that had been gently soothing the crowded sanctuary for half an hour ended. Reverend Breton prayed, "Almighty God, we have come together as mournful people to worship and to make a living memorial. Take those who have been parted from us and grant them eternal rest. Bless and heal the living who are injured. Grant us all comfort and remind us of hope for tomorrow. Amen and amen."

Reverend Gill led a hymn and read scripture.

Morty Manford, our activist Jewish associate, next came forward. "We must stand beside each other and offer our love," said Morty. "Many who died at the UpStairs Bar were gay. They knew what it was like to live in a condemning society where churches call us sinners, psychiatrists call us sick, legislators call us criminals; where capitalists denounce us as subversives, and communists denounce us as decadent!

"The irony of all this is that we are loving, feeling, productive human beings. In the face of such knowledge we stand together proudly. The pain we feel in our hearts today is not borne alone. The spirit of community, of concern, of caring and of love from sisters and brothers in faraway cities is with us. This must make our burden lighter."

Telegrams of sympathy were read by Reverend Lucien Baril. One telegram Lucien read was from the American Baptist Convention. Unlikely as the probability then seemed, I prefer to believe that some Baptist leaders knew to whom they were sending their condolences.

Etched in our memories were Bill Larson, who had worked so hard to build Metropolitan Community Church in New Orleans and died in a window on public display; George Mitchell, who fought his way back into the inferno in a vain attempt to rescue his lover, Louis Broussard; Inez Warren, who burned with her two sons, James and Eddie; David Gary, in death still seated at a baby grand piano; Adam Fontenoit, whose lover, Buddy, was able to lead so many to safety but could not help him; Dr. Perry Waters, the community dentist; and others, including Reginald Adams, Hubert Cooley, Horace Getchell, John Golding, and Glenn Green, all members of Metropolitan Community Church.

Twenty-nine died during the fire. Hambrick, Boggs, and Stratton ended their struggles at the burn unit in Charity Hospital. In addition, a dozen slightly less severe victims of the UpStairs arson were scattered among other medical facilities around Louisiana.

Three of the deceased were so badly incinerated in the bar that there was never a way to know for certain who they were. Of the bodies that were positively identified, two would not be claimed. They were disowned, even though they might not have been gay! We said the Lord's Prayer for all of them who went before, and for all of us to follow.

I concluded with a memorial address. "We are thankful for men like Reverend Kennedy and Bishop Crutchfield who have the guts to support us today," I said, "but as long as one brother or sister in this world is oppressed, it's our problem. Such names as faggot, queer, fruit, and fairy are language of the bully and the bigot—insensitive, stupid labels that will never put us down.

"Those human beings, our friends who died so horribly, have dignity now. It doesn't matter what unknowledgeable people have stooped to say, our friends will always have respect because they are forever in our hearts. The memory of our loved ones is so viable that I can almost feel their presence. If they could speak they would tell us to hold our heads up high.

"Remember their last song, the one they always sang on Sundays? It keeps running through my head:

> United we stand, divided we fall—
> And if our backs should ever be against the wall,
> We will be together—
> Together—you and I."

We had the lyrics printed for that memorial occasion. The sentiment of the words is universally beautiful. All of us sang and there was not a dry eye in the building. Hundreds of voices joined in a clear melody that will haunt me forever.

Few in St. Mark's that afternoon were not acquainted with someone who died in the fire, and they, like I, had recurring visual flashes of those who were no longer with us, of friendly people who had relaxed and drunk a mug of beer before their premature journey to paradise. Sublime was the moment. However, unwanted problems have ways of intruding. While the music continued, a handwritten note was passed to me. I read it, and then, frustrated, I interrupted the singing of the assembly of people packed within St. Mark's.

"My friends," I said, "I want to thank you for being here, and I want to apologize for making a promise I cannot keep. I told you no cameras would be allowed, but I have just received a note telling me that television and press cameras have been set up across the street to photograph us

100

when we depart. I asked the media not to bring cameras or take pictures, and I had hoped my request would be understood and honored. It has not. Now I'm told there's no legal way to remove the cameras."

A buzz of conversation spread through the gathering. Raising my hand for attention again, I continued. "For those who are concerned, I want to tell you right away that we didn't expect this, but we still made contingency plans for such a situation. Anyone who desires can leave without being observed. Reverend Kennedy can show you out through the alley by way of the back door."

Discussion in the sanctuary grew louder and numerous people, including women with babies in their arms, began shouting, "No, no! We're going out the front door!" Soon all present, without exception, were voicing their agreement. It was an extremely positive statement.

"Thank you," I told the crowd. "You have confirmed my faith!"

Without hesitation, a woman resumed singing the UpStairs song. Once more the group raised their voices, but the accent was different. Before, there had been a pure wash of music that was like brilliant crystal. The alteration was significant. Voices became stronger, more determined. Singers were no longer merely vocalizing the sweet, melodious song of unity. The singers were living what they sang. They were convinced. They believed. And when the strains of music faded away, many in the church linked arms, feeling an inner strength some had never known before.

"They all filed out," reported New Orleans' *Times-Picayune* the following morning. "None was seen leaving through the rear."

"We are not ashamed," I heard a tall man say.

The memorial service was barely over when the somber bell in St. Mark's began to toll. I listened carefully for a response. St. Mark's bell pealed alone for more than ten minutes. Then, from somewhere in the distance, another church bell also began to ring!

7

Ministry of Women:
1972–1973

*And it shall come to pass afterward, that I
will pour out my spirit on all flesh; your
sons and your daughters shall prophesy, your
old people shall dream dreams, and your
young people shall see visions. Even upon the
menservants and maidservants in those days,
I will pour out my spirit.*

—*Joel 2: 28, 29*

AUNT Lizzy Smithy was not really my aunt. She was my father's
brother's wife's sister. That made her a shirttail relative, and, where I
came from in the South, that properly entitled her to be called "aunt."

With a strong religious zeal in her own ministry, Aunt Lizzy was a
powerful influence when she supported my call. As with other Pentecostal
women in the Church of God, from which I stemmed, there was never
any reason why she should not preach. We had always accepted female
preachers. Consequently, when I began Metropolitan Community
Church, it never dawned on me that society in general had a terrible
religious prejudice that often excluded women from ministry.

Originally, all of our ministers were male, but our congregation, which
was also predominantly male in the beginning, knew a time would arrive
when Metropolitan Community Churches would not only have women
officers but would provide equal opportunities for women clergy as well.
I had occasionally made it clear that I had no objection. However, in the
late 1960s when we were writing our first bylaws (a relatively simple
document compared with what it is today), the word "he" was innocently
used throughout to refer to ministers, deacons, and other offices; only

the masculine pronoun was used because it was considered—at least by men—to be nonexclusionary.

Never in my wildest imagination did I ever think there would be a problem for our ministry to embrace women. Having been raised by female preachers, it was the last thing to occur to me. Therefore, in June 1972, when Bonnie Daniel, a zealous young lesbian, seven months pregnant and in the extended process of separating from her husband, came to me during the early days of our Mother Church at Twenty-second and Union and asked if she could begin a ministry near the beach, it was without any apprehension that I said, "Go, and do it with my blessings!" Thus, Bonnie, a recent convert to Christianity, became our first woman preacher to have her own congregation.

Bonnie had a zeal for the Lord! She was filled with so much excitement that sometimes I had to say to her, "Bonnie, Bonnie—calm down for a minute!" Like myself when I was young, she sometimes spoke before she thought, but her candor when polished became an asset. Her title was exhorter, a term we once used to denote unlicensed student clergy. As such, Bonnie Daniel established a branch of Metropolitan Community Church in Unity by the Sea's chapel in Santa Monica, and Bonnie was accepted by her congregation for herself and because she was accepted by me. In those days I had a habit of approving some people on faith, telling them to "Go—preach!" Our denomination was very small then, and we were able to be intuitive about our operating procedure. The same is not true today.

A second milestone was achieved in September 1972, at our Third General Conference, when Reverend Freda Smith became the first woman in our denomination to be officially licensed as a minister. Freda was then acting as the assistant pastor for our Metropolitan Community Church in Sacramento. Reverend Bob Wolf was pastor. Today, as I write eighteen years later, Freda is vice moderator of the Universal Fellowship of Metropolitan Community Churches (our second highest elected position) and is pastor of Sacramento's Metropolitan Community Church. The road from then to now has been strewn with pitfalls, but Reverend Smith's journey resulted in important contributions to our denomination and provides us with a fascinating story.

Freda Smith was born in Pocatello, Idaho. Judy Garland used to sing a song about being born in Pocatello—in a trunk—in the Princess Theater, but there was no Princess Theater in Pocatello. Freda was born at home.

Her great-grandmother had been a Nazarene preacher, and Freda was baptized into that very emotional denomination when she was two weeks old. As she grew, Freda was lovingly attracted to religion, but she had to learn that there were many sins to avoid. For instance, display of one's limbs, even elbows and ankles, was not allowed.

On one particularly pleasant day during the Christmas season, Freda saw a new woman in Pocatello standing near a kettle and ringing a bell. The woman wore a Salvation Army uniform with its red-lined cape and a military hat. Several days before, while on the way to school, Freda remembered having ridden on a bus with her. "I could not believe I had ridden on the same bus with someone who would stand up in public and do what she was doing," said Freda. "It was shocking to me!"

But so fascinated was the young girl, and so sheltered had been Freda's life—she rarely even came into town except to attend high school—that she went to the woman and asked, "Why are you ringing the bell?"

"I'm doing this for God," replied the woman.

"Are you sure that's what God wants?" persisted Freda.

After receiving positive assurances, Freda was invited by the woman to attend a Salvation Army meeting the coming Sunday. Filled with curiosity, Freda accepted, and a few days later went to their church. Pocatello's Salvation Army was a small unit, but the majority were in uniform—and they were, among other things, beating a large drum!

"I felt so embarrassed for them," Freda later admitted, "not realizing how constricted and narrow was my view of the world and religion. But I sat down and watched and listened, and it didn't take long before I learned that people in the Salvation Army were just the same as Nazarenes, singing all the same songs, praising the same Christ, worshiping one God—the only difference being that the Salvation Army wore uniforms.

"My great-grandmother died when I was eleven, and since there was no longer any great pressure to constantly attend the Nazarene church, I allowed myself to be recruited with other soldiers. It was to be a grand adventure. After all, religion was in my blood!"

The big drum sounded as Freda Smith signed her name to the Articles of War. Henceforth and forevermore, she swore, she would hold forth against encroaching forces of darkness. And all the while, encouraging Freda with a smile, was a beautiful Salvation Army girl, one grade ahead of Freda in high school.

"I joined the Salvation Army partly because of her," Freda recalls. "I thought she was the most wonderful person you could ever imagine. We both became very involved with religion and with each other. When we stood together and were singing, I would hold her little finger under the hymnbook. I knew, somehow, that it was something we shouldn't have been doing because we hid it from view—but her secret touch was wonderful!

"I was fifteen when my friend graduated from high school. We remained close for a time afterward. One day I told her that my English teacher, as part of a class assignment, insisted I go to a theater downtown to see the motion picture *Hamlet*. I had never before seen a movie. Attending films was not allowed. I had been taught going to movies was a sin."

"Can you get out of going?" asked Freda's friend.

"No."

"Well, then I'll come with you."

What a relief, not having to venture unaccompanied into the unknown. Yet when Freda entered the theater it was with a heightened sense of consciousness she described as "a delicious sense of sin I had, knowing I couldn't help what I was doing!"

In the darkened orchestra, the two young women sat removed from a few other afternoon patrons, watching Laurence Olivier, and holding hands. Caught by the passion of the film, Freda impulsively pressed her friend's hand and whispered, "I love you."

Years afterward, Freda recalled, "I didn't know until I had said the words that they were true. And my heart sank because I understood the meaning of what I had said. No one had ever told me about homosexuality or lesbianism, but somehow, I knew I was—doomed! And when my friend replied, 'I love you, too,' then I knew for certain—we were both doomed!"

After the motion picture, Freda went home fearing that what she was feeling was terribly wrong. She became obsessed with the idea that her only salvation would be to get away from the "situation" in which she had placed herself. Having a standing invitation to stay with her aunt and uncle who lived in Houston, Freda desperately found herself talking her mother into letting her finish high school in Texas.

"I thought getting away from my friend, away from temptation, could somehow change my situation," said Freda, "So, with my mother convinced that a change would be good for me, I went to Houston, joined the Salvation Army there, and enrolled in senior high.

"Often I would come home from classes, get down on my knees, and pray for God to save me. I believed I could reach a state where all desire to 'sin' would depart.

"I began reading every book on the subject of homosexuality that I could get my hands on. But in the 1950s, there weren't many books, and those which existed were both awful and inaccurate. From them I primarily learned the names of intimate acts that were classified as perversion. And every new thing I read seemed infinitely worse than whatever I had read before!

"In those days there was a theory that the younger a person was, the easier it would be to eradicate the 'terrible' thing. I couldn't talk to anyone about it, but the sense grew in me that somehow I had to find a way to purify my heart. In Houston, the Salvation Army was a very large organization, and there were many altar calls. Our leader, the brigadier, would take the stage and we'd all sing together:

> Have thine own way, Lord,
> Have thine own way;
> Thou art the potter,
> I am the clay.
> Mold me and make me after thy will
> While I am waiting, yielded and still.

When the song ended, I would move like a streak of lightning down to the altar where I would fall to my knees and breathlessly say, 'Oh, have your own way, Lord, have your own way! You need to change me. And this is exactly how you're going to change me: You'll take this feeling of love out of my heart. You'll take this obsession out of my mind!'

"Nevertheless, I yielded no more than a hard rock yields! And, after a time, I decided people were going to see what I was doing and begin to seriously wonder why I felt a constant need to run to the altar. What they might speculate about me became a source of worry. So I tried to resist the public calls. I fought battles with myself to remain in my seat. But another evening would come when the brigadier, in sepulchral tones, would say, 'There's someone out there who needs to get right with God. We'll hold this altar open all night if necessary until that one person comes forward.'

"And I'd begin thinking the brigadier was looking directly at me. I'm the one who is keeping everybody else here! Then I'd run to the altar again! But what I didn't realize was that God was having God's own way, only I didn't know it. I had yet to understand that God made me and wanted me the way I am, and God wasn't about to be intimidated by our brigadier."

A year after moving to Houston, Freda attended a huge Salvation

Army conference in Dallas wherein participants were constantly urged, as in militant verses of Ephesians, to put on the "breastplate of righteousness," take up the "shield of faith," grasp the "sword of the Spirit," and speak boldly to people in order "to make known the mystery of the Gospel." When that Houston conference was nearing its conclusion, there came a call for members to sign up for officers' training at the Salvation Army college in Atlanta.

Profoundly impressed, Freda expressed her dedication to the ministry, signed papers, and threw herself upon the altar where she cried to heaven. She said, "God, I want to reach the people I'm supposed to reach, and after I'm trained, I'll go anywhere for your people. I'll go anywhere you say, whether it be Appalachia or Africa. I will obey."

Never in her wildest dreams did Freda Smith consider that she might eventually be called to carry the Gospel into an affluent American community populated by homosexuals! Poverty-stricken places and faraway continents seemed considerably more exotic and promising. Nonetheless, Freda was overwhelmed by such tremendous emotion that she concluded she had been blessed with a profound religious experience.

"I thought it was sanctification—or any number of other things of which I had heard," she said. "The intensity was so great that I was convinced God had touched me and 'healed' me of my homosexuality. To be free of shame felt so wonderful!"

The idea of being "healed" became Freda's obsession. Prior to the date scheduled for training in Atlanta, she returned home for a visit. As she rode the train to Idaho, Freda inadvertently began thinking of her friend in Pocatello. She thought of holding hands in the movie. Then she tried to blot her friend from memory, repeating over and over, "I'm healed. I'm healed. I'm not going to see her. I'm not looking for her."

At home, Freda resisted calling her friend on the telephone. She kept track of the hours that passed in which she didn't call. Then a day had passed. Then two. On the third day, Freda was walking down the main street in Pocatello, when her friend approached unseen from behind and threw her arms around Freda. Freda turned.

"My heart nearly stopped beating," she said. "I loved that young woman so much. Part of me could have walked into hell with her. But at that same moment, I knew who I was—sexually—and my mind wasn't ready to accept it.

"I fled. I picked up a prayer that is used in Alcoholics Anonymous. One line of it reads, 'God grant me the serenity to accept the things I cannot change.' To me, the thing I could not change was that I was a lesbian. I was 'queer.' I knew that! 'Homosexual' was my identity all the way down to the marrow in my bones. And it wasn't ever going to change!

"I said to myself, 'Okay, this is who you are, but you don't have to live a gay life-style! I went into a kind of schizophrenia. I began to filter every move I made and every thought in my head, to make certain they were proper and acceptable. Nothing I did was any longer spontaneous or authentic. Those two attributes became frightening to me. People live all their lives that way, but I couldn't. The situation can drive people insane. I felt I was going over the brink.

"Nobody knew of my problem. In the 1950s, in Pocatello, Idaho, there was nobody to talk to. Making matters worse, hysterical Catholic and Mormon homophobes in nearby Boise were generating dramatic national newspaper headlines by entrapping and sentencing peaceful homosexuals to life imprisonment for having committed what they chose to call 'infamous crimes against nature.' It was the largest and most vicious witch-hunt against personal privacy in American history.

"No wonder I was having so much trouble with my sexuality. Everything I heard about or read about it ended with flagrant condemnation. To be homosexual was definitely criminal in those days. It was also said to be a crazy condition. And certainly sinful! The latter attribute was my reason for drifting away from the Salvation Army and for abandoning religion. I couldn't live that way. I needed some reality.

"There came a time when most of the truth I found was not in my life, or even in regular books, but in poetry. The works of A. E. Housman, a don at Cambridge, appealed to me. His poems were witty, sentimental, and seemed to have honest sentiments which one homosexual might decode from another. His words, 'I am a stranger and afraid, in a world I never made,' pierced my heart. 'I hunger for my own,' written by another poet, also had considerable meaning for me. It allowed me to come to my conclusion that I was not the only homosexual in the world. There had to be many other people out there like me with whom I could communicate.

"Yes, I hungered. Not that I wanted to run out and make love to people in the streets, but I wanted to find individuals who would know who I was, who would know what I was feeling, people with whom I could relate and be my natural self. My desperation grew, but I couldn't even discuss the anguish with my girlfriend in Pocatello. I kept finding myself saying to her, 'I love you, but I can't see you.' The emotion we experienced between us was platonic, and yet neither of us could handle it because we were both extremely rigid, moralistic, evangelical people.

I didn't know how to be in love with her, or even how to articulate how I felt."

Freda enrolled at Idaho State College and began to major in speech and journalism. The subjects were chosen because she continued to feel she was chosen to preach—even though logic seemed to refute her belief. Freda's desire to find her own never diminished. Listening carefully when people told antigay jokes, her small store of information grew. When she failed to locate one gay person in Idaho, Freda decided to move to a place where gay people were said to congregate and, according to the joke tellers, those places were California and New York (leaving an amazing vacuum in between).

Freda was eighteen when she arrived in California in 1954. At a temporary job in Los Angeles, she overheard another worker denigrating a bar for lesbians, and after memorizing the bar's name and its location, Freda hurried to learn if either was correct. What she discovered was a large, noisy establishment with lots of drinking and smoking, where some women wore men's suits and others had feminine makeup and beehive hairdos. Because she was underage and frightened by a security guard at the door, Freda only went into the bar on a couple of occasions, and even then, had only one soft drink before she would flee.

Freda watched the customers, usually about fifty in number, and wondered what many had endured to arrive where they were. However, because of an ingrained inhibition, Freda was unable to speak to anyone. "I looked and looked and looked," she said, "from outside and inside, but I couldn't leave my religious base behind and go inside and sit down at the bar and say, 'Here I am!' The best I could do was observe, and then run home frightened, and think about what I had seen."

Six months later, Freda's parents moved from Idaho to Sacramento. Since being gay was still illegal, immoral, and sick, with never a happy ending for a homosexual (according to everything Freda continued to hear or read), she decided to join her parents in California's capital city, resuming her studies with language arts, then English literature, before slowly gravitating into a major in psychology at the state university. Meanwhile, unable to ignore her continuing desire to preach, Freda would often slip unnoticed into various churches. Sometimes she attended Pentecostal revival meetings, or she would go to the Salvation Army in Sacramento, or she would attend services at drive-in churches. But whenever people began to know her, she would instantly pull away.

Freda worked nights for the Technicolor Corporation, processing film in their darkrooms. When overwork caused problems with her health, she discontinued her studies. Inevitably, Freda met some gay people. With another young woman, Madeline, Freda entered a relationship that lasted for many years.

"Yet God would not leave me alone," declared Freda. "I kept thinking that I was supposed to be involved in church work—but I couldn't be! It was a very stressful situation. I considered joining the Peace Corps—whatever it was God wanted for me to do, without having to be dishonest about my sexuality. But going to Africa didn't compute for me. Nor could I imagine anything like the wonderful theology of Metropolitan Community Church. That was not within my reality. To be gay and Christian was like the old saying of an irresistible force meeting an immovable object. You couldn't have both!

"I decided that the only way I could be a Christian was if God would cure me. I prayed—but God wouldn't cure me. And I continued to be tormented."

Working for Technicolor, Freda had more success. She became a very capable supervisor and expected the night-shift position to be hers for life if she wanted to keep it. Many other lesbians also worked with Freda. Their presence was not by design. Freda did not choose to hire lesbians nor did she discriminate for or against them. It merely happened that gay female workers became predominant because the larger percentage of marriageable heterosexual women was reduced by attrition. Lesbians without the potential security of husbands or some other person to support them usually stayed with their work.

However, nothing stays the same. Technicolor merged with another large company and their upper administrators changed. A plant manager who did not like gay people came to Sacramento, and his presence prompted an escalation of homophobia. Nongay workers began openly making derogatory comments about homosexuals in their presence. Freda, who did not look gay, felt gay—and she was frightened, fearing that if people really observed her, they might discover the truth.

Soon after the new manager's arrival there followed a terrible employment massacre. "I had been hearing rumors," said Freda, "and then one night the new boss started calling women who were not married into his office. The women who looked really butch went first. They were being fired one by one. I had a little office area where I had only a partial idea of what was in progress, so I went out into the main workplace and began cutting photographic prints. From there I could observe women being called into the manager's office, and then I'd see them leaving, crying, saying goodbye.

"I knew what was in the cards. I was thinking that I should quit before my turn arrived and they called me, but I tried to hang on. I thought I couldn't afford to be out of work. Madeline and I were in the habit of being 'middle-class respectable.' We owned three houses, one that we lived in and two we rented. We had a new car. As a result, I hated myself for not having the guts to walk into the plant manager's office and just say, 'Why don't you fire me?' But it didn't matter. He called me in at the end of the night and let me go also! I would never have believed it!

"In those days, before Metropolitan Community Church, before the Stonewall Rebellion, before June days were dedicated to gay pride, it was so easy to hate oneself. It was so typical to say, 'I should have been more careful—I lost my job because somewhere I let my guard down and was noticed—I lost my job because I associated with people who were too obvious—it was all my fault!' But actually, it was the system's fault, although we rarely thought or said that in the 1960s!"

Without Freda's income, she and her lover had to sell two of their houses. Their attention focused on maintaining the necessities of living. Fortunately, before a full year passed, a man for whom Freda had previously worked (who left Technicolor of his own accord) offered Freda a job with a competitor of Technicolor. She was placed in charge of production. Thereafter, Freda's life would move forward with considerably more boldness and increased self-determination.

"I became involved in causes and was very opposed to the war in Vietnam," she said, "and I worked for Bobby Kennedy's election. He was my hero because I thought Bobby was the person to do something about human conditions that I knew were wrong. During his campaign, I remember taking my nephew to see him and saying, 'That man is going to be the next president of the United States!' Hours later, on June 5, 1968, I watched Kennedy on television. He was at the Ambassador Hotel in Los Angeles and had just won California's primary election. I found the election exciting, but before the evening's final curtain, I turned off my television and went to bed. The following morning, I was stunned—what a devastating blow it was to learn that ten cents of lead had spoiled the dream!

"Kennedy's assassination was similar to a personal defeat. My own hopes deflated. I found myself struggling to cross stretches of melancholy and, as never before, frequently felt like crying. It was an incredible depression which lasted for several months. When I came out of it, I brought something with me from the depths of despair. It was my conclusion that any people who were oppressed, particularly gay people like myself, could not depend upon others to be our heroes. We could not quit struggling for survival because one man with charisma and foresight had been murdered. There had to be enough of us to carry our own banners, even though the majority of us were still unseen. If we wanted conditions to be different, it was up to us to accomplish the change. And if some of us fell in battle, there would be a surplus of gay people to continue the fight—forever!

"I came out of my deep depression knowing that if I and everybody homosexual didn't stand up for ourselves, nobody else would put themselves in jeopardy in our place. I decided I was a lesbian, and I no longer cared if everybody knew it. I was a feminist, too. Returning as a student to the University of California at Sacramento, I worked with a group to organize a program on campus for women's studies.

"It was the decade of riots at Berkeley and general unrest for other colleges. The woman's movement was not embracing lesbians, but a spirit of liberation was everywhere. Whenever I heard anyone expound antigay garbage that I had once ignored, I was quick to confront the speaker."

Among other endeavors, Freda and Madeline became parents to an eight-year-old boy, David, who had stepped off a curb when he was five and had his head run over by an automobile, resulting in his being diagnosed as epileptic and being fed barbiturates to keep him quiet. Freda and Madeline had found David outside an antique auction house, and when his mother was located, she asked if the women would keep David at their home while she was occupied with another of her many children. "We didn't even know the woman, but we said yes," recalled Freda. "David was with us for three days before the mother again showed up, and we talked her into letting us have him. David's in his twenties now, and has grown into a fine young man."

A new Freda Smith was simultaneously being born and, in 1971, a radio broadcast totally changed the course of her life. She was at work in the darkroom when an announcer said, "Tomorrow, at this time, I will have a special guest, a man who says it is possible to be both Christian and gay. He says you can have it both ways!"

Freda stopped in the middle of what she was doing. She stared at the radio. "I could not believe those words could come out of anybody's mouth!" she exclaimed, incredulous. The announcer's words kept repeating in her memory. The next day, Freda was impatient for broadcast time to arrive. She went into the darkroom alone, turned on her radio, and waited.

Joe Gilbert, a deacon from Metropolitan Community Church in San Diego was a guest on the Sacramento talk show. He began by saying that God loves us and that it is okay to be homosexual, but Freda was frustrated because the local radio station frequently interrupted their own program with updates about a morning earthquake which had struck Southern California. (It was the big 1971 earthquake with its epicenter several miles north of Los Angeles.)

"I kept thinking that I wished they'd forget Los Angeles and let me hear what Joe Gilbert had to say!" declared Freda. However, she heard enough, because on the very next Sunday when there was an organizational meeting of Metropolitan Community Church's new group in Sacramento, Freda was present.

There were only about six people in a very small room; Joe Gilbert preached to them and answered questions. Joe was six feet tall, handsome, with piercing brown eyes and a deep voice. His ritualistic manner was Episcopalian—foreign to the Nazarene and Salvation Army forms of worship Freda had always known, but the message was clear.

"The big revelation for me was when we got into passages from the Bible," said Freda, "to see what the Bible did and did not say. And it was so obvious! The hate-filled ideas I had been taught to believe for so many years were not supported at all by what was actually written in the scriptures. As Christian homosexuals, we were on better and more solid ground than anyone who condemned us!

"It was so clear that I was shocked. I had suffered before from tunnel vision. Religions I had known had always told me what I was going to see in the Bible, how I was going to see it, and they had let me know there wasn't a possibility of any interpretation but theirs. According to fundamentalists, the light at the end of the tunnel was another train, and never before had I used the reasoning God gave me to discover that what they taught me was sometimes intentionally wrong."

From that moment forward, Freda was caught up in the miracle of Metropolitan Community Church.

Our Fourth General Conference in 1973, originally intended to be held in Denver, was shifted to Atlanta after the defection of Ron Carnes and his local congregation. Representatives of all other ministries of the Universal Fellowship of Metropolitan Churches gathered in Georgia's fair city where our spiritual vitality was anything but gone with the wind.

Freda, whose instantly cured ankle had been a gift of the Spirit at our conference in 1972, came to Atlanta with great expectations, unaware that an even greater miracle might be in the offing. On that second occasion, the outcome resulted from Freda's own personality, her gentle outward spirit with indomitable strength within.

She had faced many realities of life, and been strengthened. High on her list of goals was an end to the traditional subordination of women. In Atlanta she would need all the resolve and determination she could muster to advance that cause. Years later, still striving to advance the equality of women in religion, she would eventually face more difficult challenges, but none that seemed greater than those existing at the outset of the Fourth General Conference.

Our Fellowship bylaws were originally written by men and for men, because women clergy were not only a rarity in the general population, they were nonexistent in our denomination, which, even if unintentionally, was overwhelmingly male oriented in the early, conceptual days of our church. Therefore, without intending to exclude women in any aspect of Metropolitan Community Church, neither did we specifically include them in our bylaws when we wrote generic words like *he, him,* and *his* but never specific words like *she, her,* and *hers,* although we were actually licensing both men and women.

The fact is, however, that in those early days we were not as emancipated as I would like to remember. There was discrimination although at the time few of us were aware of it. I had to unlearn what men in our society are brainwashed throughout our lives to believe, the myth that men are stud football players who bring in money and women are supposed to stay home and wash dishes! There is sexism among gay males and lesbians just as there is sexism in the non-gay population— because we are all conceived and nurtured by a heterosexual society whose prejudices are reflected in us. We are the children.

Therefore, Freda Smith came before us wanting changes, and it was no secret what Freda thought. Earlier in the year, she had attended our Eastern Ministers Conference where there were a hundred men, all clergy, deacons, and exhorters of Metropolitan Community Church. Most of the men came from backgrounds where women were not pastors. Some came from religions that absolutely forbid women to preach or to teach. Nevertheless, Freda received our permission to speak.

"I want to call your attention to the fact that I am the only woman here," began Freda, "and I do not believe M.C.C. was called to have all male preachers. I happen to have a strong opinion that an important part of M.C.C.'s ministry will be to have women in the clergy.

"Yes, I realize some of you are now thinking of the line Paul wrote to Timothy telling him, 'Suffer not a woman to teach, nor to usurp authority over the man, but to be in silence.' My answer to that is, you have to let the Bible interpret the Bible. In the second chapter of Acts, the seventeenth verse, the prophet Joel quotes God, saying, "I will pour out my Spirit upon all flesh: and your sons and your daughters shall prophesy." Prophesy means preach. So which scripture would you believe? Words from Paul's letter to young Timothy? Or God as quoted by Joel?

"The thing is, if you want to think women are inferior, or if you want to think that women should not be allowed to have any position of authority, then you can always dig something out of the Bible to beat women over the head!

"Consider this. Paul, in one place in the Bible, says that circumcision is not of any effect, unnecessary, yet he takes his young companion and disciple, Timothy, who is half Greek and half Jew, and has him circumcised. Paul, who says, 'To the Jews I become as a Jew, to the Greeks I become as a Greek, and I be all things to all men,' was teaching Timothy the ways of the Jews. You have to look at the relationships. It was a rule of Judaism that in Jewish temples women could not teach or preach or usurp authority over a man. It has nothing to do with the risen Christ.

"Paul also said to Timothy, 'Drink no longer water, but use a little wine for thy stomach's sake.' Yet we have whole religions, Mormons included, who drink water and forgo wine. Does this mean the Mormons should be condemned? Not for water. Paul was only prescribing a possible remedy for some temporary digestive ailment. It helps to keep things in perspective!

"What I would ask you to remember is that Jesus said, 'No man, when he has lighted a candle, puts it in a secret place, neither under a bushel, but on a candlestick, that they which come in may see the light.' It's right to interpret that to mean, among other things, that God has given women many abilities—and we're not to ignore them. We are not to hide our light under a bushel.

"In addition, the preponderance of evidence in the Bible is that women were teaching and preaching as a vital part of the early Christian Church.

"I would like to quote what Paul himself said in Galatians, the third chapter: 'There is neither Jew nor Greek, there is neither bond nor free, there is neither male nor female—for you are all one in Christ Jesus.' "

With those words in mind, Freda stood again, in September, to address our Fourth General Conference.

"This is the year of rewriting our bylaws," said Freda in Atlanta. "While we have been struggling to write a statement of faith, to acknowledge creeds our religion is based on, and a number of other things, perhaps some of you have noticed that the language in our bylaws is all male, especially in reference to ministers. Always it reads 'the minister, he . . .' and 'the deacon, he . . .' and 'the exhorter, he . . .' Women are always left out! I want it changed."

Not everyone approved.

"The word *he* is a universal application which has long been accepted to mean 'he and she'," complained a speaker in the assembly.

"Then why not come right out and say 'he and she' in the bylaws?" Freda retorted. "So we know we're included."

"Because it's unnecessary!" snapped a second male voice.

"Using the word *he* is a convention," lectured another man. "Without such understandings, the language would be cumbersome. You know the wording applies to everybody."

Freda would not be deterred. Everything the men said had validity, but nevertheless, there were occasions when the old conventions were, at the very least, subconsciously used to retard women's influence. There did exist a real need for all men and all women to know, unequivocally, that women are included in the church. Time has proven Freda correct.

"If the bylaws mean *she,* then the bylaws should say *she,*" insisted Freda. "If *she* is really what you mean, then say *she!* Don't tell me that *he* is sufficient, because the few of us women who are present today tell you it isn't! We don't want to be 'understood' as an equal part of the church. We want to be *named* as an equal part! We want to know these papers definitely mean us."

The minority of women who were present applauded.

Several minutes later, Freda wanted to make a motion that our bylaws be completely changed. In every place where the word *he* existed, she asked that the reference automatically be changed to read "he *and* she." Sympathetic as I was to Freda's intention, as moderator of the convention, I could not agree. A blanket change of wording was not the way that particular type of business could be accomplished. For technical, legalistic reasons that could not be ignored, the wording of our bylaws could only be changed on an individual line-by-line basis, and every change required a separate motion and a vote.

"So, during the conference," recalls Freda, "as we went through the bylaws, at every line where the word *he* was used, I stood, was recognized by Reverend Perry, and made a motion to substitute the words *he and she.* After every one of my motions there had to be discussion and a vote. It was a very slow process, and I know people got tired of me doing it, but I persisted, and I stood and made my motion for a change on every line of the bylaws. Always, the vote, which was not secret, was very affirmative. Men, all along the way, were going along with me, backing up their words with their votes, saying in effect that the total ministry of M.C.C. is open to women.

"At least half of our men had come from religions that taught women should have no clerical authority, but obviously they disagreed with old customs. It was demonstrated by their votes. Our only problem involved the awkwardness of language. Of primary concern was the person of Jesus Christ. I made it clear that Jesus as a human being was, in historical fact, not a point of contention. Because the Bible says that Jesus was circumcised on the eighth day, I'm certain his human self on earth was, in all ways, male. There was never any intention to emasculate the Son of God.

"Nor was there a lot of antagonism. I knew I was a thorn in everyone's flesh, getting up and making my motions. In the beginning, I had to cajole and persuade, but after we had made some of the initial changes, many who at first objected, capitulated. Troy would say, 'All in favor raise your hand,' and I would look at men who might be inclined to vote against the changes but, perhaps not wanting to look like sexist bigots, they would raise their hand in approval."

Opposition was primarily from a handful of articulate clergy with liturgical backgrounds. Among those men there was also a small number of women who felt that females could not, or should not, be in the ministry. Not surprisingly, Catholic laity understood arguments for equality of the sexes better than did our men who had been Catholic priests.

In the years to come, a determined struggle would ensue (which continues to this day) concerning the matter of altering language to include women. This debate about inclusive language has engulfed every religious organization in America, and it is something with which our entire culture must deal. For one thing, liberated women resent being thought of as "little old ladies" or "sweet young gals." Men can protest forever that they have no chauvinistic intentions—and this is occasionally true—but I learned in my dealings with women that too many individuals were not receiving the Gospel of Jesus Christ because of our widespread, insensitive use of language. For that reason, if for no other, the unconscious use of offensive words should be avoided.

In 1973, although few women clergy were licensed in the Universal Fellowship, women did comprise perhaps ten percent of our membership and were proportionally represented at the General Conference. A couple of thousand people were in attendance. When work on our considerably expanded bylaws was at long length completed, most of the women and a substantial number of men applauded Freda's valiant and successful effort.

Our business was not yet concluded, however. At that conference we were expanding the Universal Fellowship's governing Board of Elders from four persons to seven in an effort to better reflect our rapidly growing membership. When the meeting was opened for nominations to the Board of Elders, Freda Smith, with her newfound visibility (not to mention unmeasured admiration) was nominated from the floor. Nevertheless, there were several reasons to believe her nomination would not succeed.

First, no woman had ever served on the Board of Elders.

Second, Freda was not yet ordained and, at that time, many of our people still equated the Fellowship's elders with bishops in other denominations; therefore, our elders had to be ordained—because bishops are ordained!

Third, successful candidates had always come from our nominating committee. Spontaneous suggestions from the floor did not win. They were not politically viable. Floor nominations were usually from people who put up the name of a lover they happened to admire, and the lover's big moment would be to accept the nomination—and then drop out of the contest after receiving only two or three votes from among all the votes cast by delegates.

Therefore, I expected it was only a matter of routine when I asked Freda, "Will you accept the nomination?"

She hesitated.

Later Freda explained, "I was really thrown off balance. I had been approved for ordination, but I wasn't ordained yet. And I didn't think I would be elected. Still, I thought I needed to go through the motions since I had been saying women should be in all positions within the church. If I said no, that would be sending a mixed message to men and women alike. So I said, 'Yes, I accept the nomination.' "

When the votes were counted a short while later, Freda was elected on the first ballot!

As I read the list of winners, everybody was applauding, but when I came to Freda's name and read "Smith" aloud, instant pandemonium erupted. The women were first, jumping to their feet and screaming, but our men were only a quarter second behind, pulled up on a tide of emotion. Almost everybody became excited. Almost everybody shared the joy and crying. It was a major breakthrough!

Or maybe it had been with us all the time.

Nothing had been planned.

"I believe the Holy Spirit moved the will of our conference," declared Freda, "because over ninety percent of the people voting that day were men who marked a secret ballot. Nobody was looking over their shoulders when they made their private selections! Nobody was twisting their arms."

Top: My brothers and I in Daytona Beach, 1952. I was twelve. *Left to right:* Jim, Jack, Troy, Jerry, and Eugene.   *Bottom:* My brothers and I with our mother in 1954.

Top: My brothers and I with our mother in 1964. I am pastor of the Church of God of Prophecy. *Bottom:* My brothers and I with our mother in 1984 in West Hollywood.

(William Tom)

My mother, Edith Allen Perry, and I at the dedication of the cornerstone of the Mother Church, 1976.

(Sara Jorde)

Top: Phillip DeBlieck (my lover) and I together just after I preached, 1988. *Bottom:* Phillip DeBlieck and myself facing the press at the March on Washington, 1987.

Right: Here, I am just out of boot camp in 1965.
Below: A meeting of the Council on Religion and the Homosexual in Los Angeles, 1969. I am fifth from left; second from left is Rev. Clay Caldwell, who was quoted in the *Los Angeles Times* in 1967 as saying he would perform the service of Holy Union for gay couples in his church. One year later, he was forced to resign as pastor of the United Church of Christ.

(Anthony Enton Friedkin)

Ad taken out in *Variety* asking for donations after an arsonist burned our church to the ground in Los Angeles in 1973.

Right: This photo was taken in the Roosevelt Room of the White House. I was invited with thirteen other gay and lesbian leaders to discuss our agenda with the Carter administration. *Left to right:* myself, Midge Costanza—the first woman assistant to the President of the United States—Dr. Bruce Voeller, and Jean O'Leary—co-founders of the National Gay and Lesbian Task Force.

Left: I am with Des Moines minister Jerry Sloan (who would later sue Jerry Falwell and win), as well as Rev. Don Eastman, who would later become a member of the Board of Elders of our denomination. We have just met with Lieutenant Governor Arthur Neu to lobby for the repeal of the Iowa sodomy laws, in May 1975. The repeal later took place.

Above: Hanging out the window of the Freedom Train, talking to the press on the way to the first March on Washington, 1979.
Right: Robin Tyler and I are outside a train station in Denver on our way to the 1979 March on Washington. I am wearing my conductor overalls.

(Walker/Myers)

Top: Speaking with Los Angeles City Councilman Art Snyder *(left)* and California Lieutenant Governor Mervyn Dymally *(third from left)*. My bodyguard, Dave Glascock, is wearing glasses.   *Bottom:* Dancing up a storm at the Gay Pride festival in Los Angeles, 1980.

Top: The Gay Pride Parade, 1984. Mother and I are riding in a convertible while a fundamentalist screams at me. Several gay men have moved from the sidelines into the street to stand between me and the agitated man. *Bottom:* I am with other clergy members from the Universal Fellowship of Metropolitan Community Churches at the first prayer vigil organized against AIDS. The seven elders of our denomination led the worship in seven cities around the world in October 1986.

(Stephen Stewart)

(Fernando Orlandi/Bill Wilson)

(Fernando Orlandi/Bill Wilson)

(Fernando Orlandi/Bill Wilson)

Top: Deep in thought on the steps of the Lincoln Memorial, getting ready for the Sunday morning service at the March on Washington, October 11, 1987. *Bottom:* Facing the cameras as the Universal Fellowship of the Metropolitan Community Churches prepares to line up to march down Pennsylvania Avenue at the 1987 March on Washington. *Left to right:* Rev. Ed Helms, myself, Rev. Elder Donald Eastman, Elder Larry Rodriguez, and Rev. Elder Nancy Wilson.

(Jerry Weller)

Top: Someone took a picture of me with Leonard Matlovich during the "No on 6" fight in 1977. *Bottom:* At the 1981 Gay Pride Parade in San Francisco. I am holding Robbie, the adopted son of our pastor, Rev. Jim Dykes, and Dr. Lannie Dykes, on my shoulders. My T shirt reads: "Queer, isn't it, that you are not free to live where you want, work where you want, or love who you want."

Left: Rev. Willie Smith directing singing at our church in Sacramento, 1986. It was in Willie's and my home that the Metropolitan Community Church started.

Below: At Rev. James E. Sandmire's installation as pastor of the Mother Church in 1975. *Left to right:* Rev. Lee J. Carlton, Rev. James E. Sandmire, myself, Rev. Elder John Hose, and Rev. Elder John Gill.

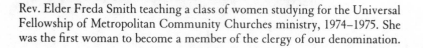

Rev. Elder Freda Smith teaching a class of women studying for the Universal Fellowship of Metropolitan Community Churches ministry, 1974–1975. She was the first woman to become a member of the clergy of our denomination.

Rev. Elder Freda Smith today, serving on the Board of Elders.

Left to right: Joseph McDuffey, my best friend outside the ministry, myself, and my assistant of fifteen years, Frank Zerilli, on a trip to Australia in 1985.

At our 1981 general conference in Houston. *Left to right:* Rev. Don Eastman (who two years later was elected to the Board of Elders), Rev. Elder James E. Sandmire, who was then serving as our treasurer, and Rev. Elder John Gill, who had just retired from the Board of Elders.

Rev. Troy Perry preaching at the Mother Church, 1976.

When Freda returned to her congregation in Sacramento, she was an ordained pastor of Metropolitan Community Church and an elder, a position she has held ever since. "I feel totally within the will of God," Reverend Elder Freda Smith says, "and I've never wavered. I articulate the Lord's will as a pastor in Sacramento, and I make policy decisions on the Board of Elders. I am very supportive of our moderator. I believe Troy is a prophet of God.

"Work for the Fellowship requires considerable travel. Between trips to cities there is sometimes an opportunity to relax with Kathleen, my lover for fifteen years. Then I often remember the early days of my youth when I was so frightened, singing with faint hope and desperate faith, 'Have thine own way, Lord, have thine own way. Thou art the potter, I am the clay.'"

8
Don't Be Afraid
Anymore: 1966–1976

Fear not, for I am with you, be not dis-
mayed, for I am your God; I will strengthen
you, I will help you, I will uphold you with
my victorious right hand.
                                —Isaiah 41:10

MY Uncle Roy had a saying that "A coward dies a thousand deaths—
a brave man (or woman) dies only once!" The essence of those words
has been the backbone of Metropolitan Community Church ever since
its inception. Five months following our initial service, a very small group
of us briefly ventured into the public. It was March 1969. We began by
picketing against an injustice which involved a gay man's loss of employment. One of our fellows holding a sign was so frightened that his
hands practically had to be pried loose from his stick after walking for
an hour on the picket line. Conditioning ourselves against fear was an
important aspect of the beginning of lesbian and gay emancipation.

The next time we demonstrated, we were bolder. My favorite picket
sign read WE'RE NOT AFRAID ANYMORE! That slogan has been with us ever
since and the words, which at first were written primarily to bolster our
own courage, today are a statement of fact. Not only do they apply to
those of us who are gay, but also to a percentage of friends, church
members, and clergy who are not homosexual.

It was courage in the face of fear that brought Reverend June Norris
to our denomination. June's story began before the beginning of Metropolitan Community Church. She was reared on a remote farm in
southern Illinois and, despite little religious training from her parents,
always seemed to have had a knowledge and an awe of God.

June was married at the age of fifteen. She was pretty, with blond hair and sparkling eyes. Her somewhat older husband, Willard Norris, was a domineering, enterprising man who came to specialize in the construction and renovation of custom homes. Willard liked to move often. After he and June had lived in many places around the United States, they settled on some property by Lake Gramley, north of Orlando, near Forest City, Florida. Their marriage lasted nearly twenty-nine years, resulting in three children and seven grandchildren (at last count). However, as the little ones grew into adulthood, June had time to take stock of her own situation and came to a vastly unsatisfactory conclusion.

"Willard was definitely head of the household," June lamented. "I never was allowed to go anywhere unless he was with me. I never even went to the grocery store by myself. In all of my entire life I had probably driven an automobile less than a total distance of sixty or seventy miles.

"My relationship with God was always close," June continued. "After the children were born, because I recognized their need to go to church, Willard and I became involved in the Adventist church, but after a while Willard lost interest and dropped away. I remained and, because I still believed that marriage is forever, an irrevocable lifetime contract, I clung to the bonds of matrimony longer than I might have done otherwise.

"Once upon a time, I believed that lifelong wedlock was God's will for me. Therefore, I debated with myself for a considerable time before I felt compelled to terminate the marriage. I knew that somewhere in the center of my being, God surely had something more for me to accomplish.

"I was in my forties when I mentioned to Willard that I was thinking about leaving him. He was terribly displeased. He let me know that he'd make certain I could not depart. With that objective, Willard even convinced me that all of my telephone calls were being recorded.

"Willard had built our home three miles from the nearest paved road, without close neighbors, and with nothing but an unmarked lane into the backwoods area where we lived. Intimidated, afraid to use the telephone, separated from neighbors, and having precious little say on any subject—I was alone and felt utterly trapped. I became increasingly afraid.

"Nevertheless, the time came when I, in desperation, decided to put a fleece before the Lord. I even named a date. I said, 'God, if it's your will, on August sixteenth, 1966, Willard will leave a set of car keys here in the house where I can get hold of them and get away. I know that if it's your will for me to escape, the keys will be available.' "

Norris had several vehicles including a truck. On the sixteenth of

August, Willard received a telephone call from Kissimmee, Florida, to drive to that nearby city and begin a job. June knew the trip south and back should take at least two hours. When her husband had departed, she anxiously went into the construction office that was built into their home, and looked for keys. On a pegboard where they were usually kept were hanging the keys for two vehicles—a 1964 Ford and a 1966 Pontiac.

"Having a choice, I took our Ford because I figured I'd have to keep that automobile for the rest of my life," explained June, "and I decided repairs on it might be cheaper than on the other. I was almost afraid to breathe, but as soon as I had the keys grasped in my hand, I hastily loaded some clothes and a few other possessions into the trunk of the Ford. I didn't begin to feel less nervous until I slipped behind its steering wheel. There I discovered the car's duplicate set of keys were waiting for me in the ignition. They sparkled in the morning sunlight, and as far as I was concerned, their appearance meant that God's message to me was made double clear!"

Unaccustomed to driving, June Norris nevertheless negotiated her way into Orlando and found a place to live. It was not a long distance from the house in the woods she had so recently called home, but she felt an undeniable sense of relief. Inasmuch as June wanted to stay close to her children and grandchildren, she obtained employment at the local Seventh Day Adventist hospital. Before a week had elapsed, however, Willard knew June's location. Orlando, she reluctantly concluded, obviously wasn't far enough away. Therefore, upon obtaining a divorce, June set out to drive across the United States. "It was a scary thing to do," she admitted, still very inexperienced in handling a motor vehicle.

Her ambition was to obtain an education. Despite having married before completing high school, June made high grades on GED examinations which opened college doors for her. June signed up for courses in Los Angeles. Three years later, her nephew, Ted Sweet, also moved to Southern California.

"Ted told me he was gay. When he said, 'I've finally learned I'm a gay person,' I thought he meant that he was happy. I didn't know what he was actually telling me. That's how much I knew about homosexuality!

"Ted was married for twelve years and has children and grandchildren now. He took a bride because he thought marriage would cure his homosexual nature, but of course that didn't work. After his divorce, Ted left Washington, D.C., and became involved with Metropolitan Community Church. I think he really blossomed after that. By 1970, he had met many people in the gay community and began introducing me to his friends. Among them was a radical young minister named Troy

Perry. My opinion at the time was that a church made up of homosexuals could be nothing but a sacrilege.

"What changed my mind was going to the church they had bought and fixed up at the corner of Twenty-second and Union. Ted was so proud of it! So, at his urging, I couldn't refuse to see the building.

"From the moment I walked into that building, I felt God's presence. I know people who don't have a good spiritual relationship will not understand, but for me it was very real. It was March 1971. Many people, mostly gay men, were getting ready for the dedication of the church building on Sunday morning, which was the next day.

"We were standing on the balcony looking down at the sanctuary when I heard God speak to me. I heard—but not with my ears. Eloquent words reached my heart. They were simply stated. 'This is my house,' said God.

"From that moment on I knew the Bible couldn't say the antigay things some people have interpreted it to mean! And I get goose bumps when I recall God speaking. I still feel God's Spirit today!

June Norris became an accountant in the business department of a Seventh Day Adventist hospital while going to college in Los Angeles three nights a week. She was also going to an Adventist church on Saturdays and a Baptist church on Sunday evenings. Then, in the summer of 1971, June sat with Ted in Metropolitan Community Church while Dr. Evelyn Hooker made a speech to our congregation. When Dr. Hooker concluded her enthusiastically applauded address, June was amazed to hear me bestow upon Dr. Hooker the title of "honorary" homosexual.

"Who would want to be an honorary homosexual?" June asked involuntarily (because the words sounded so strange in a homophobic world). "Yet," she added, "as I listened to Dr. Hooker, who was so highly regarded in the scientific community, I realized she was saying the same thing that Ted and his gay friends had been telling me all along—that people don't choose to become gay—they just are gay!

"An exhorter's class began soon thereafter," recalled June, "and I decided to become a student to learn more about M.C.C. and to learn from the course exactly what the Bible does and does not say. About halfway through those studies I realized this church with its outreach to the gay community was the ministry where God wanted me to be. On the first Sunday in November of 1971, I became a member of Metropolitan Community Church."

In 1972, June was set aside as an exhorter. In 1973, at our General Conference in Atlanta, she was licensed. And at our Fifth General Conference in San Francisco, in 1974, she was ordained. Reverend Norris was on the staff of the Mother Church in Los Angeles for eight years, preaching two or three times a month, usually at the Wednesday or Sunday evening services.

There were problems, however. In the year when she became an exhorter, June was so enthusiastic about her newfound religious knowledge that she did not hesitate to speak of it to co-workers at the White Memorial Medical Center. As a result, she was summoned into the office of the center's administrator and personally handed a letter which said that although they were not trying to dictate to her what she should do in her private life, they did not feel it was appropriate on company time for her to speak of her affiliation with a group of homosexuals.

"Other people could talk about their private lives," declared Reverend Norris, "but I couldn't! They told me the letter was just a warning. I was, henceforth, to keep my mouth shut. Of course I didn't. But it was four more years before they fired me. Their justification was that because of my friends, I was not a 'good moral example' in the Seventh Day Adventist hospital's business office. Can you imagine?"

Consequently, June opened her own office, did taxes and bookkeeping, and was very successful. The new business left her with time to give counseling two evenings a week and to perform gay marriages.

"I think Holy Unions are wonderful!" June declared. "I performed sixty of them in one year, and that's a lot. In the beginning, the couples were mostly men but gradually, after 1978, there was a shift to mostly women. Only when both partners sincerely want the union do I perform a ceremony. I feel sincerity is the first thing we have to ascertain in the mind of persons who go through the religious rite (and that's what it is, religious, not legal) uniting two persons in the presence of God and friends.

"The first thing I determine is if their spiritual lives and their lifestyles are compatible. If they are not very certain, if they doubt God's approval of the relationship, terrible trauma could result. I make certain that both persons are in agreement that their union is satisfactory with God. No person is encouraged to join with another if their beliefs are contrary. And I ask of them that if they do encounter personal problems which cannot be solved by themselves, that they agree before separating to seek third-party counseling."

Reverend Norris began to feel a call to leave Los Angeles in 1979. That awareness was strange to her because she had been of the opinion she would never leave Southern California. Her explanation was that she had a feeling God was urging that she expand her ministry.

"After I knew something was to change, I received a call from Nancy Radclyffe and Kerry Brown," said June, "telling me that there was a church in Fayetteville, North Carolina, that needed somebody like me. It was weird because it came right on the heels of my having the sensation that I was to leave Los Angeles, but not knowing where I was to go."

June shut down her bookkeeping office in March and finished calculating her customers' income taxes. On the eighth of May she departed for Fayetteville. Within several weeks, and for the next four months, she was driving back and forth between two groups, a distance of eighty miles, ministering to Fayetteville, which had a very small congregation, and to Raleigh's congregation, which was without a permanent pastor.

She would preach one Sunday in Fayetteville, then drive north to Raleigh, stay there four days and pastor the following Sunday, then drive to Fayetteville, and so forth. Eventually, a decision was made that Fayetteville would be better off with student clergy present on a more permanent basis. June was then free to be elected, on October 1, 1981, to pastor St. John's Metropolitan Community Church in Raleigh. That church had sixteen members when Reverend June Norris became its minister. Since then, during some periods Sunday attendance has surpassed an average of one hundred persons.

"We are still growing," said June, "and in Raleigh I belong to the Ministerial Association. That means we have an ecumenical relationship. Some of the other churches are unfriendly and let me know, in no uncertain terms, that homosexuality is a terrible thing, but we are making progress by raising everybody's consciousness."

A few of our members picketed the University of North Carolina in Raleigh when that university withdrew its own invitation for Reverend Norris to give the invocation and benediction at an ROTC graduation. Our people carried signs that read FORGIVE THEM—THEY KNOW NOT WHAT THEY DO and OUR GOD, TOO! and a professionally made banner proclaiming GAY AND LESBIAN CHRISTIANS. Campus security guards were nervous that the gay group would be hurt or get into trouble, but all that happened was that thanks to Reverend June Norris, a heterosexual, the homosexual presence became better recognized.

Reverend Elder Jeri Ann Harvey was the first woman to become the pastor of our Mother Church in Los Angeles, a ministerial position she filled for eight years. Jeri Ann's path toward that position was harrowing, and at one time there was genuine fear and mortal danger.

Her mother was Native American and Irish. Her father was an Irish Jew. At the age of eleven, Jeri Ann was baptized in the First Christian

(Congregational) Church of Bristow, Oklahoma. The following year, at age twelve, she openly came out as a lesbian although the word itself was not in her vocabulary. Christian ministers at various churches, who objected to the friendships they observed Jeri Ann making, called her in for counseling. Inevitably, they wound up warning Jeri that she was headed straight for hell, a course followed always with threats of eternal damnation!

"After half a dozen years, it seemed I had been bounced from every Christian denomination in existence," Jeri Ann declared, "and finally I came to the conclusion I no longer wanted any part of them. Theirs was not the God I had feelings for. The God they were serving could not have been my God. So I walked away from Christianity, took training and accepted Judaism as my religion. I figured that if Christ didn't love me, I wasn't going to love him either!"

At the beginning of the 1970s, Jeri Ann Harvey opened a bar for lesbians in Oklahoma City. Time and again she found posters stapled to the establishment's interior walls advertising a new group calling itself Metropolitan Community Church. Jeri Ann ripped the posters down, but someone kept putting them up again.

Angrily, Jeri Ann declared, "Anybody I catch with one of these posters is permanently eighty-sixed. I want nothing to do with a Christian service where a bunch of queens are getting together playing church!"

"But you don't understand!" a number of lesbians kept telling her. "There are women who are a part of it, and it's good, and we think it's something you should be involved in."

But Jeri Ann refused.

However, she had a lover who had heard about Metropolitan Community Church's rite of Holy Union, and her lover insisted that Jeri Ann find out what the ceremony was all about. Reluctantly, Jeri Ann made a phone call. Reverend Bob Falls, who was Oklahoma City's pastor at that time, answered her call and said, "Yes, you and your lover can take the vows, but there are some requirements. You have to attend our church for three consecutive Sundays, and you have to come in for counseling several times. After that, we can hopefully choose a date and I will perform your Holy Union."

"Boy!" exclaimed Jeri Ann to her lover. "Isn't he crafty? Didn't I tell you? They get you to go that church three Sundays in a row, get your money, and then preach that you're going straight to hell! It's all bull. And I think it's nuts!"

Nevertheless, Jeri Ann went to the little church which had barely begun in Oklahoma City. At one of her first meetings when Reverend

Fall asked, "Who has ever belonged to the Assemblies of God?" Jeri Ann held up her hand.

When he asked, "Who has ever been Methodist?" Jeri Ann held up her hand for the second time.

When he asked, "Who has ever been Catholic?" Jeri Ann again held up her hand, causing a perceptible murmur in the room.

"Have you been everything?" Reverend Fall asked patiently.

"Everything but Baptist," replied Jeri Ann. "Our high school was filled with Baptist kids. They couldn't dance, they couldn't play cards, and they were extremely judgmental. One of their ministers said I was going to burn in the bottomless pit forever! That's one reason I never was Baptist. It's also the reason I really turned against Christ. With great deliberation I denied Jesus because I felt he had denied me!"

After its third month in existence, the Oklahoma M.C.C. with seventeen members was suddenly hosting a District Conference of Fellowship churches. Every available row in the building was filled with Christ-loving gay men and lesbians from all over Oklahoma, Louisiana, Arkansas, and Texas.

"They were people with a sense of family," Jeri Ann said. "They really had a sense of fellowship and belonging, a feeling that God loved everybody, and the knowledge that Jesus died for them—for me—for us! It was awesome.

"I accepted Jesus Christ back into my life that day at the District Conference. I just fell on my knees in front of all those people and I said, 'Jesus, please forgive me. You know I was looking for you, Jesus, and I couldn't find you in all of the noise and doubts of this world. So please accept me back?'

"What made me change my mind was realizing I wasn't alone, seeing that Jesus was real for others, and witnessing gay people's acceptance that Christ really does care. I realized God isn't negative. God is positive! Homosexuals are God's children and God loves us! That was preached. That is lived.

"I saw lives being changed, my own included. I would cry because of hymns I wouldn't have listened to before. I'd sit in church and sing, and say to myself, 'Hey, those hymns apply to me—God loves me!' With that, I swore nobody was ever going to take Jesus away again!"

Jeri Ann became a member of Metropolitan Community Church, which grew fast in Oklahoma City in 1972. During that and the next couple of years, she tried to avoid accepting a personal ministry. Nevertheless, Jeri Ann worked for the church, was a deacon, and became our first licensed student clergy in Oklahoma City. As her belief became stronger, her involvement grew, and she applied for admittance into a little seminary located at Southwestern University.

When at first she was rejected because of her sexuality, Jeri Ann decided to challenge the school. She said, "How can you miss your big opportunity to convert me away from my 'wicked ways'? What can you accomplish if you won't even let me come on campus? Let me go through your modular course. I'll be able to show you I'm not any different from anybody else and that God really does love lesbians, and if I fail in that, you'll have your opportunity to convert me. What do you say?"

The seminary said "Yes," but they did not convert Jeri Ann. She, however, apparently had an impact on them—because thereafter several gay students from Metropolitan Community Church (including Dee Lamb, Reverend Jo Crisco, and Reverend Jeff Bishop) have taken modular correspondence courses and received Bachelor of Science degrees in biblical studies from Southwestern University in Oklahoma City.

As for Jeri Ann Harvey, those were difficult days. No longer was she involved with running a bar, but she was working full shifts at the Veterans' Hospital. During that period, she first came close to being murdered by antigay bigots who are still undisciplined in certain "patriotic" areas of America.

It was just after noon on a Sunday morning. Jeri Ann was at the church. The prayer service had just ended and every one had adjourned into the social hall for conversation and coffee. Jeri Ann walked back to the pulpit for a small notebook she had left behind. Suddenly there was— BANG—the report of a firearm outside the church.

Glass in a window shattered!

Jeri Ann heard the whiz of a bullet as it sped past her ear, and she heard an impact as lethal lead embedded itself into the wall behind her. Jeri Ann ducked automatically. People rushed from the social room to her assistance, and some went in search of the would-be assassin who was never discovered.

"Sweet Jesus," said Jeri Ann to herself. "What have I gotten myself into? Is this what I really want to do?"

Aloud, she answered her own question. "Yes, yes, it is still what I want to do!"

Time passed. When Jeri Ann had become Reverend Jeri Ann Harvey, she was offered the opportunity to pastor her own church in Houston, Texas. Her acceptance was a case of moving out of the frying pan and into the fire. Upon arrival in Texas, Jeri Ann was taken aside by Ray Hill, a local member of Metropolitan Community Church who also happened to be an important gay activist in Houston. Ray was a tall, handsome man with a brown beard and a mustache. Nearly forty, he was a couple of years younger than Jeri Ann.

"I love you a great deal," Ray said to her. "So let me give you some advice, Reverend. Number one, welcome to Houston, Texas. Number two, if you have that clerical collar on, and you're driving anywhere within the city of Houston, Texas, and a police car pulls you over—if they tell you you've gone through a red light and even if you know you haven't, you say, 'I'm terribly sorry, officer,' and you take the ticket!"

Jeri Ann shook her head. "Ray, I can't do that," she said.

"Yes, you can," he insisted. "We want you to stick around in Houston, Texas. We want you alive. But you have to know they wouldn't hesitate to kill you. And I mean the police. They know a lesbian preacher has been elected by our congregration. They know you're here and they don't want you here!"

For Jeri, the warning could be nothing but frightening. She was also informed that Houston's police department was nationally supposed to be one of the most corrupt in the United States. Apparently the FBI had investigated and exposed them. At any rate, almost every weekend, gay brothers were being found dead, slaughtered with their throats cut, and it was rumored a police officer was bragging to all his friends that he was the responsible person.

"Gay men were definitely killed by the Houston police," said Jeri. "In one case a gay man was shot because police said he was going for a gun. That was a little ridiculous when the autopsy showed he was shot in the armpit. The trajectory of the police bullet proved the gay man's hands could only have been on the top of his head. Yet, the Texas cops insisted they had been frightened by the lone, unarmed gay man, and claim they killed him because his attitude put their lives in jeopardy!"

It was legalized murder.

Temperature is not the only thing that is hot in Houston. It is the same place where a gay Mexican brother, handcuffed with his hands behind his back, was thrown into the Buffalo River and drowned. At the time of the incident, the police had him in "protective" custody. (Later, city police were successfully sued by the family of the deceased.)

Such reports were not uncommon, and in the recent past there was little in the way of gay cohesiveness—anywhere—to provide legal or political protection for our besieged community. In Houston, Ray Hill was outspoken in the local press, and a representative of the National Gay Task Force struggled to build an activist organization, but Metropolitan Community Church remained the primary gay deterrent to antigay forces. As such, our church was bitterly disliked by a disconcerting majority of the establishment.

It was not without some apprehension that we held our first parade for gay and lesbian human rights in Houston at the beginning of 1978. Having flown in from Los Angeles for the day, I joined Reverend Harvey as a leader of the march. We hoped that perhaps a thousand gay brothers and sisters might participate with us. But as often happens, we underestimated the turnout. In fact, we were joined by over fifteen thousand sisters and brothers who courageously braved the city of Houston's wrath!

Police told us to stay on the sidewalks, but when they saw how many of us were advancing, like a flash flood in a canyon, they had little choice but to let us take to the street. The amazing response was dramatic proof of how important our efforts were, and we were excited and pleased by the turnout. But there was a strong undercurrent of danger.

Jeri Ann said later, "As we marched, it was obvious that a lot of people in Houston didn't want to see us. There's the saying about safety being in numbers, but I was frightened—terrified. I knew we were in Texas. It's a whole different area of America. None of us was unaware of the fate of President John F. Kennedy in another Texas city. So before we left home, I wrote out my will."

Our pastor from Dallas, Reverend Jim Harris, a sinewy, cowboy type of street-smart preacher said. "I've never been frightened of anything in my life, but tonight I'm scared!"

At the rally following the parade, Jeri Ann made a powerful speech despite her apprehension. Holding a Bible aloft, she proclaimed into several microphones, "God doesn't make junk! We are all created to be productive, caring sons or daughters of our Maker. God doesn't have any adopted children. Know for certain: Jesus loves us!"

People who would never attend a gay rally nevertheless heard Reverend Harvey's fiery declarations rebroadcast on national television. Soon there would be repercussions. The next day, Jeri Ann received concerned telephone calls from several excited members of her Houston congregation. "The television stations and the radio stations every twenty minutes to half an hour are broadcasting the Ku Klux Klan's phone number from one end of this state to the other," one of our members said. "They're asking people to dial a recorded message. It's bad. They're giving the KKK free publicity. It's enough to make your skin crawl!"

"So what's the message?"

"The KKK's calling for the death of every homosexual in Texas!"

"They are what?"

"They want to kill pansy preachers! You better hear it for yourself. The voice sounds like a fundamentalist preacher. One who claims to literally believe every word of the Bible. I know his phone line's jammed—but keep trying until you get through. And for God's sake stay in the church. These people are dangerous!"

Alarmed, Jeri Ann agreed.

"I kept dialing," she said. "Dialing, dialing, dialing, but the number was constantly busy. When I couldn't get through anytime during the day after the parade, I forced the Ku Klux Klan out of my mind and went home. The next morning, I planned to go to the church at about nine o'clock, which was usual for me, but my home telephone rang at seven-thirty. Our church secretary had arrived at the building early.

" 'They've burned a cross on our front lawn,' " she exclaimed.

" 'You're not serious?' "

" 'I am. It's like what you see in the pictures, like what those men in sheets do with crosses on fire!' "

Reverend Harvey's heart began pounding. She finished dressing, ignored even a suggestion of breakfast, and hurried to her automobile. Our church in Houston, with sanctuary and offices converted from an old printing shop, was located in a residential area. Thus, in only a matter of minutes, Jeri Ann arrived at the Metropolitan Community Church where, on the front lawn, stood a large burned cross.

The cross was made of iron pipes and rusty rebar wrapped in heavy burlap. The burlap had then been enclosed with chicken wire. Inside this bulky assembly were .22- and .38-caliber bullets. It had been doused with kerosene and set on fire during the darkest hours of night.

Bullets fired in all directions. Some were discovered at the front of our building where they had embedded themselves in the wall. Other rounds, unspent, were found in the burned remains of the cross.

"I was mesmerized with fear!" admitted Jeri Ann. "To me, the Ku Klux Klan had always been funny people wearing white peaked hats and running around in grade B movies—but this was real. It wasn't for laughs! I didn't know what to do other than call the police. When they arrived, they asked questions of our neighbors in the area, but none of the residents admitted they knew anything."

It was a very panicky period for Jeri and her secretary. After the police departed, they went into the church office and tried to calm each other's nerves. But no sooner had the authorities departed than Jeri received her second telephone call of the day. It was actually from the Klan whose offices were located about three miles from where Jeri Ann lived. A man on the line said, "I hope you got our message this morning. Our message means that you and your kind are a blight on the land, a sore in the fair state of Texas, and we want all of you out. This is your warning! Next time it won't be a cross that burns. It'll be you or your church!"

Reverend Harvey called the police again.

"How do you know the call was really from the KKK?" asked a somewhat amused officer.

"He sounded convincing."

"Not good enough, lady!"

"You saw the cross, and you know there were bullets fired!"

"Sure, sure, but what do you want from us? We can't get fingerprints off a burned cross or a telephone call, can we? You want some advice? If I was you, lady, I'd take anything you might want to keep, and get it out of that building you call a church and lock the stuff up some other place. And I'd think about moving out of Texas."

"Thanks a lot," replied Jeri. "Yours is really heartwarming advice!"

Jeri Ann went home that evening, irritated, vowing not to run away scared, but all the while both she and her lover were actually so thoroughly frightened as to later describe their shared condition as "shaking in our boots." And, as if the situation was not sufficiently nerve-racking, Jeri Ann kept redialing the number that many Houston broadcasting stations were still urging their listeners to call. When she finally got through and heard the popular prerecorded message, Reverend Harvey was thoroughly shocked. Even so, she had the presence of mind to set up a small tape recorder and call again. On January 10, 1978, she recorded an authoritative, preachy male voice. His insidious message, word for word, was as follows:

> Pasadena, Texas. We, the Knights of the Ku Klux Klan, are not embarrassed to admit that we endorse and seek the execution of all homosexuals. While many church people are duped by their brain-washed, pink-panty preachers into believing that we should merely pray for the homosexuals, we find that we must endorse and support the law of God which calls for the death penalty for all homosexuals!
>
> Not only are we seeing the establishment of homosexual churches like the Metropolitan Church at 1214 Joannie Street in Houston in our once unblemished land, but at least two major denominations have actually ordained homosexuals into the ministry. To endorse the homosexuals as having any rights to set up anywhere in our land, we invoke the wrath of God as at Sodom and Gomorrah!
>
> God's laws on homosexuality state at Leviticus 18:22, "And you must not lie down with a male the same as you lie down with a woman; it is a detestable thing." Also, at Leviticus 20:13, "And

when a man lies down with a male the same as one lies down with a woman, both of them have done a detestable thing; they should be put to death without fail; their own blood is upon them."

It is not our intention to put this up to a discussion, or to debate the matter, or to set up a dialogue with a committee of queers as to their rights or sexual freedom. The law of God states the death penalty for homosexuals, and when God's laws are again enforced, the death penalty is what it will be!

On January ninth, on the very steps of City Hall in downtown Houston there was a meeting of the homosexuals to talk about their rights and sexual freedoms. How long will it be before the people of this land stand up for God and say, "No more of this"? Must Houston, Texas become the next Sodom and Gomorrah?

Preceding announcement made possible by the First Amendment to the Bill of Rights.

Reverend Harvey telephoned the local telephone company to complain about the message, but the woman supervisor who finally took her call complacently insisted that anybody, including the Ku Klux Klan, had every right to disseminate any kind of message they desired.

"They are protected by the laws—protected by the First Amendment to the Constitution," the supervisor said in a smug drawl, and added, "That's what we folks around here call free speech."

Jeri Ann tried to hold her temper. "You don't need to lecture me about free speech," she replied. "But that call you're letting the Klan put out is something different—it's calling for violence. I'll never forget the sound of that man's voice—calling for our death! You can hardly get through to their number because it's constantly being given out on radio stations."

"But there's nothing I can do," the supervisor said insincerely. "I'm sorry."

"Yes, you are," replied Jeri, hanging up the receiver.

The Klan's message of hate, played thousands of times, continued to go out over the telephone lines. Reverend Harvey, in response, called every member of her congregation and had each of them, and all of their friends, barrage the telephone company with complaints against what was, in reality, not a First Amendment right, but a particularly illegal activity. After three days, the message was terminated.

That evening, soon after Jeri Ann and Chris, her lover, had gone home and sighed with relief, their telephone rang. A new male voice came snarling out of the earpiece. "Bitch!" exclaimed the man. "We're gonna take care of you! We got six strong studs here what's each got more than ten inches! They're gonna take care of your sex problem what made you what you are! And we're coming to your house, so get ready now, you hear?"

The anonymous voice cackled with glee and slammed down his telephone. Then, several startling minutes later, another vicious man called to make certain the first message had been received. While the second man was on the line, Reverend Harvey decided to try a routine someone had suggested. She clicked the button up and down on her receiver and said, "Operator, are you getting this?"

A momentary pause was followed by a mean laugh on the other end of the connection. "Bitch," said the unwanted caller, "Who do you think I work for? How do you think I got your unlisted telephone number?"

Chilled, Jeri Ann lowered her receiver and let it click off. She locked eyes with Chris, and then both of them went for weapons they had in the house.

"I sat up all night in the kitchen with a thirty-eight," said Reverend Harvey. "My lover was awake in the living room with a twenty-two. At any moment we expected our doors to be broken down. Several days passed that way, until, hysterical, I called Troy. In those days, when we had trouble in our little churches, we could call Los Angeles and 'Daddy' would usually come running to help."

When Reverend Harvey called me, she started to cry. Through her tears she said, "They've burned a cross on the front lawn of the church. They're telephoning our house at all hours. They're threatening Chris and me with rape and murder. We haven't slept for three days or nights and I'm getting crazy! What can we do?"

Automatically, I suggested, "Jeri, you go through your list of people in the congregation. Find two or three of the biggest, baddest, roughest, toughest, meanest gay men you know and tell them you need help and get them to come over and make sure you're protected!"

But no sooner had I uttered those words than Jeri Ann Harvey stopped sniveling on the other end. I think she blew her nose or something, because her voice was much steadier when she replied than it had been when she first called. Unintentionally, I had pressed the correct button to make her combative.

"You have given me a good idea," she said. "But we don't need the men, thank you! I know four of the strongest dykes in the world here in Houston, and they're not afraid of anybody!"

After that, I realized that both Reverend Harvey and I still had within ourselves traces of sexism. As for Metropolitan Community Church in Houston, gay men and lesbians did ride out the storm. They tightened their security for the church, particularly on Sundays when there were services, or whenever groups were gathered. People were required to identify parcels and other measures were enforced.

It was fortunate nobody was ever hurt.

"While I was still there," said Jeri Ann, "They threatened to bomb us. It was a scary experience. A man called on a Sunday morning, just prior to service, and in a menacing voice said there was a bomb in the church and there wasn't time for us to get out. He said he wanted to hear my scream over the telephone as we were blown to bits!

"I immediately went into the sanctuary and announced to the assembly that we had a bomb threat, and I gave them a choice. Either we could run out of the building like foolish, frightened creatures, which was probably what the caller wanted us to do, or we could get down on our knees and pray.

"One person left the church. The rest of us said prayers for ten minutes, until past the time when the bomb was supposed to explode. Then we stood and I said, 'Praise God, let's continue with our service.' Which we did, raising our voices in a lusty hymn of thanksgiving.

"I think whoever called us with the bogus bomb threat was surely disappointed. I had the feeling his cronies were lurking outside, ready to take pictures of us in panic, running out of the church. Well, they waited in vain and went unrewarded."

A measure of our enemies' failure can, in this instance, be accurately described in statistics. When Reverend Jeri Ann Harvey arrived to become pastor of Houston's Metropolitan Community Church, there were eighteen members. After less than two years, when Jeri Ann departed to become the first female pastor of our Mother Church in Los Angeles, despite organized threats of death and destruction, the primarily gay and lesbian congregation in Houston numbered 360 brave persons, proving that God loves us, even in Texas!

Reverend June Norris and Reverend Jeri Ann Harvey both fought fear and won. That is how it can and should be for all people, gay and nongay alike. Such a message for the friends and members of my community was made known to me on two separate and very special occasions when I was visited by an angel of our Lord.

I have spoken of the occurrences for nearly a decade, but only now have decided to share them in writing. My earlier reluctance stems from the simple fact that many people do not like anything that has to do with prophets or mystics. Such concepts frighten them. When you speak of visions or dreams, people immediately begin to believe the individual who has received such a gift is losing his or her grip on sanity. Nevertheless, what I would like to relate in simple terms, without elaboration, is true.

On the first occasion, I was on a "bike run," handling a motorcycle in California's Sierra Nevada Mountains. It was the last place in the world I would have expected to receive a visitation!

That year was 1975, one of the best years in the "good old days" for most gay people. Our lives were filled with promise. Anita Bryant was still a year away from rattling our cages. No one had ever heard of an impossible nightmare called AIDS. Yet while 1975 was good for others, my personal ministry seemed to be in the doldrums. I had also recently had a friendly parting from Steve, my lover for the previous five years.

Depression began to plague my waking hours. "What do I do now?" I heard myself frequently ask. "What is next for our community? And in my ministry, Lord, what do you want from me?"

I awakened in a canvas tent in the middle of a starry night. My companions were comfortably asleep, high in the mountains where the temperature drops fast. I was shivering with cold. After burrowing deeper into a downy bag, I dozed again, whereupon I had a dream about being freezing cold during an earthquake. After that, I was awake once again and could not get back to sleep.

Nature was the only outside distraction as I began to feel the true spirit of prayer. I have no idea how much time passed, or how little, but all of a sudden, the tent was gone from my vision. There was no cold and there were no mountains. There was only a brilliant, almost blinding personage in a white robe standing on the ground before me, encased by light. I could see nothing else but the angel.

My attention centered on the voice, which was sweet, but sounded like that of a man. The angel's message was short, delivered with an aura of peace which my visitor transmitted. His message was that I was to act the prophet. Then I blinked, and it was morning.

The second visit was a year later, at the Lincoln Memorial. I was there with a contingent, two thousand strong, from our General Conference which was being held in Washington, D.C., that year. We were to lay a wreath, after which I led our group in making a covenant with God that we would never be afraid again. I said to those who were listening, "Perfect love casts out all fear. We will never again fear for our jobs, fear for our lives, fear our parents' disowning or denying us. We are not going to do that!"

Following our prayer, I led the group in singing, and it was during the middle of hymn singing that the same personage who was with me in the Sierra Nevada Mountains was with me again. I felt his presence as surely as I could feel breath within my lungs, but on that occasion, my angel neither spoke nor made himself seen, but by joining me, validated our covenant to cast out fear. By so doing, we would eventually be victorious over the gathering forces of religious and political intolerance.

9

This Is Our Land: 1976–1977

Blessed are they that have been persecuted for righteousness' sake: for theirs is the kingdom of heaven. Blessed are you when people shall reproach you, and persecute you, and say all manner of evil against you falsely, for my sake.

—Matthew 5:10,11

A VERY real fear engulfed gay Americans in 1977. Our vocations, our freedom, and our lives were threatened by thousands of unnecessarily frightened religious people who were whipped into mass hysteria by a handful of hatemongering preachers, politicians, and others who ignored the word *love* as I know it from the teachings of Jesus. They called *my* love perverted, and they openly prayed for the death and destruction of lesbian women and homosexual men because we dared to be visible and outspoken in our pursuit of civil rights.

On Cadillacs in Miami, bumper stickers appeared with white letters on a field of black, reading KILL A QUEER FOR CHRIST—not a loving message nor one easy to forget! It was a grim symbol of the hysteria in Dade County.

Psychiatrists and sociologists may determine what happened, but a misapplication of religion, combined with hypocrisy masquerading as morality, was the trigger. The root cause was a willingness to blame homosexuals and lesbians for the ills of society, and to attribute to us a propensity for wrongdoing that has never been true.

Reigning over Miami's frenzy of self-righteousness and bigotry was Anita Bryant Green, the overripe beauty queen transplanted to Florida from Oklahoma. Her place of worship was the Northwest Baptist Church in North Miami where Anita's husband, Bob Green, was a deacon, and where she taught Sunday school.

During the course of one of their prayer and revival meetings, Anita Bryant is said to have been persuaded by her pastor, Reverend "Brother Bill" Chapman, that God was entrusting her with a duty to confound the efforts of people who were openly involved in gay liberation. Brother Bill was apparently also responsible for Anita's displeasure at the possibility of having her children taught in school by healthy homosexuals.

Anita Bryant's antigay campaign began when she first lobbied against Dade County's Metro Commission, which intended to pass an ordinance forbidding discrimination against homosexuals in housing, public accommodation, and employment. Contrary to Anita's wishes, however, and in spite of her vocal and written objections, the ordinance prohibiting discrimination was successfully passed by Miami's Metro Commission.

Mrs. Green was infuriated! Without delay, her cohorts declared that in Miami vice and immorality would reign supreme if civil rights were guaranteed for homosexuals. Therefore, a decision to seek a county referendum for repeal of the ordinance was immediately proposed by a supporter of the antigay forces, the slick local politician, Robert Blake. He indicated to Anita that, in his opinion, a law protecting lesbians and gay men from unfair discrimination was the same as granting us undue "special privileges." With that convoluted kind of reasoning, Blake suggested the creation of a legal corporation to raise money and to legitimize their efforts. His choice for a public figure to front their organization was Anita Bryant.

"Will you head it up, Anita, as chairwoman?" he asked.

"Yes," Anita replied eagerly with her husband standing firmly behind her. Discussing her acceptance, Anita later wrote, "I would give my life, if necessary, to protect my children." However, she was never asked to make anything approaching the ultimate sacrifice. (The greatest danger Anita ever faced was to her dignity when, during a live show inside a television station, some man was passed through security guards and not prevented from splashing a creamy pie into her face.)

Mostly, Anita carried off her role with tremendous style. Eventually she became the darling of zealous hatemongers all the way from southeastern Florida to America's Pacific Northwest. Although advocates of adherence to the United States Constitution were appalled by her smiling attacks on gay civil rights, Anita and her associates continually and blatantly employed bigotry as the major justification for their actions.

In the beginning, Anita was pumped full of fiery "moral" indignation. She seemed not even to have considered the possibility that if she intentionally trampled on the rights of gay Americans to enjoy and pursue happiness, those same free men and women—who had only recently learned that they could fight back—would protect themselves. Thus, it was with impunity that Anita (as wife, family breadwinner, mother of four, prolific author of "inspirational" books, and media huckster for Florida orange juice) was pleased to become chairperson of a new antigay group. Their reactionary organization was called Save Our Children, a name appropriated without permission from a dissimilar organization. Using the words Save Our Children was the idea of Anita's husband, who took the position of treasurer.

Whoever originated the bumper sticker KILL A QUEER FOR CHRIST remains anonymous. Mrs. Green denies any personal knowledge of that, and I believe her. Unfortunately, she later took the biblical words of Paul—"Mortify [put to death] your members which are upon the earth: fornication, uncleanness, inordinate affection, evil concupiscence, and covetness, which is idolatry" (Colossians 3:5)—and readily embraced a new reinterpretation. Paul's meaning was, according to what Anita wrote, "We are to mortify such things as 'inordinate affection,' and this includes acts of homosexuality."

Naive as the beauty queen may have been, it is difficult to easily excuse Anita Bryant Green and those with her for their assault upon a gay community too often vulnerable to intentional wrong. The problem may have been that Anita and her people possessed not enough love to share among themselves, and wasted their efforts toward salvation in the unrewarding labor of condemning others. Our world would be better if each of us could discover earth's beauty and the joy brought to us by Christ.

Jesus said, "Love one another: for he who loves another has fulfilled the law," and Jesus added, "Love works no ill to his neighbor: therefore love is the fulfilling of the law." (Romans 13: 8, 10)

In Anita Bryant's opinion, she and her people never hurt anyone because they were merely fighting an "issue," not attacking "people." Anita considered her forces to be "harmless as doves" and she said homosexuals should be allowed to "live and let live so long as they do not discriminate against me." Strange statements from someone trying to terminate the employment of thousands of conscientious individuals!

Anita professed that everything she did was for love—the love of God, the love of country, the love of her children. But she also admitted, "This is what... turns us on." It was difficult, therefore, ever to be overly sympathetic toward controversial Anita, and in my travels around the United States I never missed an opportunity to present the gay side of our story to all the people I met. For instance, on the "Red Eye Special" into New York City one morning, when a very efficient airline stewardess asked if I would like orange juice for breakfast, I replied, "What kind of orange juice is it?"

"Sir?" she said. "What do you mean?"

"I mean, is it from California? Or are the oranges from Arizona or Texas? Or from Florida? What state does it come from?"

"Does it really matter, sir?"

I smiled my broadest smile. "Yes, it matters. Will you find out for me?" I said in a stage whisper, aware that my fellow passengers were listening.

A few minutes later the stewardess returned. "The carton says it's Minute Maid but it doesn't have any state or city name on it," she said, offering the empty container for my inspection. "Would you like to read the label?"

I raised my hands in refusal.

"No, no, thank you!" I quickly replied, making certain everyone around would hear, "I know what Minute Maid is. It's a blend containing Florida orange juice—and there's no way I can drink it!"

Then the stewardess asked the question for which I had been waiting all the time.

"Why can't you drink it?" she asked.

"Because I'm a homosexual," I replied.

Like nervous turtles, the heads of nearby passengers suddenly withdrew back into the safety of their shells, but I continued with my answer, secure in the knowledge that everyone around me was secretly listening.

"Gay men and lesbians are boycotting the Florida citrus industry because of what Anita Bryant's been doing in that state," I said. "Now, would you please remove this orange juice from Florida!"

The stewardess picked up the golden liquid and walked away. I proceeded to eat, knowing that every passenger in my vicinity had received the message. Not many minutes later, the stewardess returned. She had a friendly young steward in tow.

"Reverend Perry," he said with a twinkle in his eyes, "We'd be pleased if you'd come forward and take another seat—we think you'll be more comfortable in the cabin for first class passengers."

Naturally, I agreed.

Boycotting orange juice from Florida was definitely not a whim. The Florida Citrus Commission supported Anita Bryant whom they paid to promote Florida orange juice on their national television commercials.

Miss Bryant, whose primary qualification for anything was a trim figure (good enough to have made her a runner-up in bathing beauty contests), fueled with intolerant religious energy similar to that manifested during the Spanish Inquisition, wanted to have gay people fired from all teaching positions. It did not mattter to her that the overwhelming majority of us are well-trained, caring, upstanding citizens innocent of any wrongdoing.

When I spoke at meetings, I never hesitated to expand upon what Anita Bryant Green, her husband, Bob, and their cohorts were doing. "Taking jobs away from anyone, including gay and lesbian schoolteachers who have proven themselves to be dedicated in their work, is not likely to gain popular voter approval, or financial contributions from misled religious people—without some kind of emotional justification," I said. "So Anita's fraudulent crusade has concocted—and uses—the false claim that it exists for the 'protection' of God's sweet, innocent children! Does it matter to Anita and her companions that those children are really safe and no harm has happened or is going to happen simply because a well-trained teacher happens to be lesbian or gay? Or does it matter to them that many of us homosexuals have our own children, or that we are concerned about the welfare of children just as much as anybody else? Not if you listen to Anita Bryant!

"It is her contention that the best homosexual (as a nonstereotypical human being) is the worst homosexual (as a role model). The more pleasant or attractive a known lesbian or gay male teacher happens to be, or the more intelligent and helpful, or kind, or athletic—the worse that individual is for the impressionable minds of children—according to Anita!

"I know it sounds like the topsy-turvy world of Alice in Wonderland where big is little, black is white, and everything that was up is down! That is because Anita and some of the ambitious people she represents would put religion into government and prayer into schools, but they ignore Jesus' primary commandment to 'Love your neighbor as yourself.'

"The use of little boys and girls, young men and women, to cloud the judgment of adults whose thinking is otherwise fair and clear, is an old, insidious strategy. Bryant attempts to explain her attacks upon the homosexual community by declaring she is acting against out-of-the-closet gay schoolteachers because of her 'love' for children. And in her haste to emotionally inflame good citizens, she and her mentors have adopted 'Save Our Children' to be their intentionally misleading slogan! But Anita Bryant cannot love her children any more, maybe not even as much, as I love my two sons!

"Witch-hunts by people like Anita Bryant Green, supported by outfits with a book-burning mentality, are shameful! Homosexuals are not outcasts of God. We are not monsters. All of us were once children with mothers and fathers. We grew with the same love and understanding, or lack thereof, as anybody else.

"The God-given sexual difference is a small and important part of our being. It may enhance, but in no way diminishes, a gay person's compassion for others. We laugh and we cry. Nothing obstructs our prevailing desire for a shared environment in which the best possible nurture is provided for our young—including ten percent of the children who *will* grow up to be gay despite anything you or I may do or say!"

Of course, I have never contended that all gay people are perfect. Who would pretend all nongay people are without fault? It would be stupid. We, too, like heterosexuals, have outlaws who commit crimes—crimes we abhor! But because there are ten times as many heterosexuals in this world as there are homosexuals, ten times more criminal actions, including crimes against innocent boys and girls, are in fact committed by nonhomosexual individuals from the so-called straight community! The most prevalent abuses of children are felonious acts of incest in which a heterosexual father exerts parental pressure and takes full sexual advantage of his daughter. This is a *real* problem!

I have no quarrel with the idea of protecting children. Quite the contrary. But children are not endangered by gays, as Anita Bryant and her legions would have had people believe while they went about proclaiming damnation for me and my friends.

Fending off such attacks is more than a question of civil rights. It is a matter of continually supporting thousands of dedicated brothers and sisters, some only beginning to face the world, others ready to retire, all struggling to impart knowledge, creativity, and sometimes wisdom. For those who care anything about justice and preserving freedom, an action like the refusal to drink Florida's deceptively innocuous orange juice was not too large a price to pay.

The war between homosexuals who wanted liberation and the fundamentalists who wanted repression raged for nearly six months. Dade County became a topic of national interest. Night after night, Johnny Carson on NBC's "Tonight" Show poked humorous, piercing barbs into Anita's image. Show business personalities like Paul Williams, Shirley MacLaine, Phyllis Diller, and Peter Lawford, to name only a few, took public positions against the bigotry Anita stood for.

Save Our Children campaigners countered with a massive rally in

Miami's Civic Auditorium. Performers included Baptist Jerry Falwell and, singing in uniform, a discomforting bunch of police who called themselves Cops for Christ. Also, Billy Graham, Pat Boone, Dale Evans, and Roy Rogers prayed for her success, according to Anita.

Meanwhile, gay leaders and gay money from all over the United States poured into Dade County. On occasion it was a circus. The Anita Bryant forces complained we were raising a lot of money. True, but their corporation did the same. They argued that our fund-raisers sold obscene anti–Anita Bryant T-Shirts with a graphic sexual suggestion. That may also be true. I saw the T-shirts, but obscenity is in the eye of the beholder.

Nobody knew who was going to win the election. All you needed to do was read a newspaper or listen to television and it seemed obvious that antigay discrimination in Florida would soon become a relic of the past.

Victory celebrations were planned by gay organizations in most major American cities. There was a small element of uncertainty, but nothing seemed ominous. Gay unity seemed strengthened from coast to coast as a direct result of Anita Bryant's unprovoked attacks. Millions of gay men and lesbians were joining ranks. A comment often expressed was, "If there had been no Anita Bryant, the gay community would have had to invent her!"

One week before election day I flew to Miami. Although half a million dollars was raised to fight Save Our Children, Inc., I had doubts about our ability to win. Being originally from Florida, I was painfully aware of the numerous small communities that bordered on the swampy parts of the Everglades within Dade County. There was insufficient time to reason with all those people scattered in rural areas, people who knew their Bible was good but who had serious doubts about us. And the Jews in Miami Beach, and Cuban refugees who were qualified to vote, remained unknown factors.

A second problem to cause me concern was that gay leaders, who had been diligently working for months in Miami, refused to consider that the "gays are going to hell" language Anita Bryant was using to vilify us could really do our cause any harm. Gay leaders reasoned that religious fanaticism (with which we were being deluged) was invalid, and they refused to become involved with Scripture. My opinion was the opposite. If Anita could use a few selected scriptures to condemn us, someone should quote better scriptures in our defense!

I was invited to debate on television. Before my appearance, one of my gay friends stopped me and said he would prefer that I not keep the engagement. "We don't want to get a lot of press," he said. "Let sleeping dogs lie."

My response was swift. "You don't seem to understand what's happening here," I told him. "The animals in this city not only aren't sleeping—they're loose in the streets and about to eat us! Our enemies are taking the language of Scripture and running wild with it. You may think a rebuttal on their terms isn't needed, but I'm from the South, and I know we need to answer. Nobody's talking classroom civics in Miami—this is a religious issue. And I speak the language!"

Four of us appeared on television that evening. In short order, the gay man with me and his opponent, a Florida politician in the race for governor, were clashing so violently that the director of the television show concentrated his camera on me and my opponent, Reverend "Brother Bill" Chapman who was the inspiration behind all that was happening in Miami. The Baptist revival in his church had begun the struggle, and I was happy to meet him face to face.

We began talking about homosexuality and the election, which was fine until Brother Bill used the word "pervert" in reference to homosexuals. At that point I strenuously objected. It was amazing for me to realize he actually was insensitive to his callous use of the word that came so casually to his lips. Afterward, Brother Bill was more careful about his choice of language although, throughout the remainder of the program, we continued to strongly disagree on issues.

When Sunday morning arrived, I preached at the Metropolitan Community Church in Miami. The *Miami Herald* sent reporters who wrote that my sermon became hysterical. They were correct. I did become emotionally involved! Wouldn't you, with your life in danger?

I felt as the early Christians must have felt, pushed into an arena when the lions were ready for dinner. I feared we could lose the election, and I could not erase from my mind the life-threatening, antigay bumper stickers I had seen on the streets of Miami.

Dade County voters went to the polls in record numbers on June 7, 1977, and almost 70 percent of them cast ballots against us! Gay people, in public and in private, were shocked. Anita Bryant had clearly won what she referred to as "the battle for Miami." It was as though we had been slapped in the face.

Thousands upon thousands of our sisters and brothers in Los Angeles, New York, San Francisco, Chicago, Dallas, Washington, D.C., and elsewhere took to the streets and held candlelight vigils. "We're not going to give up," declared David Goodstein, publisher of *The Advocate*. But in spite of all our bravado, there was a difference in the gay community's perception of fair-weather friends among the people around us.

Something ominous had happened!

Paranoia set in—with some justification.

Forces in the United States, who would happily destroy our freedom, were proud of their success and were making new preparations to drive all gay men and lesbians back into closets after our brief glimpse of the sunlight. In a *Presbyterian Journal* interview, Anita Bryant was quoted as saying, "The greatest blessing a Christian can experience is to know you are right with God—even if the whole world calls you a bigot!"

Anita's victory ignited the ambitions of numerous petty people. California senator John Briggs was no exception. He flew to Florida to pay homage to Anita. Briggs had visions of becoming the next governor of California, and toward that end, planned walking over the bodies of homosexuals all the way from San Diego to Sacramento. His run for election was over a year in the future, but Briggs was making preparations.

Concurrently, a growing backlash against gays spread like wildfire. The next city to declare war on us was Wichita, Kansas, a city where there were more churches than gasoline stations—churches that often threatened each other, not to mention us, with eternal damnation. And again, there was no contest. No matter what the churches thought of each other, every pious antagonist in Wichita united against us. We had no time to reason with the electorate, no time to convince Scripture-quoting mobs that homosexuals are three-dimensional flesh-and-blood daughters and sons of real parents, not horned devils as we were being portrayed.

I stayed away from that election, but members of Metropolitan Community Church and a local committee fought valiantly to stem Anita's overwhelming fundamentalist popularity. Yet our people never had a chance.

The next battle was in St. Paul, Minnesota. Many felt we could win there because the city of St. Paul is part of the same urban area as Minneapolis. Unfortunately, the two cities were not twins, and were divided by more than the Mississippi River. Although Minneapolis had a gay rights ordinance, we discovered St. Paul did not. Instead, St. Paul had an antigay Roman Catholic bishop in residence. When the bishop ordered resident blue-collar workers to vote against us, the outcome became inevitable. The severity of our loss in St. Paul was equal to the disaster in Miami.

(There are Catholic archbishops who are progay and Catholic archbishops who are antigay. The Roman Catholic church is as much split on the issue as are Protestants. There are liberal Southern Baptists. In the Methodist church, Bishop Melvin Wheatley was charged with heresy for his position favorable to homosexuals, and stood trial before being found not guilty of violating Methodist doctrine. An Episcopal bishop in New York ordained homosexuals while, in Florida, another Episcopal bishop maintained that in his state being homosexual was "not fashionable.")

Anita Bryant's organization fought us as though we wore horns and carried pitchforks. Operating from headquarters in Miami Beach, they renamed themselves Protect America's Children and continued holding emotionally loaded fund-raising rallies. With three wins in a row— Miami, Wichita, and St. Paul—Anita's Brother Bill was dispatched to create religious indignation in other potentially receptive cities where gay rights were proposed.

Their steamroller of fear and falsehood kept advancing. When it rolled into Eugene, Oregon, a college city of nearly a hundred thousand residents, everyone I knew proclaimed that we finally had a 50-50 chance of winning, for several reasons: the population of Eugene is largely upper income and educated; 16,000 students attended the University of Oregon in Eugene and 10 percent of them would be eligible to vote; Eugene's school district already had a four-year-old, nondiscriminatory hiring policy regarding sexual orientation, with never a problem; and the local newspaper, politicians, educators, even religious leaders had expressed support for the gay rights referendum. But all to no avail.

Even in a compassionate city like Eugene, we lost!

With four defeats in a row, our cause was badly wounded. Gay and lesbian people everywhere felt overwhelmed. There appeared to exist no place where anyone listened to what we were saying from our hearts. We had spent a considerable amount of money and time in four different states to educate voters as to who and what we really are, and to make them realize that although we do want our civil rights as stated in the Constitution of the United States, we would not hurt anyone.

In return, we reaped a harvest of rejection and fear.

Senator John Briggs became our next antagonist. Unimpressively ranked as the worst vote-getter in a field of five who wanted to win the governor's office in California, Briggs firmly believed that a campaign of hate like those that preceded him in Florida, Oregon, Minnesota, and Kansas ("the out-of-state tryouts") would somehow enhance his image with an electorate.

For some personal reason, the antigay schoolteacher issue was obviously dear to Senator Briggs. He was so pleased with himself when he reprised the issue that he made a statement to the effect that Miami and St. Paul had been only preliminaries, like the salad and the soup part of a dinner. California was the entrée!

Predictably, gay fears spread—and while Senator Briggs was fashioning his viciously calculated antigay issue to become the centerpiece for his gubernatorial campaign, he also authored another ballot initiative aimed at winning voter approval with a wider application of the death penalty. During his campaign for governor, according to the *Los Angeles Times*, John Briggs joked that the antigay initiative would make it easier for him to get his death penalty bill passed.

Appalled gay people started wearing pink triangles cut out of cloth, which they sewed onto their shirts and jackets. The idea of the pink triangle was not original. It had been instituted by the Nazis during World War II to identify thousands of homosexuals who were annihilated in Third Reich concentration camps. Thirty-plus years later, in California, gay men and lesbians voluntarily donned the pink triangle to proclaim a renewed danger to everybody's freedom—a warning that would-be, pseudo-religious tyrants were seeking power in America.

Within the core of our being, in our hearts, we knew that if a minor despot like Briggs was successful with his misuse of the California ballot, then gay rights, the First Amendment to the Constitution, and who knows what additional personal liberties, would be down the drain for all residents in the United States for as long as any citizen could imagine!

We had no choice. We had to use all our resources to resist an evil contrary to every idea of freedom and justice upon which the American nation was founded.

California was to be the ultimate battleground!

I tried to assess strengths and weaknesses. Obviously, our strategic position was bad—with four severe defeats for gay rights prior to the issue coming into California.

Gay leaders were disorganized. Homosexual communities felt distrustful of the entire electoral process. We had essentially been disenfranchised by a well-entrenched religious minority who traded upon everybody's natural love of children—to support unreasonable efforts to codify their lust for political supremacy.

A time bomb had been activated by Anita Bryant's fanatics. And the clock was ticking! It was necessary, somehow, to convince the reasonable citizens in California that everyone in our state would be the losers (including children) if more than half of the registered voters did not come to agree with us that Anita Bryant's heir apparent, Senator John

V. Briggs, should be defeated. Nobody, homosexual or heterosexual, needed the ignorance-precipitated witch trials of Salem, Massachusetts, reenacted three centuries later on the Pacific Coast!

I knew, without exaggeration, that we faced a life-or-death issue. Yet I was uncertain about how to proceed, and everyone I knew held different opinions. There was no clear plan of resistance. Grass-roots efforts in other states to defend ourselves had not been successful, that much at least was certain.

Three times in twelve months history had repeated itself, and the only way we might break the depressing chain of events was to learn how gay activists had gone wrong in other campaigns. Toward such an objective, a conference was held in Laguna Beach late in 1977. Sponsored by the New Alliance for Gay Equality (New AGE), with helpful suggestions from David Mixner and Peter Scott, political consultant and attorney respectively, the conference brought together the leaders of losing fights. From Florida, Kansas, Minnesota, and Oregon they came, and we asked the basic question: what do we need to know in order to avoid a similar defeat in California? Their answer was simple: gay rights could not win! Period.

But there was a solution.

If the issue was freedom and justice for *all*, not just gay rights for us, we had a chance to win. Many Americans were not ready to vote for homosexuals—no matter that our cause was just. People in the nongay world were not yet prepared to give their approval to people whose presence still disturbed them.

During our period of self-analysis, Senator Briggs was at his zenith. Although I knew some things that would be productive in politics, my personal role in future community events was unknown to me. It was then that my secular thoughts became as one with the spiritual, and I again felt the presence of an angel of God reaffirming the validity of Christian social action.

Our Universal Fellowship offices were located on the sixth floor of a building at Ninth and Olive in downtown Los Angeles, not far from the Mother Church. Our habit was to hold communion in the workplace every Wednesday morning, and it was the first Wednesday in September when I arrived several minutes later than usual, wearing jeans. It only took one raised eyebrow from Frank Zerilli, my ever attentive and efficient secretary, for me to realize something was wrong.

As Frank came quickly to my side, he whispered, "Did you forget it's your turn to serve communion this morning?"

I had completely forgotten. "Oh my goodness," I gulped, looking up into the faces of about twenty people who were in the room. "Forgive me for the way I'm dressed." Without further delay, I put on my stole, moved to our little altar, and consecrated communion.

Afterward, as I began the prayer of thanksgiving, I became aware of a sudden change in my perception of the room. Everything was the same; yet not the same.

Different.

There was no visible entity, no audible sound.

Still, I became acutely aware of a new presence—the same personage who had appeared and spoken to me in the mountains of California, the same personage who had been near me at the Lincoln Memorial.

Without a sign or a sound, I knew once again that I was close to a holy angel. The message I received was unexpected. I was informed in the smallest part of an instant that Senator Briggs' political war on homosexuals was immoral—and what I was to do to thwart his objectives. I knew without any doubt that Briggs was acting contrary to the wish of Almighty God. And I knew that in the coming conflict, ours would be a moral battle.

Then the angel departed.

I removed my prayer stole and walked into Jim Sandmire's office. (At that time, Reverend Sandmire was the treasurer and an elder of our denomination.) "The Lord has just spoken to me," I said, verbalizing what I had been made to understand by the angelic visitor. "I am directed by God not to eat anymore until I raise a hundred thousand dollars to begin the fight against Senator Briggs."

Jim's Mormon background prompted him to ask, "Are you sure it was the Lord who spoke?"

I nodded. "The same personage who appeared to me on a previous occasion—the same personage I felt with me at the Lincoln Memorial," I said. "That person was here, in this building, at the altar in the other room."

Jim placed his finger beside a pencil lying on his desk, and gave the point of the pencil a tap to make it spin. "When does your fast begin?" he asked.

"Now," I replied. "It has already begun."

Sandmire looked carefully into my eyes. "Do you know what you're getting yourself into?" he asked. "Do you have any idea how long this could last?"

"I know that opposing Briggs is to be a life-or-death struggle for us," I replied, "but until now I didn't know what to do—or how or where to begin. This morning the Lord has led me to understand. And you must realize, Jim, the choice is not mine."

Without further conversation, Jim tendered his support. I had barely left his office when, unknown to me, he systematically began placing telephone calls to all the other elders in our Fellowship. "Troy's had a revelation," he told them. "He's not going to eat again until he raises a hundred thousand dollars. He is determined—and that's it!"

An hour later, David Goodstein, millionaire owner-publisher of Americas's most influential gay newspaper, *The Advocate*, telephoned. I took the opportunity to tell him what had recently transpired. "David," I said, "I know you're Jewish and I'm Christian, but both our faiths stem from a common root. And we both believe in visitation."

"Oh, yes," he responded, "but don't you stop eating now. Wait a while, Troy. Let me gear up the paper to give you some publicity. We'll do a public relations number and we'll need some time to present it properly."

I said, "No, David, you don't understand what I've told you. God spoke to me! My fast has already started and you'll have to catch up if you can. This is not debatable."

There was a pause before Goodstein replied. Then he said, "I don't want to see you starve to death, Troy. I'll contribute the first five thousand dollars toward the cause."

My fast lasted sixteen days. During that time I remained in front of the Federal Building in Los Angeles. Facilities of a recreational vehicle, which a good Mormon businessman rented for my use, were always available, but I preferred to remain visible as much as possible. I slept in the open. However, the daily luxury of a shower was welcome.

Money arrived from all around the United States. When the $100,000 goal was reached, I was physically weakened but spiritually exalted. The vast majority of the funds contributed were from friends and members of Metropolitan Community Church.

During the fast (in September, 1977), I decided to call a meeting of the gay leaders from California. Those attending were personally hand-picked by David Goodstein and myself. Included was Jim Foster, a friend long active in San Francisco's political arena.

We formed Concerned Voters of California, with dual headquarters in San Francisco and Los Angeles, to have the most impact in our fight against the Briggs initiative. We expected the fateful election would be held in June of the following year, but even in the spring of 1978 there was no unified gay opposition—although a great many different individuals were fiercely determined to resist Briggs' proposed antigay school-teacher legislation.

Morris Kight added his grass-roots campaign to others in Southern California, mobilizing rallies and marches as he has for many years. In Northern California, Michael Mank (schoolteacher member of Metropolitan Community Church) was instrumental in putting together the Bay Area Committee Against the Briggs Initiative. BACABI was formed with many diverse members listed, including Stan Smith, president of a building and construction trades council; the East Bay Dykes on Bikes; Gene Brown, sheriff of San Francisco; and others. Organizations and individuals proceeded according to their own perception of our opposition.

My intention was to be certain Concerned Voters of California could operate efficiently, with all our members functioning in harmony. Toward that objective, we did not encourage radical gay groups to affiliate with us (including those who believed that merely "coming out of the closet" would make a difference in our favor). While it is true that the majority of gays are unfortunately invisible because they prefer to be conservative, there also exists a very small minority within our minority who insist on being campy or putting on flamboyant gender-drag, which irresistibly attracts sensation-seeking television cameras. Their flagrant approach to our problem has been less than productive, no matter what they want to prove.

Concerned Voters of California avoided the pitfall of becoming partisan in politics. It could not be helpful for our organization to be either Democratic or Republican on the issue involving us all. Therefore, we resisted repeated attempts to draw us toward one side or the other. Avoiding labels was to our mutual advantage, and in such fashion, eventually, we also attracted many supportive citizens who were not homosexual.

For a time, we were continually besieged by individuals claiming to represent the "entire" gay community, but (as usual) they often belonged to fringe groups who wanted to take over our meetings and tell us what we could and could not do. When they confronted me, they were attempting to intimidate the wrong person.

In victory or defeat, we would accept our own responsibility. Outsiders would not be allowed to exert counterproductive pressure. I intended to work with professional people, and on a professional basis we would conduct a campaign of education, handling our own input to the various media. Toward that end, I invited individuals with talent, including attorneys and the wealthy, into our association. Considering the independence we strove to maintain, a few of our peers referred to us as the Lords and Ladies, a mild and temporary reproof.

When confronted with a decision of whether or not to merge with the Gay Democrats, we decided against it. The Democrats were interested in making certain that a very wide spectrum of groups was represented in their caucus, an early "rainbow coalition" with many tangential, not always cohesive objectives. We encouraged them to proceed as they were, absorbing popular grass-roots support, but we continued to believe we could do our best work if we cooperated with them but remained single-purposed and apart.

Campaign consultants of the highest caliber were what we needed, and Winner-Wagner and Associates, who had run Jerry Brown's successful campaign for governor, came to work with us. Convinced that we needed accurate information concerning attitudes of the state's registered voters, an in-depth, statewide survey was commissioned. After spending $60,000, we learned primarily that we needed to conduct an extensive program to calm California citizens' false fears and to mitigate the homophobia of a large segment of our state's population. We were also informed by the survey that the best spokesperson for us would be a person who was:

a. Roman Catholic and

b. a mother of ten children and

c. from the San Fernando Valley and

d. a popular president of her local PTA and

e. convinced that gay people are wonderful!

Additionally, we were told by the survey takers that a kind word from the president of the United States (Jimmy Carter) or from the top man in the Republican party (Ronald Reagan) would be very helpful. As for other potential spokespersons, the survey indicated that any lesbian or gay male (Harvey Milk, elected supervisor in San Francisco, and myself included) would probably be detrimental. Since Carter, Reagan, and Roman Catholic mothers of ten were not offering to speak in our behalf, I reinterpreted the survey's data to mean that since we had no one but ourselves to speak for us, I could do no more harm than any other person. With that desperate logic, and certain of God's blessing, I asked for an unpaid leave of absence from the Universal Fellowship of Metropolitan Community Church and embarked upon a year of struggle.

*   *   *

If the Briggs initiative had been voted in June as the senator desired, we would have lost by another devastating landslide. Gay efforts against Briggs' referendum were still unfocused. Money that we had raised prior to June was spent, and little more would be readily forthcoming. Gay people who read the statistics that pollsters had gathered, came to a dreary conclusion that our cause was hopeless.

The Briggs initiative, however, was not voted in June! The senator, who paid mercenary signature gatherers fifty cents for each name they obtained, had his first efforts trashed by alert voter registration officials who discovered a plethora of signature "errors and irregularities."

But Briggs, with no hesitation, began again. As Anita Bryant's hyperactive disciple, he merely intensified his drive to purge California schools of discernible homosexual teachers and anybody else who might, even inadvertently, befriend them. To qualify for the fall election, Briggs' mercenaries were ready with 405,000 new antigay signatures on the first of May. That was the Monday when Briggs personally accompanied his minions with the signatures they delivered to county registrars' offices in San Francisco, Los Angeles, and San Diego. The first bundle of Briggs' signatures, a token amount numbering only 1,000, was unveiled in San Francisco because, according to the ambitious, politically homophobic senator from the agricultural city of Fullerton, a large homosexual population made San Francisco "the moral garbage dump" of America.

After Briggs' initiative officially qualified to be on the ballot, it was assigned a number by the secretary of state, and henceforth, the initiative would be known statewide as Proposition 6. A popular anti-Briggs slogan, "No On 6," appeared on campaign buttons and bumper stickers that were distributed in large quantities. At the same time, fear continued to be the side effect of all the commotion, and that fear was a very real emotion for hundreds of thousands. In some of California's larger cities, as many as one third of the schoolteachers were male and female homosexuals. They had to decide individually whether to come out of the closet and fight, or to hide in a dark place forever.

And it did not help for gay schoolteachers to know that Oregon's primarily heterosexual Task Force on Sexual Preference had stated without reservation, "Most homosexual women and men are much more circumspect about their relationships at work than heterosexual employees."

Nor was there much comfort in the fact that *McCall's* had reported in its March 1978 issue that as a result of an unbiased questionnaire the magazine had sent to thousands of school principals, *McCall's* conclusion was, "If only the issue could be freed of the exaggerated claims and irresponsible fearmongering, no rational obstacle should stand in the way of letting homosexuals remain and become teachers, subject to those controls and standards of behavior that the profession applies to all teachers."

McCall's also invited comments with their questionnaire, and one school principal replied, "Heterosexual persons have been known to seduce or attack persons of the opposite sex—should we ban heterosexual teachers? Should teaching be reserved only for eunuchs?"

Personally, I found encouragement knowing that there were voices of reason abroad in the land, voices that had not succumbed to a steady barrage of orchestrated ignorance. Yet only six short months stood between California's gay community and electoral Armageddon. Our reprieve of extra time, the five-month postponement of the election from June to November, was a tremendous gift, but time passes quickly. Changes had to occur.

For Concerned Voters of California, it was necessary to find new political consultants, because Winner-Wagner had previous commitments that prevented them from continuing with us in the fall. They recommended someone both kind and intelligent, Don Bradley, a crusty political warhorse with many successful campaigns to his credit. Don could ably direct the conclusion of the fight, which would become intense before it ended.

Our first meeting with Don was stormy!

The full committee of Concerned Voters of California was present, and some members vociferously concluded that we could not win the contest. One member of our group, a San Francisco attorney, insisted, "We are in a no-win situation!"

Faced with that defeatist attitude, Don Bradley scowled and picked up his hat from our conference table. "Then I don't want your damn money," he snapped. "I don't accept challenges if I can't win!"

Dismissing the comment, another of our members, observing the displeasure of the man who had literally "written the book" on political science, who was the winner of 72 percent of all elections he had ever directed, murmured to Bradley, "We won't hold you responsible because we lose."

Bradley whirled toward the speaker and made no effort to disguise his annoyance. "If you've made up your mind you can't win," he asked, "why are we here?"

Quiet pervaded the room.

I looked around at the other members of our committee, and finally spoke for them. "We intend to win," I said firmly. I was determined not to fail, even if they had personal doubts. The issue for me was a matter of survival and had always been such, even from the beginning.

My determination communicated itself to the others. Their response, unfortunately, was in one particular instance terribly disappointing. "You are the only person completely convinced we can beat Prop Six," David Goodstein confidentially complained. "That's a mistake. Be realistic, Troy. This election cannot be won! Gay rights have lost in every state!"

"California is different form the others," I insisted.

"Not different enough," said David.

Nevertheless, I was not to be dissuaded. "As far as I'm concerned, this has been and will be a matter of life and death."

"Don't say that," David said frowning.

"I've always said it—from the beginning. Gays really die of suffocation in the closets. From my church, I've buried so many who died in despair."

"And so? What happens when the election's all or nothing, and we lose? Will that help anybody? Gay liberation will be finished in our lifetime. The risk is not worth the gamble. The odds aren't getting any better!"

I caught my breath. "I'm sorry," I said, "but I think this state is the place for a showdown. You know some of my reasons. I don't have any choice."

"Oh, have it your way," the publisher said angrily, beginning to turn away.

"David?" I called after him.

"What is it, Troy?"

"Will you do something?"

"What?"

"In *The Advocate*, promise to do everything in your power to help us? Promise that if we need it, you'll give us a boost in the newspaper? You know we desperately need to raise more money. Don't make it harder for us than it is already."

Goodstein hesitated, then sighed. "I'll do what I can," he said, with no enthusiasm.

Don Bradley directed operations from San Francisco, calling in political debts to help win a battle so many claimed was hopeless. In Los Angeles, after a debate within our own committee, we added to our political brain trust by hiring Peter Scott and David Mixner as consultants. Despite their youth, they proved to be more than qualified. One of David and Peter's projects was an attempt, using contacts in their informal fraternity of political advisers, to arrange a meeting between themselves and Ronald Reagan (who surveys continued to tell us would be the best, albeit the most unlikely, spokesman for our cause).

It was estimated that the mininum required to mount a statewide political campaign was $1.5 million. Appeals for the fund needed to be made throughout California and the nation. As co-chair of Concerned Voters of California (with Nancy Roth), my essential duties included the raising of money.

I could not return to Dade County for help because everyone in Miami was demoralized, yet I wanted to renew fund-raising efforts in Florida because it was there that Anita Bryant had opened Pandora's box. Consequently, I went up the coast not many miles to where Reverend John Gill had become pastor of Fort Lauderdale's Metropolitan Community Church, which was thriving under his guidance.

"My idea is to get the ball rolling in Broward County, as close as possible to Dade County without actually being in it," I told John, whose response was marvelous. John immediately contacted the gay business community in Broward County and brought its members together.

There is a bond of the Holy Spirit between John Gill and myself. It has existed since the first time we met, introduced by Bishop Clement whose Church of the Beloved Disciple administers to gay groups in New York City. It was during that same period when Gill attended a conference on homosexuality and religion and came to terms with his own homosexuality. He was so thrilled by the unexpected emancipation of his spirit that when he returned home, he revealed his sexual identity to other clergy. Immediately thereafter, however, the governing board of his Presbyterian church demanded John's resignation from their ministry.

The Presbyterians' loss was our gain. Reverend Gill founded Atlanta's Metropolitan Community Church. When the church in Atlanta was strong and flourishing, John went further south, into Florida, to become the leader of a small religious group already there, and he accomplished another organizational miracle. Today, Fort Lauderdale is one of our most successful churches.

John Gill is a man blessed with an ability to make things happen. When, at my request, he gathered Broward County's gay and lesbian business people for a $25-per-person dinner, three hundred attended. "Reverend Troy Perry will talk about the Briggs initiative, California's Proposition Six," Gill told everybody.

I walked into the hotel dining room. As I prepared to speak, the first person whose eye caught mine was an elderly man I had met earlier in the day. Since Franklin Roosevelt's administration, he had been a ranking officer in our State Department. I remembered how he had cornered me in the morning and heatedly demanded to know, "Why do you want to do this now? Why do you want to keep talking about homosexuality? We have enough problems without being in politics. We're already branded! Look what happened in Dade County!"

My first inclination was to like the man, but he annoyed me.

"You radicals!" he said with disdain.

"I'm not a radical," I instantly replied. "I'm just a preacher—but I believe with all my heart that if we don't stop this cruel menace, if we don't turn it around in California, it's never going to end. This will be the lost era. The fundamentalists and the politicians, and combinations thereof, will hound us forever. Do you remember what McCarthy did to gays?"

Unknowingly, I had struck a nerve.

The old man's eyes clouded. He turned away. Later, I learned he had been denounced as a homosexual by one of Senator Joe McCarthy's hatchet men, and had lost his high-placed job in government as a result. While I spoke to the large gathering of business people, I was aware that he listened to my words with obvious concentration.

"The twenty-five dollars you paid for tickets was enough to cover the cost of this banquet room, your dinner, and the flowers on the tables," I said. "It doesn't give us one extra penny to use for sending the Devil back to hell in California! Who is going to contribute one thousand dollars to give our struggle its start?"

Silence.

Then the clatter of a busboy's tray.

I looked around. The old man who had been with the State Department stood in front of his chair and began to speak. I couldn't hear what he was saying for the first few seconds, but his voice became stronger without urging. Briefly, he told the story of his pride and his patriotic feelings while working for the State Department. Then he told of his shame and sorrow caused by his summary, unwarranted dismissal. As he concluded, the old gentleman was crying, but with a face wet with tears, he raised his fist in an act of defiance that he had suppressed for a quarter of a century. With fierce intensity, he shouted toward me, "Here! Curse the miserable sons of bitches! I've got the first thousand dollars—and proud of it! You go get the California bastard!"

What an act of liberation!

Suddenly, everybody in the crowded room was cheering. And the old diplomat was laughing and crying at the same time.

It was a magical moment!

David Glascock, traveling with me as my bodyguard, said afterward, "I've never seen anything like it. People went wild! The political devastation of Miami, Wichita, St. Paul, and Eugene no longer seemed to matter. The gut instinct was that it had to be turned around."

Men and woman came forward and threw money at me. Literally threw it! Thus, Fort Lauderdale validated my faith. We collected $16,000 in cash that evening from people who had already paid to attend. If we could raise that much money so fast, so close to Miami, it certainly should be possible to raise funds in other places. Yet sometimes, fund-raising was considerably more difficult—like pulling teeth.

I went everywhere, crisscrossing the nation. I was still hearing people saying "You can't win—you can't win—you can't win!" My response to them was "We can—we can!" But keeping our campaign out of debt was still a chronic problem.

There was a special difficulty at home. California has a state law which requires that if any person contributes $50 or more to any political organization, that person's name and the name of the recipient must be recorded in official files which automatically become a matter of public knowledge. Anyone can examine the documents and learn not only who contributors are, but also where they live and where they work. In our particular situation, there was initially an inference that any person contributing to a committee opposing Briggs was automatically homosexual. Because of the very nature of the senator's antigay initiative, tens of thousands of individuals were afraid to voluntarily put their name on such a blacklist. Consequently, when we did receive campaign contributions, the checks were small and rarely exceeded $49.99.

One of the inspired, nongay men working with Don Bradley in our endeavor to turn the tide was named Leavitt. Leavitt was instrumental in having the *Los Angeles Times* do an important feature story with front-page headlines three inches high. The headline read FEAR STALKS NO ON 6. In the article it was explained that concerned citizens were afraid to donate more than $49.99. When the newspaper reached newsstands, outraged citizens were immediately infuriated by the unfair, adverse effect of the law as it applied to our particular situation. Aroused to action, hundreds of nongay individualists began telephoning our offices, pledging $51, and demanding that their names be included on the list of contributors. Overnight, in the spirit of right thinking that keeps America free, being on our list of contributors was the "in" thing.

Movie stars were calling and contributing. People we had never heard of were pledging money. Big checks arrived in the mail. It was a patriotic American tradition—coming to the rescue!

As I traveled around the United States, continuing to raise the necessary funds, I candidly told everyone, "California law requires a record of contributors who give fifty dollars or more. So hear what I'm saying—you can be known by what you give." And to the credit of the people who heard me, it seemed to matter no longer that their private lives were becoming less private than they preferred. Even defiant schoolteachers, gay and nongay alike, were giving us their personal checks, inevitably in sums exceeding $50.

What happened next was a complete surprise to everyone. Mixner and Scott received an invitation they had only dreamed might be forthcoming.

Ronald Reagan wanted to meet with them!

Aware of the tremendous opportunity, all of us were suddenly filled with great excitement. The meeting was to take place in Reagan's Westwood office. We had a meeting to discuss details. And if Peter and David did not need instructions from all of us, they received considerable advice nevertheless.

They were told to be absolutely factual. The man who would be president was too intelligent for any other treatment.

We wanted Mr. Reagan convinced that there was no need for Proposition 6. We wanted him, an ultraconservative who said he believed government should stay out of private business, to also believe that government should stay out of private bedrooms. (After Reagan's election, we would learn that one belief did not necessarily accompany the other, but in the meantime, many personal thoughts remained undeclared by the actor-politician running for office.)

So not only were our consultants instructed not to say anything to Reagan other than uncomplicated, fundamental truths, they were coached not to even suggest anything intended to overtly enhance a gay position. Their stated objective was to accurately explain why Briggs' initiative would cause a massive disruption of education throughout California. Only incidentally could Mixner and Scott possibly mention that Briggs' initiative would make it possible for unhappy malcontents (including bad students who received deservedly low grades) to call any teacher "queer" and have that accused person banished forever—with little or no recourse from the school system!

The Reagan meeting, when it happened, seemed to last forever. Afterward, many of us were waiting nearby, eager for a report from Peter and David.

"Mr. Reagan was very polite," said Peter. "We were with him, without interruptions, for over an hour, and he was very interested. We told him everything that might persuade him. And he listened."

"But will he help us?" I asked.

David shrugged. "I don't know if he'll help us directly," he said with apparent doubt, then brightened as he added, "but Mr. Reagan won't support Briggs. That's all he promised. As for anything else, we'll have to be patient—just wait and see."

For decades, my dream has been to see gay people liberated. In my ministry, however, I have never been a person to walk around saying, "Oh, God, please give me a sign," nor do I believe a good Christian has to speak with angels, or witness any kind of miraculous revelation to be as spiritual as anyone else. I have never prayed to receive my visions, and have always been careful not to let Metropolitan Community Church be perceived as anything other than what it is: intellectually and emotionally honest. By the same token, I believe it would be unfair to all of us to withhold genuine religious experiences that have stimulated our movement.

A full year after being told by a spiritual personage that I was to fast in Los Angeles, two additional noteworthy events happened in Texas. One embraced gifts of the Spirit. The other was a matter of fascinating coincidence.

The first occurred on a clear Sunday morning after I preached at our church in Dallas. I had just concluded my sermon, and while Reverend Don Eastman was completing his preparations for communion, I began speaking in tongues, an event which has rarely happened in the history of our denomination. (The apostle Paul said that he spoke in tongues privately—and that is the way it had always been with me.)

After the message in tongues came the interpretation. God made known that I could have anything I wanted. The idea was humbling. Before the service I had told everybody we were going to win our battle against Briggs, but there had recently developed a lack of certainty in my mind. After receiving prophecy that morning in Dallas, as I joined Reverend Eastman to celebrate communion, my optimism was rejuvenated.

"God, here at your altar I accept the defeat of Proposition Six," I said, grateful to heaven, "because this morning you have said I can have whatever I want, and what I most truly want is the rebirth of justice— starting in California."

Uneasy feelings that had earlier dissipated my energy were gone. I knew we would defeat Proposition 6. During the final weeks of the campaign, when gay leaders around the nation came to me again and said, "I'm not going to repeat anything to anybody, but tell me secretly, do you really believe there's any hope of winning in California?" I could look them in their eyes without a twinge of conscience and reply, "Yes. We are going to win!"

Later in the evening, on the same day I received the spiritual message in Dallas, I was to host ten people at dinner. My guests were to include Dr. Harryette Ehrhardt, a bright and respected elected member of the Dallas School Board. With Mrs. Ehrhardt was her husband, a prominent eye surgeon. (It was Harryette, a persuasive feminist, who, after the Dallas superintendent of schools announced that all of the city's gay schoolteachers would be fired, held a press conference fifteen minutes later and said, "No, they won't!"—forcing the superintendent of schools to retract his statement and apologize.) Others in our dinner party would include Reverend Don Eastman, David Glascock, and other gay men who had greatly assisted our fund-raising efforts in Texas.

Beforehand, Reverend Eastman approached me at the church. "You're not going to believe this," he said. "The Hyatt called about your dinner reservations."

"Is there a problem?"

"Anita Bryant is going to be in the restaurant at the same time we are. The staff intends to seat us right next to the Bryant group, so you can speak to her if you wish."

Shivers went up my spine. "Whose idea was that?" I asked, wondering what I could say to the beautiful "Dragon Lady" who had willfully been responsible for so much anger, pain, and widespread fear.

Don grinned, anticipating a confrontation later in the restaurant. "Some gay person, I suppose. Probably one of our people in charge of reservations. You know how fancy restaurants are. Half of their personnel are usually gay, or at least sympathetic."

Eleven of us arrived at Dallas' Hyatt Hotel several hours after dark. Dinner would be in the hotel's Reunion Tower, a modern, revolving restaurant high in the sky with all of Dallas spread out below. Our elevator operator, a young gay man, was excited as he took us up. I asked him, "Is she here yet?"

"No, Reverend Perry," he answered, fully aware of who we were, "and I don't know what I'm going to say to her when she does arrive. I was on a gay political caucus in Dallas. My picture got on television and I was fired from work. All because of that woman! It took me six months to get this job driving an elevator."

The youth was attractive and intelligent. "If it's important for you to say something to her, do it. But if it's not important, don't," I counseled, adding, "You can do me a favor. Whatever they say coming up, I want to know about it when we go down."

My idea appealed to the young man, who was smiling, feeling better already. I knew there was little he would overhear of much interest, but I also knew that for the rest of his life he would feel justified, hoping in a small way that he had personally repaid Anita for a little of the damage she had caused.

In the restaurant, the employee who greeted us was not the same person who had originally assigned our seating. Our replacement host, in the cautious interest of preserving harmony and/or his own employment, had recognized the names of all persons concerned and had changed the seating location of Anita's party to the other side of the room. Still, when we were at our table, it became apparent that there remained a high degree of expectancy among the restaurant help.

People seated with me kept asking, "What are you going to do, Troy? What are you going to do?"

"Why do I have to do anything?" was my reply.

Harriet Airheart finished looking at an oversize menu and put it aside. "Troy," she said, choosing her words carefully, "God doesn't speak to me in an audible voice as he does you. God only speaks to me through the Mass—I'm an Episcopalian. Even so, I believe God must have put you and that woman together in this restaurant for a reason."

As I wondered how to reply, our waiter arrived. "I hope that orange juice dame brought her food taster," he said archly. "All three of our chefs are gay!"

It was hysterical.

After twenty minutes, we were still looking around to locate the infamous Oklahoma beauty and her entourage. A little nervous, I asked, "I wonder where she's sitting?" At that moment, practically on cue, a waitress carrying a loaded tray aloft was passing. She made a fast U-turn and, looking neither right nor left, glided past me at very close range.

Hardly moving her lips, like a ventriloquist, the waitress said for all of us to hear, "Reverend Perry, Miss Bryant is at table thirty-two, around the corner to your right. You will see her from the back as you approach." Then, with her message delivered, the waitress was gone.

We noticed that people at other tables were not being served. Restaurant personnel, with a few brief exceptions, were watching me. They had decided something was going to happen. I felt it would be a shame to disappoint everyone.

"Let's surprise her," I said to Reverend Eastman. I had barely moved in my chair before Don, dependable as always, was on his feet.

We walked toward Anita's table. A woman and three men were with her. One was her husband. Another was a commander of the Veterans of Foreign Wars. He was a pompous, long-winded individual who, after we arrived at the table, continued to utter a tedious stream of words although he observed us patiently standing nearby, obviously waiting for him to desist.

Anita could not see us. And the long-winded individual, eventually realizing we would not let him filibuster us into leaving, finally said, "Mrs. Green, I think two of your admirers are standing behind you."

She turned, looking over her shoulder. We had never met. Anita and the commander were two of the few persons in the dining room who did not recognize me. "Miss Bryant," I said, "I'm Reverend Troy Perry of Metropolitan Community Church."

The smile froze on Anita's face, but the difference was barely perceptible. She was a typical Southerner, polite to a fault. "Oh, yes, you are the gentleman who debated Brother Bill in Miami," she said. "Let me introduce you to everyone here."

Don and I shook hands around the group until we came to Anita's husband. He mumbled something but kept his hands under the table. What he intended for a snub was satisfactory to me. I had no desire to touch him. My opinion was that Green used and manipulated his wife. Months later, when Anita said essentially the same thing to the press, I must honestly admit I was not disappointed by the disclosure.

"Please, don't let me further delay your dinner," I said. "I just wanted to say that tragic things are happening to many people. In the interest of everybody, I think it's time for you and me to sit together and discuss the myths that surround this issue."

She said, "I'm sure that can be arranged."

But it never happened.

Anita Bryant's star dimmed. She was replaced by a man who played the fool in California.

Senator John V. Briggs was interviewed by Robert Scheer, a *Los Angeles Times* staff reporter. Sheer asked, "Are you saying that a homosexual teacher who has taught for twenty years, who has never made an advance toward a student during that time, who has never spoken about homosexuality in class during that time, who has in no way acted improperly, and who has never said he or she was a homosexual until asked by the school board—that teacher would be automatically fired?"

Briggs responded with a long, muddled answer in the affirmative, prompting the interviewer's next question: "But isn't a man innocent until proved guilty?"

"If you look like a duck and walk like a duck ... you are a duck," responded Briggs. As the interview progressed, he added, "My bill is aimed at preventing a teacher from being put in a favored position to molest a child."

"Not a heterosexual teacher?" asked Scheer.

"That's right."

"Your bill does nothing to protect a child who would be molested by an adult of the opposite sex?"

"That's right."

"Yet most child-molesting cases involve an adult of the opposite sex ... so why have you identified the homosexuals who, at most, are responsible for a minority of these crimes?"

The answer from Senator Briggs smacked of bad theology and back-street morality. "I don't want lesbians teaching!" Briggs declared.

"No matter that they are good teachers, regardless of how much they care about children?" persisted Bob Scheer.

"Yes," replied the senator.

Political campaigns are always unpredictable, and the best things about them are favorable surprises. On September 20, Ronald Reagan gave us a present that was not anticipated. In his newspaper column, printed in perhaps as many as three hundred newspapers around the United States, he came out against Briggs' initiative. Mr. Reagan had not forgotten his hour of discussion with Mixner and Scott when he wrote:

> Proposition 6 has the potential of infringing on basic rights of privacy, and perhaps even constitutional rights. The initiative is cumbersome and has the potential for real mischief. Proposition 6 is not needed to protect our children. There is adequate legal machinery.

There it was! In print, on the newsstands, delivered to homes across America. Unquestionably, it was a major turning point in our war against those who would abridge liberty. (Also, Reagan's evaluation of Briggs' attempt to make bad law brought him the unsought gratitude of twenty million homosexuals throughout the land. Many of them crossed party lines in 1980 to elect Reagan, vainly hoping he would be a president for *all* the people.)

The final month and a half of our "No on 6" campaign was like a whirlwind. Victory became a possibility in the minds of many. Senator Briggs, infuriated at Reagan for unexpectedly taking a stand against him, telephoned Reagan's office and vehemently attacked the presidential candidate by verbally abusing his aides. It was Briggs' political suicide.

Polls that had once said gays had no chance of winning showed us gaining approval with the electorate. We were inching away from a projected defeat. Whereas the odds began at 34 percent for us and 61 percent for Briggs, the numbers changed to 36 percent for us but only 44 percent for Briggs—with a question mark representing 20 percent who had become undecided. If the voters were not switching to us in huge numbers, they were at least disenchanted with our opposition.

All who were jockeys in the race for votes knew that the time had arrived to begin running with all our resources. The Bay Area Committee Against Briggs' Initiative, operating out of San Francisco, had successfully pulled together many groups including conservative Republicans, Libertarians, and members of the Peace and Freedom party. Toward the end of the campaign, Democrats who were unable to control the Bay Area Committee spun off and formed their own group, the No on 6 Committee. Labor unions remained with BACABI, as did politicians, including the mayor of San Francisco, George Moscone.

While Concerned Voters of California spent the huge amounts of money required for statewide television advertising, members of BACABI were persistently walking from door to door throughout Northern California speaking to anyone who would listen. Michael Mank (who would become a lay elder of Metropolitan Community Church in 1981) did not advertise the fact that he belonged to both organizations. Moving between BACABI and CVC, conferring with mastermind Don Bradley, Michael was able to be certain the two groups did not wastefully overlap each other's efforts.

Mank taught in San Mateo. When the *San Mateo Times* endorsed Briggs' initiative, Michael was enraged. Ignoring personal danger, the slender, blond schoolteacher wrote the newspaper an angry letter which he and all other teachers in his school were brave enough to sign. The only person refusing to add a signature was the principal. The latter's explanation was, "If Proposition Six passes, I may someday be in a position where I have to enforce it!" From that day forward, the principal never knew why he was generally ignored or shunned by many of the teachers.

Michael and his associates passed out thousands of pamphlets on street corners or wherever people could be reached. The response was mixed. Some who saw the literature cursed, others read what we offered and searched their conscience. It was impossible to know what impact our work was having.

A small measure of accomplishment was evidenced when a woman entering a supermarket looked at one of the fliers she was handed and, seeing that it was about homosexuality and teachers, expressed relief, exclaiming, "I was afraid the butchers were on strike again!"

As October approached, California's electorate kept tilting in our favor. Then we realized we still had financial problems as before, but for exactly the opposite reasons. Some noncontributors who had said we could not win, suddenly started saying we could not lose, and therefore continued to keep a tight grip on their wallets. It was necessary that I continue speaking in various locations around the United States, always asking for financial assistance to keep our television messages on the air.

Meanwhile, David Farrell, Metropolitan Community Church's pastor in San Diego, developed arresting radio commercials that were broadcast in his area. One radio announcement began, "For homosexuals only!" and then continued with a message for everybody.

Perhaps the best commercial our media experts presented on television showed a sweet, gray-haired woman who had been a schoolteacher for thirty-five years. She sounded like a woman who had taught me civics. The mature teacher on TV commented that she believed in the Bill of Rights—but feared she could be persecuted if she ever said anything of which an eavesdropper (or Senator Briggs from Orange County) might disapprove!

There were many imaginative ways to present our position to the public. One gay man walked the length of the state of California, from Mexico to the Oregon border, stopping in all the little towns through the center of the state, attracting attention to himself in a favorable way, talking about what it was like to be a gay person, deploring the ill intentions of Proposition 6.

A lot of California's citizens *knowingly* saw gay people for the first time. On television, members of the gay community were not "freaky" and we were well able to debate issues intelligently. Whenever television stations invited our opposition to appear on camera, we made certain that we also appeared as a part of the discussions, or that we were given equal time.

No opportunity was ignored.

We went to our kinfolk and said, "All right, it's time, now or never, for you to stand up and speak for us!" And many families did. What a great comfort it was. My brother, Jerry, who works in the aerospace

167

industry, started talking to his co-workers, telling them why the Briggs initiative was ridiculous and asking his friends to pledge us their votes.

An unwelcome surprise came from Beverly Hills, a city we had taken for granted as being friendly. The Chamber of Commerce of practically every city in California was supporting us, but not in Beverly Hills. Scott and Mixner, as well as myself, were momentarily stunned! But in a matter of minutes, David was on the telephone calling everybody he knew in the entertainment industry, including spouses, guilds, and unions, asking them to call every retailer they knew in Beverly Hills to tell them they would shop in West Hollywood from that day forward unless the local Chamber of Commerce changed its position. As a result, famous patrons of expensive stores threatened to cut up their platinum-plated credit cards. An actress suggested to one dealer that her next Rolls-Royce might be purchased in Burbank, Glendale, or Pasadena. And within hours, it almost goes without saying, the Beverly Hills Chamber of Commerce was firmly on our side.

David Goodstein, having left our committee, was nevertheless supportive in *The Advocate* during the final campaign months. He wrote in his weekly column that the time had arrived for every gay person to support us. In effect, he wrote, "People, we need you! Get off your butts *now!*"

Gayle Wilson, highly successful with her own real estate office, in a continuing effort to raise money, organized a luncheon "For Women Only." When hundreds of rich females, not exclusively lesbian, were safe from the press inside the closed dining room, doors are said to have been locked. Something in the neighborhood of $50,000 had been collected when the doors were reopened. (There was an unconfirmed rumor that the only man allowed in the closed room with the women was Flip Wilson dressed as his famous character, Geraldine. I don't know if that is true, but the story goes on to say, perhaps only to embroider an amusing possibility, that Geraldine contributed $5,000.)

We continued to raise money. Although there never seemed to be enough dollars, we scrupulously managed to pay our bills. Senator Briggs did otherwise. His outburst against Mr. Conservative (Ronald Reagan) had not helped his campaign, and six weeks before the election, Briggs' income was reduced to a trickle. Thousands of dollars in debt, the senator began seeking debates wherever possible as a means of obtaining free publicity.

On the Tuesday exactly two weeks before the election, Briggs motored to Healdsburg, a small California town on the Russian River to debate Larry Berner, a thirty-eight-year-old second-grade teacher whose only offense was that he had decided it was his moral obligation to oppose Proposition 6. Of the respected teacher, Briggs said, "If you put a second-grade child with a homosexual, you're off you gourd! We don't allow necrophiliacs to be morticians!"

With his rage and indignation controlled, the debating schoolteacher replied, "Your mind is in the gutter. The children at my school are not obsessed with my sexuality, as you seem to be, Senator! If you (and your supporters) want to fantasize about my sex life, that's up to you."

A majority of the residents of Healdsburg applauded Berner. After Briggs and his bodyguards departed, a friend of the teacher said with some admiration, "I didn't think you could do so well against a professional politician."

Then Larry laughed. "I've had experience with first- and second-grade kids," he responded.

Briggs fared even worse against Harvey Milk in San Francisco. The elected city supervisor could use words of truth like a surgeon handles a knife. Milk's beleaguered opponent was cut to shreds.

Nursing his wounds, Briggs came to Southern California to debate members of the Los Angeles City Council on television. When it was Councilman Joel Wachs' turn, he said to the senator, "The only people who are supporting Proposition Six are the California Nazi party and the Ku Klux Klan!"

Senator Briggs started screaming, "That's a lie! That's a lie!"

The host moderator of the program shouted, "Shut up! This is live television! This is seen by millions of people!"

And indeed it was!

The ruckus was played and often replayed the next day on possibly every televised news program in California.

Anita Bryant had been a plus when it came to getting votes for her organization. But Senator Briggs was a plus for us. With his hopes for victory slipping away, he began unintentionally making a laughingstock of himself at every opportunity.

NBC bought a full-page newspaper advertisement reading "Is School Out for Gay Teachers?" on the day I debated Briggs. Three persons were on each side. Working with Briggs was a woman so pregnant that she looked as if she would have her baby in front of everybody on the stage. She sprawled in her chair with legs askew, delivering a self-indulgent speech to which no one was able to pay any attention. The camera people avoided wide shots of the mother-to-be whenever possible. In the background, NBC's television crew could be observed doubling over with laughter.

Dr. Johnson, the Los Angeles superintendent of public schools, also accompanied Briggs. Toward the end of the debate, I turned to the president of the teachers' union (who was on our side) and I whispered, "Why is Dr. Johnson with Briggs? I don't understand."

He whispered back to me, "If you ask the superintendent a direct question, he'll tell you there is no need for Briggs' initiative."

That enlightenment caused a wave of pleasure to wash over me, but I strategically waited until two minutes before the show would end before using it. "Pardon me," I said at the appropriate moment, "may I please ask one little question of Dr. Johnson?"

"Certainly," replied the host.

The man Briggs had brought to bolster his position turned expectantly toward me. "Dr. Johnson," I said, "is there any need for a new law, any need for Proposition Six?"

"No, there isn't," replied the candid superintendent.

Automatically, everybody instantly turned to look at Briggs. As the show was ending, the angry senator appeared about to explode. Others present seemed amused, except for the pregnant woman who may have been having contractions.

During the final ten days before the election, hymn-singing revival meetings were held by Briggs' supporters in Orange and San Diego counties, hoping to pull the senator out of a financial ocean of red ink. Opportunistic Jerry Falwell hurried to offer assistance to John Briggs (as he had assisted Anita Bryant a year and a half before). Personally, Falwell had everything to gain and nothing to lose.

"We are here because we believe this country is worth saving," the unctuous Baptist from Lynchburg, Virginia, told nearly three thousand zealots who had been bused in from mostly local California churches. "We need one hundred dollars per couple," Falwell continued, ignoring a great many empty seats in the San Diego Convention Center. "Hold up your pledge cards and wave them at me!"

The willing assembly shouted, "Amen!" They also displayed little American flags and waved their Bibles. The financial support from them, however, is reported to have disappointed Briggs and Falwell, particularly the mercenary preacher. Falwell was not accustomed to having his demands for money denied!

In vivid contrast, our largest fund-raising effort was held at the same time in the Beverly Hilton Hotel. It was a star-studded affair. The entertainment industry had finally taken our cause to heart, and after Rona Barrett mentioned on network television that our "No on 6" dinner was the place to be on Friday night, tickets sold out in less than two hours.

Influential personalities began dialing every unlisted telephone number in Greater Los Angeles, trying to obtain reservations that were no longer available. Rich society widows wanted to be included in the excitement. How they obtained my unlisted telephone number I never did know. But caller after caller would say, "I want a table. I don't care what it costs!"

People who were left out wanted to give us all the money in the world to be included, but I could only tell them, "I'm sorry. We've added every table the fire marshal will allow. There is absolutely no more space in the ballroom!"

That evening, Brenda Vaccaro, Burt Lancaster, Raquel Welch, and a cast from *Who's Who* were sitting in the audience for dinner and entertainment. John Travolta introduced Lily Tomlin who did her comedy sketch about Edith Ann with a crush on her first-grade teacher. Ronee Blakely, the star of *Nashville*, sang songs accompanied by a country-western band.

When I finished speaking, a blinding spotlight was on me. As I nearly stumbled down the steps into what seemed like a dark void, I became aware of the crowd on its feet giving a massive ovation. Somebody grabbed hold of me, saying excitedly, "Man, that was great! You were wonderful!" I tried to free myself, without results. The houselights came up, and then I could see that the happy person with me was Cher, flashing a great big smile as she stood, radiant in one of her fabulous see-through gowns.

We raised $100,000 that night.

Although the outcome of the election was too close for the experts to predict, I measured our hopes for success in a different way. Almost every religious leader in California had come over to our side. The Catholic bishop in Oakland even encouraged one of his priests to preach a sermon explaining why Catholics could not properly vote for Proposition 6. Dignity, an unsanctioned gay Catholic group, was permitted to pass out our literature at the cathedral. California's Episcopal bishops sided with us.

The only two denominations that sided with Senator Briggs across the board, were two extreme right-wing fundamentalist groups, the Assemblies of God (whose star performer was Reverend Jimmy Swaggart) and the Church of the Nazarene.

Halloween, for years, was accepted as the only day when transvestites (who often are not homosexuals) could dress in opposite-sex clothing and

171

appear on public streets without the possibility of being arrested for their suggestive, eye-stopping costumes. By 1978, some laws were considerably less restrictive, but on that October 31st, giving tradition its due, the downtown corners in Hollywood and San Francisco would be well sprinkled with scores of individuals wearing outrageous cross-dressing costumes. Those extroverts would be photographed and featured on television newscasts for the next few days—the same important days which immediately preceded the election.

Although the exaggerated, occasionally vulgar costumes in no way offended me, I knew Senator Briggs would use their public display to garner votes for himself wherever the costumes were seen. It was the first and only time in my life I wished we could cancel Halloween!

Sleep was banished during the last days of the campaign. Pollsters were hinting that we could win, but the idea was not unanimous. In spite of all our good fortune, the grim specters of defeat in Miami, Wichita, St. Paul, and Eugene were always whispering to us.

President Jimmy Carter, at the invitaiton of Governor Jerry Brown, came to Sacramento to speak at a rally held during the final preelection weekend. Carter was present to support the Democrats' candidates and not to help defeat Proposition 6. Still, those of us who had been working against the Briggs initiative since the beginning could not forget information we had obtained from our initial survey: that the two persons with national stature who could best help our cause were Ronald Reagan and Jimmy Carter. Mr. Reagan had already done his part.

The Democrats' rally was a tremendous occasion. Thousands of people, and all news outlets, were present to hear the president, and they were not disappointed. When Carter had completed his prepared speech, and while the multitude were clapping and shouting, he walked to the side of the stage where Governor Brown was waiting for him. Neither man knew that the tiny microphone on Brown's lapel was "open" and that every word spoken in Brown's presence was being recorded by a local radio station.

"You forgot to mention Proposition Six," the governor said to the president.

"Oh, I did?" replied Carter, looking indecisive.

Brown nodded. "You can't go wrong on that one," said the persuasive governor. "Every Democrat as well as just about every Republican has come out against it. You can't go wrong!"

President Carter nodded, thoughtful for a moment, assessing the validity of what he was told. Then he turned abruptly and retraced his steps back to the podium. Carter leaned toward a cluster of microphones. "And don't forget on Tuesday, vote No on Proposition Six!" he said.

The crowd went wild.

Election day was bright and beautiful, and it followed the first night in weeks that I had been able to remain in bed for anything close to eight hours. Breakfast was a quiet time. There was nothing urgent to do.

Voters went to their polling places in record numbers. There were many items of interest to vote on, including an antismoking initiative that had been the target of a media blitz. We had struggled to raise $1.5 million, which we spent on our campaign. The Tobacco Industry allocated $6 million to theirs.

At noon, with the election as much in doubt as ever, we knew we had proven that gays and lesbians could organize a major political campaign and raise large quantities of money. We had shown ourselves politically active and had proved we were willing to fight in order to protect our interests. What we still needed to prove was that we could win!

Early in the afternoon, I telephoned Mixner and Scott to learn if they had any information. All of us were worried about undecided votes, the millions of people who had refused to give any information to pollsters. The undecided had buried us in Miami!

"I have no idea how we are going to do on this," Peter Scott told me. "We are going down to the wire chewing our nails!"

About five o'clock, we finally received our first professional prediction. A pollster with a good reputation informed us, "It looks good for the gays. I think you're going to win—by about ten big points!" But three hours were left before the voting places would close and actual counting could begin. Plenty could happen in three hours. Everybody was on pins and needles.

I had always known we were going to win—but I kept praying, nevertheless!

"Dear God," I said, "it's in your hands. Please don't forget us now. Amen, amen, amen!"

Michael Mank called from San Francisco. They were ready to celebrate, but were waiting for the anticipated victory to become official. "This is one of the heaviest polling days in California history!" Mank said. "I hope the optimism in my head is the reason everybody's voting."

My mother and a few of our friends went with me to the Beverly Hilton where we intended to have a large party. It was after dark when we arrived and quickly went upstairs to a private suite. At eight o'clock the polls closed. We had the television turned on. There was no delay in the announcement of the predicted winners. I switched from station to station. All of them, immediately and without equivocation, said that Proposition 6 would be overwhelmingly defeated.

I was exuberant!

I jumped up and ran around the room, shouting. There would be time to be dignified—later. The election was a runaway. Antigay forces were losing in every county in California, including Orange County, where Briggs lived and was well known.

Amazing was the only word to describe the reports. We would not only win eventually, but we would win with well over 1,250,000 more votes than our opposition! God's work had been true for me.

We took the elevator to the grand ballroom at the Hilton where three thousand brothers, sisters, and friends were gathered to celebrate in our hour of tremendous relief. There would be dancing until dawn!

I went to the microphone and gave thanks that we had been able to communicate our message to millions of caring, thinking, holy people, and I gave thanks that we would survive.

I reached out to Tom Bradley, the mayor of Los Angeles, and he grasped my hand firmly. "Congratulations!" he said, flashing a sincere grin.

"Would you have anything to say, Mr. Mayor?" Bradley was asked while he continued standing on our podium overlooking the happy crowd. He nodded and moved to the microphone.

"How sweet it is!" the mayor declared, smiling into the sea of faces looking up at him. "Proposition Six was an evil, pernicious, dangerous measure. It was a measure against not just the rights of gay teachers, but the civil rights of all. It should be a lesson that Senator Briggs will never forget. The spirit of justice lives!"

10

The Freedom Train:
1971–1987

*Hear now what the Lord says: Arise, plead
your case before the mountains, and let the
hills hear your voice.*
                                    —Micah 6: 1

I HAVE been constantly reminded that anyone can be attacked with a
gun, a knife, broken glass, or something equally lethal. The linked murders of San Francisco's Mayor George Moscone and homosexual City
Supervisor Harvey Milk in the autumn of 1978 greatly increased the gay
awareness of personal mortality. Additionally, over the years as we have
pursued the benefits and the responsibilities of freedom, intermixed with
our joy and laughter, there have been many serious and intentional threats
to our well-being.

My way of handling an ever present, invisible menace is to push
apprehension out of my consciousness. I believe that if you sit brooding
about death, if you are afraid someone is going to assault you, then you
are not going to be able to perform your work properly. But that is not
to say I take no precautions. I do.

We have full-time bodyguards at General Conferences because, until
the 1985 General Conference in Sacramento, we had never completed a
meeting without at least one bomb threat. On those occasions (and others
when there was increased advertising or media coverage) our security
people have made searches when precautions seemed prudent. The usual
practice, however, is not to frisk an individual, but to observe anyone
who might appear suspicious, and if warranted, to check any bags such
a person might carry. We do not want a terrorist participating in one of
our meetings by shooting somebody.

Nevertheless, little incidents have happened over the years. In 1970, while I was fasting in front of the Federal Building in Los Angeles, a disturbed woman caused a commotion, declaiming that all homosexuals were disciples of the Devil. When I confronted her, she retaliated by staggering me with an unexpected fist across my face.

A year later, in 1971, a small group, including Willie Smith, Bill Thorne, and most of the old crew, were preparing to march from San Francisco to Sacramento, California's capital. Before our departure, we held a well-advertised demonstration in San Francisco's Union Square. I had just finished my speech and everybody was clapping when a man from the crowd proceeded to break a beer bottle and jump up on the stage. Without any words that I could hear, he ferociously lunged in my direction, attempting to stab me with the jagged glass. Fortunately, my defense personnel reacted equally fast. They pushed the man aside and hustled me off the stage to our Winnebago which we were using as a security post. Thirty seconds following the attack, San Francisco's police arrested the man and removed him from the scene. I never learned what had prompted his assault.

Next morning, across the Bay Bridge in a city park in Oakland, Jim Sandmire served communion to our people who would be marching to Sacramento. It was a foggy day as we started our seventy-five-mile trek with visibility reduced so we could not see more than eight feet in front of us. The press and their photographers were present, and would be for all of the trip. As a result, we had protection from the sheriff's department in each of four counties through which we passed. Sheriffs usually kept their patrol cars near us, particularly when we entered the several small cities along the way, because they were aware of what had happened in San Francisco and wanted no problems in their counties.

California's law enforcement agencies were nearly schizophrenic in those days. In one breath, they hated "queers," but in the next, they wanted us to uneventfully traverse and depart their jurisdictions. Much of the care and treatment we received must be ascribed to incessant publicity which we intentionally generated. Ahead of our scraggly marchers, gay advance people made certain that local newspapers knew we were about to arrive. We also called sheriffs' departments to be certain their law officers were alerted. That we were always able to induce officials to keep a protective eye on us was a constant source of amazement.

One sheriff's deputy who rode in a patrol car was especially concerned that nothing unpleasant should happen to our group. He told us of a place beside the Sacramento River where we could camp on a clean beach and not be bothered. The handsome deputy was six feet two, weighed about 210 pounds, and asked numerous polite questions about homosexuality and Metropolitan Community Church. I remember him vividly because he quietly displayed an admirable combination of strength and gentleness. After learning that the Greek letters on our Chi-Rho cross stand for "Christ (Chi and Rho), the Beginning (Alpha) and the End (Omega)," the deputy indicated he had a friend who was possibly gay and might like to have one. Naturally, we took a cross of ours and gave it to the sheriff's deputy. However, the next morning when the deputy again was present to accompany us, I noticed that under his shirt he himself was wearing our Chi-Rho cross. In all probability, the good deputy was a person in the process of coming to terms with his own sexuality.

We meet all kinds of characters on marches, in gay pride parades, and at demonstrations. There is never any predicting what type of person will next push forward. I am accustomed to fundamentalists screaming vile rhetoric in my direction, and their vicious intensity is inevitably disturbing to me although it usually backfires on them.

There once was a creep we referred to as "Big Harley." I have no idea whom he represented or what his name really was. Big Harley was present at three widely separated geographical locations. On each occasion, Big Harley led a group of fifteen or twenty menacing freaks of massive size, all wearing football helmets. The brutes carried professionally manufactured fabric signs stretched over illegal stainless steel frames on metal poles which obviously could be used as weapons. The law has never seemed concerned. (We, on the other hand, in Los Angeles, have always been required to use very light wooden frames meeting stringent material and weight specifications.)

The first time I became aware of Big Harley and his organized band of "religious" toughs was during a Gay Pride parade in 1971 when, almost as if from nowhere, they appeared walking alongside my open car. I heard Harley's voice saying in a menacing hiss, "Perry, you like to cornhole your converts, don't ya?"

My head turned quickly and our eyes met. Momentarily stunned, I found myself looking from close range into a face full of hate, listening to crude terminology I had not heard for years.

"God says you're going to die and go to hell, Perry. Do you know that, fucker?" hissed Big Harley, making my skin crawl. It was a very threatening situation, but physical violence never materialized.

The following year, Big Harley and his brute pack surfaced again at the Democrats' 1972 national convention in Miami. Metropolitan Community Church was there to stage a gay rights demonstration for the education of political delegates. When Big Harley and his football-helmeted toughs (with the same signs and at least four of the same people who had been in Los Angeles) tried to disrupt our proceedings, a communion service was in progress. Although they did everything in their power to provoke a confrontation, we refused to budge and continued to worship.

Using ugly phrases and intimidation was the style of Big Harley's well-financed bully boys. We never could learn who they were. Their group apparently had no name, and they never passed out literature. Fortunately, hundreds of our people were around to keep them under control—because local police never did anything to restrain them.

Looking for a place to cause a problem, Big Harley's third unsuccessful try was in New York City where he and his group appeared again. I was getting ready to speak at the annual Gay Pride celebration when his coercive gang tried to intimidate me and prevent me from speaking. They were not successful, and after the parade, Big Harley and his frustrated troublemakers followed our delegation into Central Park where gay groups had already commenced an enormous rally. Entering the park was Big Harley's mistake. The gay New Yorkers were not about to let homophobic oddballs harm anybody or disrupt the proceedings. Unlike some moderate churchpeople, the gays in Central Park were not constrained by a philosophy of nonviolence. Many of them were the same individuals who had started the 1969 gay riot against corrupt police in Greenwich Village.

The gays' message that the intruders were about to be "beaten into the ground" was quickly understood by Big Harley and his unwelcome company. After being told that their only escape was to "get lost now!" they fled, never to be heard of again, giving some credence to those outside the mainstream of our movement who believe that only with strength is there justice and that there never has been, and never will be, a tranquil resolution to our social and civil rights problems.

As for myself and members of Metropolitan Community Church, we felt that Big Harley and his bullies had been paid to travel the three-city triangle, and that their primary objective was to silence me. If I was truly their pet project, we never did have any idea who financed their activities.

The deaths of Harvey Milk and George Moscone drive home the menace that exists for all of us in our daily lives. We never know from one moment to the next when unforeseen events are about to happen. I was in the Canadian city of Winnipeg, where I had been invited to speak at both the University of Manitoba and the University of Winnipeg, when San Francisco's double tragedy occurred.

I was staying at the home of an Anglican clergyman and his lover. On the day of the murders, I had spoken at both schools. One of the schools was built underground so they could have a controlled environment in spite of the worst icy weather on the surface. The university's commons was located where the tunnels intersected, and that was where I spoke to a large crowd. After my speech, I was answering students' questions about gay liberation in the United States as compared to the Canadian experience when my Anglican friend came to me.

"You heard about George Moscone and Harvey Milk being assassinated in San Francisco?" he said.

I looked at him, and with a big smile replied, "No, I didn't—what's the joke?"

His hand went quickly to cover his lips. Then I realized he was serious. "Maybe I was mistaken," he said. "I just overheard what I thought was somebody saying they had been murdered this morning."

I felt a sudden chill. I knew how fast, with ruthless confirmation, rumors can become reality. The priest and I found a radio and tuned it to an all-news Canadian station. The newscaster was in the process of telling about the bloody killings in San Francisco. I found myself having great difficulty believing what I heard. All of it was shocking.

When Harvey Milk had run for city councilman, he had not been my choice. My help had gone to a friend, Rick Stokes, who had asked for my support. Harvey was not well known to me at the time, but when he beat Rick and was sworn into office, I flew to San Francisco for the historic moment. An openly gay person had finally won a California election!

In his acceptance speech, Harvey said all the right things so far as the gay community was concerned. The chambers were packed, and easily half the people present were gay. Everybody applauded. At the same time, Dianne Feinstein was elected president of the City Council. Afterward, a large reception was held in City Hall.

One of Harvey's aides came to me and whispered that Harvey would like to see me. I went to his office where we sat and talked. "I know you supported Stokes," Harvey said, "but now that I've won, it's time to bury the hatchet. I need your support. Your church influences a lot of voters in this area. At least peripherally, you influence even those who are not members. When I run for election in two years, I want to be sure I can win again. It's important for all of us to draw our resources together."

"We will," I said. "You won, Harvey. I'm glad, and I also think it's important for our community to keep a gay person sitting here."

As for George Moscone, I was closer to him than to Harvey Milk. My friendship with George began when he was a state legislator, before he became the Mayor of San Francisco. In Sacramento, we had worked hard to pass the consenting adults bill which Jerry Brown eventually signed into law. Moscone was a considerate, Catholic politician with a loving family. As far as the Italian population was concerned, he did everything right. He was never the typical politician who does things because they are expedient.

Moscone could have easily let gay issues slide, as did many other politicians. But not George! He was a leader and he took the forefront for the simple reason that, somewhere along the way, he had decided that sexual liberation was an important issue. George went out of his way to meet gay rights leaders and to attend Gay Freedom Day celebrations. On such occasions he was forever joining in brief conversations with the crowd. George had a sense of humor that could break barriers and dissolve tension.

So when I learned that the two men were actually dead, I felt a terrible loss. With sorrow I called my headquarters in Los Angeles. There, my executive secretary, Frank Zerilli, was nearly hysterical.

"We've tried to reach you everywhere today," Frank said quickly, blasting his words of concern into the telephone like a rapid-fire machine. "We were worried about you. We didn't know if this was some kind of conspiracy that could spread through the gay community—if this was some kind of group out to kill queers, or whatever! That was all before we knew Dan White was arrested and before we got the full story of the murders."

It didn't take long to learn the vicious details. White had resigned from the City Council, then asked Mayor Moscone to reinstate him. The mayor said no, and Harvey agreed with him. So White, with his gun, bypassed metal detectors by entering City Hall through a window. Inside there was everything he hated: the liberal mayor and the faggot Jew! White shot Moscone first. Then he walked down the hall before anybody could figure what was happening and entered Harvey's office, reloading his weapon in the meantime. To himself, Dan White must have been saying, "There just ain't no queer gonna tell me what I can't do!"

It is easy to imagine the hatred boiling in White's head as he followed his premeditated plan. White caught Harvey in the wrist and stomach with his first bullet. Then White shot Harvey twice in the chest—and shot him again, in the head, as he was falling. When Harvey was on the floor, at point-blank range, White emptied his gun, spattering the gay man's brains in a bloody mess.

In his own defense, ex-policeman White claimed that eating too much sugar, including Coca-Cola and Twinkies, had depressed him and impaired his judgment. As a result, a grossly biased jury found the Irish ex-cop guilty of manslaughter instead of murder, proving something is often awry with the justice system in this country. What else can we think when an adult can be sentenced to more years in jail for what he or she consents to do sexually in bed, than Dan White received for the horrendous murder of two innocent people?

His defense attorney pictured Dan White as the All-American Boy. We're not certain what that is, but often since, we have speculated that if Dan White had been Dan Black, or Dan Mexican, or Dan Gay, the confessed assassin would have been whisked off to the gas chamber fast enough to make your head spin!

Immediately following the murders, when I arrived in San Francisco, I found the gay and lesbian communities operating heroically, although emotionally devastated. At the same time, the city authorities, not wanting more problems, were very concerned about people like myself who were arriving for the funerals. There was no desire for more publicity of "nuts shooting queers"! Consequently, I was met with a limousine on that sad occasion and, as were many other prominent gay people, accompanied by a sheriff's deputy during my entire stay.

I was numb. The city was on edge. I knew of no threats of violence at that time, but San Francisco's police were tense. A memorial service was held to calm the populace. Joan Baez was remarkable, mesmerizing tens of thousands with hymns which she asked us to sing along with her. People in front of City Hall were visible as far as the eye could see. Acting Mayor Dianne Feinstein and a member of the Moscone family spoke to the assembly, and the San Francisco Symphony participated.

Many tears were shed.

When the time arrived for grieving thousands to pass by the closed coffins in City Hall, I proceeded into the marble rotunda close behind Moscone's family. The setting was enhanced by the largest and most beautiful arrangement of flowers I have ever seen. It was a massive botanical offering. (Flying back to Los Angeles, I learned how the floral extravaganza had been accomplished. Two men who had been sent from Oklahoma to San Francisco by the National Florists' Association were on my airplane. They introduced themselves to me, and in the course of our conversation let me know that they had been sent to direct the use of thousands of flowers that had been wired from all over America. I learned, too, that florists in San Francisco had agreed that no matter what anybody ordered, the immense floral presentation would be color coordinated in autumn hues. They felt it was important that the televised viewing of the caskets not have the appearance of a circus. Thus, no matter what people paid for, appropriate flowers were invariably delivered.)

George Moscone's funeral was held at St. Mary's, a beautiful Catholic cathedral where his children read from the scriptures. One of them prayed that a tragedy of this sort would never happen again, but in my heart, I knew with regret that it would be repeated somewhere, sometime, because until the Prince of Peace comes, the Prince of Darkness lurks.

Milk and Moscone were very unlike in many ways, so very much alike in others. Their point of nearest similarity was that both men were dedicated to the notion of fighting for human rights.

Official memorial services for Harvey Milk, an atheistic Jew, were planned by the gay community and held at the San Francisco Opera House, which most likely was exactly what Harvey would have wanted. He had a tremendous sense of the theatrical. And Harvey loved opera—although he could rarely afford to attend. His small salary continually left him in debt, but when all seats in the opera house were sold, for two dollars he would occasionally purchase one S.R.O. ticket and stand to hear an entire performance.

Milk's memorial at the San Francisco Opera House was a positive, crowded affair. An overflow of thousands stood outside and listened to the proceedings on loudspeakers. Inside, the first four rows were reserved for politicians. I sat directly behind Governor Jerry Brown and Lieutenant Governor Merv Dymally. The program included a work for chorus and orchestra, operatic selections dedicated to Harvey, and several orations. Finally, there was an Episcopal priest who had come out as a gay person. In Harvey's behalf, he made a passionate plea to the attending politicians.

"It is now time for you to change the laws," the priest declared. "Time for you to make the difference for us! And it is time for us to stand up for our rights. Today it is time for gay people to *stand up* for themselves!"

Lesbians and gay men began to rise throughout the large auditorium. Even politicians who were not gay began standing. Everybody but Jerry Brown and a few other scattered individuals were up from their seats. It was a highly charged, emotional thing.

The voice of the Episcopal priest became insistent. "All gay people should STAND!" he reiterated at the top of his lungs.

Politicians were on their feet because most of them had misunderstood the priest. They thought he had said they should stand up for gay rights when in fact he had said they should stand because they were homosexual. Nevertheless, people were cheering! Governor Brown, having heard correctly, steadfastly retained his seat.

People began to be amused by the bachelor governor's discomfort.

Whereupon, shouting over the tumult, Lieutenant Governor Dymally said forcefully, "Come on, Jerry, stand up! They're asking for all of us to stand!"

Brown was nearly the last to rise, which he did with a sheepish grin. It was a cute little footnote to history.

A month later, Governor Brown signed an executive order banning all discrimination against homosexuals in California's public employment. The governor's determination may have been a direct result of the martyrdom of Harvey Milk.

Those who have been riding the freedom train for many years have been happy to welcome aboard supporters from all walks of life, and included among our prominent passengers have often been foresighted nongay politicians. In 1974, the year after fires in Los Angeles and the holocaust in New Orleans, Metropolitan Community Church in San Francisco was also torched. Dianne Feinstein was then a member of the City Council, and she and her husband publicly offered us their support.

On that occasion, our San Francisco church had being destroyed by arson. In addition, the announcement board in front of the burned building had a message written upon it. Large, crude letters declared AND YOU SHALL DIE, BASTARD, with an arrow pointing toward the name of the pastor, Reverend James Sandmire. It was an ugly challenge that needed to be met.

Sadly, defiantly, we marched from the burned structure to a new location, a Presbyterian church which offered us the temporary use of their facilities. Walking with us in our procession were many of our clergy, our choir and, prudently, a police escort. When we arrived at the new location, Dr. and Mrs. Feinstein were waiting for us. During the service that followed, Sandmire made a plea for all the help we could receive for rebuilding a church of our own.

As a result, the Feinsteins handed us the first contribution toward that objective. It was their personal check that actually began the building fund for property we now own. In my opinion, Dianne Feinstein, as friend, as councilperson or mayor, has always been supportive of the gay community.

In 1975, I was one of about eighty persons who were invited to meet with Jimmy Carter in Los Angeles. Although few seemed to be taking Georgia's ex-governor seriously at the time, Carter was nevertheless seeking the Democratic party's nomination to run for president of the United States. Our meeting was held at a luncheon downtown in the Hyatt

Hotel. With me were three other gay persons, all of us invited by County Supervisor Ed Edelman, who had made arrangements for the candidate's visit.

During lunch, Governor Carter stood at the head table and stated, "I will answer any questions you have. If a person is not willing to candidly answer questions, he has no right to be president."

While polite waiters placed and removed plates from the tables, every guest was given an opportunity to ask one or two questions. Since the majority of people present were activists of some sort, but not related to the gay community, their topics covered the standard, predictable subjects of finance, Israel, human rights, defense, communism, et cetera. However, when my turn came, I stood and asked *the* question.

"Governor Carter," I said, "I have something my community would like to know. If you become president of the United States, are you willing to sign an executive order to ban discrimination against homosexuals in the areas of military, housing, employment, and immigration?"

Instantly the noise level in the room dropped so that small sounds, like the clink of a glass, became magnified. Waiters stopped moving around. I heard a loud whisper off to the side asking, "Who let him in?" Taut faces everywhere turned and stared in my direction. From the reaction, you would have thought I had poo-pooed in candidate Carter's peanuts!

Of all the people in the room, the only one who registered no shock whatsoever was Jimmy Carter. With an amused glint in his eyes, he smiled, and in his deliberate fashion said, "Yes, I can answer your question, but you talk kind of fast—although I can tell you're a Southerner. Where are you from?"

"Florida," I replied.

"I thought so," said Carter. "Now, would you please repeat the four categories you just mentioned—military, housing, and what?"

"Military, housing, employment, and immigration."

Governor Carter nodded. "I could be supportive of all of those areas except one," he said.

I was certain his objection would relate to gays in the military because I knew that he had been an officer aboard a nuclear submarine. But his answer surprised me.

Carter said, "The place I would have difficulty with is the area of employment where security clearances are involved, when there are employees who are not open about being gay."

The statement meant he would have problems with closet cases but not with openly gay persons. That was brilliant, and light-years ahead of what other national politicians were saying in their campaigns. And Carter did not even concern himself with the pseudoproblem of gays in the military. For those reasons, I joined and led "Gays for Carter."

Many months later, when Jimmy Carter was elected thirty-ninth president of the United States, I received a personal invitation to his inauguration. And, of course, I was very pleased to attend. Later in the same year, 1977, there was another invitation to the District of Columbia, less ceremonial, but also with the blessing of President Carter.

The event was a meeting consisting of individuals representing various gay interests throughout the United States, with a fact-finding mission to determine and begin the resolution of problems concerning homosexuals in America. The idea was conceived by co–executive directors of the National Gay Task Force, Bruce Voeller and a brilliant ex-nun lesbian, Jean O'Leary. They worked in harmony with Midge Costanza, previously a popular vice-mayor of Rochester, New York, whom Carter had appointed to the post of Assistant to the President. Midge was the first woman in American history to hold that prestigious position.

Fourteen gay persons were invited to the White House, and each was expected to prepare a paper on a designated subject which was close to his or her primary field of endeavor. My area, not surprisingly, was gays and religion. On the subject I filled a thick folder, including a list of many religious denominations that had made positive statements about the rights of homosexuals. My purpose was to show that not every established nongay church in America is filled with hatred when it comes to allowing gay and lesbian people to live happy, productive lives.

Being invited to the White House was exciting. For the occasion I wore a conservative three-piece pin-striped suit and made certain I looked good. At the gate my credentials were checked on a computer and my briefcase was scanned with a detector that was run back and forth over it. Then I walked to the wing of the White House where the Oval Office is located. A young man wearing a blazer opened the door for me. He was briefed and knew who I was without my telling him. "Reverend Perry, will you come this way?" he said.

Our first stop was Midge Costanza's office immediately adjacent to the president's office. Those of us who were to attend assembled there, and it was not long before all were present. With our group was Franklin Kameny, a crusty gay activist who, during the McCarthy era, had been fired as a government astronomer for being gay. We were determined Frank should be with us. Kameny, a thorn in the side of many administrations, was almost single-handedly responsible for initiating changes in some of the federal government's antigay bias, but the poetic justice of his presence inside the White House was that Frank had organized and led the first gay pickets who protested outside of the White House fence!

Nevertheless, wiry Midge Costanza, small in stature but with highly developed political skills, had the ability to put everyone at ease. With a broad smile she said to Kameny, "Frank, I've read all the reports about you—and I'm still going to let you stay!" Everybody laughed.

Minutes later, Midge showed us the famous office of America's chief executive. President Carter was absent. Nevertheless, we did not proceed beyond the entrance, but stood in the hallway and peered inside.

(On a different occasion, Sergeant Leonard Matlovich, the decorated air force hero and gay activist, did enter the Oval Office. In a fine moment of stolen pleasure, Matlovich had his picture snapped while sitting behind the President's desk!)

Our party, with a unanimous feeling of awe, moved farther down the hall until Midge guided us into the impressive Roosevelt Room. We were informed that it was the place where meetings of the National Security Council are normally held, and there we were seated.

We took our places around a large, polished conference table where for decades, events vital to our nation had often been discussed. Oil paintings of historical significance were on the walls and there were bronze statues, works of art I had seen in my high school civics books. Recognizing the well-known pictures, unavoidably being impressed with our own small part in contemporary history, and being present within the working heart of the White House did not intimidate or make anyone self-conscious—not, that is, until our business inside had been completed and we were on the outside reconsidering what had happened within!

Subjects discussed in the Roosevelt Room included immigration, housing, civil rights, prison reform, media representation, and other items. Attorneys from various governmental departments, including the Justice Department in particular, were brought in. The chief counsel for Civil Service was present. Everybody had a turn. When mine came, I said, "You have my written statement. Please read it later, for I would like to use this moment to talk from the heart." Whereupon, I spoke of what it was like to be a homosexual in America.

"I want to tell you how it feels to be told you can't be loved," I said, "I want you to know what it's like to have the church of your childhood dictate that you can't belong if you're homosexual. I can tell you these things because I know what it's like to be treated as if you don't fit in with others. Because I know what it's like to start a church and have that church burned to the ground around you. Ten Metropolitan Community Churches have been destroyed by fire and we don't see the end to it. And I want to tell you about something that really scares me—fire! I want to tell a horror story about a gay holocaust four years ago in New Orleans. More than thirty of our people died in that tragedy of arson with its aftermath of homophobic inhumanity!"

Not for a second did I back away from truth. All I was asking was to be treated like anybody else in my country—not any better or any worse. I said, "We merely want the Constitution of the United States to apply to us also. We want to be able to work for a living, not to be subservient or intimidated. We want to be able to worship without being fearful that some terrible retribution will be thrust at us. That's why we're here—to plead for gay America—twenty-two million viable gay and lesbian Americans!

"We need to know that our government, the government of our birth in most cases, cares about us! I remember how difficult growing up as a gay youth was, and I don't want young men and young women who follow me to have to put up with the anxiety and the misery that millions of us have already endured. There has been enough suffering! Those of us here are proud to represent the gay community because we know that we are whole persons, know we're not sinners, know we're not perverted, know we're not monsters, know we're not mentally ill! You may continue to believe what you want. Maybe I can't change that. But to be given our fair and Constitutional rights—that's what we are asking for."

An emotional charge seemed to have filled the room from the moment we entered. Even the White House stenographers who were dexterously recording everything that was said became misty-eyed. Our meeting lasted an hour and a half beyond the scheduled time. Important departmental representatives had many questions. As for us, those several hours were wonderful. At long last, *our* federal government was hearing us!

Bruce Voeller, Jean O'Leary and I were the last to depart. As we stood to have our pictures taken outside on the White House lawn, a chilly March wind was blowing, but no one cared. Each of us was filled with positive emotion. With some frequency I had to wipe tears from my eyes. I remember saying, "Just never forget how momentous is what has happened today! Do you realize where we have just been? How few people in the world, even in America, ever really get to meet with their government? It's mind-boggling for me, coming from a background of being told God couldn't love me, of being a renegade because of my sex life—and then coming to Washington! In a dramatic way, it's the validation of every American's dream!"

Many of my relatives around the country saw me on television that evening, emerging from the White House and photographed in the ensuing press conference. No incident could have done more to break the last of the tension which had once existed between my aunts, uncles, cousins—and me. Their altered attitude was that if I was gay and still good enough for the president of the United States, I was good enough for them. No longer did it matter that I was "queer." The president had invited me into his home.

Previously, when I had gone as a gay adult to visit in Florida or Georgia, I was always able to feel disturbing undercurrents of disapproval from my many relations. When I was growing up, my aunts and uncles had considered me the best little boy in the world. I was their favorite of all the cousins and nephews. But when I came out as a homosexual person, it was their reason to turn off the warmth. Not that they did not want to see me. They did—but our relationship became *so* polite! The extreme politeness that Southerners can assume better than anybody else! I hate that. Having everything perfect—perfectly wrong, that is! When they will not ask a single question. When they do not want to know about your church. When they want to know nothing about anything! But it all changed the moment they saw me on television, walking out of the White House—that made the difference!

A follow-up meeting was held in Washington. On that occasion, the president's religious liaison, a Southern Baptist preacher, asked to meet with a gay religious group, and he expected that only members of Metropolitan Community Church would attend. However, I asked Reverend Nancy Wilson and Mr. Adam DeBaugh to organize the participants, and as a result of their planning, the White House was surprised by a list we presented of people coming to Washington: gay Mormons, gay Lutherans, gay Seventh Day Adventists, gay Catholics, gay Jews, gay Jehovah's Witnesses, gay Methodists, gay Presbyterians, and gay Orthodox Greeks.

All those present could ably articulate their beliefs to the Southern Baptist preacher. Each had maintained his or her faith even though churches had attempted to drive them away; they were, and would remain, children of God. We also maintained that government has a responsibility to us, as citizens, because if federal prejudice can be stripped away, it follows that the prejudice outside of government will eventually also fall by the wayside. We explained that that was what had happened in other countries like the Netherlands, where the successful official attitude is that homosexuals can hold any occupation and do honorably serve in the military.

When the second meeting arranged by the White House was finished, President Carter's Southern Baptist religious liaison, who really did listen to what we said, had a very different feeling about us from what he had before we began. "You have broken every stereotype I've ever had about homosexuals!" he declared.

National injustices can best be addressed in the nation's capital, and for that reason, the reality of American masses taking their shared grievances to Washington, D.C., has a precedent in history dating back to the earliest years of our republic. Closer to the twentieth century, militant sign-waving suffragettes demanded their right to vote, disappointed veterans of World War I (the Bonus Army) camped in the District of Columbia until routed by Douglas MacArthur, and in 1963, hundreds of thousands of blacks in the Coalition of Conscience listened to Martin Luther King, Jr. speak of his dream from the steps of the Lincoln Memorial.

Gay activists, a decade and a half later, also began suggesting a great march into Washington, D.C. Among those calling for such action were Harvey Milk (who would be assassinated before it could happen); comic Robin Tyler; plus activists in Minneapolis, New York, Los Angeles, Philadelphia, and several other major American cities.

In no way demeaning is the little-known fact that the idea for the march began with what was intended to be a joke. Robin Tyler was performing in Minneapolis. Some humorous lines she intended to use were: "I think we should march on Washington. We'll set up tents. We know how gay men love camping." However, what the audience of four hundred lesbians and gay men heard was somewhat abbreviated.

"I think we should march on Washington," were the only words Robin had spoken when the people in the crowd, which believed they had heard a genuine call for action, spontaneously jumped to their feet and started cheering wildly. In tune with the unexpected excitement, Robin alertly cut her punch line and went along with a growing chant.

"March on Washington! March on Washington!" demanded the impassioned assembly.

Next day, a committee for the march was formed in Minneapolis. Six months later, Harvey Milk in San Francisco called for massive participation, and by the end of 1978, a national organizational structure existed to plan such a highly visible demonstration.

Our demands of the leaders of the United States would be (1) a national Gay and Lesbian Civil Rights Bill, (2) repeal of existing antigay laws, (3) an executive order from the president banning military, federal, and federally related discrimination on the basis of sexual orientation, (4) an end to unfair bias in gay father and mother custody cases, and (5) the protection of lesbian and male homosexual youths from discriminatory legislation.

October 14, 1979 was set as the date for our march. People from every state in the Union were planning to attend. From San Francisco, an Amtrak train, dubbed "the Freedom Train," offered gay camaraderie and an affordable ticket across the North American continent to Washington, D.C. Hundreds of gay people were prepared to roll through the purple mountain majesties, across the azure fields of grain to the great Atlantic seaboard, but I intended to travel using more expedient air transportation—until a self-described "radical, feminist, Jewish dyke" who believes that the way to a man's heart is through his stomach invited me to dinner at her house and changed my mind.

When I was full of turkey, Robin Tyler said, "Troy, there's going to be a special train to Washington. Why don't you and I go on board, and every time the train stops, we'll do a whistle-stop thing, à la Franklin and Eleanor Roosevelt? We'll go out on the caboose at the back of the train and give a little speech in every big town or hick city where the train stops, day or night, across country."

Robin is very persuasive. Inasmuch as I liked her ideas from the beginning, we were already making plans before dessert. Weeks later, when the time to depart arrived, the majority of people aboard the train were gay men. Together with four courageous lesbians we quickly became a wonderful, campy family. Meanwhile, the heterosexual minority was fearful of our presence. They avoided the cars at the end of the train, where our people who could not afford sleeping compartments sat up or slept in their seats.

At first, when we boarded, news reporters assigned to accompany us were very distant. Like other nongay passengers and porters, they were extremely apprehensive. But it is interesting to note that by the end of our four-day trip, almost every passenger's illogical fear of us had evaporated. There was, however, a loud exception. He was an antigay male who refused to sit near one of our people in the dining car on the last evening aboard the Freedom Train. Vociferously, he complained not only about our presence, but about anything that concerned lesbians and gays. The result was that the maître d' (who three days before had definitely been frightened of us), defiantly said to the blustering passenger, "If you can't eat with them, you don't have to eat!" and pushed the surprised bigot out of the dining car. It would not have happened at the beginning of our trip.

That was how we affected most of the crew and passengers. Many of them enthusiastically learned to enjoy us—because we treated others with care and consideration. And we were full of life! We had brought a piano into the club car and transformed it into a bar. Lively Judy Garland songs and funny, impromptu ditties meant for ourselves were equally entertaining for adventurous nongays who came to stare and remained to enjoy our company. I am not certain exactly when reporters became sympathetic toward us, but we received great press everywhere.

Robin Tyler was wonderful. "That train was so happy!" she said, "We sang songs, told jokes, and laughed just as gays have always done through the years. Camp has been a wonderful part of our culture. From it stems half of the humor of Broadway and movies, but only recently have we allowed ourselves to be identified. Before we had to sublimate, twist our humor around so nongays wouldn't recognize it. Now we are visible. And on the train, we became like a moving gay city, with consciousness—ministry—outreach—and humor!"

Robin Tyler always seems to find something to enjoy. In Winnipeg, Canada, when teenage Robin had discovered she was a lesbian, she wasted little time before making a sign and holding it up at the corner of Portage and Main. "The sign read GAY IS GOOD," Robin said, "and people thought *gay* meant merry and they gave me a buck. The year was 1958 and I was sixteen. In a lesbian magazine, *The Ladder,* I read an article by a lesbian activist, Del Martin, who wrote, 'If you are a woman who loves another woman you are a lesbian. If it feels right, it is right. Don't let anybody tell you different. P.S. Move to a big city!'"

Robin went to New York. Eventually she accompanied a friend to the Stitch and Bitch Club on Halloween. It was a night when male club members wore women's costumes—and fatefully, police raided their drag ball. Robin, despite many protests, was arrested along with a wagonload of men. The police refused to believe she was not another dressed-up man. When Robin was allowed her one telephone call, she contacted the *New York Post.* Next day, the newspaper featured her story of mistaken gender. The *Post*'s headline read: WOMAN ARRESTED FOR FEMALE IMPERSONATION.

After the unusual publicity, Robin worked for two years pretending to be a female impersonator. She became famous at New York's 82 Club using the name Stacy Morgan. "That club is the reason I became a comic," says Robin, "because the gay men taught me camp, their kind of humor. And I needed it. At the end of every show, the audience would be asked to guess who was the real woman in the show, and nobody ever guessed it was me. They always thought it was one of the guys!

"But with all the experiences, I've never been on anything as exciting as that 1979 Freedom Train," Robin continued. "We lived together for four days, worked together, and gay people in rural areas set their alarm clocks and got out of their beds in the middle of the night when we rolled through their cities. They met us at the tracks and some lesbians and gay men in mid-America became liberated as a result. Many of the gay people who came to meet us in the middle of the night were members of M.C.C. That was the big advantage of having Troy there to speak—Christians will get up at any time if you tell them something is happening!"

There was no rear platform on the Amtrak train from which to address the crowd; nevertheless, even if the schedule only allowed three or four minutes, we would hop off and give our speeches. The result was always tears and laughter. And sometimes people were so filled with joy from seeing a train packed with gay people that they impulsively decided to join us. They jumped aboard, and bought themselves a ticket to the first of the great gay marches in Washington, D.C.!

Occasionally, when we stopped in the middle of nowhere, there might at first be only a few people in small towns to greet us, but then regional reporters were suddenly impressed when a hundred or more latecomers came running to join them. That was a little game we kept in reserve for media emergencies. The late arrivals were our own people who jumped off our train on its other side and ran around to swell the ranks. The playful stunt was used on several occasions when local crowds seemed inadequate to keep the gay presence newsworthy.

Our speeches to those who met us were tailored to the length of time the train stopped. Robin, a professional comic (which she defines as an X-ray perceiver of the truth who makes pain and anger seem funny), was, like myself, always ready to address the people. Mostly we urged them to come out of their closets. "The reason 'straight' people don't want us to come out," Robin would say, "has nothing to do with what we do in bed. Ours is not a movement from the waist down! Sex is not the main part of our existence.

"We are fighting for the right to love. If I was never with a woman again I would still be a lesbian. That is why I do not not refer to being gay as a lifestyle. It is more than a lifestyle—it is our life.

"The reason our enemies want to keep us in the closet is because as long as we're isolated from each other, we can't ever achieve our civil rights. The closet is a divider. It prevents us from affirming our right to work, our right to be fairly paid, and our right to exist. There are over twenty-two million gay men and lesbians in the United States. If each of us took just one step forward into the light—millions and millions of us would all be free. The bottom line is a matter of power and economics!"

Robin, however, is quick to admit that on one occasion she was not ready to affirm her homosexuality. Canada's national television news had referred to Robin as "a world-famous dyke" and afterward, her relatively innocent mother telephoned to ask, "What does *dyke* mean?" Robin replied, "Don't worry about it, Mother. *Dyke* means Doctor of Young Karate Experts." Presumably, the answer was satisfactory.

To lesbians who met us along the route of the Freedom Train, Robin was more candid. She often said, "Gay men have been the biggest supporters of women's liberation because the gay men, even if they are not feminists, do not rely upon women to be their servants. All of us, as gay people, want only our civil rights. We don't want to see ourselves as victims. We're not asking for special privileges. And we don't care if heterosexuals understand us. Misconceptions about homosexuals are not our problem. If nongay people hold hands it's called sharing—if we do the same thing it's called flaunting. So it's important to teach people who have felt guilty all their lives that now is the time for us to love and respect ourselves. Let us be leaders with our examples of commitment and courage. I was told by everybody that if I came out as a lesbian on stage, I'd never get anywhere. Actually, I've never worked so much in my life!"

Robin's message was always popular. At every train stop we were overwhelmed with applause and affection—with one notable exception. In Ogden, Utah, in the middle of the night, a gaunt, black fundamentalist minister in a dark blue suit, with a hand-lettered cardboard sign hanging from a string around his neck, came to meet us. The five-inch-high letters on his sign read: HOMOSEXUALS—YOU DEVILS ARE NOT WELCOME HERE! The minister proceeded to lie down on the railroad tracks as if to block our progress, but he only lay down long enough to have his picture taken by the local media. (He was said to have been running for political office.)

"My name is Reverend Robert L. Harris," said the preacher. "Mighty right! Mighty right! This is a religious state. They'll appreciate me doing something like this. You have no rights. Yeah, you have no rights. The only rights you have is to turn to the Lord."

"God loves everybody," replied a voice.

"No. The power of God is against you!" railed the minister.

"You are degrading the good name of Jesus Christ!" retorted a lesbian bystander.

The minister would not be deterred. "The Lord is talking to you through me!" he declared. "Repent of your sins! The power of God is against you!"

"Start up the train and run him over," Robin kept yelling with mock sincerity. But, of course, we did not do that.

Eventually, police told the preacher-turned-politician to get on his way or be arrested. Since by then Harris had all the photographs he wanted, he dusted himself off without so much as waiting for the train to start, and departed. So much for demonstrations. He was not even lying on the correct track!

Other incidents also come to memory, but one of the best was the sight of the mostly nongay Amtrak crew, all sporting our March on Washington lapel buttons as the Freedom Train pulled into its destination. Crew and travelers had become our friends, people who four days before, in San Francisco, would never have given the time of day to lesbians and gay men. From my point of view, the events that followed were something of an anticlimax for those of us who had taken the train across America.

One hundred thousand homosexuals were present for the activities, a lower actual attendance figure than the march organizers anticipated. And although a small minority of gay socialists usurped control of the program, the majority of us, including myself and the Universal Fellowship of Metropolitan Community Churches, remained because we felt it was important for gays and lesbians, in all our diversity, to present a unified face to the world. We would not be deterred from revealing our growing political abilities and expressing, simply and eloquently, that we want our rights.

Like every large movement in America, we have participants from all segments of the political spectrum, from the far right to the extreme left. Sometimes we get along with each other, and sometimes we do not. The 1979 March on Washington was no exception. In that instance, some members of the march committee were opposed to having a "gay clergyman" speak. I was told that they had decided that the last thing they wanted to hear was a gay-white equivalent of the martyrized Martin Luther King, Jr. Yet, as my friends will tell you, I was not prepared to leave quietly or remain silent. Nor was I content to be the thirty-seventh speaker who would probably be addressing remnants of a crowd long since departed!

Aware of the ensuing difficulty, Robin Tyler came to me. Little did those who opposed my speaking realize that she and I had become close personal friends, although she was a Jewish entertainer and I a Christian minister. "Don't worry, Troy," Robin said to me. "You will not be speaker number thirty-seven. You will be first! I'm the emcee, and I'll do what I think is right, once I get up on the stand."

And do what she wanted, Robin Tyler did.

She had me waiting in the wings. After the program began, I was the first person to address the tens of thousands of gay and lesbian people who had come to Washington. Even though I had developed a sore throat from speaking across country, day and night, at every train stop, and from endlessly shouting our cries of freedom along the route of the Washington march, I was still ready to proclaim our message of hope and determination.

"We have had our setbacks," I said. "We lost to Anita Bryant in Dade County, Florida, and we're still smarting from civil rights losses in Wichita, Kansas, St. Paul, Minnesota, and Eugene, Oregon. But we turned it around in California. That's important to remember. There have been setbacks, and there will be more setbacks, but in the end, we will win because we are right!"

As the 1979 March on Washington ended, even though it was not all that we had hoped, it was still a success. The main thing we had accomplished was simply to prove that we could handle the logistics, and that we could assemble large numbers of vocal, visible homosexuals to demonstrate for freedom.

Steve Ault, who had been involved with the first Gay March on Washington, came to my office seven years later and said, "Troy, I think it's important to do it again!" I immediately agreed, having independently arrived at the same conclusion. The 1979 march had been for "gay rights and immigration reform." As we planned the 1987 National March on Washington for Lesbian and Gay Rights, our objectives were similar, but in some ways more sophisticated—and more desperate.

There were two vital reasons for the 1987 march: First, in Michael Hartwick's case, which began in Georgia and was appealed to the United States Supreme Court, the Court had recently ruled that individual states can each have their own peculiar laws telling consenting adults what they can and cannot do, sexually, in private. In effect, the highest court was saying that within any state where homophobes have control, homosexuals have no right to privacy. The second reason for needing a march was AIDS, to demand that our government (led by President Reagan) become more attuned to America's major health problem and seriously commit itself to fighting the awful disease.

Many of our national gay leaders were not initially overjoyed with the idea of a second march. "Oh, God, here we go again!" somebody exclaimed, remembering how the first program had been corrupted in various ways by socialistic brothers and sisters who were not in the mainstream of our gay rights movement. But this time there was a much better balance of gay participants. Furthermore, I remembered the old story of Nazi Germany when a victim of Hitler's dictatorship had said, "When they came to take the Communists, I said nothing because I wasn't a Communist; when they came to take the Jews, I said nothing because I wasn't Hebrew; when they came to take the Poles, I said nothing because I wasn't Polish; until finally, when they came to take me, there wasn't anybody left to speak in my behalf!"

And so it was for gay and lesbian Americans. We needed to remain united, for as President Abraham Lincoln had so vividly declared, "A house divided against itself cannot stand."

I contributed the first money toward planning what we hoped could be a major demonstration. Another contribution I was able to make was the slogan we used for our 1987 March on Washington: "For love or life, we're not going back." The words meant that not the Supreme Court, not even AIDS, would be allowed to strip the homosexual community of out-of-the-closet rights we had fought for and won in the second half of the twentieth century. By inference, in the chosen words there was also a promise of continued advancement of gay causes. And care was taken that the slogan contained no religious references, because in our gay community with millions of people, we have large devout groups of many persuasions which must be respected—Christians, Jews, Moslems, and others—plus those with no religious background. Nevertheless, our slogan evolved from a powerful hymn, well known in my denomination, that says, "Our God who gives us life, also gives us liberty!"

Over the next half year, not only was there not widespread interest in the national march, but as our plans became known, a number of gay people fought against us. Dissenters felt that our community should spend its money on other things, particularly AIDS, which they considered to be more important than a demonstration which would be over after several days. My response, however, was to increase our preparations for the march.

I felt it was vital that as many of us as possible, in a tremendous show of strength, gather at the center of government and speak in great numbers from our heart to all of America. Otherwise, given time, AIDS could greatly decimate our ranks. And the Supreme Court had already declared it cared very little about us. Nor did the president or vice president of the United States, both of whom courted fundamentalist homophobes, truly consider our plight. So it was important, as a large, organized group, to say to America, "We are not returning to the closet. We are not going to backslide. Never! Instead, we are going to urge you forward, we are going to petition the courts, we are going to push the Congress and we are going to disagree with the president. In the midst of all our suffering, nobody will be permitted to use the sorrow of AIDS, or the misery of AIDS, or the fear of AIDS to deprive us of our civil rights!"

I started receiving telephone calls from gay leaders, staunch individuals who had trusted my judgment before, and they asked, "Do you really feel this positive about a national march?"

"I sure do!" was my reply.

In July, at the Universal Fellowship's General Conference, Reverend Carl Bean, executive director of the Minority AIDS Project in the United States, requested our assembled ministers and members to raise a hand if they were attending the March on Washington. When it became obvious that few were committed, it gave me the impetus to urgently suggest that every gaybody in our denomination should make a major effort to be present. Several days later, we sent out a letter to our entire Fellowship, stating that I expected to see most of our people in Washington, D.C., on October 11—and that they should bring with them all of their signs and banners. When the event finally took place, I was delighted to realize how well my advice was heeded. There were very big groups representing well-populated states and big cities like New York and Los Angeles. Of the organizations represented, none had a larger turnout than Metropolitan Community Church.

We arrived in Washington with the good wishes of the mayor of the District of Columbia, Marion Barry, Jr. "I applaud your commitment to making the erosion of human rights a national concern," wrote Mayor Barry. "We must insure that attacks of violence against lesbians and gays will not be tolerated. We must insure that no one is denied medical insurance, health services, accommodations, or work because of sexual orientation . . . these must become the rights of all people of our nation through legislation and enforcement. Only together can we guarantee that this country will soon provide dignity and equity for all its people."

Hundreds of events were scheduled to take place over a period of six days. On Saturday, October 10, Sergeant Leonard Matlovich, a bona fide gay American hero, initiated his idea to have important homosexual Americans buried in Congressional Cemetery. The endeavor was begun with dedication of a final resting place for the ashes of the martyred San Francisco city councilman, Harvey Milk. (Sergeant Matlovich, who died of AIDS, is now also buried in the Congressional Cemetery.)

At Constitution Hall, 250 gay musicians from all over America gathered on stage to present a band concert. In the course of the program, the full audience held hands and sang a hypnotic, melodic statement: "We are gays and lesbians together—and we are singing—singing for our lives!" Our brothers and sisters sang the lyrics over and over with simple variations. "We are peaceful, loving people—and we are singing—singing for our lives!" was one of the refrains. It was all very powerful!

A red, white, and blue wreath of flowers was placed at the Tomb of the Unknown Soldier on Sunday morning. The solemn ceremony honored all of the uncounted thousands of gay men and women who, since the American Revolution and in all our wars, have sacrificed their lives for the love of country. Our wreath was received by an official honor guard and placed on a stand at the base of the tomb. Gay men and lesbians, many who had been in the military themselves, or who had gay relatives or friends in the service, stood quietly as the mournful sound of a bugler playing Taps drifted over Arlington Cemetery.

Another tribute, considerably more elaborate, took place on a section of the Mall between the Washington Monument and the U.S. Capitol. It was called the Names Project but might better be recalled as "the Quilt," an enormous cloth memorial to more than two thousand of the many persons lost to AIDS. Names of beloved deceased were poignantly presented on handmade, three-by-six-foot fabric panels that were lovingly stitched together to create colorful twelve-foot squares. Those large squares were ceremoniously unfolded and connected to wide white borders on all sides. The result was a stunning blanket of names—about thirty-six feet wide and two city blocks long! Prominent names on the gigantic quilt included Liberace, Rock Hudson, and Dr. Thomas Waddell, a gay Olympic star.

At nine o'clock on Sunday morning, members of Metropolitan Community Church met in front of the Lincoln Memorial where we held a communion service. Reverend Steve Pieters and I addressed the hundreds who came to worship. Reverend Pieters, who had nearly died of AIDS but was cured, spoke to both the gay and nongay persons who joined us. "We must give hope to the gay and lesbian community, and to everyone else who is sick and dying," said Pieters. "We must continue to struggle, letting people know God can heal AIDS. But we must not let our government off the hook. Governments must supply the money needed for research to cure those for whom faith is not the answer!"

My sermon was concerned with people who would be involved in confrontations with police on the following Tuesday in front of the Supreme Court building. I made my feelings clear that we as Christians can never back away from tackling any branch of government that treats gay members of society like second-class citizens. Anticipating the peaceful disobedience, I said, "We must let the Supreme Court know that we are protected by the United States Constitution just as much as any heterosexual, and that we will go to jail, and we will fill the jails if necessary, before we ever let any court, even the United States Supreme Court, rule away our freedom to exist."

At ten-thirty, when our service was concluded, latecomers by the hundreds were still continuously arriving. We started walking, working our way through ever growing masses of people, heading toward the Ellipse behind the White House where the march was scheduled to begin at noon. Plenty of signs and banners were held high to identify ourselves. I wanted the world to know that the Universal Fellowship of Metropolitan Community Churches was there. And, indeed, we were! Everybody watching television saw us!

There were a few organizers who would have had all religious participants walking at the end of the parade, but I fully intended for us to be up front where we belonged, in the category called National Organizations. I had seen to it that the march committee knew I intended to keep my resolve, and when some monitors, working feverishly to maintain control of growing numbers of humanity, tried to push us to the rear, I lifted my voice and pulled our people together.

"Hear me!" I said very loudly. Almost immediately there was silence. My group knew that those words indicated I meant business and often preceded an important announcement. "Do not let them separate you from me," I said forcefully. "I am your leader. Stay with me! Put your arms on each other's shoulders and make snake lines if necessary. Start a chant or anything. But let's keep M.C.C. together!"

Which we did.

As the march began, we struggled toward our place in the lineup, and like a relentless stream entering what was becoming a crushing river of people, we flowed forward. When about half of us were in position, monitors tried, for some unexplained reason, to part us from the thousands more of our people who were trying to follow, but our members prevented a separation from happening. They raised their arms and held the backs of each other's shoulders, moving forward with the rest of us, firmly holding ranks.

Like an army, led by our Board of Elders, by district coordinators from all over the world (including Mexico, Canada, Great Britain, New Zealand, and Australia), and by ministers from every state in the American Union, we were a very respectable contingent! Behind us for several blocks, which was as far as it was possible to see, were people holding our banners. When we passed troublesome fundamentalists who had taken a place in Lafayette Square across the street from the White House, we sang for their benefit, "Jesus Loves Me, This I Know," drowning out whatever rhetoric they were directing at us.

Our parade continued along Pennsylvania Avenue toward the Mall where we would eventually hold our rally with the U.S. Capitol for a backdrop. Although speeches and festivities would last throughout most of the afternoon, our march never ended in all that time because of the unbelievable attendance of lesbians and gay men. Even in the morning, at the Ellipse, I had realized that the magnificent crowd was going to exceed our wildest expectations. We had hoped a quarter of a million gay people might attend, and with that we would have been delighted, but the passionate throngs were triple what anyone had anticipated. So shocked was the National Park Service that they gave out low, ludicrously inaccurate numbers.

It was stunning!

And the march kept getting larger!

People were coming in from side streets, from everywhere. Even to viewers high on the speakers' stand, gay multitudes seemed to fill every available space for as far toward the distant Lincoln Memorial as the naked eye could see. Traffic in downtown Washington was completely jammed. The streets and subways of the District of Columbia were packed by the influx of people. For hours there was gridlock! We could hardly believe what was happening. But it was stupendous!

The CBS television network estimated that eight hundred thousand people—over three quarters of a million lesbians and gay men—were in our March on Washington! And everybody was in good humor. We had to contend with a few derogatory comments from disagreeable fundamentalists, but even with them, there were no fistfights. All along the seemingly endless line of march were bands, people singing, balloons, banners, and a genuine feeling of success. Every segment of our community was represented.

As persons with AIDS marched, or were pushed in wheelchairs, or bused in front of the White House, they sang "Amazing Grace." Smiling lesbian mothers pushed their happy babies in colorful, flower-bedecked strollers. Senior citizens chanted, "Two, four, six, eight, what makes you think your grandma was straight?" Canadian homosexuals paraded beneath white parasols with a red maple leaf imprinted thereon, and Reverend Brent Hawkes of Metropolitan Community Church of Toronto told one of his many interviewers, "If there are advantages for straight couples being married, then there need to be advantages for gay couples. If there is protection in privacy rights for individuals who are heterosexual, then there needs to be protection for people who are homosexual as well."

People chanted, "Equal justice under the law—equal justice under the law—equal justice under the law!" At a quieter moment, a woman said thoughtfully, "The close of the Pledge of Allegiance of the United States is 'with liberty and justice for all.' It's a sad state of affairs that group after group after group have to come back and fight, and continue fighting, to be included in that word 'all.' Name after name after name. Women have had to do it. People of color have had to do it. The gay and lesbian community now have to do it!"

Musicians on a giant stage, together with dancers and singers, supplied much of the entertainment. Their talent kept everybody feeling warm although the weather was cold. Amidst microphones were a piano, an organ, percussion, and other instruments utilizing some of the best sound equipment I have ever heard. There were even walk-in speakers!

An important part of the show was the intermittent presentation of well-known gay and nongay speakers. My assignment was to ask for funds. Harvey Fierstein, Robert Blake and Whoopi Goldberg represented the entertainment industry. Also included among those who addressed the gathering were the Reverend Jesse Jackson and César Chavez, president of the United Farm Workers of America, AFL-CIO.

"Our movement has been supporting lesbian and gay rights for over twenty years," said César Chavez. "We were supporting lesbian and gay rights when ten people were a crowd!"

An AIDS patient in a wheelchair said he was "fighting for more money for AIDS research . . . fighting to kill this epidemic and to get the White House off its ass." On the same subject, Whoopi Goldberg commented into the onstage microphone for all to hear, "How long is it going to take before people get smart? Educated people? Not just people with no education—I'm not talking about illiterate people. I'm talking about senators! And congressmen! And the fucking president!"

Only one candidate with presidential aspirations (from a field of a dozen or more seeking the Oval Office) was present. He was the well-dressed and well-groomed Baptist Democrat, Jesse Jackson. Reverend Jackson took the podium and addressed us, saying, "America is not a blanket all of one color, of uncut cloth all red or white or blue." Jackson said, "America is a quilt made up of many patches, many pieces, many colors, many sizes, many textures. But everybody fits, everybody counts. Everybody must have equal protection under the law in the real America!"

It was a never to be forgotten day.

On Tuesday (because Monday was a holiday), a protest was held in front of the Supreme Court. Much was said by our people about getting government out of our bedrooms, and then, according to plan, the District of Columbia's police were challenged and our people were arrested. Their efforts were not in vain because on television around the world, viewers were told why thoughtful citizens were engaged in peaceful but unlawful disobedience.

I will never forget a picture I saw on a video of the event. It showed a slender woman, presumably a senior citizen, about to be arrested. But first, the woman adjusted and straightened her hat. Then, maintaining an elfin grin that looked very much like bliss, she allowed polite policemen to drag her away. Katherine Hepburn could not have done it better!

But the event of the long weekend in Washington that received most press coverage was the one that came to be known as the Wedding, although a wedding in the heterosexual sense it was not. What did happen is that more than two thousand couples, lesbian couples and gay male couples, each in their own fashion, made a private commitment one to the other. The event transpired on Saturday afternoon in front of the Internal Revenue Service building where, in addition to the couples who participated, six or seven thousand gay witnesses, plus tourists who had been on their way to attractions like the nearby Smithsonian Institution, were present within an area cordoned off by the city's police.

As I approached with my lover, Phillip DeBlieck, and my friend and very capable bodyguard, Joseph McDuffey, we turned a corner and found ourselves confronted by members of the radical fundamentalist group that had plagued us in years past. On this occasion, instead of being led by "Big Harley," the extremists (with their metal-framed REPENT OR BURN signs) were being led by a Scripture-misquoter whom somebody dubbed "Bible Bob."

In the past, similar small contingents of hatemongers have too often been able to attract media attention out of all proportion to reason simply by being outlandish, like contestants on a television game show. In Washington, Bible Bob, who nonchalantly enjoyed the comradeship of nearby police, used his bullhorn to hurl ugly invective at the thousands of well-dressed gay people gathered for the Wedding. When our sisters and brothers hollered retorts, Bible Bob grinned with self-serving pleasure, well aware that a dozen television cameras were trained in his direction!

Since I had seen Bible Bob disrupt gay demonstrations before, I automatically decided that we had endured more than enough of his unpleasant activity. After a word to Phillip and Joseph McDuffey to accompany me, I went to a platform the fundamentalists had erected beside their truck, and I began speaking—not to Bible Bob—but to assembled couples and friends from the gay community.

"Don't listen to that man!" I declared, "He hates you. Don't reply to him. He wants only to give you hell! I want to give you heaven. Do you want to know what true joy is? This is true joy!" With those words, I pulled Phillip close to me, and we kissed—full on the mouth!

The gay crowd began to cheer.

Applauding!

All around, delighted men and women were clapping their hands. Bible Bob began screaming. He ran over to me, shouting, slobbering as he spat words out of his mouth. "Don't listen to Troy Perry, because he's a liar!" he yelled. (Bible Bob was furious because the television cameras had moved from him and were concentrating on me.)

I walked away from Bible Bob, leaving him off-camera again. "People like that," I said to the press who were following me, "are one of the main reasons we're here. People like him, who are without love in their hearts, are the reason demonstrations of this kind are important. How awful it is to have to hear someone like him get up and talk about us like we are human garbage! Something must be terribly wrong with the part of spiritual America which supports people like that!"

"Don't listen to that Troy Perry B.S.," hissed Bible Bob, pushing himself toward the press again. However, his attempts to regain on-camera attention were futile. When he realized that reporters were no longer receptive to his petty act, Bible Bob's Christian veneer fell away. I wanted to make that point with the media, but it was unnecessary. They knew already.

The Wedding was an idea of Walter Wheeler and J. Carey Junkin, whose endeavor I applauded from the beginning. However, unlike most other events of the weekend, it was the subject of public relations apprehension, and therefore, some gay persons tried to eliminate the nonsectarian celebration of homosexual union from the march's authorized program. To those who objected, my reply was, "Your complaints are ill founded. We are fighting for our gay rights as gay couples. Let us publicly show that we believe in commitment. What is wrong with that? Lesbians and gays have paid and paid and paid our taxes for everybody else's kids to go to school—now it's time we do this for us!"

The gay press, even those who were against the Wedding beforehand, were amazed by the emotion generated by more than two thousand couples making a serious, personal commitment to each other. But it was not a mock heterosexual ceremony. It was us stating that we cared, that we wanted to love each other.

We have had to fight to maintain relationships. There has been little help from most of our families. In that respect, I have been fortunate. Still, for all of us it is vital to realize that it is healthy to show affection—and we have every right to do so!

Rosemary Dempsey, an attorney who represents the National Organization for Women, spoke after being introduced by Robin Tyler. "We cannot be afraid of a ceremony like this," said Rosemary, "because this kind of ceremony, this kind of demonstration says to the world, and most importantly, to ourselves and to our community, that we are first-class citizens, we are lovers, we are family, and we will no longer be ashamed."

Phillip stood with me as the Wedding proceeded. "This is my message," I said when it was my turn to speak. "Know who you are and what you're about. We're here today because it's very important to us. Isn't it good to know we have friends? In front of this platform I see a young man who has AIDS, sitting with his other half. They are here to be a part of our celebration today, and for them my heart weeps."

Suddenly, as I tried to continue, mocking words blasted out of a bullhorn at the left side of the huge crowd. I looked over to see a handful of Bible Bob's people who still remained. The sight of them and their mean-spirited signs racked my soul with sadness as much as with anger. "Those fundamentalists on the fringes," I said, "who are shouting words of hatred at us even now, ought to be ashamed of themselves. With people here who might be dying, it makes me sick to contemplate their inhumanity. For them I feel shame. Shame!"

Immediately the crowd began chanting, "Shame! Shame! Shame!" At once, the complacent police, who had been so amused by us, realized the situation was not funny any longer. Afraid that ten thousand homosexuals might rush and pulverize a few of our irritating foes, the officers moved between them and us.

"Shame! Shame! Shame!" continued the chant.

For the safety of the fundamentalists—and of themselves—the police insisted that our antagonists depart, taking their signs with them. Removal of the unpleasant individuals was followed by cheers.

Phillip grinned into my eyes.

"Honey, when you've been shamed by ten thousand homosexuals, you've really been shamed!" he said.

Then Reverend Dina Bachelor stepped to the microphone, and said the words so many had waited to hear. As I held Phillip's hand, he and I, like the thousands of couples with us, listened, and we knew the words were beautiful and sweet for us.

"Take a deep breath," said Reverend Bachelor, "and release anything that is less than love, and let it go. Now, in your heart and in your mind, let's make a statement to this nation that we as a people choose to trust the truth and righteousness of our love. In this world that does not understand love, we have to love each other.

"We have fought with determination in our process of coming out, and now we stand together as a couple, a family, an integral part of the world's beautiful diversity. And we shall do that with honor. We are teaching the world that the word *commitment* has everything to do with love, and nothing to do with gender."

The Freedom Train continues to this day, and more and more of us are riding. Can you hear it as our mighty Constitution chugs across this blessed land? Listen! When the conductor calls, "All aboard for Civil Rights and Freedom!" remember that "commitment has everything to do with love—and nothing to do with gender."

11
World Church
Extension: 1972...

*Go therefore, and teach all nations, baptizing
them in the name of the Creator, and of the
Christ, and of the Holy Spirit: Teaching
them to observe all things whatsoever I have
commanded you: and lo, I am with you always, even unto the end of the world. Amen.*
                    —Matthew 28: 19,20

OUR Universal Fellowship of Metropolitan Community Churches grew
rapidly. It began in Los Angeles with twelve persons meeting for worship
in the modest living room of a small rented house. The date was October
6, 1968. After twenty years, the growth of that ministry, a product of
desperate and divine inspiration, can be measured in many ways. One
yardstick of success is a list of the countries in which our churches are
already located. They include Australia, Canada, Denmark, Great Britain,
Indonesia, Mexico, New Zealand, Nigeria, and forty-five of the fifty
American states (exceptions, prior to 1990, were North Dakota, Wyoming,
Maine, New Hampshire, and Vermont).

Globally, the expanding outreach is based on a desire to found evangelical centers of worship from which our compassionate Christian gospel
can be spread to many, including heterosexuals. People around the world
reveal their needs to us and we respond, undaunted by the enormity of
the task. Groups and individuals, often anonymous for their own protection, with whom World Church Extension corresponds, are located
in Argentina, Austria, Belgium, Brazil, Burma, Chili, Costa Rica, Germany, Ghana, Greece, Holland, Hungary, Ireland, Italy, Japan, Kenya,
Liberia, the Philippines, Poland, Puerto Rico, Singapore, South Africa,
Spain, Switzerland, and the Virgin Islands.

Close to our inception, only a few months after Metropolitan Community Church was one year old and we had celebrated our first birthday, it became obvious that the infant was on its inevitable way toward becoming a major denomination. Even before a permanent home for the Mother Church was located, or could be afforded, the outreach of our membership into other cities was phenomenal.

On February 22, 1970, Metropolitan Community Church in San Francisco, organized by Reverend Howard Wells, held its first service. On May 10, 1970, Metropolitan Community Church in Chicago, organized by Reverend Arthur Green, began with worship in Green's home. On May 19, 1970, Metropolitan Community Church of San Diego, thanks to the persistence of Howard Williams, initially gathered its congregation in a leased auditorium. During the same time period, successful missions began in Miami and Dallas. And on July 19, 1970, Metroplitan Community Church of Phoenix, led by Reverend Ken Jones, held its earliest prayer services in the offices of ONE, Inc.

(There is a story that when the members of Metropolitan Community Church in Phoenix bought church property, they were without a cross for their altar. Consequently, while they were preparing the sanctuary for worship, some members went into the Arizona desert and obtained a seemingly dead cactus with a vertical trunk from which two horizontal arms extended, and they used that natural growth for their cross. The next morning, according to reliable accounts, when our members entered the church for worship, there were three pale-yellow flowers, one blooming near each point of the cactus.)

Our first church beyond the shores of the continental United States was begun in 1970. Steve Jordan and I had gone to Hawaii for what was intended to be a week of vacation, but the result was that before we returned home from the tropical islands, we had founded a mission. Our work began immediately upon being met at our plane in Honolulu. We were greeted by friends of the Mother Church, including Ron Hanson, who was once a student of theology at a midwestern Bible institute. Ron had struggled against his true sexuality until he finally realized that he could be both Christian and gay, and he was powerfully motivated to accomplish missionary work. Upon being ordained as a deacon, Hanson accepted the responsibility. As a result, Metropolitan Community Church of Hawaii held its first worship service with ten people in attendance on September 20, 1970.

*   *   *

Toward the end of 1972, I made my first trip to Great Britain. I was invited by a curator of the British Museum to address a group which styled itself as the Committee for Homosexual Equality. My presence, as I was to discover, was not without controversy. It seems that the curator had attended our church in America and was so impressed that he was somehow able to persuade Britain's reluctant committee to invite me. Although it was the curator himself who contributed most of the money, many English members still were opposed to my visit and did not want to hear me. I was regarded as an American cult leader invading their "scepter'd isle" and they feared I might be disposed to decree how gay Anglicans should think!

Yet eight hundred people came into the central library in downtown London to hear me. I was billed as being a gay activist as well as a preacher, and word was passed that I would speak about "liberating gospel." When I finished talking, applause told me I had been successful not only in delivering my message, but also in making friends. Among them was Dr. Norman Pittinger, a fine man, a respected theologian, and a teacher. Dr. Pittinger reputedly was invited to be on the same program with me to refute any improper ideas I might have brought across the Atlantic, but instead, he agreed with everything I said, confounding those who wanted to discover something negative or less than proper in my presentation.

As a result of the visit, a coterie of gay men decided that the Universal Fellowship of Metropolitan Community Churches was something for which they were searching and named themselves the Fellowship of Christ the Liberator. Not long afterward, their first female member (and the only woman to join them for a long time) was Jean White, a lesbian nurse who had also heard me speak in London. Eventually, Jean White would become of special importance to World Church Extension, but in the meantime, the pastorless Fellowship of Christ the Liberator struggled to survive.

Originally, the gay Christian group was meeting in somebody's home, but then, with amazing growth paralleling what was happening to us in the United States, they moved into a larger building. By 1973, the group had grown sufficiently that they were chartered and became Metropolitan Community Church of London.

International outreach spread across the United States' northern border. Reverend Bob Wolf, an American, with his faith and our blessing, decided to organize a Canadian church as part of our religious family. Our blessing consisted almost entirely of love, for we had little in the way of funds to provide at the time, and the sad truth is that Bob, without winter clothing, nearly froze to death during his first winter in Toronto! The results of his struggle to keep himself and our struggling church alive might have been different had it not been for Bob Wolf's involvement in an event that came close to being a double tragedy.

It happened on a depressing day when cold came directly down from the Arctic. It was the day when a seriously unhappy lad decided to die. He was an appealing young man, not handsome, with eyes both sad and frightened. The youth was emotionally distraught, but not confused or lacking in determination. Having decided that life was not worth living, he made his way to the top of Toronto's City Hall.

In spite of standard safeguards, the young man managed to crawl out on the roof, about twenty-two stories above the ground, and there he sat precariously on the edge contemplating the end of his life. People gathered in the street below to watch as the sixteen-year-old shivered in the icy breeze, threatening to jump immediately when police or anybody else considered crawling toward his lofty position. To those who attempted to speak with him, he would say little, but eventually, he admitted that part of his problem stemmed from the fact that his parents had recently thrown him out of their house. They did not love him.

The sidewalk crowd remained for hours with their heads turned upward, waiting for that awful, unforgettable moment when the figure silhouetted up high against the darkening sky would plunge through the void. People looked at their watches, wondering if something would happen before they had to catch their bus or go home for dinner. Photographers and reporters drank hot beverages and waited.

After considerable time, the youth on the roof pulled part of a folded newspaper page out of his shirt pocket. The clipping was from a gay periodical. It contained a story about Metropolitan Community Church in which Bob Wolf was mentioned. "If you get him to come here," said the young man, "I'll talk to this preacher. But nobody else!"

Canadian authorities acted quickly. In a very short time they had contacted Reverend Wolf and escorted him to the top of Toronto's City Hall, whereupon our pastor, ignoring the fact that he is himself terrified of heights, cautiously made his way out on the roof. Controlling personal fear and choosing his words with care, Wolf spoke softly as he made his way forward and took a dangerous seat near the roof edge. He was not consoled with knowledge that he was the only person the suicidal fellow would allow to approach.

Crisis prevention is taught by our church. Reverend Wolf remembered all that he had learned. "What's wrong?" he asked, shivering as worsening cold penetrated his cloth jacket. When the teenager beside him began explaining, Bob listened and assessed the situation. He knew there was no way he could wrestle the youth away from the edge. Twenty-two stories in the air, one wrong move would most likely topple both of them over the brink.

"If we splashed on the sidewalk, they'd all be happy down there," said the young man, unnerving his confidant, then adding, "Nobody loves a queer, and that's what I am. I guess you know already. I guess that's what you are from what this paper says. Well, I read what you said but I still think nobody loves us. I know nobody loves me!"

"Listen," said Bob, "you've got the wrong slant. There *are* people who love you. There *are* people who care. I care! And people in Metropolitan Community Church care! We are your friends. Give us a chance and we'll prove it."

During the next nerve-racking quarter of an hour, Reverend Wolf encouraged the unhappy young man to feel considerably better about himself. Most importantly, he came to feel that there were some, at least a few, people who did care. Even though times and relationships were difficult, there could be better days.

Together, Wolf and the youth made their way back toward the inside of the high building. Well-wishers pulled them to safety. Soon the sensational, nonsexual aspects of the story were on the front page of every newspaper in Canada. A headline read: CLERGYMAN TALKS YOUNG MAN DOWN. The rescue was still news of public interest when the city of Toronto decided to honor Reverend Bob Wolf.

Bob appeared before Toronto's City Council to receive an award. Live television cameras were present and recorded his appearance. After the pastor had been acknowledged, he made an exciting speech which his elected audience had not anticipated. Reverend Wolf took full advantage of the situation, declaring that suicide prevention does not stop on a rooftop but should be part of a plan that begins in Toronto's (and every other city's) City Council. Then Wolf added information which caught the uninitiated totally unprepared.

"I pastor a group of homosexuals," Wolf declared, shocking the unsuspecting officials, "and this sort of thing happens to our young people all too often! I would like to know what you are going to do to prevent this from happening again."

Television cameras zoomed in for close-ups!

"Do you have an idea what it's like to grow up homosexual in Canada?"

he thundered. "Well, I'd like to tell you now. And then you tell me what you plan doing for gay rights in Toronto!"

Newspaper reporters caught their breath and started writing. The shocked council members were without a clue as to how to proceed. Their main regret was that they were unable to shut off the busy television cameras which were capturing and relaying their distress.

Inasmuch as our Universal Fellowship is concerned, the most tangible result of Reverend Wolf's boldness was that, thereafter, Metropolitan Community Church in Toronto grew with considerably more speed. Canada, to our way of thinking, has always remained an international success!

July 1974 approached and I received an invitation from gay activists in Australia to visit and speak as a part of their multicity "Campaign Against Moral Persecution." Reverend Lee Carlton, who by then was my assistant pastor in the Mother Church, joined me in a journey for which he was greatly responsible. (In response to numerous letters we received from nations around the world, Lee handled the responses, and out of that correspondence developed the Australian invitation, which we accepted with considerable faith and great expectations.) Unfortunately, the beginning of our adventure Down Under was unexpectedly marred. Upon arrival in southeastern Queensland, we learned that a nonreligious faction in Sydney had decided, on political grounds, that they would not receive us.

Accustomed to adversity, Lee and I determined that we would not be deterred and would, unaided, advertise our presence by passing out religious and activist literature in front of gay bars. We soon discovered, however, that that idea would be a poor solution to our dilemma, because gay bars like those we have in America did not exist in Australia. Consequently, for several hours our mission seemed headed toward disaster, but near the end of the day, a long-distance call to us from Acceptance, a small gay Catholic group in Sydney, considerably brightened our prospects. As we apprehensively began our five-hundred-mile airplane flight south along the continent's eastern coast, it was a considerable relief to know that the Catholics would make certain that our arrival in New South Wales' capital city would not go unnoticed.

Nor was it!

We were met by representatives from every television station, radio network, and newspaper syndicate with offices in Sydney. From that moment on, wherever we went in any part of Australia, neither Lee nor

I could move, say, or do anything without rapt media attention. If a carnival atmosphere was created, we participated willingly, and in the end we won all of the games. During the month we remained in Australia, I appeared on forty-eight television and twenty-two radio shows. Every paper and magazine in the country ran daily articles about us. Wherever we went, groups formed and began thinking about religion and sexual freedom in ways they had never considered before.

We simply asked the question, "Are you interested in becoming a part of M.C.C.?" and congregations began to form with a nucleus of interested people. That step enabled Metropolitan Community Church to become important in the future of Australia, because once we had offered the suggestion, Australians set out on their own to keep the dream alive.

After Sydney, we were welcomed in Melbourne, Adelaide and Perth. Included among our hosts, which varied from city to city, were people in the Campaign Against Moral Persecution, who picked up the torch their associates had dropped in Sydney. Our host in Adelaide was Reverend Stan Harris. Reverend Harris started a group called Christ's Community Church—later to become Australia's first congregation in the Universal Fellowship of Metropolitan Community Churches.

When we departed on our return flight to North America, we left excitement behind us, and also carried excitement with us! Not long afterward, I was elected to be the first moderator of our Fellowship, and Reverend Carlton replaced me as the pastor of the Mother Church. Both of us retained fond memories of Australia, but Lee, although occupied with his ministry in Los Angeles, nurtured a potent dream of returning to the friendly continent.

Lee Carlton was born on February 16, 1947, about fifty miles south of Tallahassee where I was born, and by strange coincidence, Lee's city of birth was Perry, Florida. He had two brothers and one sister. The sister died early. His older brother was gay, and the younger brother became an ordained minister in the Church of God, following in the footsteps of their father. With a call of his own to the ministry, Lee attended Northwest Bible College in Minot, North Dakota, and while still in college, he was married.

"I wanted to be a minister more than anything," Lee recalled, "but in that church you aren't accepted if you're a single person. You can't even be a missionary if you're single. So I did what was required—I married—even though I knew I had homosexual tendencies. I told my wife of my sexual concern during our courtship, but she was not deterred.

Counselors in the church assured us that all I needed was 'the love of a good woman.'"

After graduation, Reverend Carlton accepted an assignment in Michigan. He became a civilian chaplain for the air force, and off base pastored a congregation which was also comprised primarily of military personnel. During that period, a baby was born to Lee and his wife, but the inexperienced father nevertheless continued to agonize because of his maturing homosexual feelings.

"I really began to struggle with this entire situation of being gay without ever having had any choice in the matter, and yet feeling unworthy in God's sight," Lee said. "To accentuate the problem, our denomination (which happily forgives adulterous ministers after a maximum two-year loss of credentials) passed a ruling that if you were even suspected of homosexuality, your credentials would be withdrawn and you could *never* be reinstated! Threatened by such an attitude, I left the ministry, returned to Florida, settled in Tampa with my wife and child, and sold shoes. My idea was to continue to attend church, to remain safely married—and also to secretly fulfill my closeted sexual needs.

"But my yearnings were deeper. I didn't just want to have sex with another man. I wanted to love another man! There is a considerable difference, and in my head, psychologically, I was tearing myself to pieces!

"I kept praying. I made myself feel like a sinner. Finally, one day when I felt really bad, I said, 'God, I know you can't possibly love me anymore.' Immediately thereafter, I literally received a response from heaven. God said, 'Don't you tell me whom I cannot love! Open your Bible and read my Word!'

"Three times those words were repeated.

"I returned to a church in the denomination where I had been pastoring, knelt alone before the altar, and prayed, 'Dear Heavenly Father, if there is any truth in that hymn, "Just as I am, without one plea thy blood was shed for me," well, here I am. I am a homosexual, but I know now that you love me. I don't know how, and I don't know where, but I know I will serve you again!'

"Only a few months later, members of Metropolitan Community Church from Miami walked into the Tampa store where I worked. At first, because of the collars they were wearing, I thought they were Catholic priests. Then when they asked, 'Are you Reverend Carlton?' I nearly dropped the shoebox I was holding into the lap of a customer. But an hour later, during a long coffee break, my special visitors invited me to Miami to see for myself what it is like when sincere gay people gather to worship.

"It was the year our Chi-Rho cross was beginning to be used. When a banner with that insignia emblazoned upon it was carried down the aisle, the congregation stood and nearly came to attention. It was like being at a patriotic rally! I looked around and saw that almost everybody had tears in their eyes. I must tell you I had never really experienced the meaning of 'thrilling' until that moment! The format of M.C.C.'s worship was different from what I had previously experienced, but the spirit was the same, only intensified—a positive discharge of deep inner emotions which is impossible to adequately describe!

"I returned to the west coast of central Florida, determined to found a Metropolitan Community Church in Tampa. After a month of searching for a building, I still had found nothing suitable. Then, as I often do, I put out what I call a 'fleece for the Lord.' I prayed, 'Jesus, if M.C.C. is really the place for me to be, if M.C.C. is really of God and not a heresy, I want a building. And Lord, I want it no later than Wednesday at high noon. If I don't have it by then, I will consider this all to have been a mistake and not the calling you intend for me. Amen!'

"So I met with the Presbyterian church on Monday, asking to rent from them, and I was turned down. The Women's Club turned me down on Tuesday. By Wednesday morning I was short on hope and very depressed. There seemed no reason to get out of bed. But at eleven fifty-five the telephone rang. A woman's voice said, 'Reverend Carlton? This is Sister Marion from the Franciscan Retreat Center. I understand you're looking for a place to hold services?'

" 'We are,' I replied.

" 'Good,' she said. 'The sisters and I have discussed it. If you would like to worship here, you may use our chapel.'

"Instantly, I told the sister how delighted I was. And then I asked, 'How did you find out about M.C.C.?'

" 'Oh, we have our ways,' she answered.

"How the Lord does work, I thought to myself. As I replaced the telephone, I glanced at my watch. The time was exactly twelve o'clock noon!"

Within a fortnight, when the first service was held on a balmy evening in Tampa, in April 1971, there were eighty persons present for worship. Included was the Miami Metropolitan Community Church's choir which had driven the Tamiami Trail through the Florida Everglades. In the front row sat Lee Carlton's father. Near him were all of the nuns from the Franciscan Retreat.

"Our church grew from there, and so did I!" said Lee, "My only regret was the ensuing separation between my dad and me. During that first service, he came to fully realize the meaning of my new ministry. Being a harsh, fundamentalist type of preacher, he seemed to be distressed as much by my wearing a minister's robe as he was with the idea of homosexuality.

" 'Son, I hope you know what kind of mess you're getting yourself involved with,' he said, and the hurt began a separation between us which lasted for fifteen years. When peace finally returned, it had much to do with my mother bringing Dad to the realization that his only obligation to me was to love me. When that hurdle of long duration was finally overcome, my father shook my lover's hand for the first time, put his arm around my shoulder as he had not done for many years, and made certain we would join him in his house for New Year's dinner. At the table, all of us joined hands for the blessing. In the Southern culture where I come from, that's acceptance."

Amen.

Lee Carlton had been leading Tampa's Metropolitan Community Church for a year and a half when I needed a new assistant pastor to help me minister to the Mother Church's large congregation. I prayed to the Lord to help me determine who my assistant should be. The answer was Lee Carlton.

Lee could handle problems. He was dependable in a crisis, and invaluable in 1973 during the dreadful days after our original church building at the corner of Twenty-second and Union was burned. The Los Angeles congregation liked Lee, and more often than not, there was standing room only for soul-stirring sermons he preached in the large new building we purchased downtown. As a result, Reverend Carlton became pastor of the Mother Church when a constantly expanding national membership required me to become our Universal Fellowship's full-time moderator.

One of Carlton's first appointments as assistant pastor had been for him to be secretary of our board of evangelism (which was supplemented by the board of world missions—which became the board of World Church Extension). When Lee accepted the appointment, it was partly because he was intrigued by thirty-two unanswered letters in my office containing inquiries about our gospel from such diverse countries as France, Italy, Yugoslavia, Nigeria, Denmark, Argentina, New Zealand, Australia, and a few other nations where, miraculously, word was being spread about the existence of Metropolitan Community Church.

It was as a result of Reverend Carlton's correspondence that we traveled across the Pacific in the summer of 1974. Afterward, in November of that same year, Lee also made a visit to Nigeria. It happened because of an article printed in a Jehovah's Witness publication called *The Watchtower* which had found its way to Africa. The publication mentioned that Metropolitan Community Church, with our homosexual outreach, was one of the world's fastest-growing churches. Although the writer did not intend to be favorable toward us, the printed words nevertheless attracted the attention of two good Christians in Nigeria. They read between the lines of condemnation, gleaned positive information (quite to the contrary of what was intended), and wrote to us.

We learned that the situation in Nigeria (on the western coast of equatorial Africa) was that 90 percent of the population was Moslem. The remainder were severely underprivileged Biafrans who had been exposed to many Christian denominations. According to our correspondent, the ecumenical vision inherent in Metropolitan Community Church, with successful unification of people from all Christian churches, appealed to the Biafrans.

But none of us in our Fellowship were certain the Biafrans really understood who we were. Nevertheless, in Africa, they proceeded on their own to obtain an adobe brick building with a tin roof, and found themselves a preacher, Reverend Maduka, who previously had been a Methodist minister. Then, Maduka kept writing us in the United States, asking someone to travel to Nigeria to set their church in order.

Lee came to our Board of Elders and requested money that would be needed. He explained that he had seen a worldwide vision of Metropolitan Community Church which grew from the package of thirty-two letters he had obtained from my office. His dream was persuasive, and shortly thereafter Lee embarked upon his journey into the Third World, where frequent shifts of politics and starving multicultural peoples are continuing facts of life.

"They met me at the airport," said Reverend Carlton, "carrying a sign that said, 'The Son of Man has come to seek, and to save, that which was lost,' a quotation from the Book of John. When I set foot on the ground, they bowed and we shook hands. I was introduced to Reverend Maduka. Afterward, all of us piled into their car and we drove sixty bumpy miles to Zaria.

"Over the church they were flying a U.F.M.C.C. flag which they had made. Inside, people were in the process of packing down the dirt floor, using water they had hand-carried for over a mile. Three other Christian groups existed in the town, Catholic, Anglican, and Presbyterian, each with white pastors. Ours was the only congregation with a black pastor. Maduka conducted services using the Ibo language into which a few words of English were mixed. Easier for me to understand were familiar gospel songs whose music is an international language.

"During my stay, I involved myself with church organization, recognized Reverend Maduka as their pastor, and was asked to pray for the sick. I saw all sorts of people who stood in a long line waiting to see me. Some of the members had walked ten miles to come to M.C.C."

Since that time, as years have passed, more and more church groups have been established, together with a health facility, the Metropolitan Community Clinic. Because of the clinic's success, Nigeria's government has now given our Fellowship land upon which to build a hospital, and that work is progressing with the help of local people who donate their labor.

In regard to our Fellowship's outreach to the lesbian and gay communities, Reverend Carlton was the first of our clergy to attempt to discern the sexual situation in Africa, but our Nigerian membership, concerned primarily with the fact that our denomination accepts people from all churches, provided little information. A decade later we were still seeking to expand our knowledge. As a result of some questions, Reverend Elder Jean White, current leader of our Global Outreach, received a letter from Reverend Maduka, stating, "You keep asking me about the matter of homosexuality. I can only repeat that I do not know how many homosexuals we have, or who is or who isn't. The important thing here is caring for souls and making a better world. After all, as you must agree, there is no place in the Bible that says only homosexuals can be Christians!"

When Lee Carlton returned from Africa (and a side trip to Western Europe), many ideas about missions to various parts of the world stirred powerful thoughts in his imagination. And because of the success of his visits, particularly to Australia, Reverend Carlton, even though he was pastor of the Mother Church, soon was up to his old trick of putting out fleeces for the Lord. In December 1974, Lee was wanting to know if God would like him to participate in a second mission to Australia!

It was obvious Lee wanted to return.

"I began to feel a thing for Australia," explains Reverend Carlton, "and a feeling of urgency began to grow in me. I would sit at my pastor's desk trying to work and suddenly be overwhelmed by concern for people across the sea. Behind my desk was a map of the world. On each continent I had stuck in little silver pins wherever we had an established church or a new mission—in Nigeria, France, England, Denmark, Canada— and included were pins for many of the places Troy and I had visited in Australia. Often I would turn around from my desk and place my hand on those pins, and pray for the individuals they represented—and feel that I should be with them.

"Yet there were many reasons why I should remain in Los Angeles. I loved the Mother Church and wanted to see it grow. Besides, how could I arrange for my lover to accompany me? However, as I pondered, I received word that two leaders of Acceptance, Gary Pie and Graham Duncan, were coming to visit. 'Suppose they ask me to return to Australia?' I asked myself. 'What should I do?'

"So I put a fleece before God. I said, 'God, I'm not going to say anything about this to the Australians, but if you really want me to go to Australia, the Aussies will initiate my move, asking me by name to go Down Under.'

"When Graham and Gary arrived, I purposely gave them no indication I had any interest in returning to their country. They visited our church, visited my home, remained in Los Angeles for an entire weekend. They went to Christmas Eve service in the Mother Church. Then on Christmas, the day before they were to depart, we were all sitting on my sofa. Still, nothing had been said. I began telling myself that the Lord didn't want me to go to Australia, and I knew that I loved the L.A. church and leaving its congregation would be the hardest thing I'd ever done in my life. I was thinking all of those things when suddenly I realized what my guests were saying.

" 'Lee, we have a whole continent full of people, but we have nothing like this church!' exclaimed one of the visiting Australians. 'You know we have a lot of gay people who are really hungry for a Protestant denomination. We have Acceptance, but it leaves a wide-open door for M.C.C. If you come to Australia, we'll offer you any support we can give!'

After that, there was no stopping Reverend Carlton. When he expressed to me his concern about leaving the Mother Church, I told him, "Lee, you know I also had to agonize about leaving, but you have to obey God and do what you believe. If God is calling, go."

Happily, Lee made preparations to move. He gave notice to his congregation that he was resigning. His lover ended a lucrative career to accompany him. Everything seemed in good order until Lee's visa was unexpectedly denied. Reverend Carlton was on the Nixon "Enemies List" of suspected subversives!

Never before had any of us realized what a threat to the government gays can be! The worst thing Lee had ever done was to speak in behalf of America's gay and lesbian population, asking that we receive the same rights under the law as all citizens are guaranteed by our Constitution!

Fortunately, a knowledgeable gay brother in the Australian consulate was able to sidestep the ridiculous problem. (And, years later, the inaccurate list was discredited.)

Reverend Carlton and his lover arrived in Australia in March 1975, and because our requirements for chartering a church were much less stringent at that time than they are now, by the Fourth of July the church in Sydney, with only about thirty-five members, became part of our Fellowship. Thereafter, the Metropolitan Community Church of Sydney continued to grow very rapidly.

"At first, my intention was to begin as many works as possible during the two years I planned to stay," said Lee. "I merely intended to show our Australian friends how to look for clergy, how to put a church together, and encourage them to join the Fellowship. But it was God's time. Even though the work was hard, everywhere we turned our efforts were blessed.

"We soon became the largest gay group that met in Sydney on a regular basis. I was pastor and I began training lay people as quickly as possible to assume pastoral duties. Gay clergy from other denominations came over to M.C.C. and were vital in our development.

"I spoke freely while in Australia, commenting to the press about gay issues even though I recognized the necessity of choosing my words carefully. I didn't want to be expelled. Homosexuality had not yet been decriminalized as it now has in all of Australia's states except—wouldn't you know—Queensland!

"On the day of arrival, I was attacked in the press by the dean of Sydney's Anglican cathedral, Lance Shelton. Sydney's *Morning Herald* had been full of the news that I was coming to their continent, and Dean Shelton's reaction was a declaration that all homosexuals should be severely condemned. My response to his attack came two weeks later. After checking to be certain that Shelton would personally be celebrating Mass on a particular Sunday, I gathered my little band of about fourteen M.C.C.'ers. All of us donned lavender armbands and in a group attended the Anglican cathedral.

"A vestry committee began whispering the moment we entered their echoing, gray stone building. Not knowing why we were present, nervous Anglican guardians remained throughout the service, standing at each end of several front aisles where we were located. Our only transgressions were to sing louder than anybody else, and after the hymns, to resume our seats only when the regular congregation had already taken theirs. After the service, when the vestry asked their big question, 'Why are you here?' I walked past them and approached Lance Shelton, who had been watching from what he considered a safe distance.

" 'I'm Reverend Lee Carlton of Metropolitan Community Church,' I told the dean. 'We did not, nor would we, disrupt your services, but we are willing to come here to let you and yours look upon us. If you are going to talk about homosexuals, condemn us, or continue to be uncharitable, then let us see if you will do so face to face in the house of God!'

"The dean nearly dropped his teeth! He had never dreamed that a gay person would dare to come forward and challenge him. His country, unlike ours, was not founded for religious freedom. His Anglican cathedral had enjoyed the myopic privilege of heading their State Church until the year when Australia became an independent member of the British Commonwealth.

"To be told by an opinionated Dean that one cannot be a gay Christian is bad enough, but to hear similar drivel from another homosexual is something else again. That irritation occurred on another occasion during my first year when I was speaking at Australia's First National Homosexual Conference. I had just taken the stand to talk when a lesbian shouted from the back of the room that she didn't want to hear me because, 'There's no such thing as gay and Christian!'

" 'Sister—,' I said, as I would often say sister—or brother—to address someone in the States.

" 'I'm not *your* sister!' she roared back.

"For a moment I hesitated, hot under the collar. Then I said, '*Person!* Let me tell you one damn thing!' and the entire conference suddenly became silent. 'A long time ago I stopped apologizing to Christians for being gay. Now you want it the other way. Well, I'll be damned if I'm going to start apologizing to gays for being Christian! So I'd be pleased if you'll remember I have the floor!' And with that there was applause because, although M.C.C. was not one of the founding pillars of gay and lesbian liberation Down Under, all of the Aussies at least realized I was sincere and that we meant business!"

With Lee's audacity and courage, Metropolitan Community Church came to stand among the other lesbian and gay organizations in Australia. After two years, when Reverend Carlton left the western South Pacific (which at that time we called the District of Australasia), there were eight of our churches in Australia and one in Auckland, New Zealand, with a combined membership in excess of 750 persons. We could not have hoped for greater success. Recollecting those early years, one of the most interesting confirmations of our prayers for Australia occurred in Sydney while Lee was pastoring.

"After a worship service," Lee tells us, "a lesbian in her sixties and her friend came to me with tears in their eyes. 'I've got to tell you a story,' the older woman said, and although I had never met either of them, I immediately felt as if we had known each other for a long time.

" 'Until recently, I was head of women's ministry in the Anglican church,' the lesbian told me. 'They didn't ordain women, of course, but we had input where women's issues were concerned. On one occasion, I was called and asked to go to a home to be with a neighborhood woman who had just discovered that her only son, who was gay, had killed himself. The date was the sixth of October, 1968. I remember it very well. I was dreadfully shaken because I knew I was also gay, a secret which at that time I had never divulged to anyone. I remember getting down on my knees beside the dead son's bed and consoling his mother. There was a note saying he was taking his life because he was homosexual and could no longer suffer being unacceptable.

" 'His mother said, "I pray that someday, somehow, someone will bring into existence a church that will accept gay people and let them know they don't have to do this—that God loves them!" And now, seven years later, here you are in Sydney. God bless you.'

"Then I told the kind lesbian the remaining part of the story, which she didn't know, that the first worship service of Metropolitan Community Church had taken place in America on October 6, 1968—the exact same date as the mother's prayer!"

In 1979, at our General Conference, Reverend Jean White, pastor of Metropolitan Community Church of London and nursing administrator of a large English hospital, was the first non-American elected to our Universal Fellowship's Board of Elders. Reverend Jean White inherited the portfolio of everything relating to World Church Extension.

"I knew there would be hardly anything in the files," recalled Jean, aware that in the preceding three or four years (the Anita Bryant and John Briggs years), gay groups throughout the United States had, of necessity, trimmed many activities and focused on our threatening home-grown enemy (in a series of battles that nearly seemed to have been won in 1979—until the advent of AIDS several years later brought hate-mongers out of the woodwork again). "Nevertheless, in the portfolio there was correspondence about our churches in England, New Zealand, Nigeria, and our affiliate in Denmark which had not yet become a member of M.C.C.," said Jean, "but there was little else!" (Australia and Canada are in individual districts and, consequently, not within the jurisdiction of World Church Extension.)

Since then, our global outreach has grown tremendously. What was begun by Reverend Carlton was carried forward by Reverend Freda Smith and then by Reverend White. Strategically located in England, Jean adds effective organizational skills to her expanding sphere of compassion. Reverend Jean White's education, her understanding of people, her realistic desire to serve, and foremost, her religion and her faith, are constantly refined and tested.

"We have contacts throughout the world," Jean can say today. "I write everywhere, even to people in Kuwait and Saudi Arabia where death is the penalty for being homosexual! We have contacts in Poland, people who don't meet in their own church, but who worship at M.C.C. when they come to London. There was a group behind the Iron Curtain, in East Germany, who managed to get together once a year and secretly take communion. And for one man in the Middle East, I write in code. We use the word *elephant* to mean homosexual. I might write, 'I met an elephant today in Piccadilly Circus,' which sounds crazy—if you don't know that the real word could cost the man his life."

Our work is never-ending. There are always letters to compose, always more words of wisdom, more hope, more love of God to send to people around the world. Jean pushes herself even when tiredness intrudes, making another visit, writing one more letter, knowing that any endeavor may raise a soul from the bitter, lonely depths of despair. To understand Jean's dedication to helping so many people she probably will never see, it is necessary to know something of the story of this amazing woman.

Jean White was reared in a puritanical, Calvinistic sect in England called the Plymouth Brethren. She was twenty-six before allowing her hair to be cut because the Bible said it was her "crowning glory." She trained as a nurse (and estimates having delivered more than five thousand babies). After feeling the call of the Lord, Jean attended three additional years of Bible school. She wanted to preach, but that created a conflict— the Brethren believed women should remain silent and not speak. Their only exception was missionaries.

"So I became engaged to a doctor and we were both called to Africa," remembers Jean. "He preceded me to the Congo, and as fate would have it, was one of several missionaries murdered when a rebellion occurred. I grieved about what had happened, but there was also a terrible, secondary feeling of relief because I was no longer obligated to be married.

I suppose I knew by then, although with considerable uncertainty, that heterosexuality was not the path for me."

Having impeccable credentials, Jean joined the China Inland Mission (later called Overseas Missionary Fellowship) and, as a single woman, she was sent to Macao, Portugal's colony not far from Hong Kong on the South China Sea. Twice a week missionaries were allowed to enter a narrow, overpopulated strip of territory separating the Portuguese colony from China. It was a no-man's land where desperate refugees, lepers both real and political, came to a medical clinic the mission operated. The work never seemed routine, and for years Jean happily immersed herself in their religious-medical effort.

Behind a shield of righteousness, Jean White protected herself from ugly realities of the world. Instilled in her mind was the idea that a legalistic, blind belief in every word of Scripture formed the only road leading to a stern, judgmental God. And while she worked to save the lives and souls of lepers and refugees, Jean felt secure with the thought that the Plymouth Brethren's way was the only way, and that she was avoiding "the Devil's domain" of human desire.

Sex did not exist.

Love was avoided.

Jean was not even certain that women who wore makeup or cut their hair could go to heaven, but if they did, first, they would stand before God and have a lot of explaining to do!

It was a tidy, giving, but narrow-minded world.

Jean's intolerance seemed unshakable.

Then the nightmare of Cultural Revolution exploded across China. Mao's government officially purged itself, searching for national progress in orgies of blood and denunciation. Intellectuals had their tongues removed and good people died. In the south, ruthless Red Guards and army tanks swept down through Kwangtung Province from Canton, taking the narrow strip of land where Jean worked, stopping at the border of Macao.

American missionaries evacuated.

"They left because they had more sense than others," declared Jean. "The rest of us continued to go back and forth across the heavily guarded border where trainloads of outcasts with handicaps were dumped on a daily basis. Often, we could hear machine gun fire. Always, blind and maimed stragglers brought with them horror stories of students forcing people to dig their own mass graves!"

Jean and other missionaries steadfastly continued to operate their clinic.

Twice a week they passed over a bridge from Macao, walking through increasingly crowded streets which every day seemed less friendly. The numbers of frightened refugees, including crippled young people, constantly increased.

" 'If you Westerners want these children, take them!' said bureaucratic soldiers as if they were handing over sacks of spoiled vegetables," Jean recalled. "We picked up two hundred and forty youngsters in a matter of days. The United States had agencies that came in and took them, but there were so many children that the situation became close to impossible. We had to build shanties to shelter some of the inflow."

There was no special portent of danger on a day that seemed little different from others. Trouble only became evident after the missionaries had left their medical clinic late in the afternoon, intending to return home. New guards were at the border and Jean, with others, was not allowed to cross. Several hours elapsed before she realized that they were prisoners at the mercy of a merciless government out of control.

"We went back to the clinic, thinking that in a few days we would be allowed out of China. Eventually, we realized that was not going to happen. Twelve of us women were brought together—ten preaching nuns from a Catholic order, a Swedish medical co-worker who was my friend, and myself. We were all put into a very small closed room, and in that room we remained most of the time for the next two years and eight months.

"That began a time of my life which was absolute hell! There were days when I doubted God. Believe me, if you have ten Catholic nuns saying rosaries on one side of a small room, and two evangelicals praying on the other, it becomes very traumatic!

"The first year was not our worst. We came to terms with the problems of being locked up, of living in a confined space. But in the second year, the Red Guard hauled us into court, and that began a period of absolute terror. I was accused of murdering a baby because I had given it an injection of penicillin.

"The trial lasted five days. During that time we had to stand beyond the point of exhaustion. If we began to fall, the Chinese put ropes around our waists and used them as a harness to jerk us upright. On the third day they started another way of making us jump. They soaked pieces of rag in kerosene and lit them. When we began to sag, they flipped the flaming cloth at our legs. I still have visible scars.

"At first I said, 'God, just let me die,' but the Lord gave me strength instead. I learned how much persecution can be suffered in Jesus' name. We were victims of insatiable rapists. In front of everybody, they even molested a nun who was in her seventy-second year. Our captors didn't care. It was a wonder that in the third year, eight of us got out alive.

"On the twenty-first of August, 1969, after governments bargained for us, the Red Guard permitted our release, but even at the end there was no mercy. We had to crawl to the old bridge that led to freedom, and as we struggled to pull ourselves toward the other side, two of the nuns collapsed. We used all of our failing strength to drag them across the border. We thought they had merely lapsed into unconsciousness, but when we arrived in Macao, authorities informed us they were dead."

Suffering from malnutrition, Jean White was taken to Hong Kong, then to a hospital in England. One of her lungs had to be removed. Plastic surgery was performed on her legs. In the process, Jean was careful not to forget that during the ordeal of imprisonment, she had done more than merely survive. She had also begun coming to terms with herself.

"It wasn't easy to admit that all during my time as a missionary, I knew I was a lesbian," said Jean. "I still thought homosexuality was a sin. Yet I had promised God that if I ever left China alive, I would deal honestly with my inner knowledge that I preferred women. And I would find out if there were other gay Christians anywhere. But once I was safe and on the road to regaining my health, there seemed to be less urgency in confronting the problem of being double-minded. Resolutions faded with the joy of being free. Coming home to England tended to make me forget.

"It was flagrant discrimination against women that triggered the restoration of my resolve. I began to question my denomination's rules that encouraged missionary women like myself to hold services and to celebrate communion in the field, but allowed only men to publicly lead prayer at home. It was a false double standard that encouraged me to present picture slides of little Chinese children to raise money, and then required 'proper female silence' in our church. I started looking for answers.

"I went to libraries for information about being gay, and I asked questions of women friends who lived together. Someone referred me to the dean of an Anglican church in London. He was a fine married man with two children, so I thought he wouldn't know what homosexuality was all about—and he surely wouldn't be able to help me. I had little understanding of women's issues or gay liberation. The dean, however, did. He was gay! That little bit of information shook my naive psyche to its foundations."

In many ways, the dean who counseled Jean White was like an interested psychiatrist. He made it his purpose to be of help to many who needed help. Every few weeks he sat with Jean and they studied the Bible, or argued and discussed matters of sexual liberation. After three years, when she was physically healthy, back to nursing, and nearly ready to consider accepting another mission to a foreign country, the dean announced to Jean that it was time she learned something about the existing homosexual community.

"I had never been to a bar," Jean said. "I didn't drink. Nevertheless, we went to a party where there were lots of people playing roles. It wasn't appealing to me, but there was one woman whom I met and liked, a doctor, and we talked for much of the evening. Before the party was over, my new friend decided that on another evening, she would introduce me to The Rehearsal, a mixed gay club in Soho where London's theaters are located.

"About three days later, we were leaving The Rehearsal at ten-thirty in the evening when it just so happened that a group of young people training with our foreign missions were distributing religious tracts at the nearby corner. One of the trainees saw us exiting. Although the woman didn't speak to me, she pointedly revealed my presence to the others, and I was petrified.

"Less than a week passed before I received a letter from the mission board asking me to come before their committee. I thought the summons was because they were prepared to give me an overseas assignment, but a secretary who worked in the office knew the actual reason. She warned me before I went inside. 'Do you know that you're going to be accused of being a lesbian?' she asked.

"My breath went out of me. I'm sure the blood must have drained from my face. 'What are you talking about?' I said.

"Well, you were seen departing from a den of iniquity holding hands with another woman," answered the secretary.

"I immediately searched my memory. I knew I had not been holding hands. And I thought, how ironic it was to be observed the very first time I ever went into a gay club. Me, who had never even been into an ordinary pub before! At first I thought being 'caught' was a cruel twist of fate. Now I realize it was God working in God's way."

There were seventeen men and no women on the mission panel Jean White faced. All the men were grim-faced as Jean entered their domain. They wasted no time accusing her of being homosexual.

"Maybe it's because of what happened to you in detention?" asked one man. "Maybe it's because you were raped," he said.

"Did that turn you against men?" asked another.

Jean tried to answer, but nothing she said bore any weight with her judges. "You must see a Christian psychiatrist," she was informed at the end of what seemed like an interminable inquisition, "and you must allow us to pray for you to cast out this lesbian demon! The alternative is for you to resign."

Inevitably, after several months, Jean chose the latter option. "It was difficult for me," she said. "I had never envisioned my life's work as being anything other than a missionary. But that was over.

"I made a decision to remain in the nursing profession. That was logical, but where was I to worship? The year 1972 was nearly at an end when my friend, the Anglican dean, insisted I attend a speech that Reverend Troy Perry from America was to deliver before the Committee for Homosexual Equality. 'Reverend Perry's here in England not only as a preacher,' said the dean, 'he's here because of his gay activism. His talk will be about a liberating gospel, something all of us need.'"

Following that introduction, Jean White joined a rapidly growing Bible study group called "Fellowship of Christ the Liberator" which, in 1973, was chartered as Metropolitan Community Church of London. Jean, already recovered from her physical captivity, was also well on her way to regaining religious health and well-being. While becoming the nursing administrator in a large hospital, she simultaneously became one of our student clergy and sat on the London church's board of directors.

In 1978, Jean White was licensed as a minister.

In 1979, Reverend Jean White was elected to the Board of Elders of our Universal Fellowship. As an elder, Jean not only was pastor of Metropolitan Community Church in London, she also became the chair and executive secretary of World Church Extension, an important work that she has performed with skill and devotion.

"In other countries we have had to proceed according to their laws and cultures," Jean is quick to tell us. "We have already translated our literature into Polish, Chinese, Danish, German, French, Italian, Spanish, Dutch, and Russian, and must continue the translation into many more languages.

"I have had to teach people in other countries that M.C.C. is not an American church," Jean continues. "It started in America—but M.C.C. is now a Christian church on an international level. The bigger our Fellowship becomes, the more countries in which we are located, the more complex everything gets. And we must never forget that we are Christ's ambassadors to foreign lands—sometimes hostile lands—particularly for gay and lesbian folk.

"This denomination has become life to me. Not a way of life—*life*! I feel I'm a whole person now—physically, emotionally, spiritually. M.C.C. has taught me there are many different ways of going to God. I know mine is acceptable. I cannot say our way is better than a brother's or a sister's whose life-style is totally different. And they should not say I am wrong. I thrive because God has given me a message of liberation!"

The world perceives us better every day. Mick Foley defies tradition and speaks openly in Dublin, Ireland, telling of God's inclusive love. In Djakarta, capital of Indonesia, Reverend Johanna Kawengian shepherds a group of women, mostly Moslem, who are converting to Christianity. Gay Baptists in Hamburg, West Germany, are interested in joining with us. Meeting in Barcelona, Spain, a group of ex-nuns and ex-priests have voted to apply for membership in the Universal Fellowship.

But Africans who want to preach our gospel in Ghana are frightened because their national laws are very antigay. In the Dominican Republic, our people pray on rooftops and often change the place of their worship for safety reasons. We could not buy a building in Greece because we had no permission from the Greek Orthodox Church.

In Mexico, it is against the law to hold services in any place except a church, and people who have prayer gatherings in their own homes can be arrested and sent to prison. Therefore, our Fellowship asked for a special offering and raised $40,000 to facilitate a purchase. However, there was a second problematical consideration: in accordance with Mexican law, all church holdings are automatically nationalized and become property of the state! Thus, any known form of worship displeasing to Mexican politicians can theoretically be easily eliminated, or at least badly crippled, by order of the government.

Nevertheless, not long after the devastating Mexican earthquake in 1985, our elders decided to chance helping to purchase a church property in Mexico City, hoping that their authorities would allow it to exist. And they have. With the help and guidance of Dr. Armando Hernandez, church extension officer of our Hispanic ministries in Mexico, the Metropolitan Community Church—called Iglesia de la Comunidad Metropolitana (I.C.M.) in Spanish—has flourished and been a model for numerous other groups in Latin America.

Dr. Hernandez told us that Swicegood's story of the founding of Metropolitan Community Church, *Our God, Too!*, has, in a Spanish translation, always been recommended reading for church members in Mexico City. Dr. Hernandez discovered that "an immense number" of the hardcover books, printed in Spain and retitled *Tambien es nuestro*

Dios, were being surreptitiously sold from under bookstore counters in macho Mexico.

As a youth, Armando Hernandez wanted to be a priest, but became a doctor of medicine instead. Both are generally humanitarian callings. When Armando discovered Metropolitan Community Church he said, "I.C.M. united the two aspects of my being. I.C.M. has been a great help to many people and to me, making people feel welcome who were made unwelcome in other groups. In our church we have friendship. We are a Fellowship that extends from our relationship with God."

After that, Armando spoke about religion in Mexico. "Our church is growing very fast," he said through his interpreter. "According to the Mexican Constitution, we have freedom of religion, but all churches are required to be registered. Sometimes we have a little fear, but up to now the government has been fair, not dictatorial. We don't advertise in newspapers. We pass information by word of mouth. And so far there has been no violence against us."

Praise God!

The good doctor's words describing caution and secrecy sounded much like those used in the United States forty years earlier—when secret gay groups such as Harry Hay's Mattachine Society began forming in California at the conclusion of World War II.

"My family consists of my lover, my brother, and my mother," continued Dr. Hernandez. "Mother refrains from being curious about my private life. I don't live at home and she is only aware that I am involved in an ecumenical type of church. It helps that Mother is very liberal—she has never asked if I.C.M. is Catholic or non-Catholic!"

Thus, with faith and a sense of humor, and with people like Bob Wolf, Lee Carlton, Jean White, Armando Hernandez, and tens of thousands of lesbian and gay people who are similar to them in many ways, the World Church Extension of our Universal Fellowship inevitably continues.

12

Dialogue with
Christians: 1974 . . .

*For whosoever shall give you a cup of water
to drink in my name, because you belong to
Christ, verily I say unto you, they shall not
lose their reward.*

—Mark 9:41

WHEN I was a young Pentecostal minister, I was taught that ecumenical organizations perform work for the Devil! Another imaginative interpretation of the Book of Revelations thrust upon me was the fundamentalists' belief that in the last days of people on earth, there will exist a superchurch embracing the Antichrist. The superchurch, according to fundamentalist biblical belief, will precede Armageddon, after which Jesus Christ will return.

I grew up observing intensely religious people who seemed anxious to witness the end of the world. I believe some would have precipitated total destruction to arrive in glory sooner. My idea has always been different. No matter what some theologians may conclude from biblical predictions, I cling to the philosophy that is of proven importance— namely, that *prayer changes things.* Consequently, I have never held the belief that Armageddon is inevitable, and I have never been burdened with a fundamentalist fear of the Catholic church, or of ecumenical bodies like the World Church or the National Council of Churches.

My Pentecostal peers also believed that there was no reason to work or pray with other groups, because each splintered faction decided that it—and it alone—was God's true church. In doctrine, my fundamentalist acquaintances were so ultraconservative that to them Baptists were backsliders! Years later, despite my background, the temporary lack of interest I manifested in the National Council of Churches stemmed not from theological mythology, but from a suspicion that the National Council might be overly liberal.

I have never known evil to derive from an ecumenical Christian relationship. Quite the opposite. In the process of founding Metropolitan Community Church, I did not attempt to copy Pentecostal perceptions of an angry God, nor was intolerance part of the religious baggage I brought with me. Members of our Universal Fellowship come from so many different backgrounds that in diversity we have found unity.

In 1974, at our General Conference held in San Francisco, when I learned that a resolution stating we should consider applying for membership in ecumenical and interreligious organizations (including the National Council of the Churches of Christ in the U.S.A.) was to be presented by one of our new pastors from Boston, Reverend Nancy Wilson, I was not alarmed. Nor was I impressed. Some of our members even laughed at what they considered a pointless resolution. It was voted in the affirmative, nevertheless, without much concern for two reasons: there was no time limit set for making any application, and when, or if such ever occurred, it would only be at the discretion of those of us elected to our governing Board of Elders.

After the seemingly innocuous resolution passed, I proceeded to forget about it. Membership in the World or National Council of Churches was not one of my priorities. Reverend Wilson, however, whom I had met the year before on a trip to charter the Metropolitan Community Church in Boston, was a very determined woman who would not desist, as I would learn.

Nancy Wilson's mother had been a Quaker, her father a Baptist. Born in 1950, she lived her early years in Plainview, Long Island, a suburban environment where she belonged to the United Methodist Church. Her friends were Catholics and Jews, with a sprinkling of Protestants. Nancy found all religions interesting, but only in moderation.

Puberty was not an onset of joy for the girl who became aware of loneliness as her body developed but her interest in boys did not. It was an emotional crisis which the anxious teenager could not communicate to her loving parents or teachers or friends. But she was soon to learn that there would be a better time.

On a wintry evening, suffering from depression, Nancy was alone in her home. Turning away from a window, she glimpsed herself in the looking glass and recognized sadness in her own eyes. She was confused, frustrated. Then something important occurred. Nancy describes what happened: "I had a very profound experience of spiritual comfort. I believe God came to me as a friend. God said, 'It is all right—in the proper time you will understand. The friendship and the love you are seeking will eventually be found.' It was a clear message, one that did not originate from within myself. I can never forget that moment."

At thirteen, Nancy decided she wanted to become a minister, which was particularly unusual because in 1963 very few women were in the ministry. Revealing that ambition to her mother resulted in resistance rather than encouragement. Nevertheless, after graduating from high schoool, Nancy journeyed to the western part of Pennsylvania to attend Allegheny College, a Methodist school by tradition. It was there, in 1970, that she heard Barbara Gittings and Frank Kameny speak. Those two very normal-looking people told what it was like to be homosexual, creating a moment of truth (or a moment of terror) for students and faculty in that small midwestern college. Only Nancy was "enraptured," yet another two years passed before the mature woman emerged.

Coming out was a pleasure for Nancy. There was no struggle with God. By then, she had long since realized that heaven and nature were both on her side. The problem was deciding what she, as a lesbian who wanted to be in the clergy, who sought a church embracing many traditions, who had donated considerable time to work in a crisis-counseling center, could accomplish with the remainder of her life. Entering the ministry was a small, but real, possibility. Women were being recruited by seminaries for the first time in history—but seminaries were not looking for women who were gay. And that was at the same time when Nancy had finally accepted her true sexuality!

Seminary doors would slam shut for Nancy if she ever publicly revealed the truth about herself. Yet she refused to be frightened back into the closet. Fortunately, there were no questions on the seminary application that forthrightly asked, "Are you gay? Are you a lesbian? Do you like women?"

Boston's Metropolitan Community Church held its first service for a small, diverse group in exactly the same week of 1972 that Nancy Wilson began her graduate studies at Boston University's School of Theology. It was then when Reverend Larry Bernier appearerd on a radio program entitled "Gay Way" with Elaine Nobel. As a representative to the Massachusetts state legislature, Elaine became America' first important, openly gay politician to be elected to public office, but it was the homosexual minister who fascinated Nancy the most. "I'm looking for a woman, preferably in the seminary," said Reverend Bernier. "We need a women who is able to co-pastor our new, gay-oriented church. Please call my number if you are interested.

Nancy dialed immediately and left a message. "I can't believe I'm doing this," she told a friend. Everything she could ever achieve in the Methodist church was at risk. "But it was irresistible! I consecrated communion in the new church on the following Sunday and preached one week later," said Nancy, "I was out of the closet at seminary before the end of the month. It was wonderful. The unique ministry Larry and I had to lesbians and gay men grew phenomenally."

Without money, but with intelligence and imagination, Nancy joined in what she wanted, a great spiritual endeavor. "M.C.C. was so small in those days," she said, "that I knew I could make a difference. I was caught up in the emotion. And I also became a feminist. In M.C.C., religion, activism, lesbianism, and feminism all seemed to go together. I'd always had a feeling there was something for me to do with my life— in M.C.C. I found it. I knew we were on to something very important and powerful—something we could understand better only as we lived it."

Seven years after the General Conference in which she had introduced her resolution concerning interreligious affiliations, Reverend Elder Nancy Wilson was a leader in our denomination, and by 1981, she was convinced the time had arrived to make her dream come true. At Nancy's urging, members of our Board of Elders, including myself, agreed to apply for membership in the National Council of the Churches of Christ in the U.S.A. It was understood that the main body of work would be Nancy's, and I, an ex-Pentecostal, would support her efforts.

During our General Conference in Houston, we announced our decision and it was carried by the press. The National Council's response, also via media, was swift, putting us on notice that any approach toward them from Metropolitan Community Church would be "impertinent foolishness." Obviously, they were not ready for us. But Nancy, with my blessings, decided that we were ready for them!

We created our Department of Ecumenical Relations. Reverend Wilson and Adam DeBaugh were named co-directors. Together, we sought to make certain that as a denomination we were not making our application for any wrong reasons. To be precise, a wrong reason would be to believe that Metropolitan Community Church needed the National Council of Churches to legitimize our existence. The Holy Spirit legitimized us. Further authorization is not required.

However, we realized that should we be summarily rejected by the Council, our enemies would triumphantly point their fingers at us and say, "See, even the ultraliberal N.C.C. won't have them! They're not legitimate!" But such a possibility (it was informally calculated among ourselves) could be risked. If the National Council of Churches voted us down, we could endure the pressure.

Our primary objective was to give a gift and to receive a gift. From the Council's ecumenical cluster we desired fellowship with other Christians. It is not easy to stand alone. Like holy people everywhere, we gay followers of Jesus have our enemies. Some of our antagonists are from our own community, gay people who were so badly mistreated by their own churches that they will never return to Christ! Consequently, for thirteen years we had been on the battlements of Christianity, beset by Christians and non-Christians, gays and nongays, a situation never to our desire. It would take the assistance of an organization like the National Council of Churches to end our lonely devotion.

The gift we offered them was a new reality, less restrictive than their narrow theology of deified heterosexuality. We offered a broader, more inclusive understanding of sexuality, and the opportunity to reconsider their ideas concerning religion, love—and sex, which too many of them still believed to be Christianity's "dirty little secret." To be sexual but not to speak of it is an illogical idea that has plagued some churches for centuries.

Adam DeBaugh wrote our Fellowship's letter of application. It was four pages long and he intended for Nancy to shorten and rewrite his words, but she and I were both of the opinion that his work was excellent. As a result, the first draft of Adam's letter became the Metropolitan Community Churches' application for membership in the National Council of the Churches of Christ in the U.S.A. Dated September 9, 1981, the letter was signed by Reverend Elder Nancy L. Wilson and Mr. R. Adam DeBaugh, co-directors of the Universal Fellowship's Department of Ecumenical Relations. The last pages of our application read:

> In thirteen years, the U.F.M.C.C. has grown considerably—and often in the face of tremendous adversity and challenge from outside our Fellowship. Over twelve of our churches have been destroyed by arson, a percentage unequaled in any other communion to our knowledge. Our clergy and lay people have been threatened, beaten and even killed. Our church buildings have been desecrated and vandalized. Our congregations have been denied places to meet for worship. Crosses have been burned on our church property; threats have been made over the telephone, in person and in print to our people; our ministry has been vilified, condemned, threatened and slandered; and the U.F.M.C.C. has been used by unscrupulous people to frighten their constituents into giving them money to continue

their fight against us. We have been attacked in the name of Jesus whom we follow. And a small vocal minority has attacked our right to join in fellowship with our brother and sister Christians in the National Council of Churches.

Why has this been true? Why do we often feel like the early Church, set upon from every side? Why does the Universal Fellowship of Metropolitan Community Churches excite such anger and hatred from some of our Christian brothers and sisters? The answer to these questions has nothing to do with our liturgy and worship, which comes from the mainstream of the Christian Church; nor does it have anything to do with our polity, which is familiar to most communions; nor does it have anything to do with the Gospel of salvation, social action and community.

We are criticized because we minister in a loving and caring way to a despised and rejected minority—homosexuals. Our critics ignore the fact that this is not our only ministry. The U.F.M.C.C. reaches out to all people who are excluded. Our ministry includes prisoners, the deaf, the blind, the handicapped and disabled, racial and ethnic minorities, the aged, institutionalized persons, alcoholics and other chemically dependent people, terminally ill persons, the poor and the hungry, and many others. Yet those ministries are not only not criticized, they are seldom acknowledged outside of our Fellowship.

It is our acceptance of homosexuality as a gift from God in the same way that heterosexuality is a gift from God that arouses fear, anger and hatred in some of our sisters and brothers. It is our affirmation of God's love for *all* people, including homosexuals, that upsets people. It is our theological understanding, based on careful Biblical scholarship, that God does not condemn homosexuality per se anywhere in the Holy Scriptures that people seize upon to condemn us. What infuriates some people is our assertion that the traditional interpretations of scriptures to condemn homosexuality are as incorrect and invalid as the old interpretations of scriptures which permitted the holding of slaves and the subjugation of black people.

Yet while we disagree with some of our Christian brothers and sisters (and not all Christians disagree with our position, by any means), is that a reason to deny our church fellowship with other communions in the National Council of Churches? We would remind our brothers and sisters of the section of the Bylaws of the N.C.C. which requires that member communions demonstrate "a spirit of cooperation with, and respect for, the convictions of other communions." Allowing us to join the National Council of Churches in no way indicates your agreement with our position on homosexuality, either as an ecumenical body or as individual churches. Nor does our membership in the N.C.C. indicate our agreement with some policies of some of the member communions of the N.C.C., some churches' refusal to ordain women, for instance . . .

We call upon the National Council of Churches of Christ in the U.S.A. to examine our application for membership on its merits, not on false issues of our position on homosexuality. Look at the totality of what the Universal Fellowship of Metropolitan Community Churches is and preaches and does. . . .

On behalf of the General Conference and the Board of Elders of the Universal Fellowship of Metropolitan Churches, we formally apply for membership for the U.F.M.C.C. in the National Council of the Churches of Christ in the United States of America.

Our application was mailed to the offices of the National Council of Churches in New York City. After months of delay, Dr. Robert Campbell, head of the American Baptist church (and chair of the Council's Constituent Membership Committee), told Adam that he considered our submission a "hot potato." Fortunately, he was replaced by Reverend Dr. Oscar McCloud and, finally, a meeting was called on March 15, 1982, to determine if the Membership Committee (*a*) found us worthy to be recommended to their Governing Board (*b*) who would then be asked to decide if they thought us eligible for (*c* and *d*) two separate membership voting procedures! The process, intentionally lengthy and somewhat complicated, was the National Council's standard method of considering any church for membership.

With much to learn concerning the operation of the National Council, Nancy and Adam had their first meeting with them at offices located in downtown Manhattan. It was a tremendous responsibility for our innocent envoys. They were expected to convey that we were not capricious in our application, but very serious. They were also aware that publicity resulting from our application could unleash homophobic responses against our churches around the world. In that respect each of us was concerned, but we all agreed with Nancy when she said, "We have to go forward. It's part of the healing process. We must deal with other denominations."

In the National Council of Churches, denominations refer to themselves as communions. Each communion has met five qualifications for membership. They are: (1) a basis of association as a Christian body; (2) autonomous and stable corporate identity within the United States; (3) demonstrated respect and cooperation with other communions; (4) a definite church government with one responsible central body, able to train its ordained ministers; and (5) a minimum of fifty churches with a membership of at least twenty thousand persons.

We were unquestionably qualified on each count. As for the final item, we had 172 congregations worldwide, with a majority in the United States. Our growing membership in 1982 numbered in excess of 27,000 individuals.

On the negative side, the Council's associate general secretary, Arleon Kelley, had been quoted in an issue of *Christian Century* as saying, "Considering the historical position and doctrinal practices of the communions that compose [the Council], it appears to me extremely doubtful that [sufficient] members would vote for the inclusion of the MCC." In the same article, Warren Day, the Council's director of information said, "The only marriage [our communions] recognize is between a man and a woman. Any church that accepts or advocates otherwise would be hard to accept."

But as they sat around a large table with members of the Council's Membership Committee, Nancy and Adam realized we were not a totally unknown quantity to them. One woman on the Council, Reverend Callie Rogers-Witte, a sympathetic minister from North Carolina, brought us greetings from her friend, Reverend June Norris, who by then was pastor of our congregation in Raleigh. And there were other unanticipated sub-rosa hints of welcome that were sincerely appreciated.

Our representatives responded, cautioned by elders, including myself, that they should in no way attempt to be manipulative. We had no desire to embarrass the National Council of Churches. Our objective was to achieve a long-term relationship with a commitment toward their education concerning the truth about our community—and it was important for the Council's committee to hear and realize that there was more to us than sex. "Our first and major goal is to have a forum to tell the story of Metropolitan Community Church to your communions, and to engage in a shared dialogue with all of them." Nancy would repeat on many occasions, forthrightly admitting, "The question of achieving membership has to be our secondary objective."

"We know this meeting is difficult for most of you," Adam said at the outset, after which he and Nancy, carefully related the miracle of our Universal Fellowship. Using true stories for illustrations, it was soon apparent that members of the Council's Membership Committee were becoming involved, digesting the drama of our spiritual odyssey—and sometimes they were deeply moved. The committee had expected to receive a challenge from militant people. Instead, they shared our genuine Christian experiences.

"Do you have any more questions?" Adam asked during the meeting. There was a pause. Adam grinned. "I think I know something some of you want to ask but have been hesitant to verbalize," he said, "You aren't sure if the two of us are homosexuals. That's what you'd like to ask, right?" Then Adam supplied his own answer. "Sure, we're homosexual. She's a lesbian. I'm gay."

"You don't look like homosexuals," commented a committee member.

"Usually gay people don't," said Nancy, laughing.

When that was out of the way, Adam said, "I know some of you want to know about gay marriages, so let's talk about Holy Union." Whereupon, the discussion of homosexual couples went forward for a time until Adam asked, "Now, what about women in ministry?" And that was also discussed.

When the meeting, which became increasingly forthright and honest, had lasted considerably longer than anyone expected and still was not completed, Nancy and Adam were invited to relax in Arleon Kelley's office while the remainder of our application was privately discussed by the Council's representatives. An hour of nervousness for our people passed. When the committee eventually reached its decision, Dr. McCloud, who is a black United Presbyterian minister, entered Kelley's office accompanied by other committee members. Nancy and Adam feared the worst, having read Kelley's personal comments in *Christian Century,* and having been warned by friendly Presbyterians that McCloud is a stickler for church bureaucracy and would be absolutely unsympathetic to our position. As it turned out, Arleon Kelley was not an ogre, and Oscar McCloud was one of the wonderful surprises that we now and then receive in a lifetime.

"We have recommended that our Governing Board find Metropolitan Community Churches eligible for membership," Dr. McCloud was pleased to inform us. "The decision was unanimous!"

"Our committee was so touched and moved by your stories—they weren't at all what we expected," a kind woman told Nancy, who made no effort to conceal her happiness.

"Of course we recognize your Christianity!" said the minister from North Carolina, adding, "We are kind of embarrassed even to have to ask for a vote on your eligibility."

Arleon also paused in the doorway of his office and made a point of shaking our hands before departing. "Meeting you people has been a redemptive experience for our committee," he said. The words nearly stunned Nancy and Adam. Church officers do not use theological concepts such as redemption in a casual manner.

Their written decision stated: "The Constituent Membership Committee recommends to the Governing Board that it declare the Universal Fellowship of Metropolitan Community Churches eligible to be considered for membership in the National Council of Churches of Christ in the U.S.A. at a subsequent meeting."

The subsequent meeting of the Governing Board was held in Nashville, Tennessee, for three days commencing May 12, 1982. Wilson and DeBaugh were our representatives again, facing a new situation—larger, more complex, and less friendly than before. The Governing Board of the National Council of Churches consisted of 260 men and women chosen to represent thirty-two communions. A Methodist, Bishop James Armstrong, was president of the National Council, and from him, a previous champion of civil rights for all people including gays and lesbians, came the first shock of the day. In his opening address, Bishop Armstrong chose to ignore our presence, as if by so doing we would go away, and he never so much as hinted that the question of our eligibility for membership was an upcoming item on the Council's agenda.

The situation was, to say the least, delicate for everyone. *Time* magazine described it as "explosive." The press eagerly sought our representatives to learn details of our strategy, but the truth was, Nancy and Adam had little strategy, if any at all. We were merely applying for membership in a Christian organization with which we wanted to have a serious relationship.

Panic subtly ensued.

There was the perception of a potential disaster as many of the Council's board members (who amazingly had been unaware of our application) suddenly realized that a denomination with an outreach to the homosexual community—in total conformity with all of the Council's membership rules—was in their midst and ready to have its eligibility discussed!

The Constituent Membership Committee (which forwarded our application to the Governing Board) had not previously notified their individual communions that the eligibility of the Universal Fellowship of Metropolitan Community Churches was about to be considered and voted upon. The lack of prior notification, however, was standard procedure, and by treating us no differently from anyone else, they were actually maintaining their integrity. But the committee was in a no-win situation, because presenting a recommendation—in our favor—without any warning or printed information about who we are instantly ignited a furor of protagonists and antagonists within the Council.

Seated in the visitors' space in the back of the room, Adam and Nancy had been generally ignored until they were identified in conversations that spread quickly around the room. Eyes and comments were suddenly directed toward them. Prohibited from joining the ensuing debate—which threatened to burst all bounds of parliamentary procedure—our two spectators could only listen with feelings alternating between hope and anger as friendly and hostile board members were recognized and made their various emotional declarations.

Metropolitan Community Church, without question, met every criterion for membership in the National Council of Churches, and it would have been reasonable for our eligibility to be voted on schedule, but because of our homosexual ministry, nothing was settled in the first session. A decision was made to postpone consideration of our application until the following day.

"We have work to do," Adam said, rising from his seat as the session ended. Heading for an exit, Nancy was half a step ahead as they approached the elevator. In a hotel room, the two opened a bulging leather suitcase, dumping bundles of pamphlets on one of the beds. Small stacks of printed matter were quickly organized into packets of information that could be individually distributed. The literature included our Fellowship's bylaws, pamphlets entitled "The Universal Fellowship Today," and "Homosexuality: What the Bible Does and Does Not Say."

As the afternoon meetings of the Governing Board ended, our energetic duo was ready. Nancy stood on one side of an exit with Adam at the other, handing packets to whoever would take them. Despite the preceding furor, there were still a few board members who did not understand who we were. One very short, very stout man with strands of gray hair carefully combed over his nearly bald head, mistook us for the Community Churches (a member of the Council) and he said to Nancy, "But I thought you already belonged." Few others were even willing to speak to Nancy or Adam. Nevertheless, putting on a brave appearance, they continued to shake hands whenever they could, introducing themselves, handing out literature, trying to make eye contact even though it was difficult.

Many Governing Board members would not touch our literature—yet, among them we could easily detect a fair number of closeted homosexuals. Some of those individuals felt severely threatened by our openly gay and lesbian presence and, unfortunately, they were among the most aggravating people with whom our representatives had to deal. The closeted gay people were clearly frightened by the willingness of Metropolitan Community Church to deal with real issues, and unlike nongay board members, were victims as well as instigators of their own homophobia. To them the issue was not simply that we are gay or lesbian—their overriding concern was that we are not afraid to be visible!

Happily, our representatives also found new friends, more often heterosexual than otherwise, friends who squeezed Adam's or Nancy's hand with conspiratorial winks and, speaking in hushed tones, greeted us with the courage of the early Christians while indicating their support.

The press corps gave our application to join the National Council of Churches as much coverage in print as we had ever known, and more attention than the National Council had received since the previous decades when they had been in the vanguard of Protestant liberalism and a major backer of civil rights movements. The offshoot of the publicity was that not even our supporters in the Council were pleased. They feared their right-wing enemies would use our presence as ammunition to create major public relations problems.

Before coming to Nashville, the National Council was already on the defensive, fearful that Ronald Reagan's conservatives were seeking to dismantle all liberal establishments. A contrived article in the January 1982 *Reader's Digest* had insinuated that leaders of the National Council of Churches "substituted revolution for religion," while a CBS story on "60 Minutes" (also in January 1982) suggested that the Council might be using money collected from its communions to support "Marxist guerrillas." Those particular attacks had so disheartened the Council that numerous members of its Governing Board could only view us as simply another threat to their continued existence. Civil war in the Council (between those who supported our application and those who did not) could become unendurable and, conceivably, might be the last straw added to the burden of an already weakened alliance.

Nevertheless, we would not quit.

Support that Nancy and Adam could identify came from people in the Presbyterian church in the U.S., United Presbyterian church, United Methodist church, United Church of Christ, the Episcopal church, Friends United Meeting, Disciples of Christ, and Church of the Brethren. Communions vehemently opposing our very existence included all of those which, in any fashion, incorporated the word *Orthodox* in their name.

Throughout the evening, Adam and Nancy tirelessly corraled friends and foes, presenting our case, describing us with accuracy and persuasion. By trial and error, Adam and Nancy passed beyond innocence and learned what they needed to do. Complicated procedures and protocol of the

241

assembly became better known to them. Very slowly, sympathy for our application increased as they repeated the story of Metropolitan Community Church over and over, telling of Adam's experiences, of Nancy's ministry, relating anecdotes about depressed gay Christians, alcoholics, potential suicides, and others whom we had saved.

"If a church doesn't change lives, then what is the church for?" asked Adam.

"But why come to us now when we already have other pressing problems?" tense members of the Governing Board repeatedly complained. "The Council is in trouble and you and the hubbub that comes with you are making things worse. You're putting us in a bind!"

"So—when do you think would be a good time to apply?" Nancy repeatedly replied. "We could wait forever on somebody else's schedule. Do you think there will ever be an 'appropriate' time when we are acceptable to all your members, or to all of the press, or to the vocal Orthodox minority who don't like you any more than they like us?"

Never was there any positive answer.

"Our people have waited too long already," Nancy would continue. "Hundreds of years too long. And we do not know what tomorrow holds and we have no certainty that it will be any better for you."

In the morning, on the second day of meetings in Nashville, the National Council was as ready for us as it was ever going to be. Their Membership Committee had xeroxed our application and distributed hundreds of copies. Meanwhile, a growing number of their delegates were arriving at the conclusion that, in all fairness, a vote should be taken on the question of our eligibility, which in itself should not have been a matter of dispute.

Did we meet their five requirements for membership consideration, or did we not? That was the simple question the Council was initially to decide, and nothing else. The fact is that we did meet all requirements, and met them easily.

Therein existed the problem.

How was it possible to vote against our eligibility (much less our membership) without causing a furious division in the Council between those who favored justice and those who gagged on inbred homophobia? What we were later to learn was that our opposition had worked feverishly throughout the entire night in an effort to change their own rules.

When the morning session began, the ubiquitous press and television personnel continued gathering all conceivable observations concerning what they preferred to call "the gay church vs. the National Council."

Therefore, during the opening report concerning our application for membership, Jim Armstrong, president of the Council, in deference to the media, made an unusual and self-conscious move. Apropos of nothing, he interrupted Dr. McCloud's Membership Committee presentation of our case and led a prayer unquestionably intended primarily for public relations purposes. Then, after television cameras were turned off, Dr. McCloud was permitted to continue reading our application.

The letter Adam had written touched the hearts of many, and although there was foot shuffling from a few, there were tears from many others. Even Nancy, who had nearly memorized the content of our application word for word, felt her heart pounding each time Metropolitan Community Church was mentioned.

After Dr. McCloud's reading, the work of our opposition began. Dr. Paul Crow, an officer of the Disciples of Christ took the floor. His was the hatchet job of attempting an eleventh-hour change of the Council's long-standing rules—to work against our favor. "This is an event of agony for all of us," Dr. Crow said in a condescending tone. "This application is unique," he added, gesturing toward the document.

"I'm going to be ill," whispered Adam to Nancy as they sat, officially unable to respond, listening while Crow outlined a plan which could forestall the important preliminary vote we were expecting.

"This Governing Board needs time and resources to explore this matter and to discern the views of the constituents," concluded Dr. Crow, having implied, without conviction, that there might be a vote "sometime" after the ecclesiastical issues were fully studied and thoroughly resolved.

Adam groaned, physically experiencing the agony Dr. Crow had rhetorically mentioned. "We've been had!" Adam decided.

Nancy was not convinced. A black woman they knew from the Constituent Membership Committee was taking the floor, and Nancy correctly interpreted her body language. "We haven't been had yet!" Nancy said. "Adam, listen!"

The black woman was an Episcopalian, imbued with strong faith and intense beliefs. Her voice was powerful. It vibrated with anger from the patently unfair resolution that had previously been tendered. Her name was Barbara James and she needed no microphone when she faced the assembly. "The issue today is whether this church is eligible for membership," she said. "Not membership. Only eligibility to be considered for membership. Based on the rules we're currently working under, that eligibility cannot be denied. I ask you not to change the rules in order to discriminate!"

A ripple of agreement flowed among the delegates. Nancy began to smile. Adam's agony began to diminish. In the next hour, he listened with hope as Reverend Percel Alston, a United Church of Christ delegate, took the microphone and addressed the matter of delaying tactics.

"I have the strange feeling that I've met this motion before!" said Alston with measured eloquence. Many people in the room, particularly those who had known the indignity of antiblack discrimination, laughed knowingly. "The issue then was not homosexuality, but race," Alston continued. "This motion would have the effect of amending our constitution. For us to change the rules now seems to me to be unfair."

Again, there was agreement from a number of delegates who murmured in the assembly. Other speakers gave us their support and the majority of them were women. A quiet intensity gripped the room. Emotional delegates stood and had their say. One declared, "This Metropolitan Community Church is doing the ministry that we have never done—the work we have run away from!"

In response to those and similar favorable comments, a disdainful bishop stood and was recognized. He looked down his nose and said, "My church has numerous homoxexual members—who don't feel a need to make themselves obvious. There is no reason to accept this so-called church!"

Adam gave an unparliamentary snort for the benefit of those around him. "Come on, Bishop!" he said (very much out of order). "What has your church ever done for its gay members other than to intimidate them? Nothing!"

Opposition to us came primarily from white male delegates. One of them, a dandy fellow, thundered in Nancy and Adam's direction, "Oh, see these disciples of hell! This M.C.C. is a church created on the basis of *sin!*" His was one of the few homophobic pronouncements that was not in any way hypocritical or restrained. He hated us. He knew it and we knew it!

Orthodox communions were generally more subtle—but calculating. They initially claimed to be in favor of "postponement and study," but those declarations were generally misleading. Nancy and Adam quickly realized that what would really suit them best was our summary rejection. Eventually, when their actual thinking was revealed, they threatened that all Orthodox communions would walk out of the National Council if Metropolitan Community Church came in!

Reverend William Cober of the American Baptist churches also issued a stern warning to Council voters. "Favorable action will endanger our [American Baptist] relationship with the National Council of Churches," he declared.

During a lull in the proceedings, before the vote was to be taken, Adam left his seat for a drink of water. Immediately, he was set upon by the press. A tiny microphone was thrust in front of his face. "This gay church of yours can wreck the Council," said a female television commentator. "So if you really care about them, as I've heard you say, why don't you pack up and get out the hell out of here?"

Adam turned toward the woman, brushed aside the microphone, drank his water, then crushed the empty paper cup and threw it aside. "My church does not submit to any kind of blackmail," he said. "We are led by the Holy Spirit to apply for membership in the National Council of Churches. If other denominations feel led by the Holy Spirit to leave, that is not my problem. The Orthodox churches don't follow the rules. They hold the opinion that they are the only real churches—which is in violation of the Council's requirement for eligibility that says they must respect the convictions of other communions. For a long time the Orthodox churches have been looking for some excuse to leave the National Council. This may be it. Incidentally, have you noticed that they hate it when women's issues are brought before the Council?"

"No, I didn't," admitted the woman with the microphone, displaying genuine interest for the first time.

"The Orthodox have never ordained women," Adam said to her. "They never have and they never will. They haven't changed in thousands of years. If M.C.C. is admitted to the Council and ten denominations depart because of us, I'd feel diminished. We asked to join an organization that includes those people—the Orthodox. I'd feel sad because they—more than anybody else—need to have a dialogue with us."

"Which means you are willing to destroy this organization?" asked another reporter who was unprofessionally antagonistic.

Nancy joined Adam at that moment. "It wouldn't be us!" she said, controlling her anger, "The N.C.C. is only thirty-five years old—started the same year I was born. Before the N.C.C. there was something called the Federal Council, which folded for various reasons. Last night we told the Orthodox people not to do an extortion number on us. We said, 'Do what you're called to do. If God leads you out, God will take you out whether we're here or we aren't. The choice is yours, not ours.'"

Several more questions were simultaneously put to Adam and Nancy, but both shook their head. "The Council's ready to vote inside, and I want to be present," said Nancy, pausing long enough to add, "We do not come here as enemies. We are not foes—although sometimes I have to keep reminding myself. We are Christians who want a bonding relationship with other Christians. The Council is a natural home for us."

Although following strict rules of order, the Governing Board's debate had sometimes been fierce with dissension. There were speakers with elevated principles, and others with vicious tongues and depraved imaginations. It was all winding toward an end when a gaunt intruder strode down the aisle flourishing a staff in one hand and grasping a huge Bible in the other. Members of the Governing Board had just become aware of the theatrically weird individual's unannounced presence when he commandeered a microphone and began a wild oration with his own interpretation of quotations from the Book of Romans. "God gives them up to vile affections!" he shouted. "Even their women change the use of their sweet, once soft bodies into something unusable! And their abominable men burn with lust humiliating one another!"

The press moved forward and took pictures.

Naturally!

Forty seconds or more elapsed before the disturbed man was removed. Adam glanced at Nancy while order was being restored. "That kind of mentality is a part of the problem we have to deal with," he said.

Voting began shortly thereafter. A "yes" vote meant postponement. Adam tabulated the results on a small pad while Nancy kept an accurate record of who was currently for us, and who was not. She was fully aware of the inequity in the proceedings. For example, Nancy recalled what she knew of the good Christian Society of Friends. Their philosophy in *Toward a Quaker View of Sex,* which had been published a quarter of a century earlier, is an affirmation of gay relationships very similar to ours in the Universal Fellowship, yet without any disturbance, they are respected members of the National Council! (The very positive Quaker document was one of the first ever printed by a modern Christian group with any mention of homosexuality.)

Other denominations have also come to be supportive of the gay community. Episcopal churches and the United Church of Christ have been in the forefront of reform. Both have ordained openly homosexual people. The main difference between them and us is that we have an aggressive outreach, saying very clearly to gay men and lesbians, "God loves you. Come to our church. Come back with Christ!"

As the vote of members in the National Council continued, the tabulation was very close. Not until almost the end was there any certainty about the final count. Those in favor of postponing a vote on our eligibility succeeded by merely 11 votes, proving that in one day and night, Nancy, Adam and the validity of our mission had won many friends.

We were not to leave empty-handed. There was no defeat. We did achieve our foremost objective—an active and viable exchange of ideas with other Christian denominations was begun.

"This is not a delaying action, but a responsible attempt to approach a very significant and delicate subject," declared Jim Armstrong, president of the Council. "I don't think theology is the issue. It is the life-style that troubles many of the communions and could affect unity in the National Council of Churches."

An important part of the Council's official statement read:

> Recognizing that the Constituent Membership Committee has recommended that the Universal Fellowship of Metropolitan Community Churches meets the constitutional requirements for eligibility . . . and confessing that we are unable at this time to take action without study and reflection, the Governing Board . . . refers this matter to the Commission on Faith and Order for a study of the ecclesiastical issues raised by this application, including the nature of ecumenical fellowship in the N.C.C. The Commission will involve the member churches in appropriate ways and engage in dialogue with Metropolitan Community Church.

It was further resolved that the vote on our eligibility would be held a year later, in May 1983, when the Governing Board would hold its scheduled semiannual meeting in San Francisco. Although Nancy knew the Council was stalling, she was not distressed by their stopgap solution to a fractionizing situation. She had prepared herself for a negative vote that would completely terminate our precarious relationship—but that vote never materialized. Nancy was also pleased because our application received much more favorable support than anyone anticipated. Therefore, when the television people came for comments, Nancy was prepared to field their questions. "We are supportive of the Council," she said. "Let them take all the time they want. M.C.C. isn't something the Council people here readily understand because they haven't dealt with us before. So what has happened is perfect. We love the idea of talking with their Faith and Order Commission."

Adam agreed on an intellectual basis, but emotionally, he felt otherwise. Adam was particularly distressed by recurring recollections of mean and stupid unchristian comments that had now and again been uttered during the debate by some members of the Governing Board—who should have known better. Most of the intense homophobia had a veneer of politeness to casual observers, but Adam was never blind to the truth. Eventually he reacted to the understated, often intangible hostility. In contrast to his strong, urbane appearance, Adam began to cry. When tears flowed he withdrew from public view to prevent press cameras from recording his grief.

Dr. McCloud, hurrying along an aisle, followed Adam and hastened to throw comforting arms around him. Sympathetic tears were in McCloud's eyes. "It's wrong—it's wrong!" sobbed the heterosexual black bureaucrat who we had once been told would oppose our membership every step of the way!

Later, before leaving Nashville, Nancy tried to soothe Adam with her assessment of the situation. "We're here on a mission," she reminded him. "These Council people are the ones who need saving. And some of them know it. They have a tremendous amount to learn from us about what it means to be an ecumenical organization."

Six months later, the Governing Board convened for a smaller, semi-annual meeting. This time, nine well-qualified members of Metropolitan Community Church were available to join their caucuses if invited, and to meet with them at any time when we could be of assistance in answering questions concerning our polity, our faith, our life-styles, and ourselves.

Often, there would be a knock on one of our representatives' bedroom doors at some hour after midnight, and outside would stand an apologetic person from the Governing Board who wanted to talk about theological aspects of homosexuality. The caller would inevitably be shy about being observed in our presence. "I was in a long meeting and it's just over now," was the typical excuse for a late-night visit.

A few of them were apprehensive homosexuals, unfamiliar with our liberating gospel. Sometimes our visitors were parents or relatives of homosexuals. But, more often than not, they were people who merely wanted basic information about a subject that had previously been taboo. Our members went to the National Council to educate its delegates, and our members found many receptive individuals who wanted to listen and learn.

We also expected that after months of "study" by the National Council's Faith and Order Commission, the Governing Board would, in accordance with its own resolution, be sufficiently knowledgeable and ready to vote on our eligibility when the Council next convened in San Francisco. To the distress of many, however, it soon became obvious that the Faith and Order Commission had accomplished little, and had no plans to consult with us prior to writing their conclusions. As often happens, it was a case of the main subjects being discussed without having any input. Therefore, on a chilly Wednesday evening, our friends in Hartford called a special, impromptu meeting. The gathering was composed of members of the Women's Caucus (who were displeased that few female theologians were represented on the Faith and Order Commission), members of the Constituent Membership Committee (whom our people had come to respect), and all nine representatives of Metropolitan Community Church. The purpose was to institute a strategy that would realistically include the Universal Fellowship in a genuine theological study as the Governing Board had originally envisioned. There was a consensus that, after a year and a half of little progress, the time had definitely arrived to ensure an honest exchange of information between the Council and ourselves.

Lacy Camp, a woman from the United Methodist church, introduced the new resolution. She asked for "a creative and expanded process that would facilitate dialogue . . . related to U.F.M.C.C.'s eligibility and membership . . . beginning in March 1983 with the Faith and Order report to the Executive Committee."

Our representatives were consulted. We approved the resolution. At last, Metropolitan Community Church would actually be involved in discussions concerning ourselves. Our theologians would talk to their theologians. The dialogue was our top priority—but there was a tradeoff. With gain there was loss. No longer would we expect to have an early vote on our eligibility. According to the new resolution, "voting matters related to the U.F.M.C.C.'s eligibility and membership" could be studied (and thus delayed) for an additional year and a half.

We had had every reason to expect a vote in Nashville in May 1982, but it had been postponed until May 1983. With the new resolution, that vote could be as late as November 1984. We were making progress, but courting the National Council of Churches was like chasing a balloon on a windy day.

For the first time, in December 1982, members of the Universal Fellowship were officially invited to meet and have a dialogue with theologians from the National Council. Our delegation included Reverend Don Eastman, pastor of M.C.C. Dallas; Reverend Karen Ziegler, pastor of M.C.C. New York; Reverend Jennie Boyd Bull, pastor of M.C.C. Baltimore; Adam DeBaugh, and two prestigious consultants. Prior to our people's arrival at the meeting (which was held at the United Methodist's Alma Matthews House in Manhattan's Greenwich Village), they received a letter from the National Council of Churches. The closing sentence inquired, "In the spirit of the Council in Jerusalem mentioned in Acts 15, what concessions would your church make to become a part of the National Council of Churches?"

The inquiry was peculiar in that, to our thinking, it could only invite us to respond by refusing concessions. The reference was to an historical dispute initiated by the Pharisees who had said that if the gentiles wanted to be a part of their church, they were commanded to keep the Law of Moses, which required that males be circumcised. Whereupon, the apostle Peter arose and argued that God had purified the gentiles' hearts by faith, and although circumcision was an intregral part of the old Law of Moses, there existed no such commandment for Christians.

"And God, who knows the heart, bears them witness, giving them the Holy Ghost," said Peter, further defending Christians who departed from ancient beliefs.

The only parallel we could find for ourselves was that in the case of the early Christians it was not a foreskin or the removal thereof which Peter knew would save them, it was faith. And in our twentieth-century situation, it is not heterosexuality or the departure therefrom that will save us, it is faith. The same faith that had made men and women Christians for nearly two thousand years!

In the words of Saint Peter, "We believe that through the grace of the Lord Jesus Christ we shall be saved, even as they."

When the National Council's theologians gathered with us in Greenwich Village, many items, including the aforementioned "circumcision decision," were candidly discussed. After two days of intense give and take, some significant progress was made although numerous questions remained. A resulting report stated, "The participants in this dialogue understand that the U.F.M.C.C.'s reason for being is to proclaim the gospel of Jesus Christ." It continued:

> The U.F.M.C.C. also affirms that one of God's credited possibilities for loving includes physical, sexual loving between people of the same gender. The U.F.M.C.C. grounds this affirmation in what it takes to be the undeniable facts of human experience and observations drawn from the social sciences, and considers their affirmation as compatible with the Biblical message. The churches of the N.C.C. must take this testimony of the U.F.M.C.C. most seriously, since in the past some communions have come to accept positions which their founders had originally denied.

Several of the lingering questions were: "What are the limits of legitimate diversity that can be tolerated within the N.C.C.? What are the theological and practical implications of recognizing the U.F.M.C.C. as a church eligible for membership? What would be the effects of a yes or no vote on the unity and inclusiveness of the N.C.C.?"

In March 1983, a report consisting of 467 pages, including papers from the Universal Fellowship and sixteen other denominations, was presented to the full thirty-two-member Faith and Order Commission. Karen Ziegler and Don Eastman were our well-qualified representatives at that meeting. Don later reported, "I felt like the apostle Peter, unlearned because, academically, everybody there was way beyond me. And we were presenting the only thing we had to stand upon, our faith—the faith which has changed our lives."

Reverend Eastman's modesty notwithstanding, an excellent new report ensued from their four-day dialogue with the National Council's Faith and Order Commission. A portion of their distilled "reflections" contained the following:

> A. For some member communions, there would be no theological problems in accepting the U.F.M.C.C. for membership.... For others there are problems.... Several member churches have expressed serious reservations about the U.F.M.C.C. as church. It is clear that within the N.C.C., however, those same churches might also express similar judgment's about present member churches with whom they are now in covenant and have a long history of valuable and responsible relationships.
>
> B. The application of the U.F.M.C.C. raises many issues concerning pastoral ministry among constituent congregations, as well as with, to, and by the gay and lesbian community. Some churches already engaged in this ministry, would welcome the U.F.M.C.C. as a partner in ministry. Others find that the presence of the U.F.M.C.C. would further polarize their own membership and make pastoral ministry less possible.
>
> C. Members of the Commission confess our complicity in these issues that divide us. Fear of homosexuality has brought many to evade, judge, and reject gay men and lesbian women. When our churches have failed to extend compassion and nurture, guilt and failure are often expressed as hostility. Under rejection many homosexuals have turned from existing churches and have come together in a new Christian community.

Important among the Faith and Order Commission's recommendations was the following: "In light of our experience of the importance of personal interaction, [we suggest that the Governing Board] engage in dialogue with and experience the worship of U.F.M.C.C. congregations in order to better consider the ecclesiastical character and quality of ministry of this community."

Thus, in view of their Commission's recommendation, it naturally followed that when the full Governing Board met in San Francisco two months later, in May, Metropolitan Community Church would be ready and anxious to meet with them on a scale bolder than ever before. Also, we would conduct a real worship service. The entire Governing Board would be invited to personally attend "the homosexual church" with a gay and lesbian congregation at prayer.

Nancy Wilson and Adam DeBaugh had been making all the plans, handling negotiations with the National Council of Churches from the very beginning. My input was through Nancy and I would tell her if anything disturbed or impressed me. As elders, we had worked together for so many years that when the 1980s rolled around, Nancy intuitively knew what I was thinking. Everybody understood that my role was to be the emotional homosexual who knows God loves me, and Nancy would be our expert theologian. Consequently, it was a surprise when, on an overcast Wednesday morning, she came to me after communion in the office and said she wanted me to represent the Universal Fellowship in our Faith and Order presentation to the Governing Board of the National Council of Churches. "Most of their attention will be focused on us in San Francisco," she said. "The Council have all heard about you. Now they want to see what Troy Perry looks like."

I said, "Wait a minute now, Nancy! Don't be too hasty! Let's talk about this," and I motioned her into my office.

Nancy shut the door while I looked for a telephone that was ringing somewhere on my big desk, which, as usual, was stacked with notes and papers. Nancy took a seat and relaxed, but as soon as I said goodbye to my caller, she began. "The first of the National Council's meetings about us will be held on Tuesday evening," she said. "Their Faith and Order Commission will present a report to the N.C.C.'s full two-hundred-and-sixty-member Governing Board, with speeches from six of their people—and one of us. I know you don't like church politics, and I know you didn't want to be involved with N.C.C. negotiations, so I've kept you in the wings as long as possible, waiting for just this occasion."

I had to laugh at Nancy's candor, although I disagreed. "You don't want me to give a speech before the National Council," I told her. "We don't speak the same language. They won't identify with my style. Half of them think I'm Satan incarnate, and the others are uncertain. I might be a detriment and I don't want to be. We need somebody they can relate to, those mainline churches."

"Yes, but, but—!"

"No buts, I know I'm too emotional for them."

"Well—then who?"

I looked at pictures on the office walls for a moment, considering, then turned back to Nancy. "Let's call Don Eastman in Dallas," I said. "He just met with their Faith and Order Commission and that was successful. If anybody can represent us any better than Don, I'd like to know who it is."

Nancy agreed.

Reverend Elder Don Eastman is one of those individuals that people generally like. He has a clean-cut look about him, and the ability to look anyone in the eye and make that person listen and understand what he has to say. The church he was pastoring in Dallas (before he came to our Fellowship office in Los Angeles) has a contemporary ranch-style look, and was usually filled by the congregation that came to hear his sermons.

Don had grown up in Wisconsin, attended Central Bible College in Springfield, Missouri and, after graduating in 1966, served as a Assemblies of God pastor in northeastern Wisconsin for six and a half years. "I was indoctrinated into the values of the Assemblies of God, and I could defend those values, many of which I still believe," Don told me, adding, "but time and experience have modified my views. Back then I was fanatical, convinced of the unyielding correctness of Assemblies of God doctrine, believing other religions might have some elements of good in them, but that ultimately they were wrong!"

Don Eastman's parents, although their relationship with the Assemblies of God dated back to its beginning in the United States, did not have the narrowness of mind which sometimes characterizes some members of religious organizations. Don's father even went so far as to admit that devout Catholics with whom he worked might "possibly" have been sincere and redeemable Christians! Suffering constantly from the pain of severe arthritis, Mr. Eastman was crippled for the last twenty years of his life, but he imbued his son with a foundation of objectivity that would guide Don's journey through life.

A long-standing habit of Don's, even as a young Assemblies of God minister, was mentally wrestling with himself until ideas became clear. Around 1972, he moved to Des Moines, Iowa, and started wrestling with his sexual orientation. He began reading every sex treatise he could obtain, and on Saturdays would methodically search for informative new books at the neighborhood newsstand. When he read about Metropolitan Community Church, Don was interested, but never expected to become a very important part of our Fellowship. Two more years passed before he visited Chicago's Good Shepherd Metropolitan Community Church—where he felt comfortable. A couple of weeks later, Don attended another Metropolitan Community Church that we were just forming in Des Moines. By then, Reverend Eastman was so impressed that he decided to terminate his mind-wrestling, and he moved rapidly toward a major decision.

He visited our Mother Church in Los Angeles during the Christmas season of 1974. I met Don at that time, when he was about thirty years old. Another person who met Don then was a visitor from Australia, an older man, who asked Don if he was gay.

"I'm exploring the possibility," Don admitted, "but it isn't easy for me. I'm a minister in the Assembly of God."

"Well, why don't you become a minister in M.C.C.?" asked the forthright visitor.

"I really don't know," answered Don.

"Then give it a try," said the Aussie. "We need good people like you."

Thus, the seed of an idea was planted. In 1975, Don resigned his credentials with the Assembly of God and began a process to become credentialed with Metropolitan Community Church. Soon thereafter, Don Eastman's ministry with us began. He became the pastor of our infant church in Des Moines.

Before he began his new ministry, I remember stressing to Don that it was absolutely essential for him to "come out" to his family and tell all the persons who cared about him that he was homosexual. It was important to tell them that his new religious affiliation included an outreach to the gay and lesbian community. In Don's new position, as whenever there is the potential for publicity, it would be unwise, possibly even cruel, to allow those he loved to learn about his life-style from unfriendly outside sources.

Don returned home and informed his sister that he was gay. She told another of his sisters. That sister told his mother and his mother told his father. It was a strong intrafamily network. One day, before much time had passed, his mother said to Don, "Why don't you go in and see your father? I think he wants to talk with you."

Mr. Eastman was not well when Don, a little apprehensive, sat beside the bed. "I guess you've been told?" Don said, speaking softly.

His father hesitated. The older man was thoughtful for what seemed a long time as Don waited for any response. When Don's father turned to look at him, there was no anger. "Donald, I want to talk to you because I don't know how much longer I'm going to live," said Mr. Eastman. "I wouldn't want to die without you knowing how your dad feels about things."

The man in bed motioned to Don who moved his chair closer. His father reached out, touched his arm, and then continued. "I don't know why things are as they are in life. I don't know why I've had to live with pain every day for the past fifteen years. The only thing I do know is we have to accept the circumstances of our lives as they are."

Mr. Eastman paused thoughtfully for a moment and resumed. "I don't know why people are gay," he said. "I think it's because they're born gay. Anyway, I don't have to tell you that gay people are not very well accepted. I think you know that. You may have the opportunity to be of influence to gay people. If you have any influence at all, tell them to give society a standard of morality to look up to instead of down upon. Can you do that?"

"I can try," Don said.

His father died in 1981.

In the family, Don was the oldest child. His brother, Richard, was next, followed by three sisters. Don had always been close to his brother, who is also a minister. For years they had lived with the idea that one day they would be working in a ministry together. Don had to break the news that their plans might have to be changed.

They met by arrangement in a lounge at Chicago's O'Hare Airport. Don was flying north from Dallas after our General Conference in which we had presented him with credentials, and Dick Eastman was en route to Sacramento from a revival meeting in Toronto. Both of them had to change planes in the Windy City. It was ten o'clock on a Monday morning when they sat down to talk.

"Dick, I'm leaving the Assemblies and I'm going into M.C.C. This is a denomination with a special ministry to homosexuals. The reason I find a calling to this church is because I'm gay myself."

With a set jaw, Don's brother looked him in the eye. "You know, Don, that doesn't surprise me," Dick said. "Not because of anything you've done. But because of your age and still being single. Well, I can tell you one thing. If you don't change, you won't be in heaven!"

Resentment started to well up in Don. "I can also tell you something!" he immediately replied. "I *will* be in heaven, because that's not your decision to make, or your right to say! I will be in heaven because my faith is in Jesus Christ!"

The two men stood, walked away from each other, and then walked back toward each other again. Dick was obviously as distressed as his older brother. Dick said, "Don, I don't know. I just don't know what I'm going to say to my wife and children. They have loved you so much. It's going to be like you died!"

There were tears in the eyes of both ministers as they stood apart looking at each other, their stomachs churning with a mixture of love, hate, anger, and pain. It was a blessing when Richard's flight to the West Coast was announced. He managed a goodbye for his brother and ran for his airplane.

The blood was drained out of Don's face as he also walked away. He felt nearly paralyzed as an escalator moved him down to the baggage area. Shaking inside, he managed to find a telephone booth and placed a long-distance call to Des Moines. When his best friend answered, Don related what had just happened. After he finished, Don broke down and sobbed for a while.

A week later, Don received a telephone call from his brother. Dick had another concern he had neglected to mention in Chicago. "Don, you don't know how bad this is going to hurt me. What are my friends going to say? What will they think about me?" he asked.

The gay brother shook his head. Feeling hurt and disappointed, he said into the mouthpiece, "Dick, your friends are your problem. All I know is that my time of weeping has ended—and the rejoicing has started. I'm going to live my life as best I can. You'll have to deal with your friends in any way you wish."

Several years passed before the brothers spoke on the subject again. It occurred when Don had become pastor of Metropolitan Community Church in Dallas, and Dick was also in Texas for his annual address to the area's evangelical groups. The brothers had dinner together. Don refused to allow Dick to avoid a discussion of their differences. And his brother's uncompromising response was much the same as before. "There's no way I could openly say you can be gay and Christian," Dick said, "I'd be ruined. I would immediately be ostracized by all the people I associate with!"

Don nodded. "I understand that, Dick, and I know you're correct. But I need you to understand that resistance to the gay issue is not spiritual, not biblical, not theological—it is social and it is political. You are dealing with a political issue within your group."

Dick was not convinced, but the two brothers continued to have their

256

occasional dinners together. Nearly ten years had passed when Dick, without bending in his oppposition to Don's life-style, unexpectedly put down his fork in the middle of a dinner and said to his brother, "There's something I need to tell you. I need to apologize for something I said at O'Hare Airport in 1975. I said you can't go to heaven. That was not my right to say."

Our Board of Elders agreed that Reverend Eastman was the person to represent us in San Francisco before the Governing Board of the National Council of Churches. We gave Don very little advance warning, however, and he began writing the speech he was to make while on an airplane flying toward the Golden Gate.

When Don arrived on Tuesday, May 10, 1983, the lobby of his hotel was alive with activity. A large number of the National Council's Governing Board were being helped by the Universal Fellowship's Bay Area residents to ensure that their caucuses met with every success. Many gay and lesbian persons were also present to participate in the momentous worship service we would conduct on the following evening for the Council's benefit.

Adam DeBaugh and Reverend Nancy Wilson, who for two strenuous years had been overseeing our application for National Council of Churches membership, took a few minutes to relax and to playfully consider our objective. In jest, one said to the other, "What we ought to do is have a demonstration. Where could be better than in San Francisco. We might get a hundred thousand gay and lesbian people to mob the outside of this hotel while the Council's meeting within. Can you imagine it? Think of a hundred thousand of our people with lighted candles, all chanting at the top of their lungs? Then, in the middle of everything, one of us goes to the Council's Governing Board and, feigning a great display of consternation, says, 'I can't control the mob. They're getting more impatient by the minute. And we have news of lesbian commando units in the hotel! You know what that means? What it means is this: Deal with us—or deal with them!!' "

It was a private joke—of course—but as one local resident said with a grin, "You never know about San Francisco!"

Reverend Eastman completed writing his speech in the hotel. It was ready when the National Council members (all 260 of them representing thirty-two communions) met in the evening for their first session of the current agenda. Lesbian and gay people crowded into the rear of the large room provided by the Holiday Inn. The general atmosphere was considerably different from the previous year in Nashville when Reverend

Wilson and Adam DeBaugh bravely stood together and confronted the entire National Council and the world press.

The San Francisco meeting consisted of seven reports, six from the Council's Faith and Order Commission, plus final extended comments from Reverend Don Eastman. As proceedings began, Paul Fries of the Reformed Church in America made his verbal presentation. Concerning the homosexual outreach of our Universal Fellowship, Fries allowed that "the N.C.C.'s preamble and purpose ... is vague about a number of important concerns relevant to U.F.M.C.C.'s application [but] ... the final word on this subject belongs to God and not to us."

Barbara Brown Zikmund of the Pacific School of Religion raised the justice issue. She asked, "What authority do we rely on to exclude some Christians? All admit that homosexuals are children of God, but ... to whom and how you minister is a theological question the U.F.M.C.C. raises."

Father Alexander Doumouras of the Greek Orthodox Church had negative comments. "The Orthodox churches cannot accept the U.F.M.C.C. as a church on the basis on which it has been formed," he said. "For the Orthodox, it is not debatable."

Reverend Roy Sano had a different opinion. "Without personal inter-action with U.F.M.C.C. congregations and participation in U.F.M.C.C. ministries," he said, "our theologies can turn into transcriptions of scribes. We will find ourselves copying down the letter of the law written by our forebears, but closing our ears to the living word of God. If elected officials and Governing Board members of the N.C.C. only experience the membership application as a problem—and are not captivated with the potentials for deepening unity and authenticating mission—I raise questions about the state of your soul. We have been called for a day such as this. Praises be to God for possibilities the U.F.M.C.C. membership application opens up!"

The position of the African Methodist Episcopal church was read by Reverend Cecil Murray. "God wisely separated humankind into man and woman," he said, and went on to state that his communion is not "against homosexual persons—but opposes the practice of homosexual-ity." That comment I have often heard.

Repetition does not make it valid.

When Reverend Murray was finished, Reverend Eastman took the podium and prepared to deliver his address. All of his audience was eager to hear him. Television cameras with telephoto lenses were focused from the back of the room. A microphone at his side was rechecked by a technician as Don cleared his throat, adjusted his necktie, and began:

"First, let me express gratitude for the process of dialogue we have been involved in for the past several months," he said. "More than anything else, I believe that dialogue such as this provides a hope for the greater understanding of some very difficult issues.

"I do regret, however, the fact that our dialogue has been limited to so few among you. I urge you to take seriously your Faith and Order Commission's recommendations for continuing dialogue with the Universal Fellowship of Metropolitan Community Churches. I ask that you get to know us better at your local level. We sincerely invite you to worship and to dialogue with us in your community.

"We, in the U.F.M.C.C., understand and regret that underneath it all, the issue is not whether we are a Christian church that qualifies for membership. The issue really is homosexuality! I want to point out that we did not choose to make homosexuality the issue in this process, but at the same time we are not going to avoid the issue. Quite frankly, I don't think that your church can afford to avoid it any longer either.

"Let it be known that the church of Jesus Christ through your action on this issue is sending a very important message to twenty-two million people, the millions of gay men and lesbians in our society. Will it be the Gospel message? Or will it be a continuing message of rejection and alienation?

"If the church does nothing else in this whole process, it ought to confess that it has been absolutely bankrupt when it comes to pastoral ministry to and with gay men and women. Most lesbians and most gay men in traditional Christian churches have really only two options. Some take the option of living a double life, concealing their sexual identity, and staying in the church. They choose to live a lie and live in hypocrisy.

"Many others take the second option, developing their own personal theology which goes something like this: 'I know that God has created me—I know that God loves me—yet the church rejects me—so to hell with the church!' Then they leave your churches. By the thousand they come to U.F.M.C.C.

"You need to know that simple pronouncements that 'homosexuality is sin' according to your interpretation of biblical proof texts, or your point of view regarding the order of creation, do not provide a foundation for an effective pastoral ministry to gay men and lesbians. The bankruptcy experienced in your churches with regard to pastoral care for and with lesbians and gay men finds its genesis in ignorance and fear.

"I am very concerned about the lack of information that so many of you have on the subject of homosexuality and of recent biblical scholarship on the issue. Most knowledge about the issue of homosexuality is less than three decades old and most of the excellent biblical scholarship on the subject is less than five years old. Consequently, it has not found its way into many of your libraries.

"For instance, there is a growing body of biblical study that acknowledges the Scripture is silent on the issue of homosexual orientation, and it rarely speaks to the issue of homosexual behavior, and only then regarding selected forms of behavior. Some biblical scholars now conclude that the often-quoted proof texts which presumably condemn homosexuality, do in fact, refer to specific behaviors such as cult prostitution, sexual violence, active and passive male prostitution, and homosexual conduct by individuals assumed to be heterosexual.

"It is well accepted today that sexual orientation is not a matter of simple moral choice. It is much more complex than that.

"It is in our capacity to love that we are created in the image of God. The unique dimension in human sexuality is its powerful capacity to express love in and through a sexual relationship.

"If one sees only heterosexual duality as evidence of the divine image in humankind, one imposes a terribly limited view of creation's order. It seems to me that such a viewpoint ignores the fact that God made room for the exceptions. In the sense that most people (some ninety percent in our society) are heterosexual, heterosexuality may be seen as a numerical norm. But are the rest of us not created by God? Are we any less God's creation? No! God makes room for the exceptions, whether barren women, eunuchs, a celibate apostle—or homosexuals. God makes room for the exceptions. Why shouldn't the church make room also?

"When you make simple pronouncements based upon your view of Scripture or your view of theological anthropology, and ignore the facts of experience and of recent scholarship, you impose on lesbians and gay men a burden of guilt for that over which we have absolutely no control, our sexual orientation.

"You may talk about compassion and you may talk about justice to relieve the oppression that gay men and women experience, but nothing is more oppressive to me than to be told that 'it's okay to be gay'—as long as I never express my sexuality. That does *not* come to me as good news! You may not be prepared to accept us into membership yet, but I urge you to get to know us better. I urge you to become informed on the issues. Every week a new M.C.C. congregation is being established somewhere in this world and, invariably, it is being established because people are being turned away from your churches. I urge you to give us good news to take back to them."

Applause was never encouraged in the meetings, but nevertheless, it occurred spontaneously, not only from our people in the back of the room, but also from National Council delegates standing by their seats. As Reverend Eastman stepped away from the microphone, a man with press credentials stepped toward him and said, "You get an A for that speech!" He was a leading writer for the *National Catholic Reporter*.

Representatives from *Christianity Today*, the *New York Times*, and *Time* magazine then asked for interviews. Don was also invited to appear, and did appear, on ABC television's prestigious network program "Nightline."

Reverend Eastman's speech was the last of the seven prepared texts delivered to the Governing Board by the Faith and Order Commission. In closing, Paul Fries of the Reformed Church in America stepped forward again and added these final words: "If a vote was taken today, my church would vote the U.F.M.C.C. down. But! As I went through the process, I knew a strong case could be made for the admission of the Universal Fellowship of Metropolitan Community Churches into the National Council of Churches of Christ. The burden of proof rests on those who would oppose their application."

Other meetings, many of them considering issues raised by our application, were held the next day, but the event of primary concern to members of my denomination was the worship service Wednesday evening. The program had been organized by our Bay Area clergy with Reverend Michael England and Reverend James Sandmire providing leadership. Use of the grand Old First Presbyterian Church, located a very short walking distance from the hotel where the National Council was meeting, had been arranged for us by their Constituent Membership Committee, which had steadfastly supported the matter of our eligibility.

Nancy Wilson asked that I preach the sermon that evening, and as with her earlier request for me to speak, I found myself looking for avenues of escape. "Why don't you do it?" I said to Nancy, who was prepared for my response.

"Absolutely not!" she replied without hesitation. "They want to hear you even if you get loud and scare them. You're the one God gave our message to. You're the person they need to hear."

I worried for days, evaluating what I should say in a sermon to many of the most important Christian leaders in America. It was an opportunity that would have been beyond belief only a few years earlier.

At first, I thought about preaching a sermon without any mention of homosexuals or homosexuality, but I knew that would be an unforgivable evasion. I prayed, "Dear Lord, what shall I say to this special gathering? You've got to give me the message!"

My lover became annoyed when I continued to be upset. He eventually broke the tension by laughing at me. "This is when you're best—when you don't know the way," he said. "Relax! Preach what God leads you to preach. You be you. Don't change a thing."

After the mini lecture, I regained my composure, deciding that the Council's Governing Board should witness us as we are. I would not even suggest to anyone how they should dress. Although a couple of our members wear opposite-sex clothing, I was not about to tell them not to do it. Nor would I take it upon myself to ask individuals who outfit themselves in leather to dress otherwise. The decision was not easy, but it was the right decision. My only residual uneasiness was that some people might arrive at our service flaunting intentionally outlandish costumes (which the media love) just to prove they could do it!

When the time for our service arrived, San Francisco was at its wonderful best. Hundreds of our members from Bay Area congregations eagerly arrived to participate in gospel songs and prayer. As they entered the beautiful old Presbyterian church, I suddenly realized that I had never suspected so many of our men owned conservative three-piece suits! And a female friend I had never seen in anything but slacks arrived wearing a dress. She wobbled from pew to pew in high-heel shoes she had not worn since her mother's funeral fifteen years before. "Don't—you—say—a—word!" the woman cautioned when she caught me smiling in disbelief.

There are perhaps twenty-eight steps up to the entrance to the church's sanctuary. As the Council's Governing Board arrived from their other meetings, they discovered some of our members hauling several people in wheelchairs up the stairs. When all were inside, nearly seven hundred Christians were present, including approximately one hundred and fifty Governing Board members (57 percent of the representatives) from the National Council of Churches.

The evening began with several hymns sung by our congregation. It was an emotional and rousing icebreaker called Singspiration, which Reverend Willie Smith had instituted at the very beginning of Metropolitan Community Church. Next, Elder Michael Mank played the organ while a double line of our clergy processed into the chamber wearing a fine array of robes in celebration colors. After the Gloria, our choir stood. Some of our visitors from the other denominations expected the choral singers would try to impress them with a classical arrangement, something like the Hallelujah Chorus from Handel's *Messiah,* but what our choir did sing was a very moving, traditional rendition of the beloved children's hymn: "Jesus loves me, this I know, for the Bible tells me so." Before the song was over, people throughout the church were crying. They were still wiping their eyes when Reverend Wilson introduced me to the assembled congregations.

I took a moment to observe people before I began my sermon. There was a sprinkling of gay and lesbian persons from the National Council of Churches. There were also many nongay guests who were the foremost leaders of America's Christian churches. For the most part, the mixture appeared deceptively homogeneous, with little to alert a chance observer that this was not a typical congregation—although Episcopal and Methodist church leaders were located in close proximity to several men in leather, and I spied a transsexual seated beside a bishop. But nobody seemed to care. It was wonderful while it lasted!

My sermon was a little longer than my usual self-imposed limit of twenty minutes. I needed more time because I wanted to retell the story of Metropolitan Community Church and to relate some of the good things that had happened to us—and some of the terrible things, too, like the tragic fire with its aftermath of discrimination in New Orleans. It also seemed appropriate to recite the stories of two young men who lived in different periods of history:

"We have become accustomed to being told that we're going to die and go to hell!" I said to the leaders of many National Council of Churches communions. "We've been told that all our lives. It's nothing new, but it came as a shock to a young man in Texas who had been attending a fundamentalist church ever since he was born. One Sunday, when the man's mother and father were visiting, he received a phone call from his pastor asking him to be present in the church that day. The young man, whose parents were not aware that their son was gay, invited his relatives to accompany him. At the end of the service, the fundamentalist pastor announced that a congregational meeting was going to commence immediately.

"Suddenly, the preacher began ranting about damnation. When he was worked into a fury, he unexpectedly turned and announced to one and all, including parents, that the young man was being excommunicated—for being homosexual!

"The youth had never been so embarrassed in his life. He broke down. He started crying. I don't know what was the reaction of his parents. I can't even imagine!

"But the preacher wasn't finished. He continued his vicious condemnation. After a while it was too much. When the preacher shouted, 'You're gonna die and go to hell!' the young man refused to accept any more abuse. He stood and shouted back at the preacher, 'No, I'm not going to hell—because I never want to be around people like you again!' "

Lesbians and gays who were listening to me in the sanctuary that evening laughed quickly. They had heard, or been a part of, similar stories. People from the National Council laughed, too, but I could see that many of them were hearing something new. As I continued, they remained attentive and seemed particularly thoughtful.

"I have another story I would like to tell," I said. "This happened a long time ago. You will know it from the Bible. There was a man who was blind. One day, Jesus touched him and healed him. Of course, the fellow was really happy, but the busybodies of that day rushed to his parents and complained about Jesus working a miracle on the Sabbath! And they also inquired, 'How is it that your son can see?' Well, the mother replied, 'He's free, bar mitzvahed, and old enough to answer for himself—so go ask him.' Which they did. The young man had just started to give thanks to Jesus when the hyprocrites crowded around and they said, 'Save your praise for God. This Jesus is a sinner, he worked on the Sabbath.' Whereupon, the young man answered Jesus' detractors with words that have rung in the hearts of humanity for two thousand years, 'Whether he be sinner or no, I know not—all I know is that once I was blind, but now I see!'

"And that has been true for Metropolitan Community Church. Once we were blind but now we see. Nobody is ever going to take our sight away from us again!

"To members of the National Council who are in church with us tonight, I particularly want to say, don't worry about how you vote on the Universal Fellowship for eligibility in your Council. Do what the Holy Spirit leads you to do. What more can I say? There are twenty-two million homosexuals in America. In Metropolitan Community Church we have thirty-five thousand. Those figures ought to tell you something. They say to me that the majority of gay men and lesbian women in the United States are in your churches, not in mine! You may not know who they are, but they are hurting because of you.

"Most certainly, you will have to decide what you're going to say to God on Judgment Day when God asks, 'What did you do to, or do for, the lesbians and gays who are members of your churches? Amen?' "

"Amen!" responded the congregation.

I took my seat.

The service, made beautiful with splendid group singing, which is favored in our churches, continued until we arrived at an historic event. Most of us were unaware as we approached Holy Communion that the National Council of the Churches of Christ did not, and had never been able to, offer the Blessed Sacrament. Although in their thirty years of existence they had managed to bring members of their various communions together in worship, Council services had always been abbreviated and noncommittal because, among other things, they could not agree upon what constitutes the Eucharist.

Metropolitan Community Church, on the contrary, needing to be truly ecumenical with so many different denominational wellsprings, never had any difficulty celebrating Holy Communion, which we have served since our very first service in 1968.

We believe in a communion open to all who will partake. Since we never try to keep anybody away, it is not part of our consciousness that there are those people who are determined to prevent others from receiving the Holy Sacrament.

On May 11, 1983, at our services in San Francisco, two lesbian ministers, Reverend Freda Smith and Reverend Nancy Wilson consecrated communion with faith, grace, and devotion—but being women, their role in the proceedings was as foreign to some representatives of the National Council as was the ecumenical communion itself. Many of the Council's denominations had never permitted women to have any active participation at the altar, and certainly not in celebration of the holiest of all rituals of faith. Yet our presentation was so free from self-consciousness that the leaders of many churches quickly recovered from shock and joined with our gay and lesbian community at the Table of the Lord.

People streamed forward toward the altar. We welcomed people from mainline churches, black churches, and Orthodox churches. Many were the highest-ranking officials in the National Council. Important leaders from America's churches stood in line to receive Holy Communion from Metropolitan Community Church. At separate stations, eight of us—the Reverends Nancy Wilson, Freda Smith, Sandmire, England, and Evans, myself, and two lay participants, Michael Mank and Adam DeBaugh— were honored to serve.

Adam felt a surge of excitement when, during communion service, he saw an Episcopal bishop walking in his direction. Because of early conditioning, Adam admitted afterward that he wanted to say, "Oh no, Your Grace, you serve me!" Meanwhile, Nancy received numerous gay members of the National Council coming to the altar side by side with their lovers. Nongay members of their Governing Board were able to adjust to what was happening.

The moment was historic!

Gay people were ecstatic!

I saw a fellow who works for one of the wire services standing some distance from me in the line to the altar. His reporter's notepad was protruding from a coat pocket, forgotten as he waited, inconspicuously crying. He just stood, patiently waiting in line for his turn to move forward, not trying to reach for a handkerchief to wipe away the wetness. I think that writer was not gay, but merely overwhelmed by the service.

When it was over, a woman on the Governing Board said, "I've never felt the Holy Spirit in my church like this. I don't know what you people do. Why do you have it when we don't?"

Another woman, obviously amazed, said to Nancy, "You used inclusive language. It's wonderful!"

Reverend Wilson smiled. "Yes, inclusive language works," she said. "Some people don't even notice a difference."

"Women ministers at the altar. I never thought I'd live to see the day!" was another dazed reaction.

A dignified, almost stately black man shook hands with me as he was leaving. "You preached a fine sermon," he said. "It brought back memories when you were speaking about the terrible fire in New Orleans. You told about the minister who offered you the use of his church when all others had turned their backs. That same minister was the man who first brought me to the Lord."

"Wonderful!" I said, and asked, "Where is Reverend Kennedy today?"

The man became more solemn. "Reverend Perry," he said, "We miss him. Reverend Kennedy is deceased. He is gone on to be with Jesus. Amen."

I shared the stranger's feelings. "Brother, who are you?" I asked. He was the bishop of the Methodist church in Seattle, Washington.

Other people continued to pause as they were exiting. Somebody said to Reverend Freda Smith, "You people really know music. Is everybody in the congregation a member of the choir?"

Smiling, Freda replied, "Our people like to sing. We've discovered that if there is enough bellowing, it does sound wonderful!"

The leader of a major denomination stopped by Nancy. "This service and the Lord have changed my mind," he told her. "I don't know how long it will take my church to do right by gay people, but I know it's something we have to do." Turning to me, he said, "Your testimony rings true. We've heard God's spirit in your preaching. We can't walk away without knowing that we've heard something profound."

A clerk who works for the church said, "You M.C.C.'ers really mean this stuff, don't ya?"

"Yeah, you bet!" said Adam.

In the fall of 1983, the meeting of the National Council of Churches in Hartford, Connecticut, was the end of a chapter—but not the end of our story, which will continue to be written for many years. In Hartford, after a long and torturous session, the Governing Board voted to postpone indefinitely any vote on the matter of our eligibility. Chess players would call the decision a stalement; yet we considered ourselves winners. The people who opposed us wanted an immediate "No" vote in order that they might finally be done with us, but the overall membership of the National Council was not willing for that to happen.

The most decisive factor operating against us was the continuing threat from ten Orthodox denominations to withdraw from the National Council if we were so much as declared eligible to be voted upon for membership. It is the Council's tragedy that they were unable to vote their hearts and their conscience.

Several members of the National Council came to us in Hartford and tried to talk us into withdrawing our application for membership. They said it would be a "loving" thing to do, that it would get the Council "off the hook." Our representatives were in turn saddened that friends did not realize that a retreat on our part would be poor strategy and a dishonest thing to do. In the beginning, their leadership was of the opinion that we might be an instrument to destroy the Council, but our application and the debate which followed probably contributed to increased communication between their communions. The result was greater knowledge for them, greater strength for them, and even possibly, the foundation of their ultimate survival.

Sexuality, unquestionably, was the paramount issue. In that regard, Metropolitan Community Church has had a tremendous impact on the National Council of Churches. Some of their communions, but not all, are willing to admit we have influenced them in a positive manner. When it comes to matters like nuclear proliferation, Council members courageously speak of principles and values, but in matters of love or homosexuality, their otherwise bold men and women have a tendency to become pale. Not many have honestly faced such issues in their own churches.

The National Council of Churches now holds worship services, something they never did before they came to ours. I know we played an important part in that achievement. I also realize that they are utilizing everything we had to offer—without accepting us. Nonetheless, we continue to participate. We are invited to their meetings although we are unable to vote. We meet with their Faith and Order Commission and join in their commission concerned with family life and human sexuality.

When the Orthodox churches declared that Metropolitan Community Church was not the real church, it was discovered that the Orthodox felt that none of the other communions in the National Council were real churches either! The Orthodox were motivated by a belief that they were building a bridge to help everybody else come forward to *their* supreme belief. Such narrow interpretations are contrary to one of the Council's basic requirements for eligibility—that one communion must respect the convictions of another.

There may always be Orthodox churches saying, "Let M.C.C. become a member of N.C.C. and we will get out!" I cannot say differently. Those Orthodox churches have not changed in a thousand years. Maybe they will pull away from the National Council. It is not unusual for them to be out of step with other mainline churches. No matter what happens, we have a large hurdle before us. Membership would be nice, but we can go on for centuries just the way we are. Perhaps we can stretch out our educational process to help bring the Orthodox along.

One of the bright moments in our continuing dialogue was when, in a private conference, an Orthodox theologian turned to one of our theologians and said, "I think what M.C.C. is saying about religion not centering on sexuality is much like what Copernicus said—that the earth revolves around the sun, and not the sun around the earth."

But change and enlightenment evolve slowly.

Galileo defended Copernicus' hypothesis that the earth spins around the sun and, for his efforts in 1632, Galileo, a Catholic, was declared to be a heretic and was condemned to house arrest for the latter part of his life. Not until 1983, after 351 years, did his church admit the error.

13

AIDS: 1981 . . .

As Jesus passed by, he saw a man blind from
his birth. And his disciples asked him,
"Rabbi, who sinned, this man or his parents,
that he was born blind?" Jesus answered, "It
was not that this man sinned, or his parents,
but that the works of God might be made
manifest in him."
                        —JOHN 9:1-3

IT Came from Outer Space, It Came from Hell, It Came from Under the
Sea — all are, or sound like, titles of old horror movies. Their monsters
are nothing, however, compared to the dreadful, uncompromising HIV
virus that, in real life, stalks the earth. Where it originally came from is
still debated. Scientists continue the search for answers while discovering
new questions.

What might have seemed reasonable ten years ago is antiquated sup-
position today. It was only in 1981 when an acquaintance, knowing that
Haitians were one of four groups manifesting a high incidence of Ac-
quired Immune Deficiency Syndrome, postulated that since Haiti has a
moist, tropical climate, it was reasonable to assume that AIDS—in much
the same manner once ascribed to the spread of athlete's foot—was
contracted in damp places. His faulty conclusion was that AIDS lurked
(with an emphasis on public swimming pools and steam baths) where
people walked without their shoes.

Meanwhile, a large group of researchers generating considerably
greater scientific validity, was compiling evidence that AIDS probably
stemmed from the Eastern Hemisphere. Learning that in Central Africa
as many as three hundred thousand had already died of AIDS—with

five million more African men, women, and children at risk because they were already infected —researchers had strong reasons to believe, without absolute proof, that the terrible, rapidly worsening global calamity began in the jungle. Scientists have found "green" African monkeys in dense tropical areas, living happily, although all of them are carriers of what is perhaps the deadliest mutation of AIDS ever discovered. A widely presented theory holds that one of the monkeys scratched a human, and thus began ever expanding circles of death and fear, spreading around the globe.

In the mid-1980s, several Third World countries (apparently prompted by Russians to embarrass Americans) expounded still another hypothesis, one that suited their own propaganda purposes. It was no more scientific than the "athlete's foot theory" for the sudden virulence of AIDS, yet considerably more intriguing than the green monkey speculation.

According to nations unfriendly to the United States, AIDS was not a major problem in centers of world population until the U.S. Department of Defense, in conjunction with secretive technicians working on germ warfare, captured a relatively unknown virus in a testtube (or however you capture such things), took it to a laboratory in Maryland, not far from Washington, D.C., and cultured it into the monstrous and deadly virus that now strikes universal fear!

We may never know the chilling truth about the sudden prominence of AIDS, evolving from obscurity to omnipresence in less than a decade, but if there is any possible veracity in the last hypothesis, how sickening it would be to imagine top national politicians trying to decide upon whom to test the deadly virus. I shudder at the thought of a White House attorney saying, "Test it on the Jews"; a Cabinet member suggesting, "Test it on the blacks"; and both of them being overruled by even higher authority using words like, "I say test it on the queers!"

Although the foregoing is patently implausible, the reluctance of President Reagan to make any great effort to halt the spread of the plague as long as it seemed concentrated in the gay community, was equally difficult to believe —but true for most of his eight years in office.

In 1983, the White House was presented with a statement by Dr. Marcus Conant of San Francisco, in which the doctor detailed the public health AIDS problem in no uncertain terms. In his submission, Dr. Conant desperately tried to penetrate President Reagan's bureaucratic shield, emphatically warning, "Western civilization has not confronted an epidemic of this magnitude in the twentieth century. . . . Emergency action is desperately needed . . . to slow the spread of this epidemic and to prevent a calamity of incalculable magnitude."

In reply, executive aides told Dr. Conant something to the effect that gay men deserved AIDS and we had asked for the disease because of our behavior—that the only cure needed for "the gay plague" was for homosexuals to become celibate. What was really meant was that we should return to the closet—to hide and die! It was an unfeeling, fundamentalist chorus speaking.

To the best of my knowledge (and not to the president's credit), in his speeches Ronald Reagan was never able to utter words that even slightly indicated he had any knowledge of the existence of homosexuals, one tenth of the nation's population! Worse, although AIDS—with its sexual aspects—came into public awareness entirely during the Reagan administration, our nation's former leader, unlike his successor, consistently remained reluctant to forthrightly discuss the burgeoning health crisis.

Originally an affliction primarily of male homosexuals, AIDS had such a low priority with President Reagan that during his first administration, the critical early years when education and public awareness could have considerably contained the pyramidlike spread of the HIV virus, our chief executive intentionally kept government funding to less than the cost of *one* fighter airplane! While thousands of gay people died horrible deaths, and with millions more threatened, a see-no-danger attitude was maintained in the White House.

(To be fair, it must be added that homophobia did not infect the entire First Family. Lack of official sanction did not prevent the president's son, Ron, from chalking up a first to his name by hosting a nationally televised film in which, in an effort to demonstrate AIDS prevention, a condom was displayed and then carefully unrolled on a sturdy yellow banana!)

"The problem cannot be solved by throwing money at it!" was a favorite expression of the Reagan administration during the same period when our national debt became a scandal. Money that was available in an attempt to create enormously expensive, futuristic killing machines, was not available to deter a contemporary lethal disease. Nevertheless, a hypothetical attack from our enemies overseas was hardly more dangerous to America's well-being than the assault already in progress from an essentially invisible virus—the tiny enemy within.

AIDS, as politicians would learn, can be likened to Pandora's box. Once the lid is off, there is no getting all of the horrors back inside again. Now the AIDS virus, wherever it came from, is loose upon the world. It is not just a gay plague! It is no longer just killing homosexual men and several other minorities.

271

AIDS is now a danger to everyone! To men and women, children and babies. Today AIDS is no longer a word to be whispered, as it once was. It is all out in the open now. But the gay community suffered first, and in the years of greatest need, the gay community suffered almost always alone. All of us knew somebody who died. All of us had friends who were going to die. All of us came early to a knowledge of grief.

Most of us came to know what it is like to be ostracized by relatives and fair-weather friends.

It was sad.

And it was frightening.

Steve Regalado continually heard people on television referring to people like himself as victims instead of patients, and Steve lost the will to live. Steve was worn down by derogatory comments. I kept trying to change Steve's depressed attitude, but even though I made every effort to talk him into living with AIDS, it was impossible. Steve could only think about dying with AIDs. There was no way to comfort him.

I remember saying to my lover, Phillip, "Steve's not going to last. It's like he's rushing to embrace death to get away from the embarrassment, the guilt, the mean things people say."

Actually, Steve was infected with two diseases. AIDS was first. The second was a debilitating personal homophobia that exists within our gay and lesbian communities as much as in the nongay communities which oppose us. It is not surprising that many of our people suffer from oppression sickness, having been relentlessly brainwashed for years to believe that we are something less than good! Once a false idea like that becomes ingrained, it often becomes difficult or impossible to disregard.

Steve Regalado was a fairly quiet young man who did not stand out in a crowd. In the company of friends a pixie's twinkle came into his rich black eyes. He was dark in complexion, not tall, and of slender build. When I first met Steve, he was like a little hippie with long hair and a special charisma. Steve had an easy sense of humor then, and the ability to laugh. He became president of our M.C.C. youth group in Los Angeles for a time—before he drifted away from the church, searching for some other fulfillment, another dimension in life. Eventually, he became a cameraman for a local television station.

Years had passed when Steve unexpectedly telephoned me at my office. It was a Monday morning, and my joy of hearing from him was soon dampened by anguish. Steve had a story that he related to me without any prompting. In the middle of the previous week he had been to a doctor with a blue spot on one of his limbs, an ominous symptom which he pushed toward the back of his consciousness because for the entire weekend he was having house guests. They were his only living relatives, his brother, his brother's wife, and their two young children. On Friday, when Steve and his family were preparing to go out for dinner at a local Mexican restaurant, Steve's telephone rang. It was Steve's doctor with terrible news.

"Your tests are positive," said the doctor. "You have Kaposi's sarcoma."

"What's that?" asked Regalado.

The physician hesitated, took a breath, and replied. "We're talking about cancer," he said to the young man. "You have AIDS."

Steve nearly collapsed. For a moment everything around him seemed unsteady. In a daze he cradled the telephone. His world shattered. Simultaneously, another anguish swirled through his head. What could he do with guests who would be with him for the next three days, for an interminable weekend that had barely begun? His family, in Steve's hour of feverish despair, seemed alien.

What would they do if they knew the truth?

And what would Steve do?

During the next seventy-two hours Steve forced a smile, pretended to laugh, and suffered in a way which would allow no one but the most intuitive to suspect that inside, panic was tearing Regalado apart.

He was unable to speak of AIDS because he knew the words would automatically be translated to mean homosexual. For his brother and their pseudomacho culture, open homosexuality meant indefensible shame. It was automatically a cause for derision and dishonor. Consequently, on that infamous Friday evening, all day Saturday and all day Sunday, until ten o'clock Monday morning, Steve never spoke a word about his AIDS infection, keeping the knowledge contained within himself, creating a miserable, volatile mixture of terror and self-hatred.

He was numb. As he entertained, nothing diminished his reluctance or fear of sharing the awful secret. Finally, on Monday morning, Steve's brother, not any wiser, departed with his wife and children. By then Steve had already decided to call me for help.

The telephone rang as I walked into my office.

Almost as soon as Steve identified himself, he blurted out the horror that had been percolating within. "Reverend Perry, I have AIDS!" he exclaimed. "What have I done? I'm being punished! God forgive me, what can I do?"

We talked for a few minutes. I tried to calm him. Then I asked, "Can you come to my office?" When the answer was affirmative, I said, "Well, get over here right away."

Steve came through the doorway with a drawn, woebegone look that conveyed an unforgettable message. I went to him immediately and put my arms around him. Steve clenched my shirt with both hands and held on to me. He began to shake with sobs and he cried with his head against my chest. Words conveying the mental agony Steve had repressed throughout his terrible weekend tumbled out of him for most of the ensuing hour.

I listened to old myths, clichés dredged up from the gutter, stupid redneck insults, Catholic condemnations that Steve would never forget, and the corrosive, overriding guilt that he was the one to blame for having been invaded by a miserable "homosexual" virus. Everything he said made him hate himself more. So much trash was crammed into Steve Regalado's head that, try as I might, there was nothing I could do to sweep it away.

"I don't know if I believe in God or not," Steve told me.

"That's okay," I replied. "Right now, I'll believe in God for both of us. Don't worry about that. At this moment it's not important what you believe. Let's just talk. Let's talk about living."

But all my words were in vain.

Nothing I said changed anything. There had been too many years, formative years, of irreversible social condemnation which were having a morbid effect upon their victim. He wanted only to talk about death. Then and there I could tell Regalado was not going to live. He stubbornly clung to the idea that he was ill because he was sinful. He was punishing himself.

"I guess people will be happy that I'm dying," Steve persisted in saying. His attitude was horrible. His condition worsened with frightening speed.

Not many months after AIDS had been diagnosed, Steve's death was near. He telephoned me from the hospital. "Reverend Perry, I need to talk to you," he said.

"I can be there in thirty minutes," I answered. "I'll leave at once."

"No," said Steve. "Would you mind waiting until one-thirty?"

"Okay," I said. I knew Steve liked to space his visitors. He never liked it when people overlapped each other or showed up unannounced.

When I arrived, Steve turned off a religious program that was ending. I placed a chair beside his bed and after a few moments of conversation, Steve took a small spiral-bound notebook from the tray between us. "I've been writing down some things," he said.

Steve knew he was having a problem with loss of memory and was making notes to himself. The Kaposi's lesions, as sometimes happen, were attacking his brain and impairing Steve's thinking abilities. Nevertheless, he still knew very well who he was.

"Should I have a funeral?" Steve asked.

"I think you should," I replied. "Funerals are for friends, for those who are left behind. They are a way of giving us permission to feel grief."

"Well, I don't want sad music."

"What do you want?"

"Barry Manilow."

The choice surprised me. Frankly, because of his youth, I had expected that Steve was going to ask for something more radical, like rock and roll!

"And Reverend Perry," he said, "if you're in town, I want you to preach at my funeral."

I nodded in agreement and Steve made a notation.

"Is your brother in L.A.?" I asked.

"He was here—when I was in the hospital—the time before."

"But not now? Where is he now?"

A pained expression dulled Steve's eyes. "My brother hasn't called lately. It's my fault. I've made them ashamed."

There are so many things about AIDS that make me angry. At that moment it was a pattern of selfishness a few families have displayed. I wanted to kick Steve's brother's rear end!

"Can I call him?" I asked.

"No, Reverend Perry," Steve replied softly.

He sat up straight in the hospital bed, withholding emotion, but I could see how the situation bothered him. He was badly hurt, carrying all the world's guilt, believing he deserved to suffer.

Four days later, Steve Regalado was dead. Before the end, he had been unconscious, in a coma. Elizabeth, who was president of our youth group, had patiently kept a vigil at his bedside.

"I've read that people in a coma can still hear," Elizabeth told me, "so I stayed and talked to him. I wasn't sure what to say. I didn't want to see him suffer. So I said, 'Steve, it's okay. It's okay to release.' Two hours passed. I talked about everything, about television, and the youth group and how Jesus loves all of us, and every so often I repeated, 'Steve, it's okay. It's all right. It's okay to let go of life.'

"For a while, I cradled his head in my arms. Then all at once a tear ran down Steve's cheek and he was gone. I like to think a guardian angel took Steve away and left his pain behind."

When we were in the initial phases of coming to grips with AIDS, it was popular to associate and limit the syndrome to four definite groups: Haitians, Hemophiliacs, Hard-core drug users, and Homosexuals. For those who like their diseases tidy, it was neat to have the name of each of the four groups begin with the same letter. Moreover, for those who wanted to keep farther than an arm's length from the frightening, vaguely defined menace, it was very popular to be smug and say, "Well, I'm safe—thank God I'm not in one of those H categories!"

And while shock, dismay, disbelief, and fear—gut-wrenching fear—spread across homosexual communities, religious opportunists with no love in their hearts for gays, completely devoid of honest spiritual sensitivity, seized an opportunity to further their own ministries of disinformation. From their pulpits and anywhere else, hatemongers pointed their fingers at gay men and attacked us at a time when—if they had been true Christians—if they had even the slightest understanding of the Gospel of our Savior, Jesus Christ, they would have prayed for the physical recovery of AIDS patients. Instead, they sent such a stream of vitriolic condemnation in our direction as to shame the Devil!

While this was happening across America, in San Diego in 1986, people of all faiths assembled at the Metropolitan Community Church, pastored by Reverend David Farrell, to take part in a weekend prayer vigil. The meeting was held in behalf of people with AIDS—and for the friends and loved ones of people with AIDS. It was not an exclusively homosexual gathering. The general public was invited and welcomed. A mother in attendance had lost her three-year-old daughter. Another mother had lost her son.

Nearly a thousand printed invitations were sent to local priests, ministers, and rabbis in that area of Southern California. Some attended. Many others either ignored the proceedings or graciously declined. One misguided fanatic, leading a collection of evangelistic hoodlums, created a dramatic and ugly commotion, but that was not until the final day of the fifty-hour vigil.

In the beginning there was calm. On Friday, workshops formed in the evening to disseminate medical advice, symbolic candles were lit, and a solemn prayer meeting began on schedule. Their theme for the weekend proceedings was well described by vocalists. They sang:

> *For the times when we're apart,*
> *Close your eyes and know*
> *These words are coming from my heart;*

And then if you can remember,
Keep smiling, keep shining,
Know that you can always count on me—
For sure—
That's what friends are for.
In good times, in bad times,
I'll be on your side forevermore.
That's what friends are for.

Reverend Farrell stepped forward to speak after the singing. David is well known and well liked in San Diego. At one time, he had been the private secretary of his uncle, San Diego's Roman Catholic bishop. David left that vocation because he could not stomach the hypocrisy of being a homosexual in a church he knew would throw him out if his sexuality became public knowledge. (It did not help him to know that Cardinal Spellman was gay and was probably never reproached.)

The weekend prayer vigil, first conceived in San Diego, was typical of David's ideas of confronting social issues. He wanted to challenge other Christian churches to really become the truly caring churches they say they are!

"We begin a vigil of prayer in which we are going to be praying in all kinds of ways," Farrell said from the pulpit. "We've invited every man, woman, and child of goodwill in the city and county of San Diego, no matter what their faith, to come and share with us in this vigil of prayer throughout this weekend—to come and pray to the Lord in the best way that they understand, in the way that they know God—and to ask God to unite us as one people, to unite us as one in prayer against the heartbreak and the suffering that is caused by AIDS, and by the issues surrounding AIDS.

"Often this weekend, I've been asked by people calling on the telephone, and by members of the press, why we're reaching out and asking other churches and other religious groups to join with us in this prayer against AIDS. I explained to them what many of you here tonight already know: that not only these people that have AIDS, but their brothers and sisters, and fathers and mothers and relatives, and friends and neighbors and co-workers—who probably represent every congregation in the city and county of San Diego—they also are feeling the loss and the illness of loved ones.

"These people need the comfort and the ministry of their pastors and rabbis and priests and other religious leaders. So we're asking the pastors and rabbis and priests to unite with us in this vigil of prayer, to join with us in our sanctuary for a moment or for an hour, at any time during the weekend, to take advantage of the educational opportunities we're offering, the informal panel presentations, and discussions with people in various areas of expertise.

"Most of all, we ask these men and women to lead their congregations in public prayer to create in our community a climate of compassion and care and concern for all those whose lives are affected by AIDS. Brothers and sisters, you know as well as I do, that means everybody. Everybody's life is affected by AIDS.

"We hope from what we are beginning here in the city of San Diego, a movement is going to sweep right across the United States of America, and that in every city they will hold a vigil for AIDS, uniting brothers and sisters of all faiths in prayer."

When he was finished, Reverend Farrell stepped away from the pulpit, and voices arose in song. They proclaimed, "We are the world, we are the children," and they also sang:

> We'll stand together, forever,
> As servants of the Lord.
> We're one in our commitment
> In answer to the call.

On Saturday and Sunday, day and night, the prayers, songs, and workshops continued. There were numerous testimonials. Then came the disruption. There was shouting from outside. Debris struck the church. Suddenly, fanatics were screaming through the open door. "Homosexuality is sin!" they shouted. "AIDS is your punishment. You are all going to hell!" It made no difference to the yahoos that individuals within the church were trying to pray.

People who wanted to be with us fought their way inside through an organized, shouting mob. The mob's carefully dressed leader was a man with thin lips, chubby jowls, permanent-waved gray hair, and dark glasses pinching tightly at the bridge of his nose.

That evening, on San Diego's Channel 10, Michael Tuck, a particularly handsome, vastly better than average newscaster, said to his television audience, "I'm about to break a cardinal rule that says ignore the fanatic— to even acknowledge his presence is to give him credence. Usually in the past, it's been easy enough to follow that rule with the Reverend Dorman Owens and his little band of sanctimonious bigots, but this weekend, I have to admit they got the best of me.

"The whole thing started because of plans by the Metropolitan Community Church of San Diego to hold a fifty-hour prayer vigil for victims of AIDS—prayer that God would heal both their physical and spiritual woes. The Reverend David Farrell was careful to point out that the vigil was not about lifestyles, was not to condemn or condone anybody's sexual preference. Indeed, some of those who attended the vigil, praying for some degree of comfort, were not homosexual. They were the parents of small children who either died or will die from that terrible disease.

"Our reporter Mark Matthews' story about the service had barely aired last night when the phone rang at our news assignment desk. It was the right-wing agitator, the Reverend Dorman Owens, incensed by what he had just seen. 'Don't you know that's a homosexual church?' he demanded to know.

"Owens is always looking for someplace to picket, and he had just found his target for the next day. He and his followers would do it loudly so the people inside, many of them already grief-stricken from losing a loved one, could hear. They would disrupt prayer. And why? 'Well,' said one of Owens' followers, 'because they're praying for a cure for AIDS.' His exact words!

"The Owens people don't want a cure. They think of AIDS as some kind of divine punishment, of themselves as some kind of avenging angels. Actually, they're just hair-trigger fanatics, totally devoid of compassion. If there ever is the final judgment they so often talk about, maybe the cardinal rule will be in effect—and they'll just be ignored.

"I'm Michael Tuck, and that's my perspective."

During that same period, I was on a program that was nationally televised in Canada. The show, similar to "60 Minutes" in format, electronically brought me face to face, by television satellite, with Jerry Falwell, who has made no secret of his homophobic feelings. The subject was AIDS, and my intention, shared with many secular leaders in the homosexual community, was to do all I could to educate the still complacent public, both gay and nongay, as to the sudden presence of great danger, and to ask for immediate help in combating the growing menace that was killing hundreds, would soon kill thousands, and eventually millions.

Surprise showed on my face as soon as I heard what Falwell chose to say. It had been a long time since I was innocent, but I did actually expect that this fundamentalist preacher, in my community's time of greatest human need, would at the very minimum extend his sympathy for people like Steve Regalado, for our dead and for our dying. Nothing was further from Jerry Falwell's intentions.

His weak smile and cloying piety made me cold for a moment, and then hot with anger. I listened in disbelief to what Falwell had to say to millions in Canada's television audience. The gist of Falwell's statement was that AIDS is God's gift to gay people—just as herpes was God's gift to promiscuous heterosexuals!

Only with the greatest difficulty was I able to retain my seat in front of the camera. It was one of the few times in my life when I wanted to do something terrible. "God's gift?" I heard myself shouting into the telephone receiver that joined us verbally across the North American continent.

Ignoring my outburst, the fundamentalist preacher blandly continued to expound upon his unchristian bigotry, but I would not allow it. My words roared out, drowning his verbal diarrhea. "What a nasty god you must worship! A god that gives herpes, a miserable little itch, to one class of people, and gives agony and death to another? How can you even associate the two diseases? That's the stupidest comparison I've ever heard—a lip sore for your people and a horrible death for mine!"

Jerry Falwell, ever the calculating master of debate, tried to put me off with a puckish smile and a condescending tone of voice, but I would have none of it. My composure returned. My voice became more controlled. "I do not believe AIDS is God's gift to gay people, Reverend Falwell," I said to him, staring hard into the television camera's eye. "It is not a gift of God any more than sickle cell anemia is God's gift to black people, any more than toxic shock syndrome is God's gift to women, or any more than Legionnaire's disease is God's gift to members of the American Legion for being too patriotic!

"I do not believe in a theology of the common cold!" I said, aware that Falwell had become defensive and was willing to back away from the subject. He apparently sensed that our vast Canadian audience would sympathize with a more humane and enlightened position than that which he had originally put forward.

To this day, I still do not believe, not for one minute, in the type of god who passes out diseases. What an awful, erratic god it would be! Nowhere in Scripture did Jesus once say, "If you don't straighten up and fly right, God's going to give you a disease." Read the Bible for yourself! Disease is exactly and only that—disease.

At the present time, as we approach the third millennium A.D., fewer knowledgeable or educated people are inclined to suggest that AIDS might possibly be a gift from God! For example, when I was a guest on the Donahue show, I mentioned what Jerry Falwell had said on Canadian television and one of his embarrassed lieutenants vehemently tried to deny that Falwell had ever uttered such a crass, unfeeling statement. The reason for their radical change was, most obviously, that AIDS now exists even among the nongay inhabitants of Reverend Falwell's once smug community. AIDS is no longer just a homosexual's nightmare!

As it was said on the television show "Brothers," "This is an equal opportunity disease—you don't have to be gay to get it."

I was asked by a well-meaning friend if it was my intention that this chapter would be a definitive work on AIDS. My reply was, "Far from it." To begin with, it would be impossible. Some of the best scientists in the world are working at maximum speed to discover immunizations, cures, and everything in between. Those dedicated men and women could be very close to answering our prayers as this is written, and I prefer to believe that is true, but despite what any of us desire, the solution may just as easily be long years in the future.

Statisticians draw unhappy predictions of what will happen if this disease continues to run unchecked. The future may be grim—extreme caution is advised! Antiviral self-protection must be the norm. Any person who engages in a promiscuous sex life without considering such realities would indeed be foolish. On the other hand, any person who contracts the virus should not wither with nonproductive guilt. Yielding to despair would be acting most unwisely. Promising vaccines and drugs are available. AIDS is not an automatic death sentence. You *can* live with AIDS!

The story of Reverend Steve Pieters is inspirational. I met Steve some years ago when he was pastoring Metropolitan Community Church in Hartford, Connecticut. Steve knew that he had a theological call, but in spite of his intelligence, education, and skills, Steve's early work had never met with great success. The Lord had reserved a special task for him, one that would require energy and great courage from the dedicated minister.

It is Steve's belief that he contracted AIDS in New York, although it was not until after 1983, when he had relocated to Mount Washington, a wooded hilltop community in the center of Los Angeles, that the illness felled him with massive blows. Initially, Steve, who had always eaten properly, conscientiously taken vitamins and exercised regularly, had great difficulty in convincing anyone that he was not well. Even after he was diagnosed as having a cancer of the lymph glands, Steve could not immediately qualify for federal AIDS therapy because, at that time, such a cancer was not yet known to be among the many forms of AIDS that were being manifested.

Nevertheless, doctors did eventually realize that Reverend Steve Pieters had AIDS—and then they were quick to inform him that he had only one precious year to live! The death sentence produced a cataclysmic shock for the young minister. His was the dubious honor of being the first member of our clergy to have contracted AIDS, and I am uncertain if many others could have handled the terrible situation as well as Steve.

In a short time, Pieters went from being Sad, to being Mad, to being Glad. I will admit those words sound like catchphrases—but they are not hollow, nor are they unique with Steve. By way of an explanation, his attitude is the best example I can give. When Steve was Sad, there was only pain, useless despair, and endless mental torture. Sometimes the anguish was overwhelming!

Being Mad was better. At least, with the anger came intelligent responses, a determination not to surrender, and the fierce idea of beating all the lopsided odds. Steve Regalado never reached the second stage, but for Steve Pieters it was accomplished in a matter of days. He clearly decided that he was not going to die with AIDS—he was going to *live* with AIDS! And that made a tremendous difference.

Pieters refused to bend like some preceding him who, with their minds made up, decided, "Too bad—I'm gonna die—and that's the end of it." No! Steve refused to accept what for too many had become a foregone conclusion.

Within months of being diagnosed as having AIDS (including terminal cancer), Steve began writing extensive articles about his illness and his latest reactions to numerous subjects, including the art of living. He became involved in helping our community and working in behalf of AIDS patients. With seven other individuals in a scientifically monitored group, Steve began taking an experimental but not newly discovered drug for AIDS. It was a serum that had been administered for forty years to persons with African sleeping sickness.

Also, Steve appeared at a private Hollywood benefit for AIDS that helped to raise money to pay for research in lieu of meaningful government funding. Numerous motion picture stars were in the audience and onstage. Steve was introduced by Shirley MacLaine. She hugged him, twice, and as he stepped in front of the audience, she took his face between her hands and said, "Just speak the truth, Reverend." About that time, Steve reached the level of being Glad.

It seemed a little strange being in the spotlight and standing before hundreds of internationally acclaimed entertainers, but Steve had once studied acting and was not intimidated for long. He told the assembly how, two weeks after he had been diagnosed as having AIDS, he had delivered an Easter sermon in which he said, "The resurrection of Jesus Christ means to me that I am free to dance, even in the presence of my deadly enemy, AIDS. It means I am free to have joy, to feel God's love and have peace in my life. And so are you, my brothers and sisters, so are you."

Then Steve surprised everyone. He began to tap-dance in the bright circle of light that surrounded him, and his staccato footwork had moments of brilliance. When it was over and Steve was leaving, Stevie Wonder and Shirley MacLaine were in an elevator with him. "You spoke the truth," said Shirley, "and you tap danced for AIDS. Imagine!"

Pieters was not one to let grass grow under his feet. He attended more successful benefits and he enjoyed meeting other celebrities. Elizabeth Taylor, who argued before Congress that increased funding for AIDS research could easily be taken out of an enormous budget for national defense, was one of Steve's favorites.

Steve was appointed to an AIDS task force convened by the mayor of Los Angeles. He gathered awards. And he appeared with Tammy Bakker on her religious program. "Tammy's House Party" on the Praise the Lord (PTL) network joined Steve's image with Tammy's via a coast-to-coast satellite hookup. "Tammy's House Party" was a fundamentalist forum where, even before Jerry Falwell and his confederates took over, I, personally, would probably never have been welcomed.

Reverend Pieters was invited, however, and encouraged by Tammy's skillful interview, told his story of AIDS and homosexuality. Before the segment was concluded, Tammy was in tears, with wet streaks of mascara running down both sides of her face. To our way of thinking, she could not have looked more beautiful.

Tammy said, "How sad! That we as Christians who are to be the salt of the earth, who are supposed to be able to love everybody, are so afraid of an AIDS patient that we will not put our arm around him and tell him that we care!"

Speaking directly to Steve, Tammy added, "I want to tell you, there are a lot of Christians here that wouldn't be afraid to put their arms around you and tell you that we love you." From the audience in the studio there was heartfelt applause.

Steve, close to tears, replied, "You have a wonderful way of reaching people, Tammy. Your courage in doing this interview is giving me life, to know there are Christians who really do care about people with AIDS."

"We're praying for you," said Tammy in closing. "God bless you. We want you to beat this disease!"

Well, Tammy, it's much too early to say that Steve has won his battle.

But he has already lived seven years longer than the most optimistic doctor's prognosis. The truth is that Steve, in some terrible setback, could die tomorrow, as could anybody else. But today, his illness seems to be in total remission. In his possession, Reverend Pieters has a medical certificate from the University of California at Los Angeles, stating that they can no longer find any trace of the AIDS virus in his system!

Steve's doctors are amazed.

They have stopped giving him chemotherapy.

All other people who were on the experimental drug with Steve are dead. He is the only person to survive. One doctor said to Steve, "Either the AIDS virus is gone—or it's hiding in the nervous system and we just can't find it—or number three, there is a God!"

We accept her third alternative. God cares.

AIDS is not the end for us.

Our enemies, nevertheless, have made every attempt to transform AIDS into a political issue instead of the medical issue it rightly is. They tagged AIDS as the "gay plague," and with that appellation tried to blame gay people for the disease. They attempted to reinstate all the myths, stereotypes, and falsehoods about gay men and lesbian women that we have worked so hard, for so long, to correct. Unfortunately, there will always be those who are ready and willing to capitalize on the misfortune of others.

The reactions of indemnity companies still are much to the point. It is bad enough that most insurance carriers do everything in their power to prevent single men (of any sexual persuasion in AIDS-prone areas) from obtaining health insurance. Worse than this discrimination—perhaps even criminal—are the stories we hear of how some unscrupulous insurance managers do everything in their power to avoid paying valid claims when the disease is AIDS.

It was reported (but not proven) that insurance companies refused to honor nearly one third of all health insurance claims made by AIDS patients, claiming that the deadly manifestations of the disease were "preexisting" conditions! If the report is true, this is another matter of money over principle. "They are banking on the fact that the life span of your typical lawsuit is longer than the life span of the typical person with AIDS," Benjamin Schatz, director of a national AIDS civil rights project was quoted as saying in a lengthy Newsweek article.

While insurance companies are basically interested only in protecting their tremendous financial assets, worse cases of disguised homophobia exist. They come with a pretense of "saving" America from the "gay plague." Among the earliest, and probably not the last, of those indefatigable groups to go on the offensive were the extremist followers of the notorious egomaniac, Lyndon LaRouche.

In June 1986, LaRouche's people went to the State House in Sacramento with somewhere between half a million and seven hundred thousand signatures, all from people purporting to agree with LaRouche that there should be a referendum on the November ballot to "stop" AIDS! The problem with the initiative, however, was that it was misnamed, and the people who signed the petition had intentionally been misinformed. Everybody in his or her right mind wants to stop any awful disease—but the initiative's purpose was something different: LaRouche wanted AIDS to be officially listed as a communicable disease, a condition that under already existing state law would make it possible to ban gay people, even those who do not actually have the disease, from schools, restaurants, and other public places. Furthermore, people who would be banned could also expect to be quarantined!

In Germany, in the 1930s and early '40s, when that country was still under the dictatorship of Adolf Hitler, there was a name for the places where people were "quarantined"—they were called concentration camps. We well know that millions of Jews were railroaded into those death camps during World War II, but less publicized is the grim fact that at least two hundred thousand homosexuals made up another large percentage of the victims intentionally slaughtered by the totalitarian state! Little wonder that Lyndon LaRouche, with his dreams of "quarantine," struck apprehension into the hearts of all with a memory of Nazi gas chambers.

LaRouche's only argument—that his referendum, which came to be known as Proposition 64, would stop the spread of AIDS—sounded valid to anyone who was not informed about the facts. The truth is that it is scientifically known that AIDS, unlike tuberculosis and other properly labeled communicable diseases, cannot be spread by casual contact. You cannot get it by touching somebody with AIDS. You cannot get it by kissing somebody with AIDS. You cannot get it by drinking out of a glass used by somebody with AIDS. You cannot get it if somebody with AIDS sneezes directly into your face! There is no need to smash a plate after someone with AIDS has eaten from it! The way you get AIDS is not that easy.

The AIDS virus infects the blood supply.

The AIDS virus infects semen.

To contract the AIDS virus, you must have anal or vaginal sexual intercourse with a person who has the AIDS virus, or there must somehow be an exchange of blood.

Voting an initiative like LaRouche's Proposition 64 into law would certainly have achieved one of its author's not too subtle intentions—to damage the welfare of homosexuals. But 64 was soundly defeated because many sensible Californians came to realize that passage of such legislation most certainly would strike a severe blow at the United States Bill of Rights.

Propositions like 64 would defeat the very objectives we espouse, containment of the AIDS virus. LaRouche's bill would have caused any person (who might or might not be infected with the AIDS virus) to avoid diagnosis because of the fear of being placed on a "list." As a result, inadvertent carriers would unknowingly continue to be sexually dangerous, not because of malice, but because of the threat that their name in medical records could someday lead to internment.

What demagogues like Linden LaRouche do not understand is that most homosexuals are not submissive. None of us will ever go willingly to concentration camps! We do recall that hundreds of thousands of our own people, forced to wear the pink triangle, were gassed to death in Nazi Germany. Only one other minority suffered a greater loss in the mass of executions. So if you say, "That can't happen here," then I reply, "You bet it won't—because *we* won't let it!"

On the day after Proposition 64 qualified statewide, Los Angeles city councilman Joel Wachs stated, "If this is passed you're going to see the greatest rollback of civil rights that we have ever had in this country."

Councilman John Ferraro added, "Lyndon LaRouche and his ilk are breeding hatred."

And councilman Gilbert Lindsey concluded, "It's about time we stand up in a unanimous way and defeat these crackpots!"

Nearly five months later, on election day in November, the people of California proved they were not fooled by the malicious and dangerous initiative that would have been detrimental to the ongoing fight against AIDS.

Seventy percent of the voters rejected Proposition 64.

Our thoughts about AIDS are not entirely filled with shadow. When we stand upon the high ground we see more than death. I would like to be able to conclude with a cheerful anecdote or with a success story, perhaps something like that of Reverend Pieters and the wonder of his ministry; but the struggle against AIDS, bringing out the best and the worst in people, is bittersweet. And so, dear reader, is this:

Gary Wilson was a member of the Mother Church. He was a young bodybuilder and sang in our choir. When he moved from Los Angeles, he transferred his membership, always remaining close to our churches in the Universal Fellowship. Then, unfortunately, in San Francisco, he contracted AIDS. Afterward, we had a memorable conversation, which I will never forget.

Gary told me he was going to live with AIDS. He was not overwhelmed with thoughts of dying. He was preparing himself to win.

Gary had such faith! Even at the end, his attitude remained calm and not seriously troubled. He said, "I may be taken from this earth because of AIDS, but we all have to go one day. We're all appointed by Scripture. Reverend Perry, you've always told us that. But I want to remind you that you preached a sermon years ago, that as Christians we have a choice of going first class—or with no class at all! Do you recall?"

I did.

My sermon had been concerned with the prophet Jonah in the Old Testament. God had called Jonah to go to Nineveh to speak against wickedness, but Jonah was in no hurry to go to Nineveh. He booked passage on a ship to Tarshish instead. When a great storm threatened to sink the vessel he was on, Jonah decided the tempest was evidence of the Lord's displeasure. He said to the sailors, "Take me up and cast me into the sea, so shall the sea be calm for you." And after it was done, the storm subsided.

Now the Lord had prepared a great fish to swallow Jonah. He remained three days and three nights in the belly of that creature, and did not like the accommodations. "Out of the belly of hell cried I," were Jonah's own words, and when he prayed, God heard and answered. The fish cast Jonah onto dry land, whereupon Jonah finally went to Nineveh to preach as God had told him in the beginning.

Jonah could have gone first class, but no—he chose to go with no class at all. Yet Jonah still had to carry the message.

Gary remembered that sermon, and he declared, "Reverend Perry, I want to tell you I'm going first class! Even in death, I'm going first class! I know all that God's done for me in the past."

At our General Conference we reserved a full day to discuss the problem of AIDS and to decide upon an appropriate course to pursue. Gary stood proudly before the assembly and sang. He was very brave, and it was sad. Gary was a special person, and I was careful to keep in touch with him.

Finally, the time came when, two years after being diagnosed as having AIDS, Gary started walking into the shadow of the valley of death. As he did, I called San Francisco one day to pray with him over the telephone. He was very ill.

"I don't think I'm going to make it much longer, Reverend Perry," Gary said. "My glands are swollen. I'm having trouble eating and it's difficult talking on the telephone. But I want to tell you, I going to do the best I can. I know that death is close but I'm going first class. I told you that all along."

We spoke a little longer. Then, all at once, Gary, with his sweet spirit that never faltered in faith, said something I was not expecting. He said, "Reverend Perry, I'm going to make the transition. Do you have any messages? Is there some person on the other side you want me to say hello to?"

For fifteen or twenty seconds I was unable to speak, so completely had Gary's question taken me by surprise. In the Christian tradition we talk about death, but most Christians are like everybody else, resisting the hour of our demise with every living breath. We are in no hurry to depart although we believe in a spiritual life everlasting. Gary's words proved that for him life after death was not only imminent, but very real.

When my voice returned, I said, "Gary, you know a lot of folks I love are on the other side. Please tell them I said hello, and tell them we're on our way there, too. Someday all of us will meet in that heavenly city, the New Jerusalem, just inside the eastern gate."

Two weeks later, one of the last things Gary Wilson said to friends who were gathered with him was, "Tell Reverend Perry that I went first class."

Then he passed on into eternal life.

14
Up Close and Personal: 1977–1988

*Take delight in God, and God will give you
the desires of your heart.*
—*Psalm 37:4*

WE have so many stories!

Sometimes the stories fit together in neat chapters. Sometimes they are cherished anecdotes with independent lives of their own. Occasionally the stories are funny, occasionally they are sad. There are even events without a conclusion—although in my ministry, which confirms a just and loving God, we pray for happy endings.

What follows is a collection of a few memories, precious and not so precious, which have occurred during the past twenty years. They are events I like to remember—or need to remember—for a number of different reasons.

I recall a time in 1972 when Chip Garcia wanted me to accompany him to St. Ambrose Catholic Church in Los Angeles. I had no objection to worshiping with another denomination, and I agreed. We attended the seven o'clock morning mass. All went well until communion was served. We waited until nearly everyone else in the congregation had partaken of the sacrament before going to the altar. When we did, a wrathful priest unexpectedly turned upon us.

"You're not Catholic!" he said in such a way as to instantly put me on the defensive.

"No, sir," I replied, "but I've received communion in a Catholic church before."

"Not here!" the priest snapped. "I've seen you on television. I know who you are! We don't want your likes! So turn around—leave—get out!"

Anger dimmed my vision. I wanted to lash back, but instead I thought of Matthew's account of Jesus' words: "If the house be worthy, let your peace come upon it, but if it be not worthy, let your peace return to you. And whosoever shall not receive you, nor hear your words, when ye depart out of that house or city, shake off the dust of your feet."

Therefore, we heeded Jesus' adjuration, and as we turned to leave, to shake the dust from our feet, I strove to regain my peaceful composure. Yet as Chip and I departed from the "Mother Church of Christendom," I could not refrain from pausing in the exit long enough to lay both of my hands on a side of the front door. There I fervently prayed, "Lord, let me be the last gay person to walk through the portals of this church who has to put up with this kind of humiliation."

Four years later, in Washington State, I attended a conference held by Dignity (a prominent religious organization of gay Roman Catholics). About twelve hundred homosexuals were in attendance and all were invited to worship in Seattle's Catholic cathedral. As we sat in front seats reserved for us, Archbishop Hunthausen—on a specially prepared videotape—welcomed us into the tabernacle of our Lord.

On that occasion, I was of the opinion that the Catholics had made tremendous progress in combating their homophobia; and indeed they had. But what I was not aware of was that Archbishop Hunthausen had been called back to Rome to be rebuked for his Christian attitude toward homosexuals. His church was preparing their great retreat from the twentieth century. In the next decade, gay Catholics who wanted to remain with the church in which they were born would face truly wicked condemnation. Several unenlightened, fundamentally backward ideas were about to shake loose from Pope John Paul II's rigidly conservative head, and in October 1986, John Paul allowed the Vatican's Cardinal Ratzinger to release a naughty little pamphlet entitled "Letter to the Bishops of the Catholic Church on the Pastoral Care of Homosexual Persons." The pamphlet, in effect, attempted to pull the rug out from under Dignity, and also sought to run millions of homosexual Catholics (including a large percentage of Catholic priests) back into closets of fear. The effort has, of course, been a failure, and protesting Catholic gays have since frequently chosen to be arrested in peaceful demonstrations while engaging in disobedience to Rome.

In the middle of all this, Pope John Paul II decided to journey to America to quell what he correctly determined to be the unrest of a large and growing segment of Catholic Americans. Catholics were unhappy with dictates from Rome for various reasons, and Vatican homophobia was only one of many. If the Polish pope's visit to suppress threats of a religious mutiny was no surprise, what happened coincidentally most certainly was: I received an invitation to be part of their worship service, a celebration of the quasiecumenical movement involving Protestants and Catholics, which was held in a large football stadium in September 1987 in Columbia, South Carolina.

Why we were invited, at a time when vocal homosexual Catholics were actively being turned out of their churches, I will never know. I can only suppose our invitation had something to do with Metropolitan Community Church's continuing ecumenical dialogue with the National Council of Churches. But whatever the reason, I decided to attend and, since the invitation was for myself and another guest, I asked Reverend Nancy Wilson to accompany me.

Because we were guests of the Catholics and had accepted their invitation, there was little we felt we could do to address the problems Catholic homosexuals were having other than to give witness to the fact that we, a gay man and lesbian, existed as living proof that homosexuals continue to be a great part of God's ecumenical celebration. With such being our intention, Nancy and I each wore a button that read:

GOD IS GREATER THAN AIDS
Metropolitan Community Church

Our buttons attracted attention because among the four hundred invited clergy in attendance, we were the only people at the service wearing anything unusual. Ministers approached us to read the message pinned on our robes. Their reactions ranged all the way from "We're glad M.C.C. is here," spoken with warmth, to inquiries followed by exclamations like "God is greater than—AAIDSSS??!!!"

Some huffy Protestant clergy expressed shock that we (even as they) had been invited to be a part of the Catholics' large-scale public event. "Doesn't the Roman Church know who *they* are?" we heard airy preachers say.

"Evidently they do," Nancy replied.

The stadium held approximately 75,000 spectators. One of them, a gay rights protester in the top balcony, unfurled a rainbow flag and stood holding it throughout the service. It was a comfort to know that Nancy and I, like two early Christians, were not alone in the lion's den, for I had made up my mind that if Pope John Paul II mentioned a single word concerning homosexuals, I would stand beside my seat in the middle of the field. And if the pope had spoken adversely of lesbians or gays, I was prepared to respond at the top of my lungs even if such action might have meant being arrested.

But it never happened.

Many times, things that do not happen are as pleasant as things that do. For instance, in 1980, Reverend Joseph Gilbert organized a march for gay liberation across the most homophobic part of Florida, from Jacksonville westward toward Florida's panhandle, into Tallahassee, the state capital. Gilbert was accompanied by Reverend Lee Carlton. The gays were met by a sheriff opposed to their walking through Madison County, but the group continued. As a result, the *Tallahassee Democrat* wrote an editorial that said: "Freedom for all or freedom for none. You can't have it both ways! No sheriff in the State of Florida has the right to tell any group, including homosexuals, that they won't be protected in that sheriff's county!"

I joined the marchers as they came across the Leon County line, approaching Tallahassee, city of my birth. It was there, also, that an ex-masseur named George Suteck, who had become a Baptist pastor, intended to begin a counterdemonstration against us. It was Reverend Suteck's plan to stone us—symbolically, with rotten eggs instead of rocks—as we entered the capital city.

But as I said at the beginning, some of the best things are those that never happen. The sheriff of Leon County told Reverend Suteck, "Mister, you better throw symbolic eggs, too, because soon as you throw one egg, I'm hauling your ass into the depths of the Tallahassee jail!"

My hometown has come a long way!

Hallelujah!

Another story, a favorite of mine, also happened on the outskirts of Tallahassee. The story was told to me by a young man who had been a member of Metropolitan Community Church in Minneapolis. A number of years ago, he and his lover were out of work when, after considerable prayer, God spoke to him one day and said that if he went to Florida, a job would be waiting. The man's lover, although not religious, was agreeable to making the journey. "If you really believe God said to do it, then let's go," he said.

The pair had hitchhiked as far as Tallahassee when they had to wait for a ride at the side of the lonely, rural road. As fate would have it, a terrible rainstorm began.

"It was worse than anything either of us had ever seen. It was like

Lake Okeechobee was being dumped on our heads," the young member of M.C.C. told me. "We looked like two drowned rats. Of course, no one would pick us up. And then my lover started verbally chewing on me. 'Are you sure God spoke to you and told us to come to Florida?' he asked. 'Did God say we would have jobs? Or did God say we would have pneumonia? Which was it?' "

After a miserable hour, the young church member's faith was pushed to the limit. He said to his lover, "You're absolutely right. I probably didn't hear a thing from God, or if I did, I didn't understand the message. Here we are, no food, no money, and the sky's turned into ice-cold water. I guess God really isn't worried about the two of us." With that, he took a little book of common prayer from his pocket. It was a book he had carried with him since the days when he had been an Episcopalian. He looked at the collection of prayers with a sigh, then threw it with all his might into a creek that ran under the road.

"That book had been like a crutch for me," he said, "and my heart sank as I watched it drifting away." But within thirty seconds something surprising happened.

A truck pulled over to the side of the road. The door opened. The truck driver said, "Good god, guys, you look like you're going to drown out there. Come on and get in. Where are you going?"

"Tampa," said the young church member.

"Guess what? I'm on my way to Tampa, too," replied the truck driver. "I can give you a ride all the way."

The offer was immediately accepted, and the soaked men climbed into the front seat of the truck and began to get warm. A few miles down the road, the driver said, "Guys, I'm hungry. Wouldn't you like to have something to eat?"

"No," replied the penniless young church member, whereupon his half-starved lover elbowed him in the ribs.

"Well, I've got to stop and get something," declared the driver, pulling his rig into a parking spot beside a diner. "Come on in with me."

The trio took a seat in a booth where the two hungry young men were treated by the truck driver, not to hamburgers, but to steak dinners.

They began to feel good. Not only were their stomachs finally full, but their clothes were beginning to dry. All seemed well—until the ride to Tampa continued. Not many minutes after they were on the road again, the truck driver said, "By the way, I noticed one of you is wearing a cross. What kind of cross is that?"

"It's a symbol of our church," replied the religious young man.

"What church?" persisted the truck driver.

Suddenly, the young passenger wanted to panic. He thought, My God, what am I going to say? We're out here in the middle of nowhere, without a weapon, with this big redneck truck driver. If I tell him what church we belong to, he's liable to know we're homosexual. I can see it all now, tomorrow's headlines, in the *Tallahassee Democrat:* FAGGOTS FOUND DEAD ON NORTH FLORIDA ROAD.

Consequently, when the young man answered, he brushed his hands across his lips, intentionally slurring his words. What came out was, "Well, we attend Metro-blub-blub Com-blub-ity Church." His ruse, however, had little effect.

The truck driver understood completely. "Metropolitan Community Church," he said very clearly. Then he added, "Do you know Reverend Troy Perry?"

The passengers did a double-take.

"I couldn't believe that truck driver was gay," the religious young man told me later. "In fact, I'm certain he wasn't. But how did he know about M.C.C.? So I said to him, 'I know who Reverend Perry is. I know he's the founder of our denomination. But I've never really had the chance to meet him. I've only seen him preaching.'

"When I said that, the truck driver gave a kind of nice laugh, and he told me, 'Well, the next time you see Troy, tell him his brother Jimmy said to say hello.'"

People are always saying, "It's a small world," which is true. We meet gay people everywhere. That is not surprising—we *are* everywhere. Unfortunately, sometimes homosexuals are in places most people would rather not be—as "guests" of society. In prison, however, no matter what the felony or misdemeanor, for gays (or people who are young, attractive, or suspected of being gay) there has always existed a special kind of extra jeopardy. Not only are gay prisoners punished like other inmates, but additionally, our men and women are often physically abused, used, and otherwise treated with hostility.

Inasmuch as Jesus said, "I was in prison and ye visited me not," Metropolitan Community Church with Christian social action has, since our very beginning, felt strongly that visits to prisoners should be an integral part of our evangelical Christian work. However, when first our clergy tried to visit prisons to carry the Gospel of Jesus Christ as other churches do, we were stopped by the system and refused access. Consequently, we went to court and won a lawsuit against the State of California. Since that time, our prison ministry has been a success on both state and federal levels. Access to the Federal Bureau of Prisons was gained in our negotiations with Edwin Meese, who settled with us out of court.

Little by little we chip away at a host of unfair restrictions that have been imposed upon homosexuals. Every new position lesbians and gays openly hold is proof to the world that we are capable of doing good work, and every accomplishment is an inspiration to our sisters and brothers who seek justified advancement in public offices or other positions of trust. When I was appointed by County Supervisor Ed Edelman to serve as a member of the Los Angeles Commission for Human Rights, no gay person in America had ever previously been appointed to any type of commission. In protest, half of the existing members of the commission refused to come to my swearing in. Yet after three years, when I had successfully completed my work, the result was that many new doors were open for lesbian and gay people who wanted to serve thereafter.

In 1978, I received from the American Civil Liberties Union an award for commitment and leadership in the field of civil rights. The award was made by Alan Cranston, California's U.S. Senator. Twelve hundred people were present at the Hollywood Palladium. "Isn't it interesting," said Senator Cranston, "what crazy laws concerning homosexuals are still on the books in some of our states? Do you know that in Kansas, in this so-called enlightened day and age, it is still against the law for Troy Perry to drive a taxicab?"

The entire Christian religion should be a leading standard-bearer in the search for justice and freedom, but unfortunately many leaders of cults and denominations ignore Jesus' second commandment: "You shall love your neighbor as yourself."

The Reverend Jerry Falwell is such a person—unloving. Working out of Lynchburg, Virginia, he has, with malice, used homosexuals to promote his own ambitions. It is most unfortunate that his followers, good Baptists, have permitted their inbred disapproval of gay sexuality to let Falwell delude them into believing that *selected* uncharitable deeds and thoughts are acceptable within their Christian way of life. *Such an idea is contrary to every word Jesus ever uttered, and therefore can never be valid!*

Jerry Falwell is a merchant of hatred. He is not the first and will not be the last. He is like the moneychangers in John 2:13–16. Jesus whipped and ran them out of the temple in Jerusalem, saying, "Make not my Father's house a house of merchandise."

Now that you know what I think of Reverend Falwell, read what the none too subtle televangelist, on his "Old Time Gospel Hour," said about Christian people I love:

> Look at the Metropolitan Community Church today, the gay church—almost accepted into the...National Council of Churches—almost! The vote was against them. But they will try again and again until they get in, and the tragedy is that they would get one vote because they are spoken of here in Jude as being brute beasts—that is, going to the baser lust of the flesh to live immorally. And so Jude describes this as apostasy. Thank God this vile and satanic system will one day be utterly annihilated. And there will be a celebration in heaven!

Unconscionable tripe!

God will have news for Reverend Falwell!

And so did the courts in California, which ruled against him because of what happened on a talk show in Sacramento in July 1985. While the television program was in progress, gay activist Reverend Jerry Sloan, a minister of Metropolitan Community Church (who had once been a pal of rambunctious Falwell when they attended the Baptist Bible College in Springfield, Missouri), stood and asked why Falwell had, in March of the previous year, made defamatory comments concerning Metropolitan Community Church.

Falwell's response was, "I never said that ! It's an absolute lie!"

"Well, you *did* say it!" insisted Sloan. "It was on your program, Jerry. I have all that on tape!"

Falwell was furious. He made no attempt to retract his statement that Sloan was lying, but pompously went on the offensive.

"I'll give you five thousand dollars if you can produce that tape!" Falwell angrily declared.

Reverend Sloan is not the man to call a liar. He did actually possess an audiotape of the infamous broadcast. Sloan had purchased it from Falwell's merchandising outlet in Virginia. With Falwell's own recorded words as incontestable evidence that the minister had lied, Reverend Sloan wrote Falwell's attorneys and made a demand for $5,000, the sum Jerry Falwell had offered for proof of his own dishonor. Expectedly, Falwell refused payment. Sloan took him to court.

Why the pretentious preacher from Lynchburg believed he could win such an open-and-shut case, I will never understand. Falwell certainly underestimated the integrity of Sacramento's municipal court. I don't know what kind of justice the defendant expected, but in California slander is slander, no matter how high and mighty the perpetrator considers himself to be.

When the municipal court decided against him, Falwell boorishly declared that Sloan "was never a friend of mine," and he claimed that "militant homosexuals" had "duped the judge." According to Falwell, the judge was a Jew and gays had prejudiced her thinking by comparing the holocaust of Hitler's death camps with his prayer that we be "utterly annihilated." Deluding no one but himself with that type of rationalization, Falwell appealed the court's decision. His appeal, in my mind, was a frivolous attempt to avoid the punishment he deserved, and California's appellate court deplored the bluff. Jerry Falwell was found wrong and he was ordered to pay.

Typed on the reverse of the $5,000 check Reverend Sloan received from Falwell was a surprise statement. It said, in effect, that by accepting the check, Sloan promised not to hold a press conference to gloat about winning the money. It was an illegitimate condition, one that Falwell or his attorneys had no right to make. Therefore, Reverend Sloan cashed the check and immediately called all of the media—including the press.

"Praise the Lord, I won!" said Jerry Sloan.

(During the same year, in a completely different situation, Jerry Falwell was having other difficulties. *Newsweek* magazine reported that a forty-six-year-old computer systems analyst in Atlanta, having become really angry because his mother had been "taken in" by various televangelists and had contributed important sums of money to their unrelenting appeals, devised a scheme to take his revenge on Jerry Falwell. The analyst programmed a home computer to dial Falwell's 800 telephone number every thirty seconds, which the computer did day and night for a period of nearly nine months. Only computer-generated silence was heard by Falwell's operators, but when the analyst's telephone retaliation was finally discovered, at a cost of $1.00 per call received, Jerry Falwell undoubtedly was infuriated. His enterprise estimated that it was out of pocket nearly half a million dollars!)

There is a worthy saying that "Living well is the best revenge." Revenge, however, is unimportant. Justice is all that we, like many other minorities, are seeking. For that reason many gay ministers in Metropolitan Community Church have had no choice but to be interested in the politics of our detractors, and the politics of protecting human rights. For that reason I served for a time on the board of directors of the Gay

Rights National Lobby. And for that reason, I spent a considerable amount of time communicating with our elected state officials.

Following our march from San Francisco to Sacramento in 1971, a demonstration we held on the steps of the California State Capitol was one of our earliest civil rights activities to expand gay political influence. Good fortune was smiling because it was then that I had the opportunity of meeting Freda Smith for the first time, years before she became a reverend elder and vice-moderator of the Universal Fellowship.

Also, at precisely noon on that day at the capitol, immediately as we concluded an opening prayer with thousands of spectators crowded around us, someone shouted, "Look up!" Everyone did, and what we saw caused a ripple of awe to sweep over the spectators. A bright halo went completely around the sun. Such meteorological occurrences are not unusual in some areas of the world, but in Sacramento, most of us could not escape the subjective feeling that somehow the circle of light was a heavenly omen.

With us that day was one of the most powerful Democrats in California, Representative Willie Brown (who would become Speaker of the House), and he said, "I've heard of gay power, but this is ridiculous!"

And Senator Phil Burton, who was elected to the U.S. Congress, said, "It looks like someone upstairs is with us!"

But there were considerably more tangible miracles to come from the legislature in Sacramento. We sought passage of a Consenting Adults Bill that would keep government out of the privacy of bedrooms, where what was or was not going on was no outsider's business. Even though many reasonable people believed such intelligent reform could never become a reality in our lifetime, the effort was made, and legislating archaic laws out of existence became one of my primary humanitarian goals. When I spoke, I told audiences, "In California, if a husband and wife fell out of bed in each other's arms, they would break about fifty really stupid laws before they hit the floor. That needs to be changed!"

Merv Dymally was a member of California's State Assembly. He came to Metropolitan Community Church to hear Reverend Freda Smith read a poem she had written about the oppression of lesbian women, and afterward Dymally came to us, obviously impressed, and he said, "What can I do to help you?"

"We want to see a Consenting Adults bill passed," I replied.

At the time, Dymally was running for lieutenant governor, the second highest position in California's government. "If I win," he said, "I will do everything in my power to assure passage of the bill." And time would prove, after his election, that Dymally's promise was good.

Everything happened with what now seems like amazing speed. Representative Willie Brown shepherded the bill through California's legislature, and almost without warning in 1975, the Consenting Adults Bill was on the floor of the Senate for a vote. As ballots were cast, the count constantly shifted from the Pass column to the Fail column and back again. I was in the gallery keeping track of the votes as best I could, listening and counting and praying. Two fundamentalist preachers were seated next to me, and there were sparks between us as our opposite hopes shifted back and forth between winning and losing.

It was late when the final vote was cast, and the result was a tie—20 to 20—a tally that would not yield in either direction. As a result, it would be necessary for the president of the Senate to break the deadlock with his vote. Merv Dymally, by then the state's lieutenant governor, was automatically president of the Senate. But Dymally was in Colorado!

Frantic long-distance calls were placed. The lieutenant governor agreed to return to Sacramento immediately. In the middle of the night, the Senate chamber doors were shut and locked. Senators could not leave. Their votes remained unchanged.

We waited. Hours passed. There was information that fog had moved into the Sacramento area and planes were unable to land. Those of us who desperately wanted passage of the bill kept hoping Dymally could get through. An equal number of people opposed us.

The hour was very late. People were restless. I needed to use the rest room and was told I could go and return, but much to my chagrin, on my return I could not regain admittance. To make matters worse, for a quarter of an hour while I paced in the hallway, I could see that there really was fog outside, and it was getting thicker. My frustration continued increasing until I heard footsteps along the corridor. I looked up to see Jesse Unruh, the state treasurer, who had attended our church with his wife on several special occasions.

"Why are you out here?" asked Unruh. I explained, and with a laugh Jesse said, "Come with me and I'll get you in." As if by magic, at his approach the door to the chamber was opened and a sergeant at arms admitted both of us. Once inside, I took a seat in the main body of the Senate, just as if I belonged there, and watched treasurer Unruh continue down the aisle, jovially shaking hands with all the senators, asking, "How's everybody doing?"

The scene outside the capitol building looked like pictures of D-Day. Our state militia was present. Reporters were everywhere, waiting, anxious for any news.

(Hundreds of miles to the south, the *Press Telegraph* in Long Beach decided not to delay and proceeded to print their papers. In headlines two inches high, the newspaper declared: GAY BILL DEFEATED.

Everybody was nervous. Even as the midnight hour approached, I knew in my heart that Merv Dymally would arrive in time—but no one was sure he could make it. We knew that commercial airplanes were unable to land at the local airport. Nevertheless—finally—an exciting moment arrived. Through the fog, with rotors shattering damp, apprehensive stillness, a roaring helicopter belonging to California's State Highway Patrol appeared. The aircraft landed and unloaded its special passenger!

Dymally came forward through the night with great cheers surrounding him. His arrival was the culmination of a tremendous effort, and he had not disappointed us who had placed our trust in him. He strode into the building, walked along the main aisle, and nodded to friends on one side and the other as he went up to the front of the room. Without any preliminary ado, he said simply, "The president of the Senate votes aye!"

Just like that!

Pandemonium broke loose. We shouted and applauded like wild persons. And the fundamentalists were upset. But for most of us, it was a grand and glorious night!

After a time, ignoring the frantic efforts of pressure groups, Governor Jerry Brown signed California's Consenting Adults Bill into law.

Besides popes and politicians and people of the press, I have an opportunity to meet many other fascinating individuals, and because the office of our Universal Fellowship is located in a conservative business section of Hollywood, it naturally follows that there are often opportunities to meet motion picture actors and actresses. Such an occasion presented itself on one of my birthdays.

In my congregation there was a gay man who worked for his living as a film extra. I believe he has never had a speaking role, but has been a face in the crowd in literally hundreds of films, and he knows his way around the mythical part of Hollywood we always refer to as Tinsel Town. He came to me and said, "Reverend Perry, you've met a lot of movie stars over the years, but is there anybody in particular you would like to meet—and haven't? Is there a star I can give you for a present?"

I was not certain my friend was serious, but decided to go along with whatever he was pursuing. "Yes," I said, "there is one star I've always wanted to meet—and she's Mae West."

"Oh, Mae," said the man. "Wonderful choice. Her sign is Leo, too.

You'll love her. Think of Mae as your birthday present. I'll see that the two of you meet."

"Fine," I replied, trying not to be suspicious, at the same time amused and uncertain about what to believe. Nevertheless, on my birthday, Reverend Lee Carlton and I presented ourselves at Ravenswood, the apartment building where almost everybody in Hollywood knew Miss West lived. Lee came with me at my suggestion because I wanted somebody along to keep me from becoming nervous. He said he smelled a rat, suspecting our congregation was setting me up for a practical joke, but nevertheless we were dressed for a bona fide meeting with one of the screen's most famous personalities. Following our host, we went forward with fingers crossed. I figured the worst thing which could happen would be that a female impersonator from some company that sends out singing telegrams would try to embarrass me—and afterward I would be driven someplace else for a surprise birthday party.

"Reverend Troy Perry to see Miss West," our host, the film extra, told a man at the switchboard. He pushed a buzzer and spoke to someone elsewhere.

I looked at Lee and wondered if it was a joke. Was Lee in on it? Or were both of us being duped?

"Miss West is running a little late," the switchboard man told us. "If you'll take a seat near the palm, she'll see you in about ten minutes."

With that, I was certain the entire setup was a hoax. The man at the switchboard had most likely plugged in a line to the perpetrators, who were thus alerted to our presence. However, there was nothing to do but to wait, and as we did, I looked around the lobby. The apartment building built in the 1930s and owned by Mae West, was as elegant as one would expect. Everything was scrupulously clean; brass was polished. Furniture of decades past looked as if it were new.

Only five minutes had passed when the elevator made a noise and its ornate doors slid open. Three men stepped out. One of them was an affable bodybuilder who looked like a Mr. Universe, with huge shoulders and magnificent bulging muscles. He said for us to go up to Miss West's apartment. It was then that I realized we actually were going to visit the famous movie queen.

Her front door was opened by a butler named Grayson, who led us into the living room, indicated several couches, and asked us to have a seat. A regal chair was reserved for Miss West, who, we were told, was to join us momentarily.

A friend had advised me that our hostess should never be referred to as "Mae" (not that I ever would) and so it was to be "Miss West" the entire time. And she would refer to me always as "Reverend Perry." Lee and I had also been told that our hostess did not permit the use of tobacco in her presence, but since neither of us were smokers, her rule was not a problem.

All that I had the opportunity to observe in Miss West's apartment was the entry and the living room. A kitchen was close by, but I was unable to see into it. Two hallways led away from the large living room.

Everything was white. The carpet was white. The chairs and couches were white. A grand piano was white. And there was the famous white statue of Miss West that had been done in the nude in 1936. I had seen a picture of the statue in an issue of *Life* magazine which had on its cover the picture of Mae West in her white swan bed.

I was thinking, What am I going to say to a living legend, when a minute after we had been seated, she swept into the room dressed all in white which accentuated her beautiful blond hair. It was impossible to believe she was seventy-two. Her figure and makeup were perfect, her manner charming and elegant. Mae West did not seem to have aged since the 1930s when most of her movies were made. In her presence I could instantly understand why she had been such a total success.

Miss West's only departure from perfection was that she walked with a slightly halting step. And I was shocked to realize she was tiny! After the radiant star was seated in her chair, I could see she wore tall shoes with Carmen Miranda heels—big platforms with spikes three or four inches high!

I said, "Miss West, it's a pleasure and a delight for us to be here, and I want to thank you for permitting us to come in and share a happy birthday. In astrology, we're both Leos, you know."

She smiled and came right back at me with her trademark, that special sexy tone-slur that crawls through her voice. "Yesss, ayee-errr knowww," she said. Her manner of speaking was not quite as pronounced as in her films, but it was there. That was really the way she spoke!

After the introduction, there was nothing more I needed to do to maintain a conversation. Miss West immediately began talking about herself. I listened, amazed. I did not interrupt for a moment, so taken by her was I. She was something special. My only regret was that I had not brought a tape recorder with me (if she would have permitted that).

She told us how much she disliked W. C. Fields. Apparently he had changed one small line of dialogue in their movie *My Little Chickadee,* which she had written in its entirety, and for his effortless contribution Fields received equal screen credit. That piece of information was prompted following a telephone call Miss West took in our presence, in which she spoke to the manager of a wax museum. It seems that the museum was displaying wax figures of Miss West and W. C. Fields together, and she wanted them permanently moved apart.

In addition to anecdotes about her stage and screen career, she told us about her roles, most of which were from material she herself had written. And she showed us things people had sent to her. Thousands of fan letters came each year, mostly on her birthday. One person had mailed her a kaleidoscope, a clever little thing. When you peeped through a hole in one end of the revolving tube, instead of seeing mirror patterns from moving bits of colored glass, you saw random designs formed by little cutouts of Miss West herself! She was proud of that.

During the next hour, we received a descriptive history of where Miss West came from, and how she achieved success. She told us about her plays and she bragged that the popularity of her films saved Paramount from going out of business. Almost everybody, except an overly prudish minority, had apparently loved her sexual double entendres. They were risqué for that period, but in this sophisticated era seemed more like amusing quotes from a grandmother.

Her attitude about many subjects was decades ahead of those of her contemporaries. In the 1930s, Mae West was actively making statements to the press, attempting in her own way to stop police from physically beating gays in New York City. Her theory was that homosexuals were female spirits trapped in male bodies, and therefore, according to existing ideas of chivalry, should not be hurt. The entire theory of trapped identity was hokey and untrue, but not intended as a put-down. It was simply the way Miss West felt at a time before behavorial scientists began searching for the truth with unbiased sexual research.

When I had the opportunity, I said, "I want to thank you for your fair and open attitude." She quickly responded by telling us that in the 1920s she had written what was probably the first play in American history primarily about homosexuals. Entitled *Drag,* it was about female impersonators talking among themselves as they prepared to go on stage. According to Miss West, the play was successful in out-of-town tryouts, but was never performed in New York. The metropolitan police did not want it.

"They wouldn't let me take it to New York-kerrr Citteee," she said. "Tha play was tooo-errr sympathetic to-err-tha subbbject!"

We laughed knowingly. By then, a very pleasant hour had passed. I thanked Mae West for entertaining us, but she seemed surprised time had passed so quickly and obviously was not ready for our departure.

She asked if we could remain for cake. Before I could reply, Lee Carlton seized the initiative. "Yes! We'd love to!" Lee declared. So we stayed for an additional forty-five minutes.

On the following day, I wrote Miss West a note wishing her a very happy birthday, and had it delivered accompanied by three dozen white roses.

Birthdays and anniversaries always bring back memories. So many recollections are cherished. Often, I remember lovers with whom I have lived. Most of us are still friends even though some of the situations were bittersweet.

After Metropolitan Community Church was begun, I met Steve Jordan. Steve had beautiful dark eyes, and we fell very much in love. Nonetheless, living together was difficult for us because our new church was growing at an astounding speed and I was constantly traveling during those first few years. More often than not I was away from home on Fellowship business. Frequent separations were disheartening, and even when we were together, Steve was bothered by the constant realization that we were living in a goldfish bowl. After five years, public life had eroded our personal relationship so much that one day Steve said, "Troy, I can't take this anymore!" We had long conversations but few solutions, and so decided to separate and remain friends.

Ramon Garcia and I met at a Christmas Eve service. Life with "Chip" was, in several ways, a reprise of my relationship with Steve. Both were Hispanic, intelligent, and wonderful. In both instances we were together for five years, and both romances ended for similar reasons. However, with Chip it was more than just the goldfish-bowl syndrome. Chip became increasingly unhappy with the burden of being "married" to Troy Perry, who frequently appeared in church, at rallies, on television, and everywhere else. Chip needed considerable attention in addition to love and he was not forever willing to share our life with the world, while I, on the other hand, felt myself unable to stop the evangelical endeavors God had entrusted to me. And so, as with Steve, Chip and I separated, but we remain friends to this day.

Then, in the spring of 1981, I met Greg Cutts.

We did not fall in love instantly, although there was a mutual attraction from the first moment our eyes met in a popular gay bar in Vancouver. Greg looked like a cute Canadian hippie and, with an IQ of 160, had a brain full of knowledge. He was only five feet seven inches tall and had a way of looking like a little boy, although he was nearly thirty. He was rather thin, had a little mustache, a medium beard, and long hair.

(I confess that among my first thoughts was the idea that my mother could fatten him, and my barber could snip off much of the hair. There was no way I could suspect that as fate brought us together, a curtain was rising on tragedy. At that moment, moving toward him, the light in his eyes and the smile on his lips brought only joy to my heart.)

"Hi! My name is Troy Perry," I said.

"I'm Greg," he replied.

My pulse began to race. Greg returned my grin. We began talking. It was the kind of unpretentious talk that comes easily when both parties automatically comprehend that magnetic forces exist. Libido fashioned the words. After ten minutes I asked Greg if he would like to leave the premises with me. He smiled. "Yes," he said, "but I'm an interviewer for cable television, and I'm scheduled to interview Reverend Troy Perry tomorrow. Do you mind, Reverend, if I know who you are?"

"No," I said. "Does it matter to you?"

"No."

"Well, we can stand here for another hour, make small talk, and then leave—or we can leave now."

Greg laughed. "Leave now," he decided.

That night we spoke of life and of love and we laughed and were satisfied. It was fantastic! The next day we dressed and had breakfast, lunch, and dinner together. After our interview, we went sightseeing and took photographs of each other in front of tourist attractions around Vancouver. But in the evening we returned to the bar where we had met, and real life intruded.

"Tonight is different from before," I told him. "We can't make love again."

Even in the dim light, I could tell Greg had paled. "Do you want to meet someone else?" he asked. "Have I done something wrong?"

"No," I said.

"Then what's wrong?"

"Nothing. But my denomination is having a General Conference and I need to prepare myself. I seek answers from God. There is no such thing as rules, but being celibate for the while is a part of my process. Day after tomorrow when I return to California, I'm going into the desert alone—to pray and fast—and I won't engage in sex again until I return."

"Like Sir Lancelot?"

"Not exactly."

"Like Aimee Semple McPherson?"

"No, definitely not!"

"Well, tonight, just let me be near?"

"As long as you understand—"

"Sure, Troy, I do understand."

That evening Greg made love to me in a different way. He introduced me to his guitar, playing music that he had written. There was a sensual quality in his voice as he sang ballads and love songs and funny bits of patter. Before each selection he treated me to a little introduction, and when he knew I was pleased, he informed me that all of his songs and music were intended to fit together as part of a play about the gay life.

Between songs, I discovered that Greg was also a gay activist and that we had many similar likes and dislikes. He had organized gay groups in Canada and had been partly responsible for initiating Canada's first gay television program. We found much to discuss.

When Greg asked me what I believed about sexuality and spirituality, I told him what I knew and asked about his own beliefs. His replies were exceptionally candid. He told me that he had been reared in Canada's Anglican church, but had rejected the idea of being Christian.

"I've had some really bad experiences with religion," Greg told me. "Being agnostic is the best I can manage today. Do you realize that the church is the greatest oppressor of gay people there has ever been? I don't see how you can remain a gay activist and be associated with a religious organization, too!"

"That is part of the miracle of M.C.C., that we exist," I told him as I turned out the light and slipped under soft blankets. "There is a need for Metropolitan Community Church, the largest organization in the world that touches the lives of gays. When it comes to combining sexuality with spirituality, we've learned you don't have to throw out the baby with the dishwater."

Greg struggled to believe, but with mixed success. "At least," he said, "you are the most together person I've ever met." That night, I fell asleep quickly and slept as comfortably as I have ever slept in my entire life with another person in my arms. All the next day, and the night, and the next day, we spent together. Then Greg went to the airport with me and we said goodbye. Later, I had cause to wonder if it would have been better for him had our first farewell been forever.

Immediately upon my arrival in Los Angeles, I departed for the desert, a vast expanse of sand, wasteland, cactus, and distant purple mountains. My thoughts then were not of Greg, but in my mind that retreat has become a part of his story.

I was alone, miles from the town of Twentynine Palms, in a deserted campground with only coyotes and jackrabbits keeping me company.

306

Nature had been capricious that spring, and the weather during my sojourn was not any better. There was a steady downpour of cold rain on the first night. Wind collapsed my tent, and I discovered that my sleeping bag was located in a wide wash. I ran for my life when a flood of water started rising around me. The next evening was not any better. I pitched my tent on the side of a little hill, but soon after midnight fierce lightning blasted the dark sky, rain poured down from the heavens and another shrieking wind storm blew away my tent.

It was cold at night and hot during the day. The weather would clear with the rising sun, and the world became quiet and beautiful; I knew it was good for me. With my stomach hurting from not eating, I would follow paths into hills where Indians hundreds of years before had carved petroglyphs into the stones. On about the fourth day I found myself singing the chorus of a little song I had heard in Great Britain, Australia, and New Zealand. The title was "Thou Art With Me, Lord."

There were no great visions, but within my being I reaffirmed my knowledge that I had to keep our Fellowship firmly rooted in doctrine. Some of our pastors had sought to become more unitarian and less evangelical, but our Lord let me realize in the majesty of God's living desert that so long as our church continued to follow Jesus, all would be well.

My denomination was also in a major struggle concerning the use of inclusive language. "Is God both mother and father to us?" was one of the questions that has been of serious concern to many religions. The answer was not easy, particularly because of centuries of male-dominated tradition. But as I fasted and prayed, I came to understand that God is not a woman, not a man. God is both, but neither. When Moses asked God, "Who shall I say sent me?" God replied, "Tell them I am sent you. I am that that I am."

My thinking on the subject cleared. If, for example, a percentage of women feel that the word "mankind" does not include women, or if they believe the word places them in a subsidiary position, then we need to say "mankind and womankind." It does not matter that linguists for centuries have agreed that the use of both words together is redundant. If anyone is deterred by our use of the established language, then we must change our use of language so that all people will listen when we preach the Gospel of Jesus Christ.

Some women in our community, particularly feminists, felt that the generic words *gay* and *homosexual* did not apply to them, and wanted to be called lesbians instead. Yet, quite to the contrary, other women felt strongly that use of the word *gay* should not be handed over to the male segment of our population. Personally, I have no problem with either usage. Outside of Twentynine Palms, however, with the sun and the night and wind and rain to sharpen my perception, God let me know that words which anybody considered exclusionary or offensive should not be used in preaching the Gospel. Thus, I came to the decision that, from then on, whatever language will reach the largest number of people is the language Metropolitan Community Church will use.

Three days after I returned to Los Angeles, I received a letter from Greg. He wanted to spend his vacation with me, and he flew to California when I agreed. We went to all the places visitors to Los Angeles go, including the beaches, Magic Mountain, and Universal City. At Disneyland we did one thing not many gay tourists do. We held hands wherever we went. Nobody asked us to leave.

Two weeks later I flew to Vancouver again to spend several days with Greg, and early the next month he returned to Los Angeles and spent another seven days with me. As that visit was ending, I said, "Greg, commuting back and forth from Canada to California is becoming expensive! Why don't you move down here with me?"

Greg agreed.

We had no immigration problem. An attorney friend who is knowledgeable about such matters assured me that our Immigration and Naturalization Service never rounds up or embarrasses homosexual Canadians (although the Border Patrol can be very blunt and unpleasant to macho lesbians and effeminate gay men crossing the border). Greg's difficulty was inside the United States—obtaining employment. Without a work card or a legitimate Social Security number, he could not find work in television production. It helped not at all that he was very talented and bright.

After three months, I hired Greg to put together a one-hour video which we named "God, Gays & the Gospel." The informative, inspirational project, intended to combat the Jerry Falwells of the world by showing Christian gays and lesbians as real people, nearly became a fiasco. Some of our people were severely frightened by any idea of national photographic exposure. From the floor of our General Convention, one brother stood and said, "Put a show like that on television and our enemies will have a field day. Who's gonna pay for the insurance if more of our churches get burned to the ground?"

When I sought funds for the production, there was another problem. I was accused of nepotism. Everybody knew that Greg and I were intensely in love. It was a well-known secret that our relationship was becoming stronger and more intense with every passing day. When we walked through West Hollywood we never hesitated to put our arms around each other. Sometimes "brave" people speeding past at sixty miles an hour would shout "faggot" at us, but we always had an answer for them: "Get used to it!"

Greg cut his hair and shortened his beard so it was similar to mine. The change, while attractive, made him look considerably younger than he was, and caused members of the Fellowship to believe that Greg Cutts was not qualified to produce the $55,000 program we had planned. After disruption at the General Conference in Houston, the result was a one-sided compromise: I could proceed with production of "God, Gays & the Gospel," but all monies required would have to be personally raised by me.

At the same time, Greg learned that somebody had unkindly referred to him as my "$55,000 screw." His feelings were badly hurt. Although Joseph McDuffey and I tried to mollify Greg with humor, he would always remember what had been said. Nevertheless, we immediately began work on the television show. After some months, we had an eighteen-minute preliminary video to show for our efforts. With the demonstration tape as evidence of Greg's ability, we had no further difficulty raising money.

In addition to his own work, Greg was always supportive of my ministry. Of his own volition he began attending our Mother Church in Los Angeles. (Metropolitan Community Church is different from the conservative Anglican church he had renounced, and he loved our freer expressions of emotion.) When Greg accepted Jesus Christ as Lord and Savior, he asked if I would baptize him. Almost as if he was suddenly apprehensive of what the morrow held, he begged me to baptize him immediately—which I did by immersion in our bathtub at home!

For Greg, religion suddenly became a magnificent obsession. On occasions when he heard some of my important sermons being repeated at different locations, Greg never seemed to become bored with them. And sometimes we would sit up all night discussing Scripture because he was deeply intrigued by the entire concept of salvation.

But when I left town, Greg was lonely. Too often when I called him long distance, I could tell by the flat inflections in his voice that his attitude was depressed. He wanted me home. He wanted us together twenty-four hours a day. When I returned to Los Angeles by airplane, Greg would always be waiting at the terminal gate.

We kissed publicly. As role models, we thought it was important. I have contended that if people are honest in their actions and not blatantly trying to prove anything, openness is more than acceptable. To me, if we are natural, the most revolutionary act in America today is to let the public actually see two men holding hands in places where it is least expected—like at football games, or standing in line for a movie. That is the only way we will change nongay people's attitudes. Over a period of time it is important for them to become accustomed to seeing us, to realize there is nothing shocking about our love.

With Greg, being open was easy. He was a gay activist, as I am, and we loved each other. He was genuinely affectionate. We reached toward one another all the time. We laughed, we talked, and we kissed—not to push an idea or to threaten heterosexuals, but just to be ourselves. Greg liked walking arm and arm. It took guts to do that in public, because we never knew from what direction somebody's wrath might be directed toward us.

Occasionally, the danger was more imagined than real. We took a vacation aboard a cruise ship in the Caribbean, and one evening decided that we were going to liberate the dance floor—by dancing together. We were a gay couple, and although neither of us was a great dancer, our feeling was that it was something we should attempt. When we arrived at the shipboard festivities, we were both amazed to find that the only people dancing were youngsters under the age of thirteen. Neither Greg nor I was about to liberate the dance floor from a group of children! We had many laughs remembering that.

But two years was all the time we had.

Then came Death.

Still, in memory, Greg has a habit of returning.

Our last meeting was in Vancouver where he was doing some important technical editing on "God, Gays & the Gospel." I had been thousands of miles away, seeking pledges of cash to support our production, but to be with Greg I flew to Canada. Today, I know those last precious moments will never be enough. Even then they seemed inadequate, but upon both of us, work exerted pressure.

Three weeks after my visit, on Greg's final weekend, a fundraiser for our video was held in the Canadian gay bar where we had met. The event was a disappointment for Greg. Few arrived to view his production, and among the acquaintances who were present, some laughed and spoke throughout the viewing. The video had been a success everywhere—except in Greg's own home city.

He was devastated!

We spoke on the telephone afterward. Greg said, "I just miss you so much. I wish I could fly home now. I'm lonely."

I said, "Baby, it's only two more weeks—two weeks before you go in front of the U.S. Consulate in Vancouver. You'll have your final interview. You'll get your green card and then you can come back. Hold on."

He said, "I want to see you, Troy."

"It's almost time," I told him.

"Okay," Greg said, "I'll wait."

"Be patient. You'll be home. It will all be legal. Two more weeks is all it takes."

"Don't worry, I'll make it."

"Of course. I love you."

"Good night," he said.

And I said, "Good night, baby."

Our telephone call seemed like nothing out of the ordinary—but as deadly hours ticked away, I lay awake in my bed in Los Angeles. Across two thousand miles Greg was with me in my mind. I knew he wanted desperately to be home. I had heard familiar intonations. I wished that I had been able to travel less. I knew that Greg had wanted us to be together twenty-four hours out of every day. Very often, I felt the same way.

I contemplated how one of us could think of something, and the other would think of the same thing within a matter of thirty seconds. Was it body language or some special kind of perception we had between us? The reality was that our minds were on the same track. We liked doing things together and we liked conversing with each other.

Greg told me everything. There was nothing about which we could not speak. Perhaps the best part of our relationship was that we talked to each other. Sometimes we stayed up half the night, speaking about spiritual things.

He was a loving person, but with a temper. Greg could stand his ground with me, and that can be difficult to do. Fortunately, it was a rare occasion when we argued.

When he moved in with me, Greg was very good about helping take care of my mother. Her health was not the best even then, and he wanted to make certain that nothing happened. When I went away, he kept me posted about Mother's condition, letting me know all was well. And he always asked me to hurry home as soon as I could.

That was the same way I felt on the last evening of his life. Greg's spirit was with me, but I wanted a more tangible presence beside me so that we could really talk and touch each other, make love and go to sleep in each other's arms. I wanted to tell him to hurry home.

But Greg died before the morning.

*　　*　　*

It happened during the first weekend in three months that I could spend in Los Angeles. With no speaking engagements, I intended to rest and clean house. My mother was in Florida visiting relatives. On Sunday I went to our downtown church. Jeri Ann Harvey preached. In the afternoon Joseph McDuffey visited, and as best friends can, we talked for several hours about nothing in particular. That evening I called Vancouver to tell Greg how much I loved him, but nobody answered the telephone. On Monday morning, I called again and reached Mary Ann McKuen, Greg's close associate on our video project.

"Is Greg at work?" I asked.

"No, he's not," Mary Ann replied. "But it's a gorgeous, warm day here in British Columbia. And it's a holiday, Queen Victoria's birthday. Greg has my truck and I have a feeling he took off for the beach."

"Then everything's okay?"

"Yes."

"He was kind of down the other night."

"Just being moody. No problem."

"All right."

Later in the day, I tried again, without success, to reach Greg. It was then an alarm went off in my head. Greg and I had agreed to talk to each other that day, on Monday—and we never missed each other's telephone calls. I hoped that Mary Ann was correct, that he had forgotten and gone to the beach. Also, I thought that maybe he had been in and out of the place he was staying, and our schedules had not connected.

On Tuesday morning I was really worried. I called Mary Ann again. She still had not seen Greg, nor had she heard from him. She was irate that he had her truck and had given her no indication where he would be with it. "I hope to God he hasn't wrecked it!" she declared.

"You know Greg better than that," I told her. "Something is wrong, Mary Ann—bad wrong!"

"I hope you're not right," she said.

I made several more futile telephone calls. Mary Ann gave me the telephone numbers of two men, Barry and David, for whom Greg had been house-sitting. I tried to call them at the Bureau of Indian Affairs where she said one of the men worked, but there was never a time when the Bureau's telephone lines were not busy. Then, at exactly 5:25 that afternoon, I called the men's residence, estimating that was the time when a bureaucratic office worker in the United States would most likely arrive at home. It was the same in Canada. The two men had just walked in their front door when their telephone rang.

312

I said, "This is Troy Perry. Is Greg Cutts there?"

The person who had answered the telephone said, "Yes, he's here. His hat and overcoat are on the chair. He's in his room."

"You've seen him?"

"The door to his room is closed."

"Well, fine. Would you mind getting him and telling him Troy's on the telephone?"

"Hold on."

I waited, relieved, until a minute later I heard the man who had gone to find Greg shout a few exclamatory words to his friend. I could tell there was urgency in his voice, but was unable to discern the words. I had the impression of agitated movement.

Then the telephone was dropped on the floor. Breathlessly, one of the men picked it up. He said, "We'll call you back!"

Quickly, I replied, "Wait, wait, wait—you don't have my telephone number!"

He said, "We'll get it."

Click! He hung up.

I was stunned. I knew for certain that something was wrong. But how wrong? Very wrong! And what? My imagination raced! I felt my heart pounding! There is no way to adequately describe the fear that suddenly overwhelmed me.

I was seated, staring at the wall, trying to figure out why the person in Canada had dropped the telephone—when my own telephone rang. It was Burt, Greg's ex-lover in Vancouver, returning a call I had made to him earlier. "Hi, Troy, how are you doing?" he asked.

"My head's in a mess!" I told him. "Something's radically wrong and I can't get any information." Then, after I filled him in with the details, I asked, "Burt, do you know those two people?"

"Yes, I do."

"Well, they don't know me. They don't have my number. Would you please go to their house and then call me? Let me know what's going on?"

"I'll get right over there."

"Find out why they dropped the phone on the floor."

"Right away. Stay home and I'll call you."

I eased the telephone receiver back into its cradle. There was nothing more I could do but wait. Joe McDuffey came over and tried to keep me calm as leaden minutes passed.

"Nothing's wrong, Troy," he said. "Get that into your head. I'm sure there's an explanation."

"I know, Joe, but—"

My telephone rang. It was Burt. He said, "I've got some bad news, Troy. The police are here now. They found Greg and he's dead. He's been dead at least three days."

With that, my emotions snapped. I think I shouted. The furniture in the room became like abstractions, and in the middle of it all the only real thing was my friend, Joe, talking to me, holding me, telephoning others to come to us, trying to keep my sanity from leaving.

Within the hour, Jeri Ann Harvey, Nancy Wilson with her lover, Paula, and several people from the church had rushed to be with me. They kept me from disintegrating. Their touch, their kind words, their love kept my shattered being together.

We tried to figure out what had happened to Greg. Was he murdered? It was possible. In the back of my mind was a dark, debilitating thought. I could not forget that one of Greg's best friends, the director of the Gay and Lesbian Center in Vancouver, had hanged himself shortly before Greg and I met. Greg had told me that his friend was a gentle person, the only individual Greg felt he could confide in, and that everyone was shocked by the friend's untimely death. That impressed Greg. No one had realized that the affable gay activist was becoming increasingly depressed. Greg said his friend hanged himself in a closet so as not to disturb the rest of the household. What a terrible surprise!

I began trying to make plans to fly to Canada, but was unable to function. I was unable to stop crying. Jeri Ann and Nancy, viewing my condition, told me that I could not travel alone. Joe said he would accompany me.

Burt met us when we arrived in Vancouver.

"I want to see Greg," I said.

The request brought a trace of dismay to Burt's face. "You can't," he told me. "His body has already been cremated."

Burt's words struck me. The effect was like being battered by a baseball bat.

"The Cutts gave instructions for cremation," Burt explained.

I felt enormous stabs of mental pain, pain so real it became physical. I went into shock. "I can't see him?" I said, dazed.

"No, Troy," answered Burt patiently. "You didn't want to see the body. When a person has been dead that long it's swollen. I saw the body and it was not the Greg that you remember."

I continued crying. Burt called our local pastor, Reverend Ernie LaCasse, who joined us and was very helpful. At about the same time, Greg's parents arrived in Vancouver from eastern Canada where they had several homes, and where they raised world-class horses for Olympic competition. Mr. Cutts, a retired naval commodore, was Canada's director of Oceans and Fisheries.

That evening, the commodore and Mrs. Cutts, Burt, Joe, and I had dinner together. The Cutts' way of handling grief was different from mine. They were considerably more reserved, but when I broke down and started crying again, Greg's father started crying with me. Greg's gracious mother did what she could to comfort both of us.

I could have fallen in love with Mrs. Cutts—she was intelligent and charming, so much like Greg—but I knew Greg had been troubled because she had difficulty accepting his lifestyle and coming to terms with having a gay activist for a son. For his part, Greg was disturbed because he felt like an outcast, believing that his mother should accept him as readily as did my mother. It did little to bolster Greg's morale by explaining to him that through Metropolitan Community Church Edith Perry had received an early, very practical, field education in political science, sociology, and psychology concerning matters of gay rights, gay people, and gay sex. (Mother had helped us almost from the beginning of Metropolitan Community Church. As one of our earliest switchboard operators, she was the word-proof recipient of many obscene phone calls that frustrated, dirty-mouthed gay-baiters had directed at me!)

I felt very sorry that I was unable to meet Mrs. Cutts before our loss. Somehow, I think I could have helped her. Uncomfortable with the knowledge that Greg was homosexual, she really dreaded the idea that he might somehow embarrass her by making news as a gay activist. As it happened, Greg's exploits were often amusing and from the heart—but not otherwise earth-shattering.

One occasion that he told me about happened soon after gay activist Harvey Milk's tragic death in San Francisco. Greg decided, in a burst of frustration, to mount his own midnight miniprotest in Vancouver. It was contrary to his nature to be destructive. Nevertheless, with a full can of spray paint, Greg rode his bicycle through nearly deserted, star-lit streets on his way to Eden's, one of Canada's largest department stores. There he apprehensively went to work. After he had written GAY RIGHTS across Eden's locked front doors, he was ready to spray the final word, NOW. But a uniformed guard walked around the corner. Gregory fled! Left behind was his three-speed Schwinn. When he returned later in the day, the bicycle was gone from in front of the store. Although without transportation, Greg was not about to ask that his bicycle be returned.

*   *   *

Before dinner was completed, the Cutts began discussing where Greg was going to be buried. They said Greg had been raised in Halifax and could be buried near his grandmother. But Greg's mother mentioned that Nova Scotia was a place they rarely ever went, except for perhaps a two-week vacation during the year, and that it might be better for Greg to be buried in Vancouver, which he loved and where he had friends. Then they turned to me and asked my opinion.

Without thinking, I impulsively complained about what was burning in my mind! I said, "If Greg and I were a heterosexual couple, this conversation would not be happening! The decision would be mine—not a subject for discussion no matter how kind you intend to be. Greg would be buried in Los Angeles where I live, where he and I lived together as a couple for the last two and half years!"

There was silence for a moment. Then Mr. Cutts nodded, looked at his wife, and then back at me. "Is that what would be right? Would you like that?" he asked.

"Yes, in answer to both your questions," I replied, my voice softening.

"All right," said Mr. Cutts, "after the funeral service, you take the ashes with you back to the United States."

In some ways I was lucky. There are so many true horror stories of families moving in at the death of a gay son or lesbian daughter, grasping possessions, taking big and little treasures, trashing precious mementos, running roughshod over shocked, grief-stricken lovers. Too often the surviving partner can be legally ostracized and is even brutally, viciously unwelcome at his or her loved one's funeral! Fortunately, the Cutts were much too fine for anything like that.

We were devastated, and the pain of our grief was magnified by not knowing how Greg had died. All I learned in Canada was that Greg had not been murdered. Mr. Cutts obtained that information from police. I knew the coroner had performed an autopsy, but in accordance with their standard policy, they refused to tell me anything. That Greg and I had lived together meant nothing to Canadian authorities. In their eyes, I was not a member of Greg's family.

Mr. Cutts said, "The autopsy is inconclusive. We have to wait. More information should be forthcoming in about six weeks."

I asked that a second funeral be arranged to include our friends in the Los Angeles church. Jeri Ann Harvey and Nancy Wilson preached. In the chancel, a seat that had been Greg's was filled with flowers. The gospel choir sang my favorite hymn, "It Is Well With My Soul" (which are the words I would want on my tombstone).

My family and I sat on the front row with preachers who had flown in from all over the country. Our church was filled, but the only person I distinctly remember was Joel Wachs. Joel was president of the Los Angeles City Council, and he cried with me.

Night after night I went home feeling that I would succumb to despair. For a time I kept Greg's ashes in our bedroom. My faith in the Resurrection grew stronger. Greg seemed to come to me, and I tried to tell him that I loved him and not to be lonely. I tried to hear his guitar and remember his singing. I read his short diary once, and put it away, to be kept forever.

Always there was the pain of not knowing how he had died. I prayed to God that he was taken by some painless accident. Not an hour passed when I did not have to fight with myself to maintain equilibrium. "God," I heard myself saying, "I don't believe you brought me this far just to leave me now." I had repeated the same thing many times when, as I began losing hope, I received my answer. The telephone rang and it was Greg's father.

"I wanted to call and tell you that he died from a toxic reaction to two medications. It was the lethal combination of a prescription sedative that Greg had just received from a doctor taken together with an over-the-counter pill to make you sleep. It was a histamine and an antihistamine—a collision of drugs that can kill you."

With that information I did not sleep well, but I slept more easily.

One morning, Frank Zerilli came into my office with the day's mail and said, "Guess who you have a letter from?" It was not unusual that Frank answered his own question. "Oral Roberts' son," he said.

Wondering why Roberts would be writing me, I quickly opened his letter. It read:

Tulsa, OH 74105
3 Sept. 1981

Dear Mr. Perry,
I just received your kind letter thanking me for my contribution to your TV ministry. It was a very small gift, and I'm sorry I cannot send more at this time, but I will keep you in mind in future giving.
Mr. Perry, I thought you might be interested to know also that

*I am the son of the evangelist Oral Roberts, not the one on TV
with him—that's my brother Richard. I'm the eldest son and the
eldest surviving child. I am gay and have been "out" more or less
for many, many years but am only now coming into an awareness
of what being out of the closet really means. I'm not quite to the
point of being ready for a public announcement of any sort, but
I did think this information might be useful to you when dealing
with some other person from a very strict fundamentalist family who
might be having problems with his homosexuality and his religion.*

If I can be of further service, let me know. Thanx again.

Sincerely,
Ron Roberts

It was several weeks before I was able to respond:

Dear Ron,

*Thank you for your contribution and also for being so honest
with me. I will admit that for several years it has been rumored
in the gay community in Oklahoma that so-and-so knew one of
the sons of Oral Roberts was gay, but it was your brother Richard's
name that was always mentioned.*

*I will be in Tulsa, November 5–8, to conduct a revival for
our Church there. Is it possible for me to treat you to either lunch
or dinner, so that I can meet you personally? I never know but
that I might hear from one of the sons or daughters of Billy
Graham, Jerry Falwell, or whomever, who might need to talk to
someone like yourself who also was raised in a strict fundamentalist
family. That is some missionary work you could do for us if you
are willing.*

*Even though I might disagree with your father in some areas
of theology and human sexuality, I can assure you I am an admirer
of his work. I heard your father preach in Tallahassee, Florida,
in 1948 when I was just a child....*

In Christ,
Reverend Troy D. Perry

Ron Roberts replied on October 19, 1981:

Dear Troy,

*I should mention that I am not especially a religious person
nor a church-goer, tho I do admire your work among the religious*

gay community. I too have major disagreements with my father's point of view, tho like you I maintain an admiration for what he has accomplished, and he and I do get along. I am not at all sensitive about him or our relationship, so I will give more details when we meet, if you are interested.

As to the rumors you mention, I have to chuckle, for my brother is often the unhappy and incorrect recipient of such assignations when people unknowingly are really talking about me. For a short period over 20 years ago, I was somewhat active in the Tulsa gay community, then left for Stanford at age 17 and stayed away almost 15 years. By the time I returned to Tulsa, Richard had become the very visible son of Oral Roberts while I had been all but forgotten, even unknown totally to the younger group. Yet the information that "Oral Roberts' son" was gay was still very much alive, having been passed down, so naturally the rumors centered on Richard. So strong were the stories—you know how gossip becomes "fact" and never mind the details—that even now friends of mine insist that they "know" my brother is gay, tho I can assure you that is not the case.

As to the children of other famous evangelists, if any of them does prove to be gay, I would be more than willing to offer whatever service that might be within my ability. . . .

Indeed we have much to talk about. . . .

Sincerely,
Ron Roberts

Our meeting was during November 1981, in the Tulsa home of a member of Metropolitan Community Church. Reverend Alice Jones, pastor of the church, welcomed us and made us comfortable. Reverend Brad AnderSon, who was student clergy at the time, was invited and remained with us for most of the conversation. We had coffee and visited for half the afternoon.

Ron was portly, as tall as I am, and probably in his mid-forties. He somewhat resembled his father, but wore a beard and mustache, which Oral Roberts did not.

I remembered having seen Ron's father for the first time when I was a child of eight. Reverend Roberts had come to Tallahassee and was having a meeting in a gigantic tent. My mother and father took a friend, Fred Heisler, who was dying of advanced tuberculosis, to see Roberts, and I went along. I had never before observed anything like that meeting! It was fascinating! Oral Roberts was the original—the first of the Big-

Time Evangelists. Going into Oral Roberts' bigtop was like going to the circus!

Roberts preached from a platform and prayed for the sick who came to him in a long queue. There was a ramp up which wheelchairs were pushed. Most people were moved rapidly along, with a laying on of hands and perfunctory prayer, but sometimes, as for Fred Heisler, Roberts stopped the line, asked questions, prayed extra hard, and started crying. The result, in truth, was that when Fred eventually died, his death was from natural causes—he was healed of tuberculosis.

Ron Roberts had very different recollections of his father. "I almost hated my father while I was growing up," he told us. "I didn't understand the Oral Roberts ministry. I had to endure people who spoke of him as a faith healer and, therefore, a freak. After college I was away from home for more than a dozen years. When I returned, I was pleased to realize my father was not an oddball. He was one of Tulsa's city fathers, a businessman on the board of directors of Oklahoma Gas and Oil, and on the board of directors of one of the richest banks in Oklahoma. Everything was changed."

Not everything, however, was better. Ron was concerned about a pending separation from his wife, fearful that there might be some difficulty in his being allowed to continue seeing their children. He knew how generally effective locked doors and bodyguards could be because that was the way his father and younger brother were forced to live for reasons of safety. Ron found traveling in a van and selling Chinese porcelain at antiques shows considerably less restrictive.

From an early age, Ron had known that he was homosexual (and believed his parents were most probably aware of it also). Reverend Roberts had refused to send him to Columbia University because, as Ron quoted his father, there were "too many homosexuals in New York City." Roberts sent Ron to the University of California at Berkeley instead. "Out of the frying pan and into the fire!" Ron smiled, adding, "It was paradise."

When Ron married, he said he had made his wife fully aware that he was homosexual and she had told him not to worry. "Of course, it's never that way!" Ron bitterly complained when it was much too late, and I tended to agree. Millions of gay men and lesbians want children, and most are very capable of becoming fathers or mothers—but an inherent parental love for children does not permanently redirect a homosexual's sexuality toward the opposite gender. That is a different matter, and it is a very basic fact which, if ignored, will continue to bring pain to many generations—despite "healing" quacks who ignore our God-given sexual orientation. Understanding—not condemnation—may lead to tolerable solutions for people who are loving parents but who cannot be heterosexual.

Ron was depressed as his separation moved toward divorce. He told me that was when his mother finally asked him if his was a sexual problem. "Is it homosexuality?" asked Evelyn Roberts, who had an independent ministry of her own with friends.

The son hesitated, recalling that his mother had once discussed a letter from an older missionary out in the field who wanted to know if it was a sin to masturbate. Aware that the missionary had felt he could ask such a question of Evelyn Roberts, Ron decided his mother had to be more knowledgeable than he had previously thought, and therefore, he could summon the courage to acknowledge his own sexuality.

"I'm gay," Ron Roberts told his mother. After that admission, Ron said he never had the feeling that his family withdrew from him. Unlike a few well-known preachers who have sought to raise millions of dollars for their own purposes by using homosexuals as whipping boys, Reverend Roberts never felt an obsession to attack gay people. Yet Ron admitted to feeling that he did not fit in with the family. He was aware of stories about the powers that be at Oral Roberts University who had made an issue of homosexuality and who, every so often, had purges to force gay students (as well as fat people) out of the school.

It was a strange dichotomy.

I wondered if his gay son caused Oral Roberts to have a personal understanding more Christian than was exhibited by some of the administrators of his university.

The only time I ever heard Oral Roberts mention homosexuality was during the time when I was married and living with my wife. Pearl and I had gone to Roberts' "Crusade" in Santa Ana. He said, "Last night a young man came up in the healing line and threw himself into my arms. The young man said, 'Reverend Roberts, I'm a homosexual. Can Jesus love me?'"

Listening to Oral Roberts, I was stunned. At that time I had *never* heard homosexuality mentioned in the pulpit. Today, Reverend Roberts might tell you that being gay is a sin, but twenty years ago, soon after his oldest son had left home, he said, "I told that young man, 'Jesus loves you.'" That was all Roberts said in public. Not a condemnation as I had expected.

But speaking to Oral Roberts' son in Tulsa, there was no question that he was depressed. "I'm burned out on religion," Ron said. "It's too hard, not being as close to the family as I would wish. And maybe I'm going to lose sight of my children. Can they be taken away? If people could only deal with their children as *their children*. Nothing more, nothing less. As kindred. Blood ties and loving relations. Does everything have to be distorted? Is all my life reduced to nothing but labels? Fruity and faggy and flitty and queer!"

I said, "Ron, God loves you, I want to assure you of that. You have to accept that people are not always perfect and can be wrong on some issues and right on others."

"I don't even know if I believe in God anymore," he said.

At that instant I realized I had lost Ron Roberts. Maybe if I had sought the opportunity to talk with Ron's parents, that might have made a difference. But at that point, I could only hope they could come to terms with him as a whole person.

Ron Roberts killed himself six months later. My mother found the story in a newspaper, and knowing that Ron and I had met, she brought the sad information to my attention. Mother never understood parents who, in effect, reject their children. She would say, "I want to take parents like that and just shake them—shake them and say, 'They're your kids! Don't you know they're your kids?' "

Mother has always been supportive. She started the first group of parents and friends of gays in America, although at the time we did not call it that. It was a group that met with gay children and their parents to help soften the trauma of coming out.

"I have some bad news for you, Troy," Mother said point-blank as I came into the house one day.

"What is it?"

"Oral Roberts' son. He evidently committed suicide."

I went inside and read the newspaper.

I felt so sad. I could not stop thinking that no home in the world is exempt, no family can be certain of remaining untouched by the will of God. I don't care who is involved, whether the father is a famous evangelist or anybody else. We have had presidents of the United States with gay children. And vice president's children. And governor's children. On down the line. Believe me!

How families react makes all the difference in the mental health of their children. I see one example after another, and I always think, If parents could only come to terms with love, justice, and reality. I ask parents to remember that your children are your children. They are the same people three seconds after they come out to you that they were three minutes before! They are no different!

I am so sorry when I meet gay children, of any age, who cannot get beyond the disappointments of their life. We sent a remembrance to Ron's funeral and afterward received a card:

> *Dear Brother Perry,*
>
> *Thank you for the beautiful flowers. The thoughtful expression of love from you and the Universal Fellowship of Metropolitan Community Churches is so much appreciated by all the Roberts family. Our faith in Jesus is strong. With his help we can make it.*
>
>
>
> *In Christ's name,*
> *Oral and Evelyn, Richard and Roberta*
>
>

There followed a period in my life when death and sorrow were with me like unwelcome friends. I was still very much disturbed by Greg's untimely death when I was approached by a nervous, distinguished-looking man of about my own age. Our encounter was near the vestibule of a family restaurant in the San Fernando Valley. The man had been having dinner with his wife, grown son, and daughter when he saw me departing. He hastily slipped away from his family and, out of their view, stopped me before I went out the door. "Are you the gay preacher?" he asked.

When he was certain of my identity, he suddenly began telling me that while I was having dinner, his family thought they had recognized me, and the subject of homosexuality had adversely been initiated by his outspoken son. Not knowing how to respond to the young man's negative comments, the father, according to his unexpected confession to me, had mercilessly condemned homosexuals and everything pertaining to our life—although he himself had been surreptitiously, but actively, gay for years!

"Why are you telling all this to me?" I asked.

He waited a moment, until a waitress passed out of hearing range, and whispered with intensity, "I really feel like a hypocritical louse— but I don't know how else to react. I want you to know I don't mean what I say. There's no way I could march in parades or be on television like you guys do. I have a family, you know? I guess I just want you to agree with me that how I've handled things is the right way, you know, to keep under cover in my circumstances."

"No!" I heard myself exclaim. Then, in a lower voice I said, "You did the wrong thing—the worst thing! Do you have any idea how many sons and daughters die each year—simply because of the terrible things people say to condemn us? And you're telling lies, despicable lies, just for some kind of verbal camouflage? Mister, that makes you worse in my eyes than our worst religious-political enemies! Go talk to Linden LaRouche, not to me! Do you understand what I've said?"

Frightened, the man stared at my face.

"You're not going to say anything to my family?" he asked in sudden panic, envisioning all kinds of peril.

"No," I replied, "that's not my style. I think you know what you've done is wrong. You wouldn't be taking the chance of talking with me if you weren't asking for help."

"I don't know what to do. I can't ever tell my family."

"That's up to you."

"But I want you to forgive me."

"No, I'll do something better."

"What?" he asked.

I took a pencil from my pocket and wrote three sentences on a slip of paper. "Here," I said. "You read this—memorize it—and the next time you are frightened and think you can only be safe by saying something awful about homosexuals, take a safe, first step toward the light of decency and say the words I've written for you. In today's world, they won't jerk you out of the closet but they may keep you from going to hell!"

The gay father looked at what I had written. A sheepish little smile appeared on his face. "Thanks," he said. "That's what I really wanted. I can learn this, memorize it word for word, and repeat what you wrote like I just thought of it. Before, I never knew what to say. I didn't know where to begin. I never spoke with a liberated person before."

With that, the father returned to his family. I hoped that in the future he, one of our own people, would be one less person to unnecessarily cause gay people death and damage. Maybe we will meet again someday and I might learn the answer. In the meantime, the first step toward emancipation I had written for him was:

> *I guess some people are made heterosexual and some people are made homosexual. I don't think anybody can help the way they are born. I believe they shouldn't be condemned for what they can't help.*

After Greg died, I thought I would never have a lover again. There was the dreadful feeling of unshakable personal grief. I dated people, went to dinner and motion pictures with them, but that was the extent of my social activity.

Two and a half years passed until, in June 1985, I met Phillip DeBlieck, a tall, intelligent young man who has since brightened my life. One of the things Phillip asked during our first meeting was, "What do you do for a living?" and the question gave me some satisfaction because I realized he was interested in me without being aware of my work in our community.

"I'm in public relations," I replied. (Public relations director is one of my auxiliary titles as moderator of the Universal Fellowship of Metropolitan Community Churches.)

When we met a second time, Phillip told me much about himself. He was from a small desert community in California. While in high school he had fallen in love with and been taken to bed by a teacher who was a heterosexually married father of two. When Phillip's mother discovered a compromising written communication that revealed their relationship, she had the coach arrested.

A trial was held.

"I was very much in love with my schoolteacher," said Phillip, "and I was scared. The police said he was evil and forced me into testifying against him. Waiting in court, however, I prayed and asked God to show me the way. Then, when I was questioned, I gave intentionally vague answers and was intentionally unconvincing. And the Lord was with us. The jury chose to disbelieve my testimony, although it was true, and the man I was in love with was found not guilty."

Even though Phillip's teacher was not convicted, the school asked Phillip not to return. Soon afterward, at age sixteen, he ran away from home. He came to Los Angeles where he completed high school. We met some years later.

When I introduced him to my mother, Phillip did not merely say "hello" and leave. Not Phillip! He sat down beside my mother on a couch and they started talking. Several weeks later, Phillip moved in with me, and we have been together ever since.

So it would seem that my life had become complete again, but it was not. If someone was to ask if I had lived a happy life since accepting myself as a gay person, I would say, "Yes, except there's one area of my being that feels cheated—not having been able to see my sons grow up."

After Pearl and I separated, she moved back to the Midwest. When my wife returned to her parents' home, we were still friends, but after a fortnight with her mother and father, Pearl's attitude changed and a bitter breakup became inevitable. We had, between ourselves, planned to be rejoined, but some unanticipated difficulty in selling our old car delayed my return for two weeks. By then, verbal poison put into my wife's ear had done its work.

One evening, Pearl angrily telephoned me. She said, "I don't ever want to see you again. You were supposed to be here by now!"

"I just finally unloaded the car," I protested. "Nobody wanted to buy it, but now it's sold. I'll be there in three days."

"No, you won't!" Pearl declared, "It's all over with us—and that's final!"

In Pearl's voice there was hard-edged hostility that I had never heard before. It was undoubtedly instilled in my wife by her parents, both Pentecostal ministers, who had been forgiving as far as their own children were concerned, but toward me were fanatical on the subject of homosexuality. And they always had their own answer for everything!

It was bad enough (and incorrect!) when society equated homosexuality with illness, but that was not a sufficiently terrible condemnation to mollify Pearl's parents. They would not be satisfied until they went considerably further, equating homosexuality with demonic possession and associating me, the father of their grandchildren, with Satan and spiritual darkness.

"Hallelujah!" said Steve Sands, my boss at Sears Roebuck, who was unimpressed by the attitude of my prejudiced Pentecostal in-laws. "You're gay and never should have been married," he said. "You're well out of it!"

As for myself, speaking as a gay person, Pearl did the best thing in the world she could have done for me. In retrospect, I know that—except for being estranged from my sons—there is little in my life I would want changed. However, at the time, that was difficult to realize.

Pearl immediately began cutting the bonds between us. My letters to her were constantly returned unopened. She definitely wanted to prevent me from ever again seeing the kids. In the middle of all that, thirteen months after the beginning of our separation, I was drafted into the army and shipped overseas. Pictures of myself in uniform that I sent to our boys were returned, with *refused* written on the envelopes.

While in Germany, I learned that Pearl wanted to remarry. She had her Church of God attorney write me a letter. It said, in effect, "Dear Mr. Perry, Your wife has reported certain revolting facts to me, facts that if the military knew about them, would mean your immediate expulsion from duty. With this in mind, I am certain you will not want to contest the enclosed divorce decree. Sign and return it without delay."

I took the the letter from her Church of God attorney to the U.S. Army judge advocate's office on the base. The army lawyer read the communication and asked if I wanted to give Pearl a divorce.

"Not this way," I said.

"Fine," the military attorney said. "I'll just write the judge in the States and inform his court that you're a G.I. stationed in Germany, and when the war in Vietnam is over, you'll be sent home, and that you feel certain you can effect a reconciliation. The court won't refuse us. Not in the middle of a period of hostilities during which soldiers are being killed!"

"Thank you, sir."

"Happy to help, soldier," said the officer.

His official military letter was quickly dispatched.

I also wrote a letter of my own to Pearl's attorney:

> *Dear sir,*
> *I am in receipt of your letter. I don't know what 'revolting facts' my wife may have discussed with you, but if she has given you information to get me out of the military, please use them. I hate the Army! But, of course, my dismissal will create two problems. (1) Mrs. Perry's monthly allotment will be cut off. And (2) my expulsion from the Army will make it impossible for me to find employment when I return home—which will mean I may no longer be able to contribute child support! With those facts in mind, you can better make your own decision as to how to proceed!*

Shortly thereafter, I received the only letter Pearl ever wrote me in all those years. It was very angry. She told me how evil and terrible a person I was. And the last thing she said was that if I had ever loved her, et cetera, et cetera, I would grant her a divorce. So I did—but not until after I was honorably discharged from the military.

As the years continued to pass, when being interviewed or speaking before university groups, the question was often asked, "When was the last time you saw your sons?" And as the years kept slipping away, the period of separation kept growing longer and longer. I would admit that losing them was the only major disappointment in my life. Not only did I not see my sons, I had no good information as to where they were.

I kept praying God would bring us together.

In my churches, I would ask friends to pray for our reunion. The entire Fellowship knew I needed their prayers. Everybody realized, year in and year out, that what I most wanted and longed for was the day when I could see my sons. Sometimes people in kindness would say, "The day will come, Troy, when the boys will become men enough to know who you are, and they'll seek you. God will answer the combination of our prayers, and someday your sons will return."

Such hope creates a heavy burden.

But then, what seems like a perfectly wonderful miracle began to unfold in July 1985. I had just returned to Los Angeles from our General Conference in Sacramento, a wonderful conference, the best in our history with five thousand people in attendance. It was the first time we had ever used our new closed-circuit equipment to translate discussions into foreign languages. The preaching had been fantastic! On Friday, Reverend Harvey had asked people with special needs to stand at their seats or come forward in prayer. I prayed for several things. I prayed for my mother who had been twice hospitalized, first for a small stroke and then for a minor heart attack. I also prayed, "Dear God, don't think I'm being selfish. I don't want you to think I'm being selfish, but I also have a need. My need is that I want my mother to see her grandchildren— my children. And I want to see them myself!"

The first day when I was back in my office was a Thursday. A note with a telephone number was on my desk stating that someone had called from San Diego with information that my youngest son was trying to reach me. I looked at the message. I thought of how many times over the years, well-meaning people had come to me with erroneous reports about having seen my sons. Often they said they had seen one and he looked exactly like me—even before the boys were of an age when they could grow a mustache and beard like those I had worn for years!

It was a matter of self-defense when I refused to elevate my hopes. Instead, I asked Frank Zerilli to contact whoever had called from San Diego to determine whether or not that person really knew what he was saying. Ten minutes later, as I was leaving my office, I stopped by Frank's desk and asked, "Did you call that number? Did you find out who it is?"

"Yes," he said, and then hesitated.

"Well? What did they say?"

"They said they are U.S. Naval Operations. The person who left his name is out to lunch and I left a message for him to call when he returns."

I said, "Oh," and went to my car and began driving. Halfway home, an intuition struck me. I suddenly had a strong feeling that one of my sons *was* trying to reach me. Pulling off at a service station, I called my office to ask if the person in San Diego had returned our call. But Frank had gone out for a long lunch.

Frustrated, I felt myself becoming apprehensive. In a minute it dawned on me that since the note had been put on my desk, it would have necessarily gone through our Fellowship receptionist. I called him.

"Have you logged a number from San Diego?" I asked.

"Yep, I have it right here."

"Please give it to me."

I called Naval Operations. That time our caller came on the line himself. He was a civilian employed by the navy, and a deacon in Metropolitan Community Church.

"I have a story for you," he said. "A young man stationed here in San Diego came to our office a week ago. He's a GI and said he's also a computer programmer. He told the woman I work with that he wants to find his real father.

" 'Oh,' she said. 'What happened to your real father?'

" 'Well, my father and mother were divorced when I was one and a half. I don't remember him, but I want to meet him.'

"She said, 'I know something about genealogy. Here's the way you do it. Do you know anything about your father? His name, anything? Is there anything different about him?'

"He said, 'The thing I know is that my mother told me he's a homosexual. And I remember, when I was fourteen, she said something about him starting a church. His name is Troy Perry.'

"My associate's eyes immediately lit up. She sent Michael over to me. 'This young sailor says he's the son of Troy Perry,' she said.

"But I didn't know if there was any truth in the lad's story at all. 'I might be able to help you find your father, and I might not,' I told the young man. 'Tell me what your mother's maiden name was, how many brothers or sisters you have, where you were born, characteristics that will identify you, and if they check out, and if I can locate this person you are trying to find, I'll notify you.' "

"What did he say?" I asked, trying to restrain my impatience.

"He said his name is James Michael Perry."

Chills went up my spine!

"That is the name of my son," I declared. "My baby boy! After nineteen years!"

The hair on the back of my head felt as though it was electrified. It was pounding pulse time! The man on the telephone continued giving me information from his list.

"He said his mother was Pearl Pinion."

"Absolutely!" Even louder, I shouted. "That's my son!"

"He said your oldest boy is Troy Perry III, but you had a nickname for him. You called him 'Punkin.'"

By then I was nearly hysterical! Everything checked. I said, "Read my lips—*that's—my—son!*"

"I don't have a telephone number for him right now," the man said. My heart despaired. "But if you'll call me at home tonight I can give you a number to reach him," he concluded.

By then it was nearly three o'clock in the afternoon. I waited until after dark and called again, but there was no answer. After that I called every fifteen minutes, until ten-thirty at night. Finally, much to my relief, the man I had been speaking with earlier answered the telephone.

"I am so sorry, Reverend Perry," he said, "but I went to choir practice tonight and it lasted late. However, Michael called while I was out and left his telephone number for you on my machine. He's working tonight. If you call there now, you'll be able to get him."

I dialed without a moment's delay.

A GI answered the telephone. "I would like to speak to Michael Perry, please," I said.

"I'm sorry, but he's not here."

My heart sank! I feared fate was playing games with me.

But the fellow on the other end of the line had more to tell. "He would have been here," he said, "but Michael thinks he just found his father—after nineteen years! The navy let him off to celebrate."

I gasped and started to cry; great happy tears of joy were soaking my face. With my handkerchief I kept mopping my eyes. It was long moments before I was able to speak. When I could, I said, "Well, when Michael comes in, can you give him a message? Tell him his father called. This is my home telephone number. Let him know I won't leave this location until he calls!"

"Yes, sir!" snapped the voice on the other end.

Next morning, at 7:05, the telephone rang and I scrambled across my bed to grab it. At the same time, my mother was grabbing for the extension in her room.

"Hello?" I said, nervous with anticipation.

"This is Mike Perry," said the voice.

"This is your father," I replied.

It was so emotional! I can't remember everything. I know that I finally said, "Can you come up here to L.A.?"

"Yes, sir."

"Do you have a car?"

"Yes, sir."

"If you didn't, I'd come down there."

"I'll drive up."

After that, I gave Michael directions to reach my home. Several hours later, before noon, mother, Phillip, and I sat on the balcony of our condominium—waiting for Mike. I told Mother to quit forever looking for his car to be coming, yet I was unable to relax myself. I kept staring down the street. The only movement was a pair of squirrels playing follow-the-leader on our telephone wires.

"A watched pot never boils," said Phillip, trying to maintain our good humor when it became obvious Michael was late.

"Where is he?" said Mother, "I hope nothing's happened."

"Oh, Mother, nothing's happened!" I declared.

"Well, I hope he knows how to drive on freeways."

"He's a good driver."

"How would you know how he drives?" she asked.

"It runs in the family," Phillip replied, answering for me with a sly grin.

Finally, a red Camaro roared up the street, making a U-turn below and directly in front of us. A tall young man with blond hair stepped out on the sidewalk. I knew it was Michael and I hurried to meet him. Both of us were nervous. He was looking for my residence code-number on the large building directory when I arrived downstairs.

"Mike?" I said.

"Dad?"

We reached out, threw our arms around each other, and hugged. It was a fantastic experience. The last time he had been in my arms, Michael had only weighed a few pounds.

"How're you doing?" he asked when I partially let go, reluctant to release him entirely.

"I'm as nervous as you are," I said, and we both laughed and that broke the tension. I didn't know that Michael had, very unnecesarily, been fearful that I would reject him because I was gay and he might remind me of the problems with my heterosexual marriage.

"Come on inside," I told him. "Your grandmother's waiting."

Her presence was like a revelation to Michael. He looked quizzical when I mentioned relatives. Then he said to me, "Do I have aunts and uncles, too, and cousins?"

"You bet!" I declared. "You have a whole big family. All wanting to meet you!"

My mother threw her hands in the air when Mike walked into the room where she was waiting. She took hold of her grandson and said, "Thank God! Thank God!" and began to cry. "I've been waiting for this moment for nineteen years!" she said, ignoring her tears.

All of us started talking, being frank and honest as we filled in some of the blank spots of so many years. Mike told us where he had been, about his stepfather, of his half brothers (twins) by Pearl's second marriage, and of my oldest son, Troy.

Early in the afternoon, the four of us went to a neighborhood Mexican restaurant. I had kept my emotions under control until I began to say grace. Before I could complete the blessing, I began sobbing. There was no help for it. I was unable to stop, and soon everybody at the table joined me. The Hispanic waitress, who spoke not a word of English, came to our table and was very concerned about what was happening. She thought something was wrong, that perhaps the tamales were too peppery hot! And through her tears, my mother, who speaks no Spanish, tried to explain to the waitress what was really happening. The result was hilarious. In spite of our blubbering, we laughed ourselves silly!

At the condominium we talked for an additional three hours. By then I was emotionally drained, and none of us, particularly Mike who had been out celebrating all night, had had enough sleep the night before to prepare us for the day. Consequently, I suggested a nap for all. But while I slept, Mike read parts of *The Lord Is My Shepherd and He Knows I'm Gay* and Tom Swicegood's *Our God, Too!*, which Phillip handed to him. As a result, while the rest of us slept, Mike had a fast education into my life and the miracle of Metropolitan Community Church.

Upon my awakening, Mike who had just finished reading one of the books, put it down and grabbed and hugged me. "Dad, I'm so proud of you!" he said.

Since then, ours has been the best relationship a father and son could have. The only cloud over our happiness was the absence of my older son, Troy III. As of this writing, he and I have yet to meet, but with God's help we will.

On the first Friday Mike spent with us, he came "to hear Daddy preach." When it was over, Joseph McDuffey, who knows me so well, pulled me by my robe and said, "I think you were showing off tonight, Troy! You really preached your behind off!"

Of course, he was right!

I was in rare form. God was with me. The title of my sermon was "Yes, you can!" and I spoke of the tens of thousands of gay men and lesbians who have their children taken away from them each year. I gave examples of bigoted individuals who kidnap their young so the other parent can never find them. I stressed that our court system must do more to protect the privileges of loving gay parents. Just being homosexual is not a good reason for never being able to be with your daughters and sons.

"In this denomination you all know I have prayed for many long years. Prayed to find my sons. At one point, I was ready to kick in doors to see them. Well, your prayers and mine have not been in vain. My son is seated with us tonight. James Michael Perry. He prefers to be called Mike. He's the handsome young man in the front row. His presence proves that yes, with faith, you can have everything!

"Don't ever give up on your dreams!"

15

Celebration:
April 1985

*All the ends of the earth shall remember and
turn to the Lord; and all the families of the
nations shall worship before God.*
                                    —Psalms 22:27

I RECALL experiencing a surge of pride as, braced by gentle sea breezes
from beyond the Golden Gate, we gathered near the top of Nob Hill on
a Saturday afternoon. San Francisco's Metropolitan Community Churches
were commemorating the fifteenth anniversary of their founding, and
we were all invited by the Episcopalians to worship in Grace Cathedral.

My role in the celebration was to preach an inspirational sermon. I
was thinking about the event-filled road our denomination had traveled
in nearly two decades when Michael Mank, our lay elder who planned
the event in San Francisco, approached. At his elbow was another smiling
member of our church.

"Troy, I know that we in M.C.C. have our own meeting places," said
the jovial member, a twinkle in his eyes, "but our churches are as nothing
compared with this magnificent Episcopal landmark. Here is a building
so elegant that it is unquestionably the ideal place for grandeur-loving
gay people to pray! Why don't you lay hands on the walls of Grace
Cathedral and claim it for us now?"

A coordinator of ours who had been endeavoring to coax laity and
clergy into a processional formation, overheard the comment, smiled, and
then resumed his efforts at crowd control. His readiness, however, was
slightly premature.

Twenty minutes later, we continued to wait outside. With growing
concern, Jim Sandmire, founder of Oakland's Metropolitan Community
Church, and I compared time on our watches. As we did, a young

Episcopal cleric wearing a fine purple robe anxiously burst out of the building and rushed in our direction.

He was practically out of breath as he nearly skidded to a stop before us. "I have some information that I've been directed to tell you," he said, not waiting to regain his composure, "It's about those big gilded bronze, main-entrance doors you are looking at. I must tell you they are only used on very special occasions. Nobody but the bishop can order them to be opened."

My good humor began to evaporate. In one place or another our people had been rudely disappointed too many times. But a moment later we heard a heartening sound. It was the satisfying rumble of the cathedral's heavy, impressive doors moving outward, opening like great arms outstretched toward us in welcome.

"Our bishop said he would not ask you to come in through our side door," the youthful clergyman told us, "and he certainly didn't want you to sneak in the back. Our bishop wants all of you to enter by the real front doors of Grace Cathedral. You are to know you are wanted here as you visit with us this afternoon!"

What a day!

How indescribably nice to be greeted with a little kindness!

The organist played a resounding fanfare, and with festive ribbons and banners held high, our self-conscious procession advanced through the golden doors to where 650 proud members of the Universal Fellowship of Metropolitan Community Churches were waiting for us.

A bespectacled church member, wearing a kilt, took his cue and began to play "Amazing Grace" on a bagpipe. The sweet melody of that old hymn enveloped everyone. It was an auspicious beginning for our meeting.

When the time arrived for me to preach my sermon, I walked to the front of Grace Cathedral's exceptionally large altar. There, a lofty pulpit is positioned about fifty feet forward of the congregation. The pulpit's microphone, in order to minimize echos in the vast sanctuary, feeds into an expensive, computerized audio system designed to adapt itself electronically to any preacher's speech pattern. However, those familiar with my oratorical style know that when Troy Perry gets to preaching, he has a tendency not only to speak loud, but also fast and downright "Southern!"

Consequently, it was amusing but no surprise to any of our people when, in only a matter of seconds, my amplified religious exhortations were rebounding from one masonry wall to another. I had merely begun with "As a former Pentecostal..." when, throughout the immense architectural enclosure, echoed and re-echoed "Pentecostal . . . Pentecostal . . . Pentecostal . . .

There was some good-humored laughter, especially when the cathedral computer, after a vain effort to catch up with me, suffered a nervous breakdown and was mercifully switched to rest.

After a few moments, when the congregation was quiet, I recalled how, in the Bible, God often spoke to prophets. "God does communicate with us," I said. "God speaks in God's own way and in God's own time. I was reading in the Old Testament how one day God took the prophet Ezekiel and placed him in the middle of a valley that was full of dry bones, and God asked him, 'Can these bones live again?'

"The prophet, fully aware with whom he was speaking, replied, 'O, Lord God, thou knowest!' Ezekiel wasn't about to get into an argument with God! He knew whatever God said was the way it would be.

"Then God gave Ezekiel an order, saying, 'Prophesy upon these bones, and say unto them, O ye dry bones, hear the word of the Lord: Behold, I will cause breath to enter into you, and ye shall live.'

"So Ezekiel started preaching, telling those bones, 'I want to tell you something, bones, you can live again. I don't care what you heard before when you were alive. I don't care what you were told when you had ears. God said it and I repeat—you *can* live again!'

"While Ezekiel was prophesying, there was a shaking, the bones joined into complete skeletons and flesh came upon them. Eventually, God caused breath to enter into them and they stood of their own accord, a miraculous living army. After it was done, God said, 'Ye shall know that I am the Lord when I have opened your graves, O my people, and brought you out of your graves. I shall put my spirit in you, and ye shall live, and I shall place you in your own land. Then shall ye know that I the Lord have spoken.' "

My voice carried into the vast recesses of Grace Cathedral, and I hesitated. There came a silence broken only by the presence of so many attentive individuals. The majority were gay men and lesbians, but there were others, also. There were some with special reasons for needing to know God loves them. They were all my brothers and sisters, and I raised my voice and spoke carefully so everyone would hear.

"To the lesbian and gay community, to the oppressed everywhere, and to our friends and visitors," I said, "It is important to know God loves you, to know you can be gay and you can be Christian at the same time. It is important not to be intimidated by any misguided individual or group who would, for evil reasons, for egotistical purposes, or for selfish economic gain, attempt to keep us from God.

"Seventeen years ago God spoke to a young man from North Florida, and he, Troy Perry, stands here before you this day. I didn't clearly understand God's meaning then because I had much to learn. Now I think the message is clear.

"God said, 'Say unto the people, I will bring them out of their graves. They are my children who once thought they were not. They shall not be afraid anymore.'"

Appendix A
Not a Sin, Not a Sickness: Homosexuality and the Bible

HOMOSEXUALITY AND THE CHURCH

The most beautiful word in the Gospel of Jesus Christ is "whosoever." All of God's promises are intended for every human being. This includes gay men and lesbians. How tragic it is that the Christian Church often has excluded and even persecuted people who are homosexual!

We are all created with powerful needs for personal relationships. Our quality of life depends upon the love we share with others, whether family or friends, partners or peers. Yet, lesbians and gay men facing hostile attitudes in society often are denied access to healthy relationships. Jesus Christ calls us to find ultimate meaning in life through a personal relationship with our Creator. This important spiritual union can bring healing and strength to all of our human relationships.

For many centuries the Christian Church's attitude toward human sexuality was very negative: sex was for procreation, not for pleasure; women and slaves were considered property to be owned by males; and many expressions of heterosexuality, like homosexuality, were considered sinful. Such tradition often continues to influence churches today. Many teach that women should be subordinate to men, continue to permit forms of discrimination against peoples of color, and condemn homosexuals. They say that all homosexual acts are sinful, often referring to their interpretation of Scripture.

Other churches today are influenced by a century of psychoanalytic thought promoted through a powerful minority in the field of medicine. They see homosexuality as some kind of sickness. Although this view has now been soundly discredited by the medical profession, some churches and clergy continue to be influenced by the idea. They say that homosexuals are "imperfect" and in need of "healing."

The good news is that since 1968, when Metropolitan Community Church was founded, the emergence of a strong lesbian and gay community and the conclusions of new scientific studies on homosexuality have forced the Christian Church to re-examine these issues. A growing number of biblical and theological scholars now recognize that Scripture does not condemn loving, responsible homosexual relationships. Therefore, gay men and lesbians should be accepted just as they are in Christian churches, and homosexual relationships should be celebrated and affirmed!

ABOUT THE BIBLE

The Bible is a collection of writings which span more than a thousand years recounting the history of God's relationship with the Hebrew and Christian people. Consequently, the Bible was written in several languages, embraces many literary forms, and reflects cultures very different than our own. These are important considerations for properly understanding the Bible in its context.

There are vast differences in doctrines between various Christian denominations, all of which use the same Bible. Such differences have led some Christians to claim that other Christians are not really Christians at all! Biblical interpretation and theology differ from church to church.

Biblical interpretation and theology also change from time to time. Approximately 150 years ago in the United States, some Christian teaching held that there was a two-fold moral order: black and white. Whites were thought to be superior to blacks, therefore blacks were to be subservient and slavery was an institution ordained by God. Clergy who supported such an abhorrent idea claimed the authority of the Bible. The conflict over slavery led to divisions which gave birth to some Christian denominations that exist today. These same denominations, of course, do not support slavery today. Did the Bible change? No, their *interpretation* of the Bible did!

What influences lead us to new ways of understanding Scripture? New scientific information, social changes and personal experience are perhaps the greatest forces for change in the way we interpret the Bible and develop our beliefs. Scientific awareness of homosexual orientation did not exist until the nineteenth century.

Most Christian churches, including Metropolitan Community Church, believe the Bible was inspired by God and provides a key source of authority for the Christian faith. Therefore, what the Bible teaches on any subject, including sexuality, is of great significance. The problem, however, is that sometimes the Bible says very little about some subjects; and popular attitudes about those matters are determined much more by other sources, which are then read into the biblical statements. This has been particularly true of homosexuality. Fortunately, recent scholarship refutes many previous assumptions and conclusions.

GENESIS 19:1–25

What was the sin of Sodom? Some "televangelists" carelessly proclaim that God destroyed the ancient cities of Sodom and Gomorrah because of "homosexuality." Although some theologians have equated the sin of Sodom with homosexuality, a careful look at Scripture corrects such ignorance.

Announcing judgment on these cities in Genesis 18, God sends two angels to Sodom, where Abraham's nephew, Lot, persuades them to stay in his home. Genesis 19 records that "all the people from every quarter" surround Lot's house demanding the release of his visitors so "we might know them." The Hebrew word for "know" in this case, *yadha*, usually means "have thorough knowledge of." It could also express intent to examine the visitors' credentials, or on rare occasions the term implies sexual intercourse. If the latter was the author's intended meaning it would have been a clear case of attempted gang rape.

Horrified at this gross violation of ancient hospitality rules, Lot attempts to protect the visitors by offering his two daughters to the angry crowd, a morally outrageous act by today's standards. The people of Sodom refuse, so the angels render them blind. Lot and his family are then rescued by the angels as the cities are destroyed.

Several observations are important. First, the judgment on these cities for their total wickedness had been announced prior to the alleged homosexual incident. Second, all of Sodom's people participated in the assault on Lot's house; in no culture has more than a small minority of the population been homosexual. Third, Lot's offer to release his daughters suggests he knew his neighbors to have heterosexual interests. Fourth, if the issue was sexual, why did God spare Lot, who immediately commits incest with his daughters? Most importantly, why do all the other passages of Scripture referring to this account fail to raise the issue of homosexuality?

What was the sin of Sodom? Ezekiel 16:48–50 states it clearly: the people of Sodom failed to meet the needs of the poor, and they worshiped idols. The sins of injustice and idolatry plague every generation. We stand under the same judgment if we create false gods or treat others with injustice.

LEVITICUS 18:22 AND 20:13

Christians today do not follow the rules and rituals described in Leviticus. But some ignore its definitions of their own "uncleanness" while quoting Leviticus to condemn "homosexuals." Such abuse of Scripture distorts the Old Testament meaning and denies a New Testament message.

"You shall not lie with a male as one lies with a female; it is an abomination." These words occur solely in the Holiness Code of Leviticus, a ritual manual for Israel's priests. Their meaning can only be fully appreciated in the historical and cultural context of the ancient Hebrew people. Israel, in a unique place as the chosen people of one God, was to avoid the practices of other peoples and gods.

Hebrew religion, characterized by the revelation of one God, stood in continuous tension with the religion of the surrounding Canaanites who worshipped multiple gods of fertility cults. Canaanite idol worship, which featured female and male cult prostitution as noted in Deuteronomy 23:17, repeatedly compromised Israel's loyalty to God. The Hebrew word for a male cult prostitute, *qadesh*, is mistranslated "sodomite" in some versions of the Bible.

What is an abomination? An abomination is that which God found detestable because it was unclean, disloyal or unjust. Several Hebrew words were so translated, and the one found in Leviticus, *toevah,* is usually associated with idolatry, as in Ezekiel, where it occurs numerous times. Given the strong association of *toevah* with idolatry and the Canaanite religious practice of cult prostitution, the use of *toevah* regarding male same sex acts in Leviticus calls into question any conclusion that such condemnation also applies to loving, responsible homosexual relationships in our culture.

Rituals and rules found in the Old Testament were given to preserve the distinctive characteristics of the religion and culture of Israel. But, as stated in Galatians 3:22–25, Christians are no longer bound by these

Jewish laws. By faith we live in Jesus Christ, not in Leviticus. To be sure, ethical concerns apply to all cultures and peoples in every age. Such concerns were ultimately reflected by Jesus Christ, who said nothing about homosexuality but a great deal about love, justice, mercy and faith.

ROMANS 1:24–27

Most New Testament books, including the four Gospels, are totally silent on same sex acts, and Paul is the only author who makes any reference to the subject. The only clearly negative statement by Paul regarding same sex acts occurs in Romans 1:24–27 where, in the context of a larger argument on the need of all people for the gospel of Jesus Christ, certain homosexual behavior is given as an example of the "uncleanness" of idolatrous Gentiles.

Does this passage refer to *all* homosexual acts, or to *certain* homosexual behavior known to Paul's readers? Romans was written to Jewish and Gentile Christians in Rome, who would have been familiar with the infamous sexual excesses of their contemporaries, especially Roman emperors. They would also have been aware of tensions in the early Church regarding Gentiles and observance of the Jewish laws, as noted in Acts 15 and Paul's letter to the Galatians. Jewish laws in Leviticus mentioned male same sex acts in the context of idolatrous cult prostitution.

Significant to Paul's discussion is the fact that these "unclean" Gentiles exhanged that which was "natural" for them, *physin* in the Greek text, for something "unnatural," *para physin*. In Romans 11:24, God acts as an "unnatural" way, *para physin*, to accept the Gentiles. "Unnatural" in these passages does not refer to violation of so-called laws of nature, rather implies action contradicting one's own nature. In view of this, we should observe that it is "unnatural," *para physin*, for a person today with a lesbian or gay sexual orientation to attempt living a heterosexual lifestyle.

Romans 1:26 is the only statement in the Bible with a possible reference to lesbian behavior, although the specific intent of this verse is unclear. Some commentators have seen in this passage a reference to women adopting a dominant role in heterosexual relationships. Given the cultural expectations on subordination of women to men in Paul's time, such a meaning may be possible.

The homosexual practices cited in Romans 1:24–27 were believed to result from idolatry and are associated with some very serious offenses as noted in Romans 1. Taken in this larger context, it should be obvious that such acts are significantly different than loving, responsible lesbian and gay relationships seen today.

Any consideration of New Testament statements on same sex acts must carefully view the social context of the Greco-Roman culture in which Paul ministered. Prostitution and pederasty (sexual relationships of adult men with boys) were the most commonly known male same sex acts.

In I Corinthians 6:9 Paul condemns those who are "effeminate" and "abusers of themselves with mankind" as translated in the King James version. Unfortunately, some newer translations are worse, rendering these words "homosexuals." Recent scholarship unmasks the homophobia behind such mistranslations. The first word, *malakos* in the Greek text, which has been translated "effeminate" or "soft," most likely refers to someone who lacks discipline or moral control. The word is used elsewhere in the New Testament but never with reference to sexuality.

The second word, *arsenokoitai,* occurs once each in I Corinthians and I Timothy, but nowhere else in other literature of the period. It is derived from two Greek words, one meaning "males" and the other "beds," a euphemism for sexual intercourse. Other Greek words were commonly used to describe homosexual behavior but do not appear here. The larger context of I Corinthians 6 shows Paul extremely concerned with prostitution, so it is very possible he was referring to male prostitutes. But many experts now attempting to translate these words have reached a simple conclusion: their precise meaning is uncertain.

The rarity with which Paul discusses any form of same sex behavior and the ambiguity in references attributed to him make it extremely unsound to conclude any sure position in the New Testament on homosexuality, especially in the context of loving, responsible relationships. Since any arguments must be made from silence, it is much more reliable to turn to great principles of the Gospel taught by Jesus Christ and the Apostles. Love God with all your heart, and love your neighbor as yourself. Do not judge others, lest you be judged. The fruit of the Holy Spirit is love . . . against such there is no law.

One thing is abundantly clear, as Paul stated in Galatians 5:14; "the *whole* law is fulfilled in one statement, *"you shall love your neighbor as yourself."*

OTHER INSIGHTS

"The homosexuality the New Testament opposes is the pederasty of the Greco-Roman culture; the attitudes toward pederasty and, in part, the language used to oppose it are informed by the Jewish background."

—Robin Scroggs, Professor of Biblical Theology
Union Theological Seminary, New York City

"Once cannot be absolutely certain that the two key words in I Corinthians 6:9 are meant as references to male homosexual behavior."

—Victor Paul Furnish, Professor of New Testament
Perkins School of Theology, Dallas

"The strongest New Testament argument against homosexual activity as intrinsically immoral has been derived traditionally from Romans 1:26, where this activity is indicated as *para physin*. The normal English translation for this has been "against nature." Two interpretations can be justified concerning what Paul meant by the phrase. It could refer to the individual pagan, who goes beyond his own sexual appetites in order to indulge in new sexual pleasures. The second possibility is that *physis* refers to the "nature" of the chosen people who were forbidden by Levitical law to have homosexual relations."

—John J. McNeill, Adjunct Professor of Psychology
Union Theological Seminary, New York

"A close reading of Paul's discussion of homosexual acts in Romans I does not support the common modern interpretation of the passage. Paul did not deny the existence of a distinction between clean and unclean and even assumed that Jewish Christians would continue to observe the purity code. He refrained, however, from identifying physical impurity with sin or demanding that Gentiles adhere to that code."

—L. William Countryman, Professor of New Testament
Church Divinity School of the Pacific, Berkeley

"The Hebrew word *'Toevah,'* here translated 'abomination,' does not usually signify something intrinsically evil, like rape or theft (discussed elsewhere in Leviticus), but something which is ritually unclean for Jews, like eating pork or engaging in intercourse during menstruation, both of which are prohibited in these same chapters."

—John Boswell, Professor of History
Yale University, New Haven

HELPFUL READING

The following books are highly recommended for those wishing to carefully study issues of homosexuality as related to the Christian Church:

Boswell, John (1980). *Christianity, Social Tolerance, and Homosexuality.* Chicago: University of Chicago Press.

344

Countryman, L. William (1988). *Dirt, Greed, and Sex: Sexual Ethics in the New Testament and Their Implications for Today.* Philadelphia: Fortress Press.

Edwards, George R. (1984). *Gay/Lesbian Liberation: A Biblical Perspective.* New York: Pilgrim Press.

Furnish, Victor Paul (1979). *The Moral Teaching of Paul.* Nashville: Abingdon Press.

Horner, Tom (1978). *Jonathan Loved David: Homosexuality in Biblical Times.* Philadelphia: Westminster Press.

McNeill, John J. (1988). *The Church and the Homosexual.* Boston: Beacon Press. Orig. pub. 1976.

Scanzoni, Letha, and Virginia Ramey Mollenkott (1978). *Is the Homosexual My Neighbor?* New York: Harper and Row.

Scroggs, Robin (1983). *The New Testament and Homosexuality.* Philadelphia: Fortress Press.

AN INVITATION

Thousands of lesbians and gay men, along with many friends and family members, have discovered new freedom and deep inner peace in a personal relationship with Jesus Christ. Their association with Metropolitan Community Church has brought a new measure of fulfillment and meaning to their lives.

Whoever you are, wherever you may be, whatever the circumstances of your life, it is important for you to know that Jesus Christ died to take away your sins, not your sexuality. Christ accepts you as you are, and so do we. You are always welcome at MCC!

METROPOLITAN COMMUNITY CHURCH

Calling people to new life through the liberating Gospel of Jesus Christ

Confronting the injustice of poverty, sexism, racism and homophobia through Christian social action

Creating a community of healing and reconciliation through faith, hope and love

For additional resources on this subject, contact:

UFMCC, Suite 304
5300 Santa Monica Blvd.
Los Angeles, CA. 90029 U.S.A.
Phone (213) 464-5100

By Rev. Elder Donald Eastman, Second Vice Moderator of the UFMCC Board of Elders.

Appendix B
Doctrine, Sacraments and Rites of the Universal Fellowship of Metropolitan Community Churches

A. DOCTRINE: Christianity is the revelation of God in Jesus Christ and is the religion set forth in the Scriptures. Jesus Christ is foretold in the Old Testament, presented in the New Testament, and proclaimed by the Christian Church in every age and in every land.

Founded in the interest of offering a church home to all who confess and believe, the Universal Fellowship of Metropolitan Community Churches moves in the mainstream of Christianity.

Our faith is based upon the principles outlined in the historic creeds: Apostles and Nicene.

We believe:

1. In one triune God, omnipotent, omnipresent and omniscient, of one substance and of three persons: God—our Parent-Creator; Jesus Christ the only begotten son of God, God in flesh, human; and the Holy Spirit—God as our Sustainer.

2. That the Bible is the divinely inspired Word of God, showing forth God to every person through the law and the prophets, and finally, completely and ultimately on earth in the being of Jesus Christ.

3. That Jesus . . . the Christ . . . historically recorded as living some 2,000 years before this writing, is God incarnate, of human birth, fully God and fully human, and that by being one with God, Jesus has demonstrated

347

once and forever that all people are likewise Children of God, being spiritually made in God's image.

4. That the Holy Spirit is God making known God's love and interest to all people. The Holy Spirit is God, available to and working through all who are willing to place their welfare in God's keeping.

5. Every person is justified by grace to God through faith in Jesus Christ.

6. We are saved from loneliness, despair and degradation through God's gift of grace, as was declared by our Savior. Such grace is not earned, but is a pure gift from a God of pure love. We further commend the community of the faithful to a life of prayer; to seek genuine forgiveness for unkind, thoughtless and unloving acts; and to a committed life of Christian service.

7. The Church serves to bring all people to God through Christ. To this end, it shall arrange for regular services of worship, prayer, interpretation of the Scriptures, and edification through the teaching and preaching of the Word.

B. SACRAMENTS: This church embraces two holy Sacraments:

1. BAPTISM by water and the Spirit, as recorded in the Scriptures, shall be a sign of the dedication of each life to God and God's service. Through the words and acts of this sacrament, the recipient is identified as God's own Child.

2. HOLY COMMUNION is the partaking of blessed bread and fruit of the vine in accordance with the words of Jesus, our Sovereign: "This is my body ... this is my blood." (Matthew 26:26–28). All who believe, confess and repent and seek God's love through Christ, after examining their consciences, may freely participate in the communal meal, signifying their desire to be received into community with Jesus Christ, to be saved by Jesus Christ's sacrifice, to participate in Jesus Christ's resurrection, and to commit their lives anew to the services of Jesus Christ.

C. RITES: The Rites of the Church as performed by its duly authorized ministers shall consist of the following:

1. The RITE OF ORDINATION is the setting apart of duly qualified persons for the professional ministry of this church. It is evidenced by the laying on of hands by authorized ordained clergy, pursuant to these By-laws.

2. The RITE OF ATTAINING MEMBERSHIP IN THE CHURCH shall be conducted by the pastor or Pastoral Leader before a local congregation at any regular worship service. After completing classes for instruction in the beliefs and doctrines of the church, a baptized Christian may become a member in good standing of the local church group through

a letter of transfer from a recognized Christian body or through affirmation of faith.

3. The RITE OF HOLY UNION and the RITE OF HOLY MATRIMONY are the spiritual joining of two persons in a manner fitting and proper by a duly authorized clergy of the Church. After both persons have been counseled and apprised of their responsibilities one towards the other, this rite of conferring God's blessing may be performed.

4. The RITE OF FUNERAL OR MEMORIAL SERVICE is to be fittingly conducted by the ministers of the Church for the deceased.

5. The RITE OF LAYING ON OF HANDS or prayer for the healing of the sick in mind, body or spirit is to be conducted by the ministers of the Church, at their discretion, upon request.

6. The RITE OF BLESSING may be conducted by the ministers of the Church for persons, things and relationships, when deemed appropriate by the minister. This includes the dedication of a Church building to the glory of God.

Index

Mitchell, George, 79–80, 85–86, 93–94, 99
Mixner, David, 149, 156, 160, 161, 165, 168, 173
Morris, Major Henry, 86
Moscone, George, 175, 178, 179–180, 182
Murray, Reverend Cecil, 258

Nelson, Madeline, 28, 29, 30–31, 37, 38
Nobel, Elaine, 232
Norris, Reverend June, 120–125, 135, 237
Norris, Willard, 121, 122

O'Leary, Jean, 185, 187
Owens, Reverend Dorman, 278, 279

Peachy, Paul, 55
Perry, Arthur, 8, 9, 11–12
Perry, Edith Allen, 1, 2, 3, 4, 5, 6, 11, 12, 13, 14, 17, 25, 36, 37, 47, 98, 311, 315, 322, 325, 328, 331, 332
Perry, Eugene, 1, 5, 36
Perry, Eula Mae, 12
Perry, Hortense, 8
Perry, J. B., 8
Perry, Jack, 1
Perry, James, 8
Perry, James Michael, 22, 23, 328, 329–332
Perry, Jerry, 1, 5, 167–168
Perry, Jimmy, 1, 293, 294
Perry, Pearl Pinion, 15, 16, 17, 19, 20, 21, 22, 23, 24, 25, 321, 326, 327, 330
Perry, Roy, 12, 13, 120
Perry, Sarah, 8, 9, 12

Perry, Troy D., Sr., 1, 2, 3
Perry, Troy, III, 21, 23, 330, 332
Pie, Gary, 218
Pieters, Reverend Steve, 198, 281–284, 286–287
Pinion, Pearl. *See* Perry, Pearl Pinion
Pinion, Reverend, 15
Pittinger, Dr. Norman, 208
Ploen, Reverend Richard, 51, 72
Proctor, Reverend Wayne, 17, 18

Quinn, Robert, 72
Quigley, Reverend Revel, 36

Radclyffe, Nancy, 125
Rasmussen, Buddy, 82, 84, 94
Ratzinger, Cardinal, 290
Reagan, Ron, 271
Reagan, Ronald, 153, 157, 160, 161, 165, 166, 168, 172, 195, 241, 270, 271
Regalado, Steve, 272–275, 279, 282
Richardson, Reverend William, 89
Roberts, Evelyn, 321, 323
Roberts, Oral, 317, 319–320, 321, 323
Roberts, Ron, 317–319, 320, 321–322
Rogers, Roy, 144
Rogers-Witte, Reverend Callie, 237
Roosevelt, Franklin D., 1
Roth, Nancy, 157
Rushton, Bill, 95

Sandmire, Reverend James E., 49–50, 51–53, 54, 58, 59, 150, 151, 176, 183, 261, 265, 334
Sands, Steve, 28, 37, 326
Sano, Reverend Roy, 258
Schatz, Benjamin, 284
Scheer, Robert, 164, 165